We the Women

Career Firsts of
Nineteenth-Century America

Madeleine B. Stern

With a New Introduction by the Author

Wood Engravings by John De Pol

BURT FRANKLIN REPRINTS
New York, N.Y.

Published by Lenox Hill Publishing & Dist. Corp.
235 East 44th St., New York, N.Y. 10017

Library of Congress Cataloging in Publication Data

Stern, Madeleine Bettina, 1912-
    We the women. With a New Introduction by the Author.

    Includes bibliographical references.
    1. Women in the United States—Biography. I. Title.
CT3260.S73 1974   920.72'0973   74-11307
ISBN 0-8337-5535-8

To

Miriam Y. Holden

Who suggested that this book be written.
Her enthusiasm, her fertile mind, and her
splendid library of books by and about women
helped bring it to completion.

INTRODUCTION

We the Women was first published in 1963 — a year noteworthy for the appearance of another, far more influential book in the women's movement, Betty Friedan's *The Feminine Mystique.* Like *We the Women,* Betty Friedan's book was researched in the Frederick Lewis Allen Room of the New York Public Library before it went on to become, according to the blurb, the "bestseller that ignited women's liberation."

Despite the hyperbole of that statement, *The Feminine Mystique* along with the reports of the President's Commission on the Status of Women did herald a host of books on feminism that flooded the presses during the decade that followed. With few exceptions those books looked not to the past but to the present and the future.[1] Anthology after anthology reflected the 'Voices of the New Feminism' from *Woman in Sexist Society* to *Women's Liberation,* from *Up Against the Wall, Mother* to *The New Women.* Supplementing the anthologies came the general expos´es of woman's oppression and the blueprints for her emancipation. In this field Shulamith Firestone's *The Dialectic of Sex: The Case for Feminist Revolution* comes to mind, along with Germaine Greer's *The Female Eunuch* and Elizabeth Janeway's *Man's World, Woman's Place.* Numerous other books would come to other minds.

Between 1963 and 1974, the less general, more specific women's literature has centered upon four major concerns. One of these is theological—the relation of feminism to the church—which has been explored in depth in a succession of books that include *The Illusion of Eve, The Church and the Second Sex, Women in the World of Religion,* and *Women's Liberation and the Church.*

Another primary preoccupation of writers on feminism has been black feminism, a subject investigated in a small library of books such as Toni Cade's anthology, *The Black Woman,* Josephine Carson's *Silent Voices: The Southern Negro Woman Today,* and Shirley Chisholm's autobiographical *Unbossed and Unbought.*

Sex itself has of course been a prime target for writers on feminism who have analyzed human sexual response, cogitated about sex and gender, and — like Kate Millett — "discovered" the political aspect of sex. And in the wake of books on sex have come the manuals, tomes and polemics on abortion and abortion legislation.

Finally, the literary feminists have devoted their pens to books on women's economic, political, and professional position. One recalls *Born Female: The High Cost of Keeping Women Down; Woman's Place; Women in American Politics; Women and the Scientific Professions;* and, as a kind of corollary to the books on working mothers, the vast literature on day care.

During this prolific decade, the work of the early feminists has not been altogether neglected. There have been some distinguished biographies as well as reprints of documents in the history of American feminism. Under the auspices of Radcliffe College, the monumental three-volume biographical dictionary, *Notable American Women 1607-1950,* has been published. But by and large, in the extensive feminist bibliography that has emerged from the presses between 1963 and the present, the literature devoted to the past is sparse and meager. The emphasis has been upon movements rather than upon people, and the tendency has been to neglect the past which not only becomes, but conditions, the future.

In our urgent concern with present and future it may be self-orienting to remember the past. The woman's movement had early antecedents indeed. Perhaps the first organized woman's liberation movement was that of the Amazons about whom a seventeenth-century French savant, Pierre Petit, wrote an elucidating *Dissertation.*[2] During the sixteenth century woman had champions whose names were both masculine and distinguished: Agrippa and Erasmus, Dolce and Vives — all gave her respectful attention. In 1647 another Frenchman, Pierre Le Moyne, assembled a *Galérie des Femmes Fortes*[3] and in 1674, still another — Poulain de La Barre, a strong believer in sexual equality — pleaded that universities be opened to women since no studies were beyond their capacity.[4] The anonymous author of *Truth Triumphant: or, Fluxions for the Ladies* (London 1752), though not brave enough to reveal his name, was brave enought to assert woman's scientific abilities.

The great early feminists are of course remembered — Mary Wollstone-craft, Margaret Fuller. Indeed a small but hard-working coterie of scholars today editing and making available Margaret Fuller's letters and journals and preparing her bibliography. The Modern Language Association of America allocated a seminar to Margaret Fuller Studies in December 1973, at which it was my privilege to present a paper offering a thirty-year view of Margaret Fuller scholarship.[5]

It was Margaret Fuller who gave to women their most useful rallying cry: "We would have every arbitrary barrier thrown down. We would have every path laid open to woman as freely as to man. . . . let them be sea-captains, if you will." Today we remember the rallying cry, but we are inclined to forget or to be ignorant of those who once rallied to it, those who did become the metaphorical sea-captains during the century that preceded ours.

It was my purpose in writing *We the Women* to reanimate the lives and careers of those nineteenth-century American women who had been first to throw down the arbitrary barriers of profession and industry and who had thus liberated woman economically. I purposely and deliberately omitted from my book those women, such as the first woman doctor, Elizabeth Blackwell, whose stories were thrice-told tales that were readily available elsewhere. My intention was, like that of the women whose lives I reconstructed, to walk untraveled roads and tell previously untold or inadequately told stories.

My problems were grave. To establish priority with scholarly precision is no easy task, and to establish priority in the economic or professional or industrial spheres is still more difficult. Gradually I was able to assemble my *Galérie des Femmes Fortes* and, as I had suspected, those women who were the first to enter professions previously reserved to men turned out to have lives that were rich and personalities that were colorful.

I found, in my first woman admitted to practice before the United States Supreme Court, the redoubtable Belva Lockwood, who must be remembered not only for a long activist career in law, arbitration, and the rights of Indians, but for the dramatic role she played on one historic day. On February 2, 1880, Belva Lockwood moved before the Supreme Court of the United States that Mr. Samuel R. Lowery be admitted to practice. In more specific terms, the first woman who had been admitted to plead before the Supreme Court of the United States was also requesting the admission to that court of the first Southern black. Surely there was a scene that painted more than a thousand words.

In the first woman graduate of Massachusetts Institute of Technology, the chemist, Ellen H. Richards, I found a nineteenth-century investigator of food, air, and water pollution who coined a word — Euthenics — to signify the science of controllable environment. It is high time that ecologists, organic food enthusiasts and women's studies classes harkened to her words and her career.

In my first woman stockbroker, I found the gaudy and gorgeous Victoria Woodhull who was also the first woman candidate for the Presidency of the United States and whose writings and speeches I have just had the pleasure of editing.[6]

Once priority had been established for my dozen women, another problem loomed up: that of locating sufficient source material to reconstruct their lives and careers. In the case of my first woman stenographer for Congress, Isabel Barrows (who was also the first American woman ophthalmologist), the Price of Serendip came to my aid — a story which deserves a place in a biographer's reminiscences. While researching another subject, I scoured the pages of *The Revolution,* a nineteenth-century American weekly devoted to women's liberation. In the January 5, 1871 issue I noticed a heading: 'A Lady Oculist — Mrs. Bella C. Barrows.' Her achievements were related in capsule form. She had "heroically struck out a new path for her sex . . . in thoroughly fitting herself for the profession of an oculist." She had been born in Vermont, spent some time in India as the wife of a missionary and lost her husband there. Upon her return to America she had started her medical studies and married again, this time a shorthand expert named S. June Barrows who worked as Secretary Seward's secretary. During her husband's illness, Mrs. Barrows took his place in the State Department and subsequently went to Vienna to study ophthalmology. Here was a woman with at least two "firsts" to her credit, but sources for her life were meager until I was struck by one of those productive "connections" that enrich the work of every researcher.

In preparing a book on publishing history I had once corresponded with a scholar named June Barrows Mussey who lived in Vermont. Now here was a woman born in Vermont and married to S. June Barrows. Was there a connection? Mr. Mussey had by that time moved to Germany and, with the kind of cardiac palpitation known only to biographers on the scent of sources, I sent him an airmail letter asking if he had ever heard of Bella or Isabel Barrows. His reply came by return mail. My shot had landed on target. Mr. Mussey had indeed heard of Isabel Barrows. She was his grandmother. Moreover, she had written an unpublished autobiography. Would I care to see it? Ten days later it was on my desk — the fascinating source for an extraordinary life that began on a Vermont farm and ended with an attempt to free a woman prisoner in Czarist Russia. In between had come the "firsts" — the opening of doors, the tearing down of arbitrary barriers. I had the material not only for a chapter in *We the Women* but for a full-length juvenile on the life of Isabel Barrows.[7]

I tell this story not only because it is a happy record of a serendipitous find, but because it implies a moral for researchers, for writers, for feminists. There are bridges, there are connections everywhere. We have only to find them. There are strong bridges between the women firsts whose stories are narrated in this book and the feminists who have organized today. There are tight connections between the subjects of *We the Women* and those who are now exploring sexual politics and sexual economics. Their sexual revolution had to be fought before the current sexual revolution could be launched. Their efforts at women's emancipation had to precede the women's liberation movement. Their radical feminism should be remembered because it was an essential forerunner of our own radical feminism.

If we but listen, we shall hear the echoes of their voices in the Voices of the New Feminism that besiege our ears today. They were of the past, but they were also of the future, and so they form a bridge between the two without which there can be no marchers.

Madeleine B. Stern

New York City
March 9, 1974

FOOTNOTES

[1] For a useful selected bibliography on women citing the works mentioned, see that compiled by Lucinda Cisler with an Addenda to August 1972, in Judith Hole and Ellen Levine, *Rebirth of Feminism* (New York: Quadrangle Books, 1973), pp. 450-471.

[2] Pierre Petit, *De Amazonibus Dissertatio* (Amsterdam 1687).

[3] Pierre Le Moyne, *La Galérie des Femmes fortes* (Paris 1647).

[4] [François Poulain de La Barre,] *De l'Education des Dames pour la Conduite de l'Esprit dans les Sciences et dans les Moeurs, Entretiens . . .* (Paris 1674).

[5] Madeleine B. Stern, "30-Year Survey. A Biographer's View of Margaret Fuller," *AB Bookman's Weekly* (February 4, 1974), pp. 427-430.

[6] Madeleine B. Stern, ed., *The Victoria Woodhull Reader* (Weston, Mass.: M & S Press, 1974).

[7] Madeleine B. Stern, *So Much in a Lifetime: The Story of Dr. Isabel Barrows* (New York: Julian Messner, [1964]).

We would have every arbitrary barrier thrown down. We would have every path laid open to woman as freely as to man. . . .

Women have taken possession of so many provinces for which men had pronounced them unfit, that though these still declare there are some inaccessible to them, it is difficult to say just where they must stop. . . .

. . . if you ask me what offices they may fill; I reply—any. I do not care what case you put; let them be sea-captains, if you will.

—MARGARET FULLER

What gate has been unlocked from the straitness of woman's past which tempts a headlong and multitudinous rush into the world's field of labor?

—CANDACE WHEELER

The professions indeed supply the key-stone to the arch of woman's liberty.

—JULIA WARD HOWE

ACKNOWLEDGMENT

I wish to thank the editor of the *Bulletin of The New York Public Library* for permission to reprint Chapter 2, which originally appeared as an article in that periodical. Thanks go, too, to The New York Public Library for permission to use the Frederick Lewis Allen Memorial Room, in which much of the research for this book was done.

Acknowledgment of the author's gratitude to the many individuals who have provided information and assistance in connection with the preparation of this book is made at appropriate points in the section, "Notes on Sources."

To Mrs. Miriam Y. Holden, to whom the book is dedicated, the author wishes to express again her deep appreciation for the help and encouragement that persisted at every stage of the work.

The author's gratitude to Leona Rostenberg may be stated and restated, but it is too unbounding for adequate acknowledgment.

CONTENTS

Contents

Business & Industry

ILLUSTRATIONS

"Let Them Be Sea-Captains, If You Will"

Who would count today the number of women stenographers who record in pothooks of one kind or another the sessions of Congress and its Committees?—or of the women lawyers who plead their cases before the Supreme Court of the United States?—or of the women architects with their blueprints, the chemists with their test tubes, the dentists, the women in arts and sciences, professions, trades and industry? They go about their business unremarked and all but commonplace. They have become an expected pattern in the national fabric.

The first woman lawyer who wished to plead a case before the United States Supreme Court was forced to lobby a bill through House and Senate. The first woman stenographer for Congressional Committees was required to sign her name with initials only lest her sex be detected. The first women architects and chemists and dentists—the first to enter the professions and trades, the arts and sciences—raised eyebrows when they did not raise protests. Their struggles and their eventual triumphs were as much a part of their own nineteenth century as all the other causes of the time. They, too, were part of the American tapestry, one of its most colorful parts.

These women firsts of the nineteenth century did not flock to the lecture platform to plead for woman suffrage or for equal rights. Rather, they lived equal rights quietly and without fanfare. For them the vote was only incidental, and Margaret Fuller's plea, "Let them be sea-captains, if you will," was a rallying cry nearer to their purpose. Their end was pertinent and timely—economic independence. To achieve that end, they upheld, unconsciously as often as consciously, woman's most vivid tricolor: freedom of work, equality in the rewards of work, fraternity in trade and in profession. And though, with such a feather pinned to their jaunty caps, they fought the bloodless revolution of the nineteenth cen-

1

tury, their contemporaries and sometimes they themselves were unaware of what they had accomplished. For a century, therefore, many of these women firsts have gone unremarked, unacknowledged even. Yet any woman who ventures first into a trade, a science or an art is worth at least a backward glance. Against backgrounds as varied as far-off India and Czarist Russia, Reconstruction Washington, Paris, Philadelphia, in that exhilarating nineteenth century that expanded its frontiers as it rounded out a nation, they lived their colorful lives and created their diverse careers.

Here, for the first time, a handful of those women firsts have been tracked down, assembled, brought once again to life. Here they pry open doors and enter corridors where no woman had preceded them. Here, armed with pen or test tube, legal brief or ballet slipper, drafting board or telegraph key, they charter—as they did a century ago—the unchartered, explore the unexplored, and give to the women who came after them a stronger purpose, a more possible dream.

The Arts

The First American
Ballerina to Capture the Nation

MARY ANN LEE

1837

O N SATURDAY evening, December 30, 1837, Philadelphians trooped into their own particular "Old Drury" known as the Chestnut Street Theatre, looked about them at Monachesi's superb paintings of classical scenes, and no doubt commented upon the dramatic effect of the gas fixtures that heightened the illusion of the long ago and the far away. As they settled themselves in pit and boxes, surely they anticipated with relish this last performance of the year when, for the benefit of Manager Maywood's wife, her daughter, Augusta, and another young pupil of Monsieur Hazard, professor of dancing, were to make their joint début in a Frenchified ballet opera called *The Maid of Cashmere* and based upon *La Bayadère.* The gaslights flickered. The curtain rose to the symphony of the opening chorus. The audience were transported to the principal square of Cashmere, where they could glory in the improbable as their senses responded to "a mixture of beautiful scenery, exquisite music, singing and dancing." Especially they must have responded to the dancing, as they watched the twelve-year-old Augusta Maywood perform as the *bayadère,* Zoloe, and her rival, the still younger, surely less conspicuous Mary Ann Lee, enact the role of Fatima. The dances varied. The scenes shifted. The young performers danced, mutely expressed their pantomimic emotions and intimated their thoughts, until at length they vied, one with the other, in the grand trial dance for the benefit of "The Unknown," until indeed, amid the brilliant light of an Indian paradise, the final tableau shaped itself and the final curtain fell.

The audience, some perhaps enchanted, some unmoved, considered that they had experienced, in the midst of a Philadelphia winter, an evening in Cashmere. Actually, they had witnessed one of the most extraordinary débuts in the history of the ballet—a double first appearance almost unprecedented in the annals of the dance. Augusta Maywood, the Zoloe of the evening, was to become the first internationally known American dancer, astonishing Europe with the impossible realized—an American ballerina who could evoke from balletomanes across the sea the bravos exclusively reserved for their own compatriots. Her rival, the Fatima of the evening, Mary Ann Lee, was to become the first American dancer who would bring to her land the romantic ballet techniques and choreography of Europe, laying at the feet of her country the revolutionary dances she was to learn abroad. On that December night in Philadelphia, the ballet had subtly, without fanfare, burgeoned forth.

At the time, quite naturally, the significance of the evening was lost to most of those who had witnessed it. To them, the facts in the life of the young dancer, Mary Ann Lee, seemed no doubt too unimportant to gather for recording. As a result, errors accumulated, speculations and omissions, and mysteries were manufactured to fill the gap made by ignorance. Although a biographical sketch has been written about Mary Ann Lee, it makes her two or three years older than she was—a grave error in the life of a ballerina. Her mother's name was unknown to the writer, and Mary Ann's retirement, her marriage, her own family life have all been invested with suggestions of sensational tragedy and mystery that never existed. Now, at last, the facts of her life have been unearthed, and those vital statistics that can help delineate a living, human being, have been discovered. We know now when she was born and when she died and a great deal of what happened in between. Her life was neither sensational nor mysterious. But in the field of the ballet it was sufficiently productive to warrant painting with all the rich colors restored, the shadowy outlines clearly sketched, the truth announced, and with that truth the past and its dead brought once again to life.

Mary Ann Lee was born in Philadelphia in 1826, the daughter of actors, Charles and Wilhelmina Lee. Her father was "a very useful little member of the corps" of the Olympic Circus, a "general favorite" who filled "important niches in stage and ring performances," a man of "obliging and honest good nature" which his daughter seems to have inherited along with his versatility. Mrs. Wilhelmina Lee contented herself with minor parts, playing Jessamine in *The Dew Drop* or a "character in the dream" in *O'Flannigan and the Fairies*. After Charles Lee's early death his wife was to marry again, becoming Mrs. John Broad, but widowhood pursued her, and the widow of Charles Lee eventually became the widow of John Broad.

Mary Ann, slight of build, small and graceful, began dancing "in her mother's arms," an inclination which had been fostered by parents whose lives centered in the greenroom. The smells and sights of the theater were her heritage—she was clothed in the draperies of its costumes. Its secrets were early laid bare to her, from the expectant preparations backstage to the intermissions when the audience drank or ate oysters and fruit.

At 96 S. Fifth Street in Philadelphia, Paul H. Hazard, teacher of dancing, had opened his classroom. There, along with Augusta Maywood, George Washington Smith, and other Terpsichorean hopefuls, Mary Ann pursued her studies in the poetry of motion. Hazard, who brought his memories of the *corps de ballet* of the Paris Opéra to the Philadelphia where he had made his own début in 1830, initiated Miss Lee in the study of her legs and arms and body, in those five positions that formed the basis of "The Code of Terpsichore." In his classes she was taught to "preserve a perfect equilibrium in the execution" of her pirouettes and "to twirl delicately round on the point" of her toes, "to vary" her "enchaînemens," her figures and her attitudes, to exercise her "battements" and "ronds-de-Jambes." Pantomime, she learned, was "the very soul and support of the Ballet"; it might "assume any shape, and imitate every passion." It was "a mighty Protean power" in which "every movement, every step should convey a sentiment." Practising her *pas,* her *entrechats,* she began her devoted study of ballet technique, learning also from Professor Hazard the role she would enact for her début—Fatima in *The Maid of Cashmere.*

The grand trial dance between Augusta Maywood's Zoloe and Mary Ann Lee's Fatima was metamorphosed after that début into a more realistic rivalry that titillated the audience while it spread

rancor behind the scenes. The *pas de deux* in which Zoloe and
Fatima vied for the favors of "The Unknown" was converted into
a trial dance in which two children were forced to vie for the
favors of the audience. Both had studied under Monsieur Hazard.
Both were "endowed with natural abilities for agility and grace."
To some, Miss Lee's poetry of motion was of the style of a "celebrated danseuse brought out from France." To others, Miss Lee
was "a clever little girl enough in her place, . . . but no one . . .
pretends seriously to compare her forced and trembling performances to the finished, graceful, flexible, and confident figures of
the astonishing Augusta." "Augusta had more precision, more of
the mind and the science of the artiste." Mary Ann had the "pleasing expression," the "smile that fascinated." But "the astonishing
Augusta" was older than Mary Ann, and "the astonishing Augusta"
was also the manager's daughter. A ballet *pas de deux* had been
transposed into an unsavory rivalry between two stage children
for the delectation of a perhaps jaded audience. The wreaths and
bouquets hurled onto the stage were counted. Comparisons made
way for threats. After "La Petite Augusta" was granted a benefit,
the followers of Mary Ann—"Our Mary Ann"—made their resent-
ment tangible. They sent notes and applications demanding a
benefit for their partisan to Manager Maywood, who appeared on
stage to reject them "as an interference with the private arrangements of his business." The disturbance he declared "an insult to
his gifted child." He had, moreover, he informed the audience,
"generously paid for the tuition of Miss Lee" besides "paying her
and her relatives salary regularly." A threatening letter found its
way behind the scenes. "Our Mary Ann" had become, at the age
of eleven, the center of an interlude more dramatic by far than
any ever enacted by Fatima or the Maid of Cashmere.

Public opinion, however, vindicated her, and Manager Maywood
"with enforced grace" bowed to its "popular expression." "Our
Mary Ann" was granted her benefit after all, and it proved a
"bumper" in a theater "filled from pit to dome," "a triumphant
overflow—a deserving tribute to merit, and a handsome offering
to an orphan daughter." On the last night of the ballet opera's
presentation, bouquets and wreaths were "literally showered upon
the stage by the admirers of both Augusta and Miss Lee. . . . peals
followed the bestowal of each present, and it kept poor 'Brahma'

[played by Pearson] . . . all the time walking from side to side of the stage gathering up the trophies until he entirely forgot the bestowal of the stage wreath which in his character he should have awarded to Fatima." For Augusta, twenty wreaths were thrown, along with bouquets and a garland in which glittered a "splendid *diamond ring.*" For "Our Mary Ann" there was "her fair share of the honours." The night would be long remembered by both children.

The rivalry, the backstage intrigue, the humiliation, the publicity, all these would be long remembered by Mary Ann Lee. Yet all these she took in stride. She would leave criticism to the critics and concern herself with that which touched her most closely—the improvement of her technique, the expansion of her roles, the advancement of her capabilities. To this she was dedicated. And to this she quietly proceeded.

Between rehearsing a pastoral ballet, attending Monsieur Hazard's semi-monthly cotillions, and sitting for a colored lithograph, the "pretty little danseuse" prepared herself for the strenuous life of a professional ballerina. Performing with Maywood or Madame Lecomte, she learned the popular roles of her day, roles that lay somewhere "between tightrope walking and fancy dancing" in ballets that borrowed the conventions of the eighteenth-century stage to present themes mythological and heroic and pastoral. With rope dancers and conjurers, fire-eaters and "masticators of ribbons," "Our Mary Ann" was becoming part of the American Bartholomew Fair. Like the ballet itself, she had entered her apprenticeship.

For insatiable audiences who demanded two or three plays of an evening with songs and dances in between, she must study the part of the fairy for *Sadak and Kalasrade* or of Maude for the new melodrama, *The Avenger of Blood.* The fairy's spangled shrub robes made way for the blue bodice and French petticoat of Lisette in the musical burletta, *The Swiss Cottage,* or the nankeen trousers and white waistcoat of Little Pickle in the two-act farce, *The Spoiled Child.* From a hamlet in Provence to the gardens of a villa near Utrecht her backdrops shifted, as she turned from melodrama to vaudeville, from *The Loan of a Lover* to *The Wandering Boys.* Whether she indicated her emotions in the difficult pantomime of mute roles, or sang of her passions or danced them, she was learning the varied expressions that the age demanded and that would serve her so well when she came to her artistic maturity.

When Manager Maywood's rancor became intolerable, Miss Lee joined the corps of Manager Wemyss of the Walnut Street Theatre, where, for the first time in her short career, a ballet was composed to introduce her to her new "constituents." For "Our Mary Ann," the portly and imposing Amherst of Astley's Amphitheatre wrote *The Lily Queen,* featuring a variety of lily vases arranged in a pyramid, from which sprang the *corps de ballet* along with a chubby Cupid, while from a spreading Victoria Regis emerged the Lily Queen herself. At the finale, Flora crowned the tableau of lilies with a gigantic bouquet nearly covering the stage. It was a pretty conceit, cleverly managed, and Wemyss himself was well pleased with his Mary Ann, who "danced as well as ever." But it was in quite another ballet that Mary Ann and the Philadelphians who watched her had found a foretaste of the romantic ballet that she was one day to bring in full flower to her country.

In the "operatic drama" of *The Dew Drop,* based partly upon *La Sylphide* which Marie Taglioni had first performed in Paris, both Mary Ann and her audience could view the faint beginnings of the romantic dance and the "ballet blanc." Its background of romantic forests, its Scottish tale of the supernatural, above all its danseuse, ennobled, immortal, but enamored of a mortal, all combined to adumbrate the romantic ballet that she would one day study in Paris. In the diaphanous costume of the Sylphide, with her pink tights and satin shoes and tiny wings, she danced to the music of bells and bagpipe, bringing to the stage "a sempeternal fête . . . leaving nothing to regret or to desire." Performing first as Flora to Augusta Maywood's Dew Drop, Mary Ann advanced to the title role, dancing with delicate grace the wraithlike Sylphide in her vaporous *tutu.* A few months after "La Petite Augusta" had crossed the seas for Paris, never to return, "Our Mary Ann," small and blue-eyed, presented *The Dew Drop* for the delight of Baltimore, where "The Museum continues to be nightly crowded with the most respectable and fashionable visiters" to enjoy the "operatic ballet of La Sylphide, . . . performed in a beautiful manner." To the accompaniment of the "Cornopean," she danced her way into the heart of at least one Baltimorean with her Scotch *pas seul* and echo dance, for she received a poem entitled "La Sylphide" from an anonymous admirer who effused:

Ne'er did the Grecian chisel trace,
A Sylph, a Naiad or a Grace,
Of finer form or lovelier face;
And seldom was a wreath amid
Such locks of golden beauty hid;
Nor ever beamed of heavenly hue,
Eyes of more sweet and radiant blue;
Each changeful movement of her breast,
Her varying features still confest; . . .
And while upon her speech there hung
Accents more sweet than wind harp's tongue,
Those silver sounds, so soft, so clear,
The listner held his breath to hear.

After the Vaudeville of the Four Mowbrays, or the Vaudeville of The Bachelor's Buttons, Baltimoreans were regaled in August of 1838 with Miss Lee's pleasing executions which incidentally marked the inception of a revolution in choreography.

She continued her performances and her studies in Philadelphia, leaving her home on Chester Street, where she lived with her mother and her grandmother, for the Walnut Street Theatre, where, as Zoloe in *La Bayadère,* or in Hazard's arrangement of the cachucha, the "industrious little lady" won her plaudits. She could read in *The Saturday Courier* that "Her appeal will no doubt be warmly responded to by those who are anxious to encourage native talent. Naturally modest and of unassuming manners, this young lady has through her natural abilities, aided by application and perseverance, 'won golden opinions' in her vocation; and from the rapid improvement recently evinced under the tuition of Mr. Hazard, she bids fair to become an ornament to the profession which she has selected."

A more substantial plaudit than "golden opinions" came her way in the form of a New York début. At half past seven on the evening of June 12, 1839, the curtain of the Bowery Theatre rose on the drama of *Nick of the Woods* and fell some hours later upon the last act of a farce entitled *Victoria; or, the Lion and the*

Kiss. In between, Miss Lee performed, for the delectation of the Empire City, in the trial dance from *The Maid of Cashmere.* While the equestrian drama of *Rookwood, or, Dick Turpin* featured the histrionic abilities both of John Gilbert and of a genuine horse that "gracefully flirted her tail," Mary Ann and a rival danseuse, Julia Turnbull, introduced *The Sisters,* an original native "pictorial" ballet. If Miss Turnbull charmed the Bowery boys with a Highland fling, Miss Lee delighted them with a gallopade, and when President Van Buren honored the theater with his presence, Miss Lee's cachucha made a graceful interlude between *The Honey Moon* and *The Lion King, or, The Bandit's Doom.*

While Augusta Maywood prepared for her brilliant Paris début, Mary Ann Lee moved on to less brilliant, but perhaps no less important performances on the boards of the stage in Baltimore and Pittsburgh. The "Favorite Dances" of "this interesting danseuse" enchanted the audience of Baltimore's Front Street Theatre, where, against a background of Alpine scenery, she also played Albert to Forrest's William Tell. When Van Buren visited the theater to see Forrest in *Metamora,* surely he stayed on to see Miss Lee in *The Spoiled Child.* And, having introduced her *Bayadère* to the Pittsburgh Theatre, the young and indefatigable trouper returned in the summer of 1840 to New York, this time for an engagement with the incomparable P.T. Barnum.

The great showman had opened the Vauxhall Garden saloon on the Bowery Road, where pleasure-seekers could wander along the graveled walks and flower beds and, for 12½ cents could enjoy the more mundane delights of ginger pop or baked pears in molasses. In between, they could, for only 25 cents, feast their eyes and ears upon the variety performances scheduled by P.T. Barnum, performances that ranged from ventriloquism to Ethiopian specialties, from the songs of Mary Taylor or the Albino lady to the legerdemain of a "wonderful young sybil," from the "Yankee Eccentricities" of the singer Jenkins to the strumming of Whitlock, "King of Banjo players." In this "highly respectable audity, and . . . rich fund of entertainments," "Our Mary Ann" took her place as a star. Her cachucha dance was "received with shouts of applause," and "a regular jam" thronged the Garden to see her dance "divinely." For a public who came to "laugh and grow fat," she sang "Buy a Broom" in character or executed a

favorite dance from *La Bayadère.* During intermission, while the
crowds rushed for a promenade and refreshments and the brass
band played popular airs in the gardens, she prepared for her
gallopade from *Gustavus,* and at her benefit—"a splendid bill,
at this splendid place, for the benefit of a splendid girl"—Miss
Lee varied her already rather extensive repertory with a hornpipe.
She was learning to give the public what it wanted. One day she
would be able to give the public what she wanted.

On the same night that "Our Mary Ann" danced the cachucha
for the habitués of Vauxhall Garden, a far greater dancer with
an international reputation gave her version of the dance at the
Park Theatre. Fanny Elssler, who had been told in Europe that
the Yankees "had no dancing in their souls, and that their appreciation of Terpsicorean excellence went not beyond the 'break-
downs of Virginia,' " had made her American début at the Park
in a *pas seul* called "La Cracovienne" and, overwhelmed, had
watched the pit rise in a mass to cheer her while a shower of
wreaths and bouquets was flung from the boxes. For $500 a night,
in addition to the tumultuous enthusiasm of Gotham, the "divine"
Fanny exhibited her special technique of precise steps on points
known as *tacqueté,* along with the pagan voluptuousness and vigor
of her bends and turns and gestures. For "Our Mary Ann" at the
moment, Fanny Elssler was perhaps less a rival to be emulated
than a goddess to be worshiped. But she did not worship from
afar. Elssler had come to America with her partner and ballet
master, James Sylvain, "the best male dancer ever seen" in the
country. His charms captivated the New England bluestocking,
Margaret Fuller, who borrowed his name for a story. His abilities
captivated Mary Ann Lee, who proceeded to study under him.

Despite his Gallic name, she soon discovered that his proper
patronymic was Sullivan and that he was said to be a brother of
the famous actor, Barry Sullivan. Although he never appeared to
understand English, he spoke, when he was obliged to speak, with
a brogue. But whatever his ancestry or his tongue, he proved a
useful teacher for Miss Lee, who under his guidance quickly
learned Fanny Elssler's dances, from her sparkling version of the
cachucha, provocative, abandoned, to the Spanish five-part bolero,
noble and restrained, from the Russian smolenska to el jaleo de
Jerez. She studied Elssler's handling of the castanets, her Crac-

ovienne costume of blue skirt, red boots and white jacket; above all she studied the techniques of dances as varied as the nations that had produced them. Her newly acquired techniques she put to good use in her engagements on tour, whether she journeyed to Pittsburgh in the winter, where "the stars, . . . met half frozen at the top of the Alleghany mountains," or to Boston in the spring, where she joined a "commonwealth" among the actors. For $25 a week in addition to benefits, "Our Mary Ann" ran the gamut of the ballet in America, a gamut she would one day help to extend and enrich.

As her background shifted, her rivals varied and her roles expanded. At the Olympic Saloon on Washington Street, "Miss Mary Ann Lee . . . fascinated the students of Cambridge, and the young men of Boston, by her dancing," and at the Tremont Theatre, the denizens of the hub of the world could choose between the attractions of Herr Driesbach and his lions and the performances of Mary Ann, who had begun to "rival Elssler" in *La Bayadère*. At the benefits of the equestrian director or the "gentlemanly treasurer" of the house, Miss Lee executed the steps of "L'Espagnole" or the smolenska, and in the "new dance entitled El Bolero" she "created a great sensation," managing the castanets "most admirably."

Boston's Tremont Theatre gave way to Baltimore's Front Street Theatre, where the pretty young trouper continued with her character dances, from the rustic cracovienne to the *Pas Tyrolien,* from the *Pas de Danube* to a new *pas seul.* In Baltimore, Miss Lee could be reached at a rather curious address for a ballerina— No. 72 Baltimore Street, where the Edwards lace and fancy store was located. In only a few years time, she was to marry a Philadelphia gentleman connected with a trimmings company. Is it possible that, while she was serving as journeyman in the art of the ballet, young William Vanhook was serving his own apprenticeship as a merchant in Baltimore? If they met, they quickly parted, for Baltimore must be abandoned for New York, and New York for New Orleans as the months sped by in a terpsichorean whirl. A sailing packet took nine days to reach New Orleans, but at the end of the voyage Mary Ann could find the " 'varieties' of the multiform, multi-colored, multi-lingual, multi-ludal city, which is *levée* on the banks of the Mississippi." Among the stars of the

New St. Charles, whose Corinthian and Doric columns stood between Gravier and Poydras Streets, Miss Lee took her place. And, although by the inevitable comparison with Elssler, she "dropped behind in position," the danseuse "from the Eastern theatres" had "a friendly greeting" and was "rapturously encored." Her "chaste and pretty" *Pas de Danube,* her Polish Cracovienne "captivated the hearts of half the young beaux in town, who were dying for a smile from 'our Mary Ann' " whether she danced or played the Dumb Girl of Genoa who expressed a gamut of histrionic emotions in pantomime, or the far from mute Laurette in the one-act farce of *My Little Adopted.* At the St. Charles, and later at the American Theatre in New Orleans, Miss Lee continued her performances as danseuse and mime, singer and actress. For her, a new piece entitled *Eugene—Or, The French Conscript* was expressly written to exhibit her pantomimic powers in the title role of the dumb boy. For her *Maid of Cashmere,* the scenic artist, Samuel Stockwell, painted new backdrops. In the "Original Burletta," *One Hour; or The Carnival Ball,* Miss Lee played a Julia who sang and who danced against a Neapolitan background. She evoked smiles, and consternation, too, when, "owing to some 'small potato' professional jealousy," the rival dancers, Mary Ann Lee and Emma Ince, failed to titillate their audience in a promised grand trial dance. And, practising the versatility that her contemporaries demanded, she evoked laughter, too.

Mary Ann Lee's theatrical apprenticeship was almost complete when she was able to parody herself. In March of 1843, the New St. Charles and its star, the seventeen-year-old ballerina from Philadelphia, offered a most unusual bill for the "discerning portion of the auditors." Commencing with *La Bayadère: or, The Maid of Cashmere,* in which Mary Ann played Zoloe to Miss Chapman's Fatima, and continuing with a lecture on Steam by Dr. Heavybevy, the program concluded with a burlesque on the curtain-raiser entitled *Buy It, Dear!—'Tis made of Cashmere,* written by the actor-playwright, Joseph M. Field, more popularly known as "Straws." Substituting the farcical Mlle. Solo for her serious role as Zoloe, Miss Lee now matched wits as well as steps with a Fatima transformed into an "oleaginous Beauty" named Fatty-Ma. Against the background of a parish workhouse, she led a chorus of broom girls who had brushed up their wardrobe for the occasion, and in ludicrous jumps in place of graceful bounds, "Our Mary Ann" gave evidence that she had learned to laugh at herself. In the burlesque operatic ballet extravaganza, the small, blue-eyed young ballerina who had worked so indefatigably over the years relaxed and poked fun at herself.

Her growing maturity was evinced as her roles increased in variety. In New York she had supported Madame Lecomte in the first American performance of *Robert-Le-Diable* which introduced the cult of the supernatural against a Sicilian setting. She had played Rosignol in the four-act historical drama of *The Surgeon of Paris* when the audience was transported to the days of Charles IX and to the Bastille in the moonlight. From farce to melodrama, from song to pantomime she had vibrated, learning to act by acting, to express by expressing. Especially she had studied the dance —in *pas d'action* and in ballet, and in parodies of her own ballet. She had studied enough to know she must study more—surely the most significant mark of maturity in a young danseuse.

On October 25, 1844, therefore, a letter was sent from Philadelphia to Secretary of State Calhoun, requesting passports for Mrs. Wilhelmina Lee and Miss Mary Ann Lee, described for the purpose as an eighteen-year-old blue-eyed brunette, who intended leaving in a few days for Europe. With her mother, "Our Mary Ann" set forth on a mission that would divide her professional life in two and bring to America the first fruits of the romantic ballet that had flowered abroad.

In Paris, "the great school of art, science and refinement," she would "complete and perfect . . . those 'graces' " essential to her profession; she would improve her technique; she would vastly expand her choreographic repertory. With her mother—the dancer's mother whom Parisians, regardless of any individual charms, dubbed the dragon in the Garden of Hesperides—Mary Ann Lee entered the "Foyer de la danse" behind the Opéra, descended a few steps, opened two doors, and found herself in the upper part of a grand salon surrounded by mirrors, before which she saw the bars of white wood where she would practise. She had come from a distant land to this Foyer of the Opéra, where she would be enriched, and where she would learn to enrich her country.

The eighteen-year-old danseuse from Philadelphia faced the sixty-five-year-old Jean Coralli, official choreographer and *maître*

de ballet of the Paris Opéra. The mustachioed ballet master in his
stock and velvet lapels raised his baton, and Mary Ann Lee knew
that her education had just begun. Coralli, she soon discovered,
was at once the most courteous and the most irascible of teachers.
He was Monsieur de Coislin and the King of Prussia rolled into
one. His perruque, it was rumored, he had once thrown in the
face of a dancer, and when an order was poorly executed, he
would cry out, "Sacré mille millions de tonnerres et de diables,
tas de sottes que vous êtes." He would *tutoyer* or *rudoyer* his
pupils, whom some preferred to refer to as his slaves. But when
he raised his baton, he knew precisely what he was doing.

Perhaps for the first time in her career, Mary Ann Lee learned
to view her powers and her faults objectively. Surely she knew
that she was both graceful and agile, her smile was arch and
winning, her *pas* were neat. But her knowledge of general effect
needed improvement; she lacked a certain precision and freedom
of execution. To her native grace she must add stylistic finish.
Despite her small stature, she must try to develop her muscular
power. She must learn "the peculiar tact and felicity of dressing."
She must, above all, perfect her technique.

In the inquisition of the dancing class she condemned herself,
in exchange for fifty francs a month, to the ceaseless physical and
mental labors imposed by Monsieur Coralli. At his "Tournons-
nous!" or his "Cassons-nous!" she maneuvered her knees, her
feet, her hands. In group studies she worked at her *jetés* and
entrechats, her *pirouettes* and *balancés.* In concentrated devotion
she practised and repractised the elevations, the beats and turns
and turnouts of classic ballet technique. She studied the distinction between the *ballonné* style of Marie Taglioni with its bound-
ing and leaping movements, its elevations and resilient springs,
and the *tacqueté* style of Elssler with its precise, elaborate foot-
work on the full point.

In between her lessons she took time to send to a friend at
home a letter reporting her observations of Parisian charms and
her nostalgia for the more substantial mores of her own country:

Notwithstanding the charms and pleasures which are to be met with
in Paris, I much prefer my own dear country. One can hardly appreciate the worth of home, until after having been in a foreign land.
Here all around you have a smile in readiness, which is but a prelude

to something farther, which the French call politeness,—and so far as words and language go, they are exceedingly polite, (or rather *gallant*, . . .)—but give me the politeness of own countrymen, who have sincerity in their words and will accompa[n]y them with polite actions.

Mary Ann Lee was apparently rounding out her education not only in ballet technique, but in the vagaries of human nature. Her countrymen were proud of her efforts, announcing that she was "demonstrating to a perfect mathematical nicety that Native American legs are on an equal footing with the imported article." Whether or not this was overly optimistic, there is no doubt that she would soon demonstrate that native American legs could exhibit the poetry of the romantic ballet for the delight of the new world.

Although she was in no way connected with the opera ballet proper, Mary Ann enjoyed all the advantages not only of "receiving her lessons in the Opera building," but of "a seat in the director's private box on each Ballet night." There, before her enchanted eyes, were unfolded the bewitching beauties of romanticism in the ballet. She had had a taste of the "ballet blanc" in *La Sylphide,* but never before had she seen the dance so elevated to the plane of the ideal and the timeless. In the ballets that Coralli had helped to choreograph, that the great Taglioni had performed, she found the dance converted from an end in itself to a means— a means of dramatizing the conflict between the actual and the ideal, in love themes, fairy tales and folk legends. In such ballets as these—the *Jolie Fille de Gand,* the *Fille du Danube, Giselle*— the ballerina reigned supreme, calling upon all her powers of pantomime and expression to escape from the confines of the earthly to the magic realms of the supernatural. For such ballets as these, a dancer must combine the techniques of *tacqueté* and *ballonné.* She must at once offer the voluptuous appeal of the worldly and the realistic, and suggest the ethereal and the unattainable. She must step out from the set framework of classical mythology and transform herself into a peasant girl metamorphosed into a sylph. She must doff her theatrical court costume and Empire dress for the long *tutu,* the delicious transparencies of tulle and tarlatan. She must be made of earth and of air.

Mary Ann Lee watched and studied and listened. She heard of

the great *Pas de Quatre* performed in London by four of the most splendid ballerinas of all time—Taglioni, Grisi, Cerito and Grahn —the "most famous *divertissement*" in the history of the dance. And as the months passed, her ears were filled with the sounds of romantic music, her eyes were dazzled with the joys of the new romantic ballet. Her technique improved. Her horizon expanded. She had explored a country to her unchartered and unknown.

In September of 1845, Mary Ann returned home, bringing with her the music and "business" and choreography of ballets that the majority of American enthusiasts had never seen. Almost half of her life had been devoted to the theater. Now her purpose crystallized. She had gathered together the freshest, most delicate flowers of the romantic dance that had sprung forth in Paris. Now she would lay them at the feet of her country.

It was supremely fitting that Philadelphia should have been chosen for Miss Lee's "first appearance since her return from Paris." Her native townsmen, who had read in the *Public Ledger* that "Report speaks in the highest terms of the progress she has made in her profession," could look forward with no little interest to their evening at the Arch Street Theatre, where, on November 24, 1845, "Our Mary Ann" would appear "in a new piece, and one which . . . the manager has spared no expense in bringing out."

The curtain rose on the shop of Cesarius, a wealthy goldsmith of Ghent, in the "entirely new" pantomimic ballet of *La Jolie Fille de Gand*. Zephiros, the *maître de danse,* was giving a dancing lesson to Cesarius' daughter, Beatrix, betrothed to Benedict but loved by the Marquis de San Lucar, and played by Mary Ann Lee. Through all the tumultuous passions of the three-act ballet she moved, becoming the Marquis' mistress, losing her reason, hurling herself into the abyss, and finally wedding Benedict. Through all its vivacious *pas* she stepped, from the rustic dance at the Kermess to the carnival ball with its masked revellers, from the *Pas de Diane* to the *Pas de Saltimbanques*. To the beautiful slow movement of Adam's music she danced her *pas* of *Diane Chasseresse* in splendid classical attitudes. Whether her background was the main square in Ghent or a Venetian palace, a magnificent ballroom or the park of a villa, she brought to her performance the technique and the vision she had acquired in Paris. Philadelphia responded. The crowded house received her "enthusiastically," agreeing that she had "much improved since her last appearance." Indeed, it was difficult to recognize "in the lovely woman and skilful danseuse . . . the late juvenile and hesitating tyro in the art." Well might "transatlantic visitors look to their laurels, when our own soil produces such sprouts as Miss Lee." Now, in her role as Beatrix, her portrait was painted "From Life and on Stone" by Davignon, the portrait lithographer, who would record her evanescent attitudes for all time and give the stamp of immortality to an art so transient.

To Boston, and later to New York, Miss Lee brought her next great romantic role, *La Fille du Danube,* which she had renamed *Fleur des Champs.* With her partner, George Washington Smith, the only American *"premier danseur noble,"* who had accompanied Elssler on tour and who would serve Lola Montez in a similar capacity, she dramatized this "poetic sequel" of *La Sylphide.* The two-act pantomimic ballet, set in the Valley of the Donaueschingen, introduced the orphan, Fleur des Champs, to houses crowded with "a fashionable and discriminating audience." In dances "full of grace and spirit," Fleur des Champs expressed her love of Rudolph, her contempt for Baron Willibald who chose her as his bride. As Beatrix had flung herself into the abyss, now Mary Ann as Fleur des Champs hurled herself into the Danube, only to reappear, metamorphosed from her earthly state into an intangible shade as the curtain was raised upon Act II. Beneath the Danube Rudolph found his Fleur des Champs and the lovers were restored from their watery abode to the world outside. With its charming *pas,* its galop, its veil dance, the "elegant Fairy Ballet"—"grotesque, surprising, and delightful," evinced to New Yorkers that Mary Ann Lee had "very much improved during her visit to Paris, . . . She was loudly applauded, and many of the dances encored." With her partner, she "electrified a crowded audience with voluptuous enchantment" by her witchery, her elegance and charms.

All her charms, all the resources of her improved technique had met their greatest test on the first of the new year of 1846 when, before the audience of Boston's Howard Athenæum, Mary Ann Lee had presented a ballet that marked the apotheosis of romanticism, a ballet that summed up the varied facets of the romantic dance and became its supreme achievement. All else had served as mere precursors. *Giselle,* presented for the first time in America by Mary Ann Lee on that historic night of January 1, 1846, was destined to become the *Hamlet* of the ballet, as timeless as the tale it told.

Circling about the stage in a series of *glissades,* Mary Ann—Giselle—made her entrance in some remote, mysterious portion of the Rhine at vintage time, and transported her audience to those realms of earth and air known only to the romantic ballet in its full flower. Crowned with vineleaves, the peasant girl Giselle danced gayly, for she loved and was loved by Loys. She had but two loves in her life—her passion for the peasant Loys, and her passion for the dance. Both were dramatized in the first act of the fantastic ballet, as the earthly Giselle learned that her beloved Loys was an impostor, none other than the disguised Duke Albrecht, and, in a mad and frenzied dance, perished. She who had been of the earth in Act I was transmuted to air in Act II. In a misty forest on the banks of a moonlit pool, Giselle had been metamorphosed into a Wili, a legendary maiden dead before her marriage, destined to dance and to bewitch young suitors to dance until they died. From her shoulders sprang a pair of wings. She must entice Albrecht to the fatal dance. In her most seductive *pas,* the irresistible Giselle must lead her lover to his doom, till, seized with the fatal madness of the dance, he dies. To Adolphe Adam's haunting melodies, Mary Ann must run the gamut of human emotion and passion, and then leave the realistic world of madness and death for the world of the fantastic and the supernatural. She must translate into terms of the theater a choreographic elegy, a "richly sinister phantasmagoria" of "misty and nocturnal poetry." She must be mortal and immortal, material and immaterial, earthly and ethereal, an Elssler and a Taglioni in one. In glides and leaps, in turns and poses she must bewitch not only her partner, Smith, but all who, gazing upon her, were transported to the misty, nocturnal, legendary region that was the abode of the romantic ballet.

"Such a lovely Ballet," Mary Ann described it for the Southern managers, Ludlow and Smith. And Boston agreed. "No ballet of action" had ever been produced there "that could bear comparison with Giselle." The "full and fashionable audience, . . . testified their delight by loud and continued plaudits at the grace and agility of the beautiful heroine, who, . . . evinced a truthfulness of action that conveyed as plainly almost as in language, the feelings and passions of the character." New York was one with Boston. "Miss Lee enacted Giselle with a beauty, charm, elegance and grace not to be described." New Orleans looked forward to it, for the balletomanes of the city on the banks of the Mississippi knew that Mary Ann had "the music and business of 'La Giselle,' the new ballet which has been so popular wherever it has been produced, and which she intends to bring out with all regard to effect. United to a native grace, and exquisite finish of style, Miss Lee possesses a gentleness of deportment and ease upon the stage fascinating to a degree, pantomimic powers of no common order, and her success in the ballet cannot be doubted."

Her undoubted success was more significant than her contemporaries realized. They had seen more than a charming dancer in an enchanting ballet. They had seen a new conception of the dance that would be cherished as long as ballerinas graced the stage and balletomanes the pit. They had seen the glorification of the romantic ballet presented for their delight by a twenty-year-old Philadelphian—their "own American danseuse."

Before Mary Ann fulfilled the anticipations of her New Orleans followers, her tour took her to Charleston where, in November of 1846, she drew superlatives from her admirers. "In Mary Ann Lee—our own American danseuse—the 'Ballet' has found an artiste whose classic brow is worthy the wreath of triumph she has so fairly won and so modestly wears! Small, but perfect in figure—elastic and flexible in motion—with a countenance eloquently expressive of the passions or emotions she would portray— we cannot look at her without being reminded of Sheridan's beautiful thought, that 'Nature always places her costliest essences in her smallest vessels.' "

For the small vessel that was Mary Ann Lee, the Charleston engagement required unceasing work, impeccable artistry, and enormous versatility. Besides performing the demanding roles of *Giselle* and *Fleur des Champs* with George Washington Smith as her partner, she donned moccasins and beaded headdress to appear as Narramattah in *The Wept of The Wish-Ton-Wish*, a drama based upon Cooper's "Celebrated Novel." A variety of *pas de deux,* a mazurka, a *Pas Styrien, La Polaca* and *El Bolero* punctuated the Charleston run, and upon one occasion Miss Lee enacted two roles on a single evening, those of Gertrude in *The Loan of a Lover* and Zoloe in the old standby, *La Bayadère.*

The New Orleans season was equally strenuous and equally rewarding. On December 5, 1846, Miss Lee, her mother, and George Washington Smith arrived at the St. Charles Hotel, that caravansary that was "the High Change of news, conversation, politics, scandal." For none of these, however, the Philadelphia danseuse had time—nor for gossip about a *"duel à l'outrance"* or a quadrille in the ballroom. It had been announced that "Miss Mary Ann Lee, . . . comes to us with all the native graces we have admired long since, increased, perfected, and with the Parisian polish upon them." Although, because of some technicalities, the Southern managers, Ludlow and Smith, had threatened her with proceedings for breach of contract, they had dropped the suit and now were intent upon building up a rivalry between Miss Lee and Julia Turnbull by engaging them to dance on the same evening.

The interior of the St. Charles Theatre had been remodeled and refurbished. The partitions between the boxes had been removed, and cushioned chairs placed in parquet, dress circle, second tier and family circle. There, and later on at the American Theatre, the critics and young beaux of New Orleans who had died for a smile from their Mary Ann, came once again to behold the changes that time and study had wrought. They saw her go through her paces, from *La Bayadère* to the *Pas Styrien,* from the *Grand Pas de Mouchoir* to the magic new ballet of *Giselle.* They saw, and they revelled in what they saw. In the *Picayune,* Mary Ann could find a record of their verdict. "Miss Lee, whom we consider decidedly the best of all the native dancers we have ever had. . . . has long been a favorite, and from the time she first established herself as such, has made the most rapid improvement in her art. There was always something captivating in her style of dancing, from her unaffected native grace and modesty, which won her hosts of admirers. Many of the little faults that arose from the impossibility of getting proper instruction in this country have disappeared under the hard practice of the Parisian school, where she has acquired new graces, a better knowledge of general effect, greater precision and a freedom of execution that she lacked before." As Giselle she "added new laurels to her previous high reputation." "Her pantomime is both graceful and pleasing, while her dancing is delicate and shows a finish to be attained only by long practice and study in the higher schools of the art. It is in her solos that she is most to be admired—in dances where she has not to share the faults of others—for we have seen her in a *pas seul* remarkable for its smooth and facile execution—a dance in which she delighted the beholder by the beauty of her attitudes, and at the same time left little to wish for in the strength and firmness of her poises."

Such plaudits were ample compensation for the cold of a New Orleans January, a cold that would "make a Norwegian hug his fireside" but that she must endure in flesh-colored tights. They were compensation, too, for the "indisposition" that upon at least one occasion had made her "unable to dance." Although Mary Ann recovered promptly and completed her engagement, only six months later, on June 18, 1847, a rather strange announcement appeared in Philadelphia's *Public Ledger* regarding the twenty-one-year-old danseuse.

Miss Mary Ann Lee takes a farewell benefit at the Arch Street Theatre this evening. . . . The state of her health renders her retirement from the stage necessary, and when it is remembered that she is the sole stay of an aged grandmother and a mother advanced in life, and that her earnings have been for years devoted to their support and comfort, it is not to be doubted that the public will show their approbation of her considerate and affectionate conduct, by giving her a substantial token of their esteem. Unexceptionable in her public as well as her private deportment, Miss Lee presents no ordinary claim for the notice of the patrons of the drama in her native city.

Until now, this announcement has been accepted in every detail, and it has been concluded that, with the exception of a few later performances, in one of which, in 1852, she appeared as one "Mrs. Van Hook," Mary Ann Lee retired from the stage and, to all intents and purposes, vanished from public notice. Like "The Poor Ballet Girl" about whom William Knight Northall wove a fanciful tale, she has therefore been consigned to the mysteries of speculation and the embroideries of supposition.

Yet, is it not strange that, less than a month before the "Farewell and Complimentary Benefit" tendered Miss Mary Ann Lee at the Arch Street Theatre by her admirers, Mrs. W. F. Vanhook made her "debut" at the Chestnut Street Theatre as a danseuse? There is little doubt that Mary Ann Lee had by this time married the Philadelphia merchant, William F. Vanhook, and that the "state of her health" which rendered necessary her "retirement from the stage" was nothing else than the state of matrimony. Instead of a "whole story of drama and tragedy" that "may lie behind" the "few small details of her attempts to return to the stage" as Mrs. Vanhook, nothing was involved but the concerns of hearth and home. The curtain had risen, not upon a melodramatic tragedy but upon a domestic scene.

Its setting was Philadelphia; its principals, Mr. and Mrs. William F. Vanhook. The domestic play was as undramatic as it was long-lived. William F. Vanhook, trimmings and dry goods merchant at the time of his marriage to the ballerina, varied his career as the years passed, becoming an inspector and then appraiser at the Custom House, later a deputy sheriff, and finally a member of the real estate fraternity. The same age as "Our Mary Ann"—now his Mary Ann—he must have combined his knowledge of the trimmings business with an ardent interest in the theater. Whether they lived at 8 Jacoby Street or St. John Street, at Buttonwood or North 16th, their marriage was destined to be enduring and productive. At least three children were born of the union, the eldest, Marie, then Charles Hunt, and finally Mabel. Mrs. Broad remained one of the household which appears to have been as unsensational as Mary Ann's career had been spectacular.

Her career was not entirely over. In December of 1849 she ventured again to New Orleans, this time in the stock company of Placide's new Varieties Theatre on Gravier Street. In between the births of her children, and the death of her young son, she performed at Philadelphia's Chestnut Street Theatre in the grand trial dance from *La Bayadère* as well as in *The Swiss Cottage*. There, too, she danced a *Pas de Quatre Nations,* and at her benefit appeared as danseuse, actress and vocalist on a bill that also featured Joseph Jefferson. During the early 1850's, while Mrs. William F. Vanhook was keeping house with the help of Mrs. Wilhelmina Broad, Miss Mary Ann Lee found time to dance *La Manola* at the Walnut Street Theatre with George Washington Smith or to act the role of Fenella in *Masaniello*—an unfortunate production in which " 'The awful eruption of Mount Vesuvius'

was about as effective as such fire and volcanic explosions are."
The ballet of *Nathalie* was added to her repertory at the Walnut
Street Theatre, while at the Chestnut, Manager Quinlan "collected
a highly creditable company—including the fiery Fenno, the excellent and versatile Gilbert, the quaint and irresistible Jefferson, . . .
and the worthy, graceful and popular Lee."

By 1852, when Mary Ann was twenty-six years old, she was
dubbed no longer the captivating young danseuse, but "the amiable
and exemplary . . . Mrs. Vanhook." Into the announcement of
her "Complimental Benefit" a note of nostalgia had already crept.
"We trust that none of the old and ardent admirers of the once
talented professional artist and always excellent lady, Miss Mary
Ann Lee, will forget the complimental benefit preparing for her
at the Chestnut street Theatre." A year later she had become "the
very worthy lady and accomplished danseuse, *Mary Ann Lee.*"
The critics seemed more grateful for past favors than for present
promises.

What she had promised she had already fulfilled as a performer.
As the years passed, she faced the sorrows if not the storms of
domestic life—the loss of her baby boy in July of 1853 at the age
of one year and nine months. Her daughter Mabel was born in
1854, the same year that saw the death of her aged grandmother
and of her great ballet master, Jean Coralli. By the time her oldest
daughter, Marie, was ten years old, in 1860, Mary Ann turned,
as so many ballerinas had done and would do, to teaching the art
she could no longer practise with perfection.

The dancing academy of Mary Ann Vanhook was opened on
the fourth floor of 527 North 8th Street, Philadelphia. For at least
two years she continued to give instruction in the dance, near the
Spring Garden academy of Professor David L. Carpenter, whose
annual floral *soirées* were worthy of emulation, and doubtless she
consulted with her old-time instructor, Monsieur Hazard, who was
still teaching the *gai science* to young Philadelphians. Now, for her
students rather than for houses packed from pit to dome, she
demonstrated the varieties of her figures and attitudes, the equilibrium of her pirouettes, the delicate twirls on the point of her
toes.

Disciples there were—if not of Mrs. Vanhook, then of others
who had no doubt been greater teachers. Surely with intense inter-

est she followed, as the years sped by, the events and gossip of the ballet world, from news that Marius Petipa had restaged *Giselle* in the Russian Imperial Theatre to reports that Augusta Maywood had retired. Did she journey to New York in 1866 to see the great extravaganza, *The Black Crook,* that ran for 475 nights at Niblo's Garden? Did she read, with a wry smile, the newspaper article entitled "With The Ballet-Dancers of Days Gone Bye" that recalled the début of Mary Ann Lee but concluded, "We cannot say whether Miss Lee is living or not."

Miss Lee was very much alive. In 1874 she found joy in the birth of her grandson, George Van Hook Potter, Marie's son, and sorrow in the death of the mother who had shared her life for so many years. And surely when the splendid new building of the Paris Opéra was opened, she recalled in memories as poignant as they were vivid the far-off distant days when she had seen and studied the beauties of the romantic ballet in the Opéra's "Foyer de la danse."

In 1889, during a visit to Atlantic City, William F. Vanhook died after a lingering, paralytic illness. For still another decade his widow lived on with her daughter Mabel at her home on South 37th Street. She had survived both Taglioni and Elssler, whose place was taken but not filled by the eccentric dancers and the skirt dancers and the tap dancers who invaded the vaudeville of the dying century. On January 26, 1899, at the age of seventy-three, Mary Ann Vanhook died at the home of her daughter Marie Potter and her grandson George, who had been a captain in the Spanish-American War. She died—curiously enough for one said to have retired at the age of twenty-one because of ill health—of the beneficent illness known as "Old Age." She was buried four days later in Laurel Hill Cemetery.

For the actress and ballerina who had taken so many bows, received so many plaudits, about whom so much had been written, scarcely a word was recorded now that she was gone. She had died, "possessed of Goods" and "Chattels" valued at $500. Perhaps the "Goods" and "Chattels" included the ballet slippers in which she had danced so often.

Yet the future would know that she had left a heritage as tangible as it was significant. She had been the first American dancer to bring to her country the poetry of the romantic ballet.

Although that country had forgotten her, it had been and would continue to be enriched by the gifts she had flung at its feet. She had started a chain of events in the American ballet world more indestructible by far than evanescent fame and vanishing fortune. If she had doffed her ballet shoes forever, there would be others to follow her graceful steps. If the curtain had fallen, it would rise again.

2

The Author of the
First Beadle Dime Novel

ANN S. STEPHENS

1860

O N SATURDAY morning, June 9, 1860, New Yorkers opened their
Daily Tribune to read of such imminent events as the problems of Kansas and the Senate, the Bell and Everett ratification
meeting at Cooper Institute, and the destructive effects of a tornado
in Iowa. If they glanced at the advertisements on the first page of
their newspaper, however, thcy must have scanned a notice that
was to make its own kind of history and lead, if not to civil war,
at least to literary revolution. For the publishing firm of Irwin P.
Beadle & Co. had inserted in the *Tribune* their announcement that
"Beadle's Dime Novels, No. 1" was "Ready This Morning." Characterized as "The Best Story of the Day" "By the Star of American
Authors," *Malaeska: the Indian Wife of The White Hunter* was
introduced to the public. The first of the Beadle Dime Novels
was available at all news depots, the comparative novelty of a
complete dollar book for a dime was touted abroad, and a literary
conception that would be imitated and extolled, challenged and
condemned was on its way.

The writer of the first Beadle Dime Novel should, by rights,
have been an adventurous trailer in buckskin, a scout of the Great
Plains familiar with powder horn and painted Indian, who guided
an "unfaltering steed" through "trackless woods." It is one of the
delightful paradoxes of American literary history, however, that
the "Star of American Authors" who had produced the first Beadle
Dime Novel was neither trailer nor scout nor indeed a man at
all. She was a woman, stout, fair, fifty years old, who hailed from

29

New England. Her name was Mrs. Ann Sophia Stephens, and although she was completely unaware of the fact, on Saturday morning, June 9, 1860, she joined the ranks of American women firsts with a literary effusion which was to her no more than an unconsidered trifle.

The unconsidered trifle that went under the name of *Malaeska* and regaled the public with the gaudy but sad and moral tale of an Indian princess wed to a white hunter, was worth exactly $250 to Mrs. Stephens. It was for that price that the firm of Beadle & Co. arranged with the "Star of American Authors"—not to write what would become their first dime novel—but to reprint it. For, like its prolific creator, *Malaeska* had already had a history.

The story had first appeared as a serial in a New York magazine called *The Ladies' Companion* between February and April of 1839, when Mrs. Ann S. Stephens was twenty-nine years old. Even then—on the threshold of what would become a rather amazing literary career—the author could look back upon a varied and lively past.

She had been born on March 30, 1810, in the village of Humphreysville, Connecticut, the daughter of John and Ann Winterbotham. Perhaps her forebear, William Winterbotham, a dissenting minister and political prisoner of London, who had in 1795 written *An Historical Geographical, Commercial, and Philosophical View of the American United States,* had imparted his literary leanings to the descendant who would approach the "American United States" from a somewhat different angle. Perhaps the influence of another literary aspirant engendered in Ann Winterbotham the desire to "make books." It was Col. David Humphreys, poet and patriot, aide-de-camp to General Washington during the Revolution and an intimate of the Hartford wits, who, having served as minister to Portugal, had imported merino sheep into Connecticut and invited John Winterbotham of Manchester, England, to superintend his wool manufactory in that State. In 1810, the year that Ann was born in an eighteenth-century red house in Humphreysville, the Humphreysville Manufacturing Company was formed and her father was admitted to partnership. This association meant a great deal to the observant little girl, who was never to forget the "grandly handsome" Colonel in his blue coat with large gold buttons, his buff vest and lace ruffles, who served as a bridge between Revolutionary and modern times. Moreover, Col. Humphreys was of a literary turn, and it must have been with no little inspiration that Ann watched with the apprentices while his plays, such as *The Yankey in England, A Drama, in Five Acts,* were performed to celebrate the Christmas holidays.

There was much else in Humphreysville to serve as grist to the mill of a future "literary lady," whose forte would become historical romances. After she conned her lessons under the watchful eyes of Abby Punderson, who sat in a high-backed chair holding Webster's blue-backed speller and pointing out the letters with a pair of scissors fastened to her side by a steel chain, Ann drank in the New England that spread before her—Doctor Stoddard and his saddlebags, the paper mill, the Spring Pond, the grove of white pines, Revolutionary powder horns, the valley of the Naugatuck— background treasured up for the author of the first Beadle Dime Novel.

Ann's mother had died and her father had married his sister-in-law Rachel, or, as the authoress was to put it, her stepmother "received me an infant from the arms of a dying sister." The Winterbothams were blessed with a large family, but the vagaries of the tariff took neither death nor fertility into consideration, and by 1829 or 1830 the uncertain market led to financial ruin. John Winterbotham determined to pull up his roots and move to Ohio—the "far west." Meanwhile, his daughter Ann had used her time well for, besides garnering scenes and portraits that stretched back to the Revolution and learning not only the alphabet but the domestic arts of needle and thimble, she had become acquainted with a young merchant of Plymouth, Massachusetts, named Edward Stephens whom she married in 1831.

Instead of going west with her family, Ann and Edward Stephens moved to Portland, Maine, where the Beadle Star of American Authors began her literary apprenticeship. In addition to his mercantile pursuits in Morton's Buildings where the firm of E. & E. Stephens offered West India Goods for sale, Edward Stephens ventured into the printing and publishing business in which he was most nobly abetted by his young wife. Besides reading every book in the Portland library and attending the sessions of the Augustine Club, Mrs. Stephens made her bow to the public as editor of *The Portland Magazine* published by her husband. With appropriate hesitancy she sought literary advice from the Portland author and editor, John Neal, who found her "a woman of great original genius, with poetry in her blood, patient, industrious, and full of impassioned enthusiasm." Both the poetry and the passionate enthusiasm found a vent in *The Portland Magazine,* where the editor indited her opening "Address": "Noah, when sending out the dove upon the waste of waters, could not have felt more anxiety for its safe return with the green leaf of promise in its bill, than is experienced for the success of the specimen number of the *Portland Magazine.*" She had, she insisted, no hopes for fame or personal distinction, but "poetry, fiction, and the lighter branches of the sciences are woman's appropriate sphere," and in this sphere a new and indomitable star had made its appearance. Neither her literary style nor her decorous fear of seeming unwomanly was ever to leave her. They set the tone for her life work as well as for the first issue of *The Portland Magazine* on October 1, 1834. There, along with an article on phrenology by the obliging Mr. Neal, were printed the editor's own contributions, "Romance and Realty" and her poem, "The Polish Boy," which was to enjoy a long and popular career as one of the most frequently declaimed recitations in the "Readers" of the elocuting 'seventies. Until June 1836 the magazine continued to receive not only the effusions of the editor, among them her "Lines on the Death of a Lady. Who Fell from the Passaic Falls, a few days after her Union with the Rev. H. Cummins," but also contributions from Whittier and Willis Gaylord Clark, as well as a poem, "The Muffled Knocker," by Lydia Sigourney which the "sweet singer of Hartford" accompanied with a letter of appreciation—a "token of approbation" that was to mark the beginning of a lifelong friendship.

Besides editing *The Portland Magazine* and contributing to such periodicals as *The Boston Pearl,* Ann Stephens demonstrated her knack for pulling out all the plums from the literary pie by compiling a *Portland Sketch Book* that offered the work of native authors—Seba Smith and N.P. Willis, James Brooks and Joseph Ingraham, Longfellow, Neal, and of course Mrs. Stephens herself who found that she was forced to "supply the deficiency" when original contributions were found to be "insufficient for her object."

By 1836, it is little wonder that Mrs. Stephens who, in between her literary preoccupations, had had a stillbirth, found that her health was failing. *The Portland Magazine* was, therefore, converted into *The Maine Monthly Magazine,* Mr. and Mrs. Stephens decided upon a trip West to visit the Winterbotham family, and a new phase in the career of the Star of American Authors had begun—a phase that was to carry her nearer to her status as the first Beadle Dime Novelist.

The journey, possibly through the Wyoming Valley of Pennsylvania, and then on to the farm that John Winterbotham had cleared in the heavily timbered Ohio land where deer still lurked in the woods and flocks of wild turkey threatened the wheat field, provided a harvest for Ann Stephens who not only recovered her health, but stored away enough pictures of the West to garnish her plots for many a season.

By 1837, the couple had settled in New York City, where Edward Stephens found a position in the Customs House that would yield him $1200 a year, and where his wife joined William W. Snowden as contributor and associate editor of *The Ladies' Companion,* a periodical which she had puffed in her own *Portland Magazine* and which, under her aegis, swiftly increased from a circulation of 3000 to 17000. The public was apparently grateful not only for the new plates offered by a monthly magazine "embracing every department of literature," but also for the stories of Mrs. Ann S. Stephens which were emblazoned on the first page of nearly every issue. Two such stories were to prove of particular significance. The first—"Mary Derwent"—was begun in the May 1838 issue as the "$200 Prize Article." "The following story," it was announced, "was written at a time when the author had formed a resolution never again to connect her name with a prize article, nor indeed with any species of Magazine literature; consequently the highest prize offered by the publisher of the Ladies' Companion, during the last season, was adjudged to her, under a fictitious signature, that of Mrs. Catharine Rogers. It will be remembered, that at the time the committee decided on the premium articles, the author was in no way connected with this magazine, and was, consequently a proper candidate for the prize of two hundred dollars"—a rather curious and roundabout way of explaining why a prize had been given to a staff writer. "Mary Derwent. A Tale of the Early Settlers" was important not only because it yielded

the author $200, but because it showed her awareness of the
public's interest in Indian novels. Set in the Valley of Wyoming,
the romantic tale of Lady Granby who became the ruler of a
Shawnee tribe of Indians might well have become the first Beadle
Dime Novel had it not been reprinted before the eventful year of
1860, and had its author not followed it with an even more significant serial named "Malaeska."

That Ann Stephens had made a fairly serious study of the
Indian language is evidenced by her scrapbook in which she listed
a variety of Indian words with their English meanings. Less than
a year after "Mary Derwent" had appeared in *The Ladies' Companion,* "Malaeska" was serialized there, making its bow in the
February 1839 issue along with such vivid tales as "The Saxon
Prelate's Doom" by the author of "Cromwell," and "The Wandering Steed" by William Comstock. There it was to lie, unnoticed,
despite its gaudy pictures of Indian life, for more than two decades,
in the course of which its author was to realize her ambitions,
crystallize her purpose, and establish so enviable a reputation that,
by 1860, when the firm of Beadle was searching for a novel to
begin its dime series, they could do no better than turn to the
work of Mrs. Ann S. Stephens.

By 1839, indeed, the author had begun to feel that "the novelty
of a literary life is beginning to lose its gloss and my own mind is
becoming matured." She was "anxious to do something that I
can look back upon with pleasure in my old age." "Malaeska"
had just been completed in *The Ladies' Companion,* but obviously
it was not such a tale that the author had in mind for pleasurable
remembrance in her old age. Her output between 1839 and 1860
was to be an almost ceaseless flow of storied words. Yet—such
are the vicissitudes of taste and the vagaries of fortune—although
she was completely unaware of the fact, Mrs. Stephens had already
made her major claim to fame in the three-part serial that was,
after twenty-one years, to emerge as the Beadle First.

Meanwhile she was indeed maturing. Col. Humphreys' "little
flax-head" had developed luxuriant long blonde curls and Mrs.
Stephens herself had become tall, "slightly inclined to *embonpoint.*"
Her low, broad forehead and massive features were "full of life
and intellectuality," while her brilliant blue eyes gave life to the
decorous and statuesque appearance that had begun to make its

mark on the world. As the years passed, she grew more ambitious, more energetic, more forceful. Determined to do good and yet remain womanly, she was to exhibit a tendency to have a finger in every literary and political *cause célèbre* and to develop a "lasting" friendship with every major figure who came her way. As far as Mrs. Stephens was concerned, in 1839 her life was all before her.

Within a short time, her family made its appearance—a daughter, Ann, born in 1841, and a son, Edward, born in 1845—and Mrs. Stephens' domestic accomplishments were, somehow, to keep pace with her literary achievements. Her literary achievements were becoming so marked that it was soon to be said of her that "No writer, since Sir Walter Scott, has excelled her" in descriptive power. It was seriously remarked that "her characters are described rather by their appearance and actions than by their words. In this she differs from Shakspeare." Since, in the early 1840's, "four readers out of every five . . . prefer a romance of Scott to . . . Othello, Macbeth or King Lear," the reason for her growing popularity was not hard to find. She supplied—in a never-ending flow—a popular demand.

No one was more aware of this than George Rex Graham, a Philadelphian who had learned the trade of cabinet-maker, studied law with his friend, Charles J. Peterson, and abandoned the Bar for periodical enterprises. In January of 1841 the first number of *Graham's Magazine* was issued. Within a year the subscription list had climbed so high that Graham was able to take a mansion on Arch Street, keep a handsome carriage, and engage with liberal payment the most eminent authors of the United States to contribute to his magazine. The most eminent authors at that time included Longfellow, Bryant, Cooper, Poe—and Mrs. Ann S. Stephens!

From January 1841 until May 1842, Edgar Allan Poe was an editor of *Graham's Magazine*. In December 1841, it was announced that Mrs. Ann S. Stephens would join the editorial staff. For four months, therefore, Mrs. Stephens was closely associated with Poe on *Graham's Magazine*. Such are the mutations of popular taste in literature that today she shines in reflected glory through that association. In December 1841, however, it was Mrs. Stephens who added the lustre of her reputation and her capabilities not

only to the magazine but to its editor, who happened to be writing
his own unconsidered trifles—"The Murders in the Rue Morgue"
or "The Masque of the Red Death."

Side by side with Poe's tales and Sartain's mezzotints, appeared
Mrs. Stephens' effusions, her "The Two Dukes" running along
with Poe's "An Appendix of Autographs," while the first issue of
1842 was further illuminated by contributions from Lowell, Park
Benjamin, Mrs. Sigourney, and William Gilmore Simms. Mrs.
Stephens was in good company, although at the time the general
consensus was probably that her colleagues profited as much from
her presence as she from theirs. As far as she was concerned, like
Poe she was simply enjoying Graham's policy of liberal payment
to authors—that "burst on author-land . . . like a sunrise without
a dawn."

Journeying occasionally to Philadelphia from New York, Mrs.
Stephens doubtless became an habituée of Graham's great house
on Arch Street with its glittering crystal chandelier, and may well
have been introduced to Henry Clay when he dined with the
Philadelphia editor. She was in the full tide of the literary life
both in Philadelphia and New York, one among the great. Although Poe was to state that she "had nothing to do with the
editorial control" of *Graham's*—a technicality challenged by the
listing of her name among the editors—he had discussed her
"manuscript" in his "Chapter on Autography," which was confined
to *"the most noted among the living literati of the country,"* and
he was to include her in his "Literati." Moreover, he could write
to Mrs. Sigourney, "So far we have been quite successful. We
shall have papers from Longfellow, Benjamin, Willis, . . . Mrs
Stephens," and to Lowell, regarding the appearance of his own
portrait, "When it will appear I cannot say. . . . Mrs Stephens
will certainly come before me." To Mrs. Stephens this was all
nothing more nor less than her just deserts. She had left *The
Ladies' Companion* for *Graham's* simply because Graham offered
"more money and less work," and for several years she continued
to supply him with stories that appeared side by side with the
work of Cooper and Poe, Longfellow and Hawthorne. When the
editor listed "our favorite old writers" for his subscribers, he
naturally included Mrs. Stephens' name along with Longfellow's
and Poe's. The discrimination that was to bring about oblivion

for the first, decline for the second, and exaltation for the third had not yet begun to make itself felt.

Mrs. Stephens was at home with the great, for in the 1840's she was one of them. Her presence was equally expected at the funeral of Poe's child-wife as, now and again, in the editorial offices of *Graham's*. There, the anthologist, Rufus Wilmot Griswold, had succeeded to Poe's chair, and into his life Mrs. Stephens was to weave a rather startling fabric. Having found him "a man constitutionally incapable of speaking the truth, a sycophant in your company, a serpent in the company of those who like to hear you unjustly spoken of . . . a moral coward and a dangerous person to be connected with," she declared that "nothing but my personal influence with Mr Graham, which happened to be more powerful than he dreamed of, prevented him doing me a serious injury." To Horace Greeley she had confided her opinion and her knowledge of the internal politics at *Graham's,* which he was quick to repeat to Griswold, who carried the report to Graham. As a result of the tempest in the literary teapot, Griswold, listing Mrs. Stephens' name along with those of the women writers of the day, remarked to James T. Fields, "Ye Gods! is there nought to settle my stomach after the writing of all these names!—they all have sworn admirers, and could bring witnesses into court, every one of them, to prove that they are equal to De Stael. . . . the literature of women, everywhere, is for the most part, *sauzle*." Mrs. Stephens carried her hostility farther and longer, appearing as a witness against him as late as 1856 when the notorious proceedings to annul the Griswold divorce came to court.

Into the plummy pie of every literary controversy Mrs. Stephens inserted a practised finger. And wherever literary notables congregated Mrs. Stephens was one of the company. With Poe she attended Anne Lynch's soirées on Waverly Place; with a Bayard Taylor disguised as Goethe's Faust she appeared at a fancy ball in the character of Madge Wildfire; she had passes for Burton's Theatre and her portrait was painted by Frederick R. Spencer, who doubtless exhibited it in his rooms on Canal Street. In her own home on New York's Cottage Place she entertained, arrayed in a velvet gown, swiftly developing into the chatelaine of New York's literary society, the center of a scribbling coterie that included the most prominent writers of Gotham. Between household chores and social appearances, a struggle between ill health and contracts that admitted of no indulgence, Mrs. Stephens went her industrious way. Her literary circle was enlarged as her reputation increased. And in a world where magazines were the moving pictures, the radio and the television of a public avid for entertainment, the demand for the output from Mrs. Stephens' flowing pen grew as the years passed. Many seemed to consider that no one could write better. Certain it was that no one could write more. A host of magazines entreated her services, and long before the climactic year of 1860 Mrs. Stephens had developed a willing and an indefatigable right hand.

It was natural that, for her husband's enterprises, Mrs. Stephens should have offered her literary output. When he was "engaged in the business department" of the *New York Express,* published by James and Erastus Brooks, two young men from Portland who were to make their mark in the political world also, she identified herself with its struggles and its history, and when Edward Stephens became co-proprietor of the *Sunday Morning News,* readers were promised that the columns would be enriched with the tales and sketches that might emanate from her pen. For *Brother Jonathan,* a weekly edited by John Neal and published by Edward Stephens, her "peculiar style" was guaranteed to provide a highly "intellectual feast" for avid subscribers.

Israel Post, founder of *The Columbian Lady's and Gentleman's Magazine,* solicited the services of the "popular authoress," and among her contributions to that monthly was a serial entitled "Romance of the Real; or Phases in the Life of Myra Clark Gaines," which, like "Malaeska," was one day to reappear in the form of a Beadle Dime Novel. For *The Ladies' Wreath* she plied her tireless pen, while for Frank Leslie, the future dynamo of Publishers' Row, she was to act as editor and chief contributor of his first magazine enterprise, *Frank Leslie's Ladies Gazette of Fashion,* a monthly whose prime object was "to improve the standard of our own national fashions" and "to give encouragement to the great talent that exists everywhere among us." To this end the indefatigable Mrs. Stephens supplied paper patterns and "fashionable and literary intelligence," stories and instructions in crochet, until in 1856 she turned her attention to her own magazine, *Mrs. Stephens' Illustrated New Monthly.* Published by her husband from his offices on Nassau Street, the magazine regaled the public with her serials, poems, and editorial gossip about crinolines and matrimony until, in 1858, it was merged with a more celebrated periodical, *Peterson's Magazine.*

Long before that time, Mrs. Stephens had formed what would become a lifelong connection with its publisher and with the magazine itself. Charles J. Peterson of Philadelphia, brother of the book publisher, T.B. Peterson, had studied law with George R. Graham and had been associated with *Graham's Magazine* before he had founded his own monthly and invited Mrs. Stephens to join in the new venture. Expansive and genial, a *bon vivant* with a fine capacity for friendship, Peterson was not only to attract Mrs. Stephens to his staff, but to hold her there in an association that would continue for the better part of forty years. Neither illness nor war would long interfere with the serials by Mrs. Stephens that made their bow every January and their finale every December. As the magazine put it, "Mrs. Ann S. Stephens writes an original novel . . . every year; she is the best novelist of America; and her stories can be had nowhere else." As she herself put it, "In this age authorship has a more substantial reward than attends female exertion in any other walk of life, and the privileges which a successful writer commands, are among the highest in the gift of society." Mrs. Stephens' reward consisted of payment beyond the usual remuneration of $2 a page for prose and $5 for a poem, for, as far as Charles J. Peterson was concerned, Mrs. Stephens was "above all rule." The magazine's reward consisted of climbing circulation and over a half century of flourishing life.

A successful rival of *Godey's Lady's Book, Peterson's Magazine* had a twofold purpose. It was "not only a lady's magazine, but a *national* one also." It was "thoroughly and consistently American." Produced by American authors, it was well aware that in the mid-nineteenth century "the magazines are not only the schools of future novelists, but they exercise a powerful . . . influence, on the popular taste." For $2 a year the popular taste could be elevated with Peterson's hand-colored fashion plates that proved "to be elegant it is not necessary to be trivial," with the "sentimental Victorianism" of its tales and sketches, and with the narratives of Mrs. Ann S. Stephens which, from 1843 on, titillated the women of the country. With a kind of cosmic regularity her serials and their sequels appeared—"The Widow's Revenge" and "The Trades-man's Boast," "Lost and Found," and "Palaces and Prisons"—a never-ending flow of words that "come from her pen in sentences often glowing like molten lava."

On April 17, 1850, Mrs. Stephens interrupted the verbal flow of molten lava for a grand European tour whose splendors were to be reported and exaggerated until the American public envisioned the stately blonde author as the lofty recipient of lavish attentions from Dickens and Thackeray, Humboldt and Thiers. Actually, the journey was sufficiently remarkable to need no gloss. Leaving her husband and children for almost two years, Mrs. Stephens consented to go abroad with two young members of the wealthy Pratt family of Prattsville, New York, George and his sister Julia.

To their mother, Mrs. Zadock Pratt, whose husband owned the largest tannery in the world and who had served as New York Congressman, Mrs. Stephens had recently dedicated her serial, "Palaces and Prisons." To the young Pratts—the scholarly George, aged 20, and Julia, aged 18, the 40-year-old fountainhead of words of molten lava now dedicated her services as traveling companion. George Pratt, who had already journeyed abroad and studied Oriental languages, no doubt proved as instructive to Mrs. Stephens as she to him. At all events, on April 17, 1850, the trio set sail aboard the S.S. "Hermann," and Mrs. Stephens' departure was described, for the readers of *Peterson's Magazine,* as "in one sense, a triumph." Gifts from all quarters were lavished upon her by friends, among them a locket from Henry Clay containing his portrait and a lock of his hair, and a poem "On The Departure of Mrs. Ann S. Stephens For Europe" bade a flowery farewell to the "gifted one! America's daughter!" who was on her way to lionize and be lionized.

While George Pratt collected books and languages during his grand tour, Mrs. Stephens proceeded to collect people and background for her stories. The journey itself bore testimony both to her reputation and to her indefatigability, for it covered not only the well-traveled ways of the tourist—London and Paris, Berlin and Vienna, Naples, Rome and Florence—but "places . . . rarely visited by American ladies"—Moscow and St. Petersburg, Malta and Constantinople—in all of which she found scenes and characters for her tales and sketches. Trapped by her tireless pen the notables sat for their portraits—the Earl of Carlisle, whose mansion in Grosvenor Place was opened to her for a reception at which she occupied the seat of honor and at which the evening guests included Dickens and Thackeray, who discussed his lectures on the "Four Georges"; Samuel Rogers, the aged banker-poet, who invited her to his palatial residence in St. James's Place for breakfast and who quoted Mrs. Sigourney over the French rolls and grated ham; the small, vivacious Maria Edgeworth; the massive-browed Humboldt in his home on Berlin's Oranienburger-strasse; Don Carlos in Trieste; members of the Imperial family in St. Petersburg; Abdul Medjid, reigning sultan at Constantinople; the Pope in Rome—all received the traveler who stored colorful memories for her gaudy pen until, her "heart in a glow," she returned in November 1851 to what she described as her "own nest-like home" and the "happy voices" of her children "ringing up through the grape-leaves." Prophetically she announced to her followers in *Peterson's Magazine* that "something of all that my spirit has garnered in the old world . . . will yet be blended in the romance and the song, with which it is my ambition still to haunt your firesides yet a little longer."

Through the years, both abroad and at home, Mrs. Stephens had been collecting not only literary, but political notables. Most of her friends dabbled more or less in politics, from James Brooks of the *New York Express* to George Pratt, who was to become state senator. She herself, in anticipation of a tour abroad, had at one time hoped to be entrusted with government dispatches, and among the verses in her scrapbook were her lines to John C. Calhoun and her poem on the death of President Harrison. The woman who was to provide the first Beadle Dime Novel was, in her heyday, if not a political power in Washington, at least one who had "many friends in Congress." She had been a guest of President Polk, and she could indeed boast that she "need not hesitate what to wear" at the Earl of Carlisle's mansion, since she had "often dined at the 'White House,' with different Presidents."

One of her most colorful political friends certainly was Mirabeau B. Lamar, President of the Republic of Texas, whom she had met in New York as early as 1845 and who was requested "to stand sponsor" at the birth of her son. Having written, for

The Knickerbocker Magazine, a poem "To General Mirabeau B. Lamar" who had "won the pale Lone Star/Its brightest golden beam," she was rewarded when the statesman returned the compliment by presenting to Mrs. Stephens not only a tract of land in Texas, but his own verses, "O Lady, While A Nation Pours/Its praises in thine ear." As American Minister to Nicaragua during the late 1850's, Lamar had much in common with Mrs. Stephens, whose brother-in-law, Fermin Ferrer, served as Minister-General of Nicaragua and as Secretary of State under the filibusterer William Walker. With her characteristic interest in all angles of the current scene, Ann Stephens found herself much involved in Nicaraguan affairs, secret missions, and threatened invasions of that country. Her information and her ambitions she confided to yet another political friend somewhat higher placed than Mirabeau B. Lamar—a man who happened to be President of the United States —James Buchanan.

While Buchanan was American Minister in London, Mrs. Stephens had assured him that "if all America lay at my disposal I would confide it . . . to your wisdom and your kindness." After all America had shown a similar turn of mind by electing him to the Presidency, she continued plying the Chief Executive with letters that evinced her friendship and her gratitude for past and future favors. When her husband was demoted from his clerkship in the Liquidating Department of the New York Customs House, it was Buchanan to whom Mrs. Stephens turned for help, and when she was the recipient of secret information about Walker's planned invasion of Nicaragua and Commodore Vanderbilt's part in the affair through his directorship of the Atlantic and Pacific Steamship Company, it was Buchanan to whom she entrusted her confidential report. Assuring the President that "men will learn that James Buchanan has been living for history and working for a nation instead of a mere party," she informed him also that she was "trying in my way to bring a powerful friend or two up to the mountains who shall not leave them except as your sworn supporters. So much for my small politics!"

Her "politics" were not altogether "small," since, long before, Mrs. Stephens had not hesitated to visit Governor Seward of New York for the purpose of getting "a poor . . . mother pardoned from the gallows"—a purpose which she achieved! By 1858 both her "politics" and her literary reputation were such that she was invited to write two odes to celebrate the laying of the Atlantic Telegraph Cable, and her verses were sung, one to the tune of "The Star-Spangled Banner" and one to the air of "God Save the Queen," by the New York Harmonic Society in the Crystal Palace. Even in that marriage of Albion and Columbia, the future Star of Beadle played a part, although, contrary to the popular version, she was not the "first woman that ever sent a telegraphic dispatch under the ocean" by cabling a message to Queen Victoria!

Meanwhile, both Albion and Columbia had been enjoying the fruits, not only of Mrs. Stephens' periodical effusions, but of her appearances in book form. As early as 1843 her husband had reprinted her series on "Jonathan Slick in New York" as *High Life in New York. By Jonathan Slick, Esq.* to "minister to the risibilities" of a larger audience who would be tickled by Jonathan's letters to his "Par," Zephaniah Slick, Justice of the Peace and Deacon of the Church in Weathersfield, Connecticut. In short order the book had been republished in London with a glossary of Yankee words for English readers, and translated into German at Stuttgart, while subsequently *Peterson's Magazine* was to muse coyly, "We would give something to know the witty author; for the work is anonymous." During the 1840's, several of the "witty author's" works crossed the border of the magazine world into that of the paper-covered romance, and "Alice Copley" and "David Hunt, and Malina Gray," "The Diamond Necklace" and "The Tradesman's Boast" were published by the "Yankee" Office of Gleason in Boston and by Graham in Philadelphia—forerunners in the field of cheaply priced paper-backed fiction with which the firm of Beadle was to identify itself.

In 1854 Mrs. Stephens' first full-length cloth-bound novel was issued—*Fashion and Famine*—renamed from her serials, "Palaces and Prisons" and "Julia Warren," and the author soon found herself at the zenith of her success. A domestic novel of city life, it was described as an example of the "intense school" and it swiftly became "a sensation." Published simultaneously in America and England, where it was given "terms . . . better than those yet offered for any American novel," *Fashion and Famine* was dedicated to Mrs. Sigourney and prefaced with the flowery declaration that "the thoughts of an author are the perfume of her own soul going forth on the winds of heaven to awaken other souls and renew itself in their kindred sympathies." If Mrs. Stephens' soul was not renewed by those kindred sympathies, her pocketbook certainly was, for the novel, advertised as "The Greatest of American Books," was translated into German and French, and three large editions were sold within a month of publication. *Peterson's Magazine* assured its subscribers that "Mrs. Stephens has no rival, in American literature, in the higher walks of passionate fiction," and her "passionate fiction" was dramatized in time for the 1854 season. The play opened at Purdy's National Theatre, featuring in the role of the "Strawberry Girl" little Cordelia Howard, who had played Eva—a combination guaranteed to create "as great a sensation . . . as . . . 'Uncle Tom's Cabin.' "

The pattern of Mrs. Stephens' success and of her life work had been set, a pattern quickly followed by her next literary triumph, *The Old Homestead*. From then on the Stephens stories would appear first as serials in *Peterson's Magazine* and then in book form—a "molten lava" flow of melodramatic narratives, domestic novels and historical romances that mingled the author's experience and florid imagination, that stirred in a surefire formula phrenological principles and home influences, mesmerism and flowers, seduction and self-sacrifice. Her stories were pirated or reprinted everywhere; annuals and gift books featured her artistry; even the hostile Rufus W. Griswold styled her one of the most "spirited and popular of our magazinists," and she herself was immortalized as Number 211 in the Fourth Era of Sarah Josepha Hale's *Woman's Record; or, Sketches of all Distinguished Women, from The Creation To A.D. 1854.*

By 1860, Mrs. Stephens' name was obviously one to conjure with, and the firm of Beadle was ready for the sleight-of-hand that would make literary history. In all probability, before 1860 Mrs. Stephens had not heard of the brothers Irwin and Erastus Beadle. Erastus had come from Buffalo, where his major claim to fame had been the publication of a successful *Dime Song Book*, and had ventured to New York where, with his brother Irwin, he formed the firm of Irwin P. Beadle & Co., publishers of *Beadle's Home Monthly*. Then, struck by the simple brainstorm that was to make history, they had decided to venture into the dime novel field. Perhaps it was through Orville Victor, who was to become the Beadle editor in 1861, that overtures were made to Mrs. Ann S. Stephens, for Victor had been a contributor to *Graham's Magazine* and doubtless knew the prolific source of successful serials. Perhaps it was simply Mrs. Stephens' reputation that made the Beadles turn to her for the first number of their new experiment. They were well aware that she fulfilled with perfection their requirements for dime novels, for she avoided the "offensive" and the "immoral" and she specialized in "strength of plot and high dramatic interest." As far as she was concerned, the Beadle offer of $250 for the right to reprint her twenty-year-old serial, "Malaeska," was a welcome one for, despite the success she enjoyed, her husband had recently been demoted to "an inferior post with a salary of eleven hundred—one hundred less than the pay of his clerkship." $250 was $250, especially since she had nothing to do but watch the firm transform her serial into Beadle's Dime Novel Number One—a somewhat insignificant looking pamphlet bound in plain printed orange-colored paper wrappers.

On June 7, 1860, the firm announced their first "Dollar Book For A Dime" in the *New-York Daily Tribune*. On June 9, the book was placed on sale. First 10,000 copies, then 20,000 more were issued. In time, 300,000 copies were said to have been sold— perhaps as many as half a million copies in the various reprints. By 1864 the *North American Review* could state that "an aggregate of five millions of Beadle's Dime Books had been put in circulation. . . . The sales of single novels by popular authors often amount to nearly 40000 in two or three months." Mrs. Stephens sat by, while a new best seller was in the making and a comparatively new literary conception was launched.

Perhaps she wondered why her obscure and long forgotten tale of *Malaeska* was so avidly devoured by the public. The publishers knew the reason if she did not. They had chosen it "as the initial volume of the Dime Novel series," they explained, "from the interest which attaches to its fine pictures of border life and Indian adventure, and from the real romance of its incidents. It is American in all its features, pure in its tone, elevating in its sentiments." Moreover, "This great story" was "full of power and unique delineations of Indian and forest life. The scene is laid in and around New York, in those not very distant days, when the 'dusky skins' infested the Weehawken heights. . . . in beauty of style, fervor of imagination, and construction of plot, it is quite equal to any of the numerous works which the distinguished authoress has hitherto published."

The publishers were astute. In 1860, when the frontier had receded to the line of the Missouri and the Arkansas, when the Far West had been settled, and adventure was no longer just around the corner, arm-chair pioneers and Indian fighters could revel vicariously in this romance that was indeed "American in all its features" and unfolded a tale remote enough to be thrilling, yet not so remote that it could not be remembered. Everywhere, as the 1860's catapulted by, readers devoured the story of *Malaeska*—Union soldiers in army camps to whom Beadle bundled off the paperbacks in carloads, critics who found the dime novels completely "free from any immoral tendency," young men and boys at home who would one day recall the year 1860 less as the year of South Carolina's secession than as the year of Beadle's first dime novel.

For them all, as they thumbed the orange-colored pamphlet almost out of existence, there were color and excitement, adventure and thrills in Mrs. Stephens' *Malaeska: the Indian Wife of The White Hunter*. They were transported, as they turned the pages, to the time when the region of the Catskill Mountains was a "dense wilderness" and the Hudson "glided on in the solemn stillness of nature." They were introduced to an incomparable heroine, the Indian princess Malaeska, who combined the picturesque and the exotic with a civilized sweetness and light, whose "laugh was musical as a bird song," whose "long hair glowed like the wing of a raven," whose "motion was graceful as an untamed gazelle," and whose language, despite her "broken English," managed to be "pure and elegant, sometimes even poetical," expressing sentiments that were "correct" in every principle. Neatly arrayed in her "robe of dark chintz, . . . confined at the waist by a narrow belt of wampum," Malaeska might have stepped directly out of one of Peterson's paper patterns. But, in contrast with her own docile sweetness, her tragic story assumed violent proportions.

Around hearthfire and campfire her tale was read—her marriage to the white hunter, William Danforth, son of a Manhattan fur-trader; his death after a splendid struggle with the Indians, a struggle replete with blazing guns, whizzing tomahawks and savage war-whoops. With avid expectancy her career was followed as Malaeska paddled with her baby down the Hudson to Manhattan, appeared at her father-in-law's home "in the vicinity of what is now Hanover Square," but concealed her identity from her son, who thought her a dusky-hued nursemaid. With acknowledgment as a daughter-in-law denied her, the heroine fled to the woods, leaving her son, taking only her "womanly self-abnegation." As readers lived and relived her adventures, the years passed swiftly until at length her sorrowful tale reached its climax. Young Danforth, grown to proud and wealthy manhood, found Malaeska, who revealed her identity, only to be greeted with his most unfilial response: " 'Great God!' he almost shrieked, dashing his hand against his forehead. 'No, no! it can not—I, an Indian? a half-blood? . . . Woman, speak the truth; word for word, give me the accursed history of my disgrace. . . . So I have a patent of nobility to gild my sable birthright, an ancestral line of dusky chiefs to boast of. . . . Father of heaven! my heart will break—I am going mad!' " Instead of going mad, however, young Danforth preferred the watery grave of the suicide, while his mother, whose hair, touched with the "frost of grief," had turned gray in a single night, swiftly followed him—"the heart-broken victim of an unnatural marriage."

There was no doubt that Mrs. Stephens had found the formula for dime novel success. With just the right proportion of savagery and civilization, with just enough Victorian sweetness coupled with just enough wild melodrama, she had touched the heart of the sentimental and quickened the pulse of the adventurous. The firm of Beadle knew a literary star when they saw one, and swiftly reprinted *Malaeska,* first as a Fifteen Cent Novel, then in their American Sixpenny Library for London consumption. Meanwhile, it was Mrs. Stephens' task to follow the pattern she had set by unearthing more serials for transformation into Beadle Dime Novels. It was a task she assumed with alacrity, supplying the firm with six more tales between 1860 and 1864, among them her romance based upon the real life story of Mrs. Myra Clark Gaines and her celebrated lawsuit, *Myra, the Child of Adoption.*

Her tales of the Far West: *Sybil Chase; or, The Valley Ranche* and *Esther. A Story of the Oregon Trail* followed, along with three more Indian romances: *Ahmo's Plot; or, The Governor's Indian*

Child, Mahaska, the Indian Princess, and *The Indian Queen*—
stories that stirred in the dime novel cauldron a delectable broth
of covered wagons and border scouts, fur-traders and savage Indians—thrilling adventure nicely balanced by decorous character-
ization and sentimental language. Like *Malaeska,* they were widely
read and reprinted in the various Beadle series that served up to
a nation hungry for historic romance its own romantic history. To
Mrs. Stephens all this was simply one more business arrangement
whereby the hand that wrote became the hand that fed. Yet it
was an arrangement that was to give her a niche in literary history,
for the seemingly evanescent paperback imprinted with the title
Malaeska was to make her name remembered when all her other
interminable serials and voluminous cloth-bound novels had turned
to dust.

Unaware of a literary fate which might well have appalled her,
she found that the compulsion to work and write for money was
intensified during the 'sixties. On August 20, 1862, her husband
died of typhoid fever and Mrs. Stephens was left with an unmarried daughter aged 21 and a son of 17. She spent her winters during
the Civil War at the National Hotel in Washington, that "huge
caravansary" that was to serve as headquarters to Booth. There
she may have tried to arrange a position for her son in the Treasury Department, and—in light of the confidential information
which she had supplied to Buchanan—she may possibly even have
acted as secret agent. Certain it is that her political know-how
was increasing. As she put it, "I know all about the ropes the
people and the duties." She believed, too, that "there are more
ways of serving a country than dying for it."

During the earliest days of Lincoln's administration, she tried
to serve her country in one of those "ways." Certainly her solicitude for the President's safety was deeper than the ordinary citizen's, and it was that solicitude that involved her in one of the
most provocative incidents of her political intrigues. On the night
of April 18, 1861, only four days after news of the evacuation of
Fort Sumter and only three days after the call for 75,000 volunteers, Mrs. Stephens appeared at a White House now converted
into a barracks to help report an assassination plot on Lincoln's
life. John Hay, the President's secretary, recorded the story:

To-night, Edward brought me a card from Mrs. Ann Stephens expressing a wish to see the President on matters concerning his personal

safety. As the Ancient [Lincoln] was in bed I volunteered to receive the harrowing communication. Edward took me to a little room adjoining the Hall and I waited. Mrs. Stephens who is neither young nor yet fair to any miraculous extent, came in leading a lady—who was a little of both—whom she introduced to me as Mrs. Colonel Lander [the popular actress, Jean M. Davenport Lander]. I was delighted at this chance interview with the Medea, the Julia, the Mona Lisa of my stage-struck days. After many hesitating and bashful trials, Mrs. Lander told the impulse that brought her. Some young Virginian— long-haired, swaggering, chivalrous, of course, and indiscreet friend— had come into town in great anxiety for a new saddle, and meeting her, had said that he and a half a dozen others, including a daredevil guerrilla from Richmond, named F., would do a thing within forty-eight hours that would ring through the world. Connecting this central fact with a multiplicity of attendant details, she concluded that the President was either to be assassinated or captured. She ended by renewing her protestations of earnest solicitude mingled with fears of the impropriety of the step. . . .

They went away, and I went to the bedside of the Chief *couché*. I told him the yarn. He quietly grinned.

It was supremely fitting that, when Mrs. Stephens died, she was to leave among her possessions not only the locket from Henry Clay, but a gold locket containing a lock of Lincoln's hair that had been cut from his head the night he died and given to her by Dr. Charles Sabin Taft, the army surgeon who had attended the President.

Throughout her stand had been pro-government. In 1859, after Victor Hugo had written a letter condemning the execution of John Brown, Mrs. Stephens had replied, assuring him that John Brown's fate had been "an inevitable necessity," since "Liberty with us subjects herself to the laws she has inspired." Later on she had been a moving spirit as well as Vice-President of the "Ladies National Covenant," a society "for the suppression of extravagance" and "the diminution of foreign imports" during the War. And she had, of course, turned her pen to the service of the North, compiling a *Pictorial History of the War For The Union* that followed "the ensanguined track" of events through reports from the War Department, statements of commandants in the field, and descriptions by eye-witnesses.

Taking time off from her Washington enterprises, Mrs. Stephens attended and reported the Vanderbilt Golden Wedding celebration in New York on December 19, 1863, presenting her host and hostess with "five handsomely bound volumes" of her own works, among them one dedicated to Mrs. Cornelius Vanderbilt and rather startlingly entitled *The Rejected Wife*. Everywhere during the '60's and '70's she was a figure of importance. Her "Song of the Working Woman" evoked copious tears when it was read at a meeting at Cooper Institute, and her reputation was enhanced as her output increased. By 1870 it could be said that "there are American writers, such as . . . Mrs. Stephens, . . . who, if the statistics were given, would be found . . . to have an immense constituency, outlying in all the small towns and rural districts, such as no English writer possesses here." When she mentioned the name of a florist in one of her stories, he was so inundated with customers that he sent her a bouquet every week. According to her publishers, the "great secret" of her success was simply that "her readers cannot get out of her influence."

Readers of magazines certainly found it difficult to do so. From Street and Smith's *New York Weekly* to *Frank Leslie's Chimney Corner* they found her effusions featured, and in *Peterson's Magazine* she continued her serials when advertisements of "Sozodont" were substituted for advertisements of the "Balm of a Thousand Flowers" and when the chintz costumes and cloth paletots of the '70's took the place of the Garibaldi shirts and Zouave jackets of the '60's. By that time, too, readers of cloth-bound books found it all but impossible to "get out of her influence," for as soon as Charles J. Peterson finished publication of a serial by Mrs. Stephens, his brothers of the firm of T.B. Peterson issued it in book form from their offices at the magazine's own address, 306 Chestnut Street in Philadelphia. While the star authoress' picture was emblazoned on the title-page of *Peterson's Magazine,* her books rolled from the press of T.B. Peterson & Brothers—a mutually productive family arrangement crowned in 1869 by the publication of a uniform fourteen-volume edition of the Works of Mrs. Ann S. Stephens. Whether bound in paper at $1.50 a volume or in cloth at $1.75, her set of popular novels was guaranteed as "suitable for the Parlor, Library, Sitting Room, Railroad or Steamboat." The uniform edition was enlarged in time as *Married In Haste* succeeded *Mabel's Mistake,* or *Lord Hope's Choice* followed *The Reigning Belle*. Appropriately dedicated to the many notables with whom the author had formed a usually lifelong friendship—from

John Neal to Frank Leslie, from the wife of the Governor of Minnesota to Mrs. Cornelius Vanderbilt—the novels recounted, in a demure and respectable manner, such affairs as massacres and "Love in a Log Cabin," "The Chamber of Death" or "The Maniac and the Child," "The Trail of the Serpent" or "The Midnight Walk." Only the titles changed as the years passed, for the compulsion to turn words into money continued. As Mrs. Stephens put it, when she was unable "to do my writing . . . my income . . . stopped." Perhaps her son's unfortunate marriage to one of the Sutton "beauties" contributed to that compulsion, for the marriage ended in divorce not long after the birth of a daughter—Ann Stephens' granddaughter.

In 1873 she was well equipped to convert the products of her pen into cash for her family. By that time, when her early poem, "The Polish Boy," was included in almost every "Reader" of the country, the firm of Beadle reprinted *Malaeska* in yet another series, New and Old Friends. Both that firm and its star author were at their height. At Peterson's "great palace of a house" in Newport, where she spent her summers, or at the Saint Cloud Hotel in New York, where she passed her winters, Mrs. Stephens was an imposing figure. Far from "hanging like a burr on the edges of fashionable society," she was the center of a salon, a tall, stout, dignified woman who, in her black satin cut "en princesse," with ruffles of lace at the throat, and a watch suspended from a jet and gold chain, looked the part of "*châtelaine* of our literary society." In stately manner, her hair "silvered" rather by age than by the "frost of grief" which had worked a similar effect upon Malaeska, she moved with earnest determination among the guests who flocked to her receptions, a circle that included "nearly every person of note who visited the city." At her home in the Saint Cloud, and later on East 63rd Street, her imposing figure was set against an equally imposing if somewhat cluttered background that included Worcester vases and flower stands, John Vanderlyn's self-portrait originally owned by Aaron Burr, as well as a bronze representation of the Dying Gladiator. When she rose from her marquette writing desk to entertain her friends, she found herself the venerated center of a cordon of young girls, and the admired equal of guests "whose fame was counted by their millions, or was won on the battlefield, or in science or music."

Unlike their early star whose powerful lustre showed as yet no signs of dimming, the firm of Beadle had by the 1880's entered into a decline. Although they reprinted *Malaeska* yet again in a series of New Dime Novels and printed a reminiscent article on "The Dime Novel" in *Beadle's Weekly,* both the nature and the reputation of their product were waning. The cowboy and the detective had taken the place of the Indian and the frontiersman. The West was vanishing as a literary source. The new dime novel, according to the *Daily Tribune* which had carried the advertisement of the first, was "distinctly evil in its teachings and tendencies." Its heroes were almost always "thieves, robbers and immoral characters," while its stories abounded with "descriptions of brutality, cruelty and dishonesty." The Hon. Abel Goddard was moved to make his bid for immortality by introducing into the New York Assembly a bill that would declare guilty of a misdemeanor "any person who shall sell, loan, or give to any minor . . . any dime novel . . . without first obtaining the written consent of the parent or guardian."

With all this, the first of the Beadle authors was probably not too deeply concerned. Her daughter and her friends, her visits to her publishers in Philadelphia and to her son, who worked in the Treasury Department in Washington, above all her literary commitments filled her life during the early '80's. That a "fate worse than death" might overtake her *Malaeska* was incomprehensible to its creator, whose hand might tire but never succumbed.

Yet even to such productivity there was an end. On August 20, 1886, the 76-year-old Mrs. Stephens, who was visiting her really lifelong friend, Charles J. Peterson, at Newport, died. A new 23-volume edition of her Works was rolling from the presses. Her serials were still running in *Peterson's* and would continue running after her death. As the editor put it, "There are readers, this year, of her 'Millionaire's Daughter' whose grandmothers read 'Mary Derwent' and 'Malina Gray' when they first appeared, more than forty years ago." "With her, the last of what may be called the first generation of American female authors passed away." One newspaper after another recalled her life and echoed her praises. She had been "among the most prolific authors of the age." She had made "A Fortune . . . by Her Novels, Yet at 70 She Had Not Dropped the Pen." She was "the first American woman novelist of note." The Nineteenth Century Club passed a resolution on

EL BOLERIO, AS DANCED BY MSS. M. A. LEE, AND MR. HUBBARD
—Theatre Collection, Harvard College Library

TITLE-PAGE OF *Malaeska* BY ANN S. STEPHENS (1860),
THE FIRST BEADLE DIME NOVEL
—Rare Book Division, The New York Public Library

the death of its eminent member, characterizing her as "a pioneer in the romance writing of the day. . . . a woman of genius" who "in her half century of hard literary labor . . . has not written one line which 'dying she would wish to blot.' " Nowhere, however, was she described as the author of the first Beadle Dime Novel— except in *The Banner Weekly,* published by the firm of Beadle & Adams, where *Malaeska* was recalled as "a very striking and beautiful story, which had a large sale and assisted materially in establishing the popularity of that famous 'Library of American Romance by noted American authors.' "

Despite *The Banner Weekly,* the reputation both of the House of Beadle and its "Star of American Authors" was about to pass into limbo. While Mrs. Stephens' multitudinous works gradually declined in interest and were eventually forgotten, the Beadle Dime Novel came to be regarded as "an atrocity" and by 1897 the firm reached its debacle.

Yet, like her own serials, no event connected with the life of Mrs. Ann S. Stephens would have been complete without a sequel. The "sequel" to *Malaeska* occurred in 1929, when the first dime novel was reprinted and hailed with fervor by nearly every reviewer in the country. Time had once again worked its transformations. The dime novel was re-interpreted by a new generation as a work that had its "roots in the American scene," even as "the nearest thing . . . to . . . a true 'proletarian' literature, . . . a literature written for the great masses of people and actually read by them." According to the *New York Herald Tribune, Malaeska* "may have been the principal origin of our keen interest in American pioneers and the winning of the West." According to *The Chicago Tribune,* it had "a more important effect on the reading habits of its generation than any other publication of its time." It was "a landmark on the road of American literature," "written . . . by a sedate female who unwittingly blazed the way for a new literature."

Malaeska had become an American document, and the few extant copies of that orange-colored paperback first edition were exalted into rarities, fetching almost half of what Mrs. Stephens had received for giving up all her rights to the work. The "sedate female" who had longed to do something she could "look back upon with pleasure" in her old age, might have shuddered to learn that, of all her unending line of stories, one only would be remembered in the twentieth century and that one, her unconsidered trifle of 1860. Not as the chatelaine of New York's literary society, not as the puller of political wires in Washington, not as the author of serials for popular consumption does she lay claim to memory, but as the author of the first Beadle Dime Novel, upon which time has worked its little ironies.

3

Three American Women
Firsts in Architecture

I HARRIET IRWIN
1869

A T BUFFALO, in October of 1881, an "exultant sea of femininity"—literally as well as figuratively "in high feather"—assembled for the Woman's Congress which was graced by 975 women and 25 men. Among the various discussions of scientific and artistic openings for women, no mention was made of architecture although a woman architect was in their midst. Less than two years later, a contributor to an architectural monthly mused, "It is perhaps singular that in a time when nearly all the professions are invaded by courageous women, . . . not one woman is found to try her fortune as an architect. There are women preachers and physicians and lawyers, as well as painters and sculptors; but no jealous architect finds a professional rival of the other sex." The writer was misinformed. In 1888, at the convention of the Western New York State Association of Architects, Mr. Sidney Smith, president of the Western Association of Architects, prefaced his remarks with the salutation: "Gentlemen: I wish I could add ladies, but I hope the day is not very far distant when I can. . . ." Mr. Smith might have made the hoped-for addition with strictest accuracy, for his audience included a lady architect. As late as 1902, in "A Plea For Women Practising Architecture," a writer supposed that "the reason why woman should not practise architecture is because, except in one or two isolated cases, she has not practised it hitherto."

By that time, however, the "isolated cases" had become the exceptions that proved the rule and pointed the way for women to enter the profession of architecture. Though their work stood strong, they themselves had been unknown, or if known at all, forgotten. Their names had been writ—not on stone—but in water. They had become anonymous. Yet they had lived and they had built—a trio of women firsts in architecture. At long last they may doff their anonymity and carve their names where they belong, on the structures which they planned and which survived them.

Harriet Morrison Irwin of North Carolina was the first woman actually to patent an architectural innovation for a dwelling. This she accomplished in 1869 with no formal training behind her. A dozen years later, Louise Blanchard Bethune, who had studied in an architect's office, opened shop in upstate New York where she designed schools, stores and apartments, becoming the first professional woman architect in the country. After another decade, Sophia G. Hayden, the first woman graduate of the architectural course at Massachusetts Institute of Technology, won the competition for the Woman's Building at the Columbian Exposition and proceeded to supervise its construction. Unaware, by and large, of each other's existence, this trio of women, step by step, explored the mysteries of architectural plans and specifications at a time when such mysteries were considered quite unwomanly. Together they proved that if woman's place was in the home, it might well be a home which she had built, and if woman's place was not in the home, she was quite capable of pursuing the manly art of architecture.

Harriet Morrison Irwin, whose life had run a middle course between that of Southern belle and Southern bluestocking, surely held that woman's place was in the home—provided she had designed that home. She doubtless agreed with the writer who had proposed the rhetorical question, "Who knows so well as [woman] how a house should be constructed? Men may build barns and bridges; but women know best, where they know common things at all, how to plan a dwelling in which they live, move and have their being."

By 1869, Harriet Morrison Irwin had lived and moved and had her being in a variety of homes built by men. At the age of nearly forty-one she could remember the house on the Derita Road near

Charlotte, North Carolina, where she had been born, the third of Rev. Robert Hall Morrison's large family. She could recall still more vividly the three-story house dubbed "Cottage Home" in Lincoln County, a "neighborhood noted for its excellent society, refinement, and hospitality," where her father, who had been the first president of Davidson College, "furnished the best school for his children." The pastor's lessons had been followed by the "home school" of Mrs. M.J. Brevard, and then by more formal studies at the Institution for Female Education in Salem, North Carolina, where Harriet had pursued the ladylike arts of needlework and painting, natural philosophy and the use of the globes. By 1849, when she married James P. Irwin, a cotton factor from Mobile, Alabama, only an intensely inquiring mind and a "remarkable fondness for varied reading" distinguished the twenty-one-year-old bride from the numerous Southern ladies of her acquaintance.

The twenty years that elapsed between Harriet's conventional marriage and her unconventional application for an architectural patent had been filled with enough domestic activity for her to answer that rhetorical question, "Who knows so well as [woman] how a house should be constructed?" Living at first in Mobile and later in Charlotte, she had given birth to nine children, losing four of them in infancy. With an eye sharpened by experience, she must have formed her own ideas about the housing needs of large families. And if she glanced into Mrs. Tuthill's *History of Architecture*—probably the first architectural history by a woman in the country—she must have smiled accordance with its dedication, "To The Ladies of The United States of America, The Acknowledged Arbiters of Taste."

Between bearing her large family and facing the havoc wrought by the Civil War, Mrs. Irwin probably found little time before 1869 to exercise her own architectural tastes. The War itself had been as close to her as to any North Carolinian—closer perhaps, since she was the sister-in-law of the Confederacy's hero, Stonewall Jackson. By 1869, heroic memories of the battlefield had been replaced by the no less heroic demands of everyday life. Harriet's world had changed. Out of the ruins of the old agrarian system, she observed in Charlotte a new, unprecedented industrial development. Impoverished landowners from the country were pouring into the city. Northern capitalists were reopening the gold mines.

Cotton was selling at thirty-five cents a pound. Although Federal troops still roamed the city, and the Ku Klux Klan had made its ominous appearance, buildings were rising in Charlotte almost at the rate of one a day. The time had come for Mrs. Irwin to make her own literal contribution to the Reconstruction of the South, and to demonstrate that women did indeed "know best, . . . how to plan a dwelling in which they live, move and have their being."

This she proved in an extraordinary document entitled "Improvement In The Construction Of Houses," known to the United States Patent Office as Letters Patent No. 94,116, dated August 24, 1869. The document—ambiguously signed "H.M. Irwin," proposed "an entire revolution in the method of building houses." It called for a dwelling that would be neither the conventional square, nor the less conventional octagon, but the still less conventional hexagon.

Be it known that I, H.M. Irwin, of Charlotte, county of Mecklenburg, State of North Carolina, have invented an Improvement in the Construction of Buildings; and I do hereby declare the following to be a full, clear, and exact description of the same.

My invention consists of a dwelling-house or other building, hexagonal in form, and enclosing a space separated into hexagonal and lozenge-shaped rooms, . . . also of a chimney-stack, arranged at the junction of the walls of the adjacent hexagonal rooms, and containing flues communicating with the fire-places in the several rooms.

The objects of my invention are the economizing of space and building-materials, the obtaining of economical heating mediums, thorough lighting and ventilation, and facilities for inexpensive ornamentation.

By external elevations and sectional plan views, the housewife from Charlotte, North Carolina, proceeded to "describe the mode of carrying her invention into effect." She would eliminate "the ordinary passage, and its consequent waste of the interior area of the building," at the same time affording "every facility of communication between the different rooms." For purposes of ventilation and lighting, she believed, her arrangement was "far superior to any other now used." Moreover, a greater floor-surface could be obtained in hexagonal buildings than in the oblong or square variety. She claimed, therefore, as her invention, "A building hexagonal in form, . . . its entire area . . . divided by partitions . . .

into hexagonal and lozenge-shaped rooms," in testimony whereof she signed her name to her specification in the presence of witnesses.

Whether or not Mrs. Irwin's invention did indeed "create a new era in architecture" is less significant than the fact that in 1869 a Southern woman without any formal training had conceived such an innovation at all. Whether or not Harriet's hexagons were simply a variation on the "Octagon Mode of Building" outlined by the phrenologist, Orson Fowler, some years before, is less important than the fact that Harriet actually patented her hexagonal plan. And if there are but few hexagonal houses dotting the countryside today, it is still well to remember that one of them was designed by a woman working comparatively unaided in the South of 1869.

For Harriet Irwin not only patented her hexagonal dwelling, but built it. On Charlotte's West 5th Street it stands today, a two-story frame house with a central tower, a mansard roof, an arched porch, and hexagonal apartments—a dwelling now subdivided and somewhat the worse for wear, but still it stands, enduring testimony to the fact that a Southern lady had effected a revolution, if not in a nation's architecture, then in women's opportunities. As one critic put it, "Among the new and untried fields ready for the occupation of woman is that of dwelling-house architecture. Every housekeeper knows what enormous stupidity has generally been displayed in the construction of the family dwelling; the waste of corners, the sacrifice of details necessary to convenience and comfort, to apparent size and show, and the utter ignorance of those points in the internal arrangement which promote convenience and comfort, and save time and labor. . . .

. . . Women are eternally complaining of want of closet room, of badly arranged rooms and closets, of the want of windows for ventilation, of the inaccessibility of some of the most important sections; attics, for example, and various other shortcomings, found in some of the most costly as well as the poorest houses, yet they have not seemed to think of the remedy in providing better designs and calling public attention to them.

None but Harriet Irwin, that is, had thought of the remedy. She had suffered, but not endured the "furnace-heated, carpeted and curtained rooms" designed by male architects in the throes of Victorian Gothic or French Mansard. She had pored over her copy of Stoney on *The Theory of Strains in Girders,* studying angles of economy and the tensile strength of materials. She had made notes and rough sketches that would convey "her own ideas on house planning." And she had followed her designs to their logical conclusion, from plans and specifications to letters patent, and from letters patent to the completed dwelling, the hexagonal house that would be "cheaper, handsomer," more spacious, and "capable of greater artistic beauty than the square."

Harriet Irwin followed her hexagonal enterprise with at least two other dwellings which she designed along more conventional lines and angles, and with a work of fiction almost as unusual as her architectural invention. *The Hermit of Petræa,* dedicated appropriately by the authoress in 1871 "To England's Artist, Philosopher And Poet, John Ruskin," incorporated her "speculative theories" not only on health, clothing and vegetarian diet, but on architecture. Its hero, young Harry Thorpe, who ventured in search of health to the wild regions of Arabia Petræa, finds himself in surroundings which "filled him with amazement."

I was not in a house, [he mused] and yet not quite out of doors. . . . I lay in a lofty, latticed arbor of a hexagonal or six-sided form, . . . Three sides were closely latticed with osiers, . . . The other three sides were arched openings.

Studying its "novel architecture," he saw that "the soul of the artist spoke in every line and curve, projection and recess; and the effect of the whole was as magically beautiful as though built by a painter's brush." And so he resolved that "The fine art which I will choose for my province, shall be 'the magnificently *human* art of architecture,' . . . I may possibly rear structures of such airy grace and lightness, and strength and beauty, that my name will live, in architectural annals, like that of bishop Henri de Blois."

In her own quiet, unspectacular way, the creator of *The Hermit of Petræa* had also chosen, as one corner of her province, "the magnificently *human* art of architecture." Varying her versatile pursuits with magazine and newspaper articles and a colonial history of Charlotte, she lived on until 1897, "a very gentle sweet lovable old lady," whose white hair was demurely covered with a lace cap. But the gentleness and the frailty could not conceal the strength of purpose in this domestic lady of the South. Even in death she remained devoted to her architectural theories, for in Elmwood Cemetery the monument sacred to her memory is of hexagonal shape! Mrs. Irwin's invention, described in Letters Patent 94,116, standing for all to behold on Charlotte's West 5th Street, is testimony that in 1869 a woman had pioneered in the unwomanly art of architecture. Harriet's hexagons bear witness, tangible and enduring, to Harriet's belief that woman's place was in the home that she had built.

II LOUISE BETHUNE
1881

In 1869, when Harriet Irwin was patenting her "Improvement In The Construction Of Houses," Jennie Louise Blanchard, who, as Louise Blanchard Bethune would one day become America's first professional woman architect, was a thirteen-year-old child in upstate New York. Like Harriet, Jennie Louise had been educated at home. As Harriet's father had served as president of a college, Louise's father was principal of a school. There, however, any resemblance between the two ended. There was no Southern graciousness about Louise Blanchard. No gentleness concealed her forthright purposes. Her beliefs went further than those of her North Carolinian predecessor. Woman should do whatever she was capable of doing, provided she received equal pay for equal work. And if her capabilities ran to architectural design, she should certainly not content herself with merely building a home in which to live.

Like Harriet Irwin, Louise Blanchard both reflected and moved beyond her background. But their backgrounds presented studies in contrast. Born in Waterloo, New York, in 1856, the daughter of Emma and Dalson W. Blanchard, the principal of Waterloo Union School and a mathematics instructor noted for his "mental agility and accuracy," Louise even in her girlhood "showed great aptitude in planning houses and various other structures." Having acquired in her upstate New York home "habits of study and self-reliance which led her . . . to disregard the usual class criterions," Louise continued her education at Buffalo's high school, from which she was graduated in 1874. "A caustic"—and unrecorded—"remark had previously turned her attention in the direction of architecture, and an investigation, which was begun in a spirit of playful self-defense, soon became an absorbing interest." For two years Louise Blanchard taught, traveled, and studied, hoping to prepare herself for the recently opened architectural course at Cornell University. Instead, at the age of twenty, she received an offer of an office position as draftsman with the Buffalo firm of Richard A. Waite. She knew that by far the greater number of professional architects were trained not in the schoolroom but in the drafting office. She would follow suit.

Between eight in the morning and six in the evening, she worked and studied. The pay was small, but architect Waite's library was at her disposal. For five years, between 1876 and 1881, she continued as Waite's student and assistant, spending part of the time also with architect F.W. Caulkins of Buffalo. The apprenticeship was productive, for Louise Blanchard not only mastered the techniques of drafting and the art of architectural design, but met in Waite's office her future husband, Robert Armour Bethune. Her fellow student came, she learned, from Canada, and had begun his work as a draftsman with Detroit's pioneer architect, Gordon Lloyd, before venturing to Buffalo. They soon decided that they had enough in common to share not only their lives, but their careers.

In October of 1881, when a galaxy of strong-minded women were convening in Buffalo for their Woman's Congress, one strong-minded woman gave evidence of her beliefs in equal opportunity for women by opening, with Robert Armour Bethune, an architectural office in Buffalo. Surrounded by tressels and stools, boards and drawings, Louise Blanchard gave notice to any interested party that the first professional woman architect in the country was ready for business.

Only two months later, on December 10, 1881, Louise Blanchard married her partner. The firm of R.A. and L. Bethune had flung its banner to the breeze on Buffalo's Main Street. Louise Bethune did not shun the "practical questions of actual construction"— the "brick-and-mortar-rubber-boot-and-ladder-climbing period of investigative education." To her knowledge of drafting she joined a familiarity with the Romanesque Revival that flourished in American architecture. And gradually she formed her own conception of the work of the architect. It was not "construction in any of its various branches," nor was it "arrangement of interior nor exterior, nor coloring, nor carving, nor profiling of moldings." Neither was it "acoustics, nor fenestration, nor sanitation, nor any one of a hundred other things." Rather, it was "the arranging and adjuncting, harmonizing and contrasting of all these and many other elements into a suitable and satisfactory whole."

To the application of this credo, Buffalo's young woman architect now gave herself. And Buffalo responded, assigning commission after commission, as the years passed, to the firm of R.A. and L. Bethune. To the cluster of buildings in Buffalo that reflected the Romanesque Revival the Bethunes added a goodly share. Their province was wide. They undertook any architectural design, from a $4,000 Episcopal chapel in the suburb of Kensington to a $150,000 brick factory at Black Rock, from a grand stand and fence for the Buffalo baseball club to a veterinary stable on Franklin Street, from a storage building to a bank. Mrs. Bethune, unlike Mrs. Irwin, did not hold that women were ordained by nature to specialize in dwelling house architecture. The dwelling she regarded as "the most pottering and worst-paid work an architect ever does. He always dreads it, not, . . . because he must usually deal with a woman, but because he must strive to gratify the conflicting desires of an entire household, who dig up every hatchet for his benefit and hold daily powwows in his anteroom, and because he knows he loses money nearly every time. Dwelling house architecture, as a special branch for women, should be, . . . quite out of the question." Louise Bethune knew whereof she spoke. She had helped design many a dwelling, from a $3,500 residence on Porter Avenue to a $30,000 brick and stone apartment house in Bridgeport, Connecticut, from a two-story $7,000 frame apartment house on Fourteenth Street to a whole block of flats in Buffalo.

Louise Bethune's tressels and boards and architectural paraphernalia were put to steady use, as the years passed, and her firm provided plans and specifications for the stores that were rising in Buffalo—a building for the merchant, M.J. Byrne, a block of stores for Michael Newell, the Iroquois Door Company's plant on Exchange Street, the Denton, Cottier & Daniels music store—one

of the first edifices built with steel frame construction and the
first to use poured concrete slabs to resist fire.

Buffalo needed not only stores and dwellings, but hotels for
visitors to upstate New York, and these, too, the Bethune architects were ready to design. In 1898 they were invited to plan the
225-room Hotel Lafayette that would, it was hoped, house visitors
to the great Pan-American Exposition in Buffalo. Financial troubles intervened, however, the Pan-American "came and went that
chilly Summer of 1901," and the Hotel Lafayette was not completed until 1904. It made up in imposing detail for its delay in
construction. The Bethune firm built the hotel in "French Renaissance" style. A million dollars were spent "in providing comfort
and enjoyment for Buffalo people and Buffalo guests." The fire-
proof structure, with its slabs of Numidian marble in the main
lobby, its restaurant in English oak, its red and gold grill room,
its wine rooms and billiard rooms, "excited general admiration."
Working with contractors and plumbers, masons and carpenters
and engineers, the architects had planned a hotel that reflected
Buffalo's industrial expansion and its importance as the "gateway
to the Middle West," a building that would stand long after they
had ceased building.

If Louise Bethune specialized in any branch of architecture, it
was the school building to which she gave particular attention.
Her firm designed some eighteen schools in western New York
State, from the two-story Hamburg High School, costing $10,000,
to a twelve-room schoolhouse on Miller Street, costing $45,000.
Far more ambitious was the Lockport High School, financed by
a special bond issue. The plans had been drawn by R.A. and L.
Bethune of Buffalo. On July 10, 1890, the cornerstone was laid,
and in August of the following year, Louise Bethune reaped her
rewards when "an immense crowd gathered at the new Union
School building . . . to witness the dedication ceremonies." Better
than any, perhaps, she knew the tremendous hurdles mounted
between the submitting of the architect's plans and the dedication
of the building.

Despite her special interest in schools, she refused "to confine
herself exclusively to that branch." Louise Bethune believed "that
women who are pioneers in any profession should be proficient
in every department, and that now at least women architects must

be practical superintendents as well as designers and scientific constructors." An architect, whether man or woman, must, she knew, be at once artist, scientist, and practical businessman; essentially an architect must be an artist; incidentally an architect must be a constructor, a modeler in building materials. To the harmonizing of those abilities she had given herself, combining skill in designing structures of every description and variety with "a practical knowledge of all the details of building." She could and did provide working drawings "to guide the artificers"; she was familiar with "the qualities and strength of materials, the weight of structures, and the relationship of the various operations" involved in building. She was, in every sense of the word, a professional architect. Neither the birth of her son in 1883 nor the troubles of clients in financing the buildings they had commissioned were allowed to interfere long with her art and her work. By 1889 R.A. and L. Bethune were "enjoying a justly earned reputation at their quarters on Main street, and their services were in demand from their large and varied experience in the profession and their work being conducted on good business principles."

To her artistic and professional principles Louise Bethune added another, more general ideal toward which she labored. "Woman's complete emancipation," she believed, lay in "equal pay for equal service." Perhaps to realize this distant goal she combined with her professional career years of practical work as a committeewoman. The practising architect was also an intense partisan of reform in the profession to which she was committed.

In 1885, Louise Bethune joined the Western Association of Architects. A year later she helped organize the Buffalo Society of Architects, an organization which merged into the New York State Association of Architects and finally became the Buffalo Chapter of the American Institute of Architects. In all these associations Louise Bethune was an active and effective member or officer. To the American Institute of Architects she was admitted in 1888 as the first woman associate. The work of these organizations became part of her life, whether they discussed the "Status of an Architect" or "Building Stone" and "Various Hardwoods," whether they considered the draftsman's working hours or legal decisions relating to building interests. On architectural competitions she held especially violent views, believing that "competition

is an evil against which the entire profession has striven for years."
"I never vote or have anything to say on competitions," she remarked at a meeting in Buffalo's Library Building. She doubtless
had more to say about the important subject of the Architects'
Licensing Bill which was to take twenty-five years of legislative
debate before becoming a law of the State. For Louise Bethune
was active in attempting to secure passage of a law that would
"enforce rigid preliminary examinations" for architects and that
would so closely affect the practising of architecture in years to
come.

In 1888, Louise Bethune of Buffalo, not yet thirty-two, had
become the first woman member of the American Institute of
Architects. A year later, when all members of the Western Association of Architects were automatically admitted to the Institute
as Fellows, she became the first woman Fellow. "Before we separate," the toastmaster had proposed, "let us drink a toast to the
lady member of the Buffalo chapter, Mrs. Bethune." The toast
itself was both gallant and prophetic. "Long may she live and may
there be many more."

Louise Bethune lived on until 1913. As early as 1890, with the
admission of the architect, William L. Fuchs, to her firm, she had
indulged in a semi-retirement, continuing as more or less silent
partner in the concern now known as Bethune, Bethune and Fuchs.
She kept her hand in her profession none the less, delivering,
before the Women's Educational and Industrial Union, a speech
on "Women and Architecture," supervising the plans for the Hotel
Lafayette, and no doubt observing with keen interest the architectural innovations introduced to Buffalo by Louis H. Sullivan
and Frank Lloyd Wright. As she grew older, a short, stout lady,
she spent her leisure moments on genealogical pursuits, joining
and then dropping membership in the Daughters of the American
Revolution. On December 18, 1913, she died, having left to her
husband all her "interest or share" in her "office furniture and
office library, books and papers," and all her "interest in all uncol-
lected office accounts and claims." Bethune, Bethune and Fuchs,
architects of Buffalo, now were transformed into Bethune and
Fuchs. The traces of the woman partner who had been the first
professional woman architect in the country were committed to
memory.

In 1891, when Louise Bethune spoke on the subject of "Women and Architecture," she had been asked her opinion of the Woman's Building proposed for the World's Columbian Exposition. "The chief of construction," she said, "has issued a circular inviting competition, notwithstanding the fact that competition is an evil." The competition for the Woman's Building she regarded as the "most objectionable form" of competition, since it was by women and for women, and since it was not conducted on the principle of "equal pay for equal service." She herself had refused to submit a design. Whether or not Harriet Irwin of North Carolina had similar opinions regarding the Woman's Building, she presented a copy of her *Hermit of Petræa* to the Woman's Library. Both women architects were doubtless aware that the competition for the Woman's Building had been won by yet another woman "first" in architecture—Sophia G. Hayden—the first woman graduate of the regular architectural course at the Massachusetts Institute of Technology.

III SOPHIA G. HAYDEN
1891

It is one of the ironies of fortune that Sophia Hayden should epitomize so well the advancing steps in the profession of architecture and in woman's pursuit of that profession. She was an architect who designed only one major building. Her career, although spectacular, was brief. Yet within the span of a few years she helped to dramatize the change in American architectural taste, the importance of academic training for architects, and the possibilities for women in a gentlemanly art. Like her building, her career stands for an idea.

She was born in Santiago, Chile, about 1868, the daughter of a New England dentist, Dr. George Henry Hayden, and a South American mother variously described as a "Spanish lady" and a "Peruvian beauty." Her heritage was twofold—the quiet reserve of New England, the "soft, dark eyes of the Latin race." In early childhood, Sophia Gregoria left South America for Massachusetts and began her studies at the Hillside School. In 1883, before she was fifteen, she entered West Roxbury High School. Lamartine

Street, in Jamaica Plain, where she lived, was a far cry from Santiago, Chile, but Sophia seems to have adjusted well to her surroundings, and in June of 1886 the young girl of the dark Latin eyes and the quiet New England reserve delivered at her graduating exercises the first essay on "Our Debt to George Eliot."

Surely if Miss Hayden owed any debt to George Eliot, it was to the George Eliot who had written *Romola* and reveled in the architectural beauties of the Florentine Renaissance. To the study of those beauties the eighteen-year-old Sophia now dedicated herself, entering the architectural school of the Massachusetts Institute of Technology in 1886. The young woman student soon learned that the method pursued at the Institute was modeled upon that of the École des Beaux-Arts in Paris, and that she must "grasp the principles governing composition and design, and . . . present clearly and intelligently" her "finished work." Not for her the "picturesque and free-and-easy Romanesque" that required no academic training, but rather the elaborate techniques of "Classic design" that demanded "manual dexterity and mental accuracy, . . . skill of hand and eye, the cultivation of good taste in line, form, color, and design."

Especially the classic techniques demanded study. And study she did—strength of materials and heating and ventilation, contracts and the "mathematical side of drawing." A "brilliant and earnest" pupil, she attacked the problems presented to her, making blueprints from tracings of architectural details, working at graphical statics and stereotomy, attending lectures in architectural history. The slender young woman of medium height, with soft, dark hair and a pleasant manner, grappled with Eugène Létang, the first great teacher of design in America, who fell "with almost savage intensity upon the work of the students," but who taught them to scorn sham and love a rational classic architecture. She grappled with an intensive curriculum, too, that ranged from mechanical and freehand drawing to shades and shadows and perspective, from the Orders and elements of architecture to acoustics and problems in construction. Lectures and sketch problems, drill in design, working drawings and specifications consumed her. At length, in her final year, she presented her thesis—the design for a Museum of Fine Arts which, with its Renaissance style, its portico with Ionic columns, its symmetrical proportions, foreshadowed the building she was to plan for the Columbian Exposition and epitomized the classic academic training she had received. In 1890, Sophia Gregoria Hayden was awarded the degree of Bachelor in Architecture from the Massachusetts Institute of Technology, the first woman to receive a degree in architecture from that school. Not long after, she could rejoice that President Walker of the Institute considered her "competent to build a railroad bridge, if necessary, as she has gone thoroughly into her work."

It was not a railroad bridge, however, that was to test her competence, but a building designed for women and by a woman, a building as classic in its architectural style as it was symbolic in its significance. Perhaps it was through President Walker, who served as chairman of the State Commission for the World's Fair, that Sophia Hayden first heard of "An Unusual Opportunity for Women Architects." While she may have had some brief experience in an architect's office after her graduation, she was teaching mechanical drawing in the Eliot School when she read the unprecedented "advertisement to women architects for the design and construction of a public building."

Sketches are asked for, on or before March 23, 1891, for the Woman's Building of the World's Columbian Exposition. None but those made by women will be considered. Applicants must be in the profession of architecture or have had special training in the same, and each must state her experience, in writing, to the Chief of Construction. All sketches must be sent in sealed, with only a motto on the envelope, which must contain a second envelope inclosing name and address of the designer. The selected design will carry with it the appointment of its author as architect of the building. She will make her working drawings in the Bureau of Construction, and receive an honorarium of $1,000, besides expenses. A prize of $500 and one of $250 will be given for the two next best drawings. A simple light-colored classic type of building will be favored. . . . The general outline of the building must follow closely the accompanying sketch plans, the extreme dimensions not exceeding two hundred by four hundred feet; exterior to be of some simple and definite style, classic lines preferred; the general effect of color to be in light tints. Staff, stucco, wood, iron, and equivalents to be used as building material, with discretion as to the disposition and ornamentation, so as not to render the building too costly. First story, eighteen feet high; second story, twenty-five feet high. . . . to come within the limit of . . . $200,000. The plans should show the outline desired, leaving all detail to the ingenuity of the competing architect, who is expected to give them a thorough study, locating openings, etc., so as to give easy access and exit to the constant flow of passing crowds. The main entrance will lead down a series of steps to the water landing, . . . Drawings must be made to a scale of one sixteenth of an inch to the foot. They must include elevations of one front and one end, as well as one perspective.

The announcement of this unusual competition was doubtless read in Charlotte by Harriet Irwin, and in Buffalo by Louise Bethune, who proceeded to fulminate against it. When Sophia Hayden read it, she sat down to draw her plans in India ink, omitting shade lines and brush work, and designing two elevations in line at one sixteenth of an inch to the foot. The academic training she had received at the Massachusetts Institute of Technology, the admiration for classic architecture that had been instilled in her, the practice she had had in planning a Museum of Fine Arts, were all concentrated in her drawings. When she had completed them, she sealed them in an envelope and sent them to Daniel H. Burnham, Chief of Construction of the World's Columbian Exposition, Room 1143, "The Rookery," Chicago. Then she waited.

While she waited she surely heard much of the plans and purposes behind this Woman's Building of the Columbian Exposition and the unprecedented competition that had been instituted for its design. The Board of Lady Managers, provided for by the Act of Congress which had created the Exposition, desired a building that would "direct attention to [woman's] progress and development, and her increased usefulness in the arts, sciences, manufactures, and industries of the world during the past four hundred years," that would "present a complete picture of the condition of women in every country of the world . . . and more particularly of those women who are bread-winners." Unlike the other Exposition buildings which were assigned to male architects who represented the best talent in the country—Richard M. Hunt, McKim, Mead and White, Van Brunt and Howe, George B. Post, Peabody and Stearns—the Woman's Building was to be designed by a woman chosen by competition, since "there was no woman practicing architecture with sufficiently established reputation to warrant her selection," and also since a competition "would attract

attention" to the work of women "and . . . be an advertisement
for all the women who entered" it. Bertha Honoré Palmer, President of the Board of Lady Managers, had made a pencil sketch
of a plan showing the interior arrangement of the building, and
had had it drawn on an enlarged scale by a draftsman before
Chief of Construction Burnham had prepared the "notification of
competition."

On March 24, 1891, drawing after drawing was spread out
before Mrs. Potter Palmer and the Supervising Architect until
about a dozen plans had been displayed, "almost all of which
were creditable, and five or six excellent." In one, however, Mrs.
Palmer discovered "that harmony of grouping and gracefulness of
detail which indicated the architectural scholar." The competition
was closed.

For the twenty-two-year-old Sophia Hayden the moment of triumph had arrived. She was rewarded for her intensive work at
the Institute and her devotion to architectural studies when she
received a telegram from Daniel H. Burnham informing her that
her plan had won the first prize of $1,000 and that she was to
journey at once to Chicago and prepare the working drawings.
For the next year or two the history of her life would be the
history of a building. Her moment of triumph would be over-
shadowed by days and months of labor and struggle. Her work
had just begun.

She must contend, first of all, with the Board of Lady Managers,
not all of whom concurred in the choice of the architect, but most
of whom wished to "incorporate into her building all sorts of bits
of design and work, whether they harmonized . . . with it or not."
She must contend, too, with the Board of Construction with whom
she must modify her plans. Her shy New England reserve, however, did not prevent her from insisting in her own quiet way upon
her designs when she was convinced of their beauty and originality.
Problem after problem arose and was met. The Woman's Building,
not originally intended to be primarily an exhibit building, was
swiftly being forced into that state when exhibits were denied admission elsewhere. Compared with the other Exposition buildings,
it was small—too small. Compared with the other buildings, the
sum appropriated for it was negligible—$200,000, as opposed to
over one million dollars for the Manufactures and Liberal Arts

Building. More committee rooms were needed, and a third floor must be added, introducing "the novel feature of a roof garden." Changes must be made which would affect both the sky line and the general plan. With freshness and versatility the young architectural student grappled with designs, specifications, modifications in her working plans, while contracts were awarded to carpenters and plasterers, roofers and glaziers. She must extend the time for the receipt of carved panels. She must especially solve one of the most difficult architectural problems presented by the Fair—the design of a comparatively small and inexpensive building that would include not only "a general and retrospective display of woman's work," but a library, an assembly-room, parlors and committee-rooms, a model hospital and kindergarten.

Sophia Hayden summoned up all her architectural skill in meeting the problem. The small scale of the building suggested to her ten feet as "a module of proportion," and upon this basis she developed her plan and organized her elevations. The diffuse and various uses to which the building would be devoted required, she believed, a series of connected rooms all subordinated to a great hall which she would place in the middle, freed from columns and built high enough to receive light through clearstory windows. She would surround the open central area of the hall on the second story with a system of corridors in the style of a cloister around an Italian cortile. Instead of emphasizing vertical lines, she would, because of the comparatively small scale of her building, create strong, horizontal lines in the facades. She would block out the frontage by allowing the roof of the lofty central hall to assert itself. She would mass the building in the manner of the villas of the Italian Renaissance. The first story she would treat as an Italian arcade in bays without columns, while upon the second she would impose a full Order of pilasters more or less in the Corinthian manner. Her third story of small rooms would open on each side on roof gardens which would extend over the end pavilions, surrounded by light Ionic columns. Her design would be lyric rather than epic in character, graceful and delicate, fitting for the display of feminine arts.

For the regular draftsman's pay that amounted to $977.60, Sophia Hayden supervised the construction of her building in Jackson Park. She watched it rise, with its gallery of honor, its vestibules and arches and colonnades, east of Midway Plaisance, facing the north end of the lagoon. From its center she saw the grand landing erected, and the staircase leading to a terrace above the water. Its principal entrance was a triple-arched pavilion. Its rotunda was surrounded by a two-story open arcade, delicate and chaste in design. A series of open colonnades surrounded her building; from its balustrades vines would trail; above the second story stone caryatids would support the roof garden. In the midst of the Windy City, a twenty-two-year-old girl had evoked the classical elegance of the Italian Renaissance.

As the architect herself described it:

The plan of the Woman's Building was laid out to serve the dual purpose for which the building was intended—that is, to be the headquarters for the women connected with the Fair, and also to afford space for exhibits. . . .

The . . . details of this building are modeled after classic and Italian Renaissance types, and on account of the comparative small size and scale of the building, are more delicate and refined than those of the other main structures of the Fair.

The Woman's Building "went up with marvelous rapidity," and was the first to rise on the site of the World's Columbian Exposition. Its architect could be gratified when it was filled with exhibits from all over the world, water colors from Queen Victoria and oil paintings from Princess Christian, "a map of Italy made by an English woman of the time of Dante" and the sword of "Her most Catholic majesty," Isabella of Spain, paintings by Mary Cassatt, court laces, the works of Miss Edgeworth and Miss Austen, mannikins and needlework. She could be gratified, too, when her name was inscribed on the south end of the building she had created.

By October of 1892, the Windy City was fast becoming the White City, the Dream City. Under electric lights and decorations, State Street was thronged for the grand military procession and the great parade of tradesmen. Sophia Hayden was on hand for the inaugural celebration, despite reports that had begun to circulate to the effect that "as a result of overwork she had broken down mentally." Surely she applauded Mrs. Palmer's optimistic if inaccurate remark at the dedicatory ceremonies of the Exposition, "Even more important than the discovery of Columbus, which we are gathered together to celebrate, is the fact that the General Government has just discovered woman."

On the first of May of the following year, the Woman's Building was formally opened. In the court of honor, the hall of the Rotunda, the arches and columns were decorated in white and gold. The flags of all nations flanked the national colors and festoons of crimson and yellow bunting mingled with roses and lilacs, palms and ferns. Amid cheers, applause, and the fluttering of innumerable white handkerchiefs, Mrs. Potter Palmer arose to open the exercises. After the grand march and the reading of the ode, she delivered her address.

The moment of fruition has arrived. . . .

. . . We rejoice in the possession of this beautiful building in which we meet to-day, in its delicacy, symmetry, and strength. We honor our architect, and the artists who have given, not only their hands, but their hearts and their genius to its decoration.

. . . We now dedicate the Woman's Building to an elevated womanhood.

With a golden nail Mrs. Palmer gave the finishing touch to the building planned by a young girl to honor the women of the world.

Theodore Thomas had waved his baton and the audience had joined in singing "America." Elsewhere, President Cleveland had placed his finger on the golden key that opened the Exposition, and the drapery had fallen from the figure of the "Republic." Crowds poured through the Woman's Building and to its library Harriet Irwin presented a copy of her *Hermit of Petræa*. But the architect herself, it was said, was succumbing to "brain fever" or a collapse from the "responsibility for the execution of the prize-winning design."

Perhaps the critics had a hand in Sophia Hayden's breakdown. They pointed out, as if it were a fault, the fact that her work was the work of a student and a woman, allegations to which there could be no answer except perhaps to remark that her building competed with the structures of the most notable architects in the country. "The Woman's Building," *The American Architect* sniffed patronizingly, "is neither worse nor better than might have been expected. It is just the sort of result that could have been achieved by either boy or girl who had two or three years' training in an architectural school, and its thinness and poverty of constructive expression declares it to be the work of one who had never seen his or her 'picture' translated into substance. As a woman's work it 'goes' of course; fortunately it was conceived in the proper vein and does not make a discordant note: it is simply weak and commonplace." The roof garden that crowned the building was a " 'hen-coop'—for petticoated hens, old and young." The same periodical deliberated further, "It seems . . . a question not yet answered how successfully a woman with her physical limitations can enter and engage in . . . a profession which is a very wearing one."

Actually, had Sophia Hayden studied all the reports, she would have found more pros than cons among the critics. The medal awarded her by the Exposition jury was, she knew, for the "delicacy of style, artistic taste, geniality, and elegance of the interior hall." She had, according to some, created the "most unique building" of the Exposition, in which she had perfectly succeeded in conveying the Renaissance style. Daniel Burnham himself, who congratulated Miss Hayden "upon the success of your plans, which is further evidenced by the Construction," described the building as "purely classical, developed with taste and judgment," and tried to induce the young architect to open an office in Chicago, assuring her "that she could soon be at the head of a lucrative business." As Mrs. Palmer put it, "the delicacy and beauty of Miss Hayden's creation . . . have received the highest encomiums from all the artists who have seen it. While our building is smaller and less expensive than most of the others, its scholarly composition, beautiful proportions, refined and reserved details, hold their own, . . . It is remarkable as being the first creation of a young girl." Hubert Howe Bancroft replied to the detractors when he wrote that the Woman's Building was "the work of a professional architect, and not, as some would have us believe, of an architectural scholar; for if Miss Hayden was before unknown to the profession, she has here given proof that she is far above amateur rank. If in her design its feminine features are somewhat pronounced, that is as it should be." As the great architect, Henry Van Brunt, remarked, "It is eminently proper that the exposition of woman's work should be housed in a building in which a certain delicacy and elegance of general treatment, . . . a finer scale of detail, and a certain quality of sentiment, which might be designated, in no derogatory sense, as graceful timidity or gentleness, combined however with evident technical knowledge, at once differentiate it from its colossal neighbors, and reveal the sex of its author."

The Woman's Building must stand or fall upon the fact that it was, for better or worse, the work of a student and a woman. Precisely because it was created by a woman architectural student, it dramatized the advance not only of woman, but of architecture. "The Exposition found the country Romantic, and left it Classic," and with that change in architectural ideals, schools of architecture "automatically assumed a new importance and usefulness." No longer could an architect learn his profession in the drafting room alone. Like Sophia Hayden, he must be academically trained; and with Sophia Hayden, he must learn to master "the highly technical demands of Classic design." The work of the dark-eyed young architect from Massachusetts, the first woman "to whom had been intrusted so important a commission in architecture," marked "an era in woman's progress" as well. Her success—for, despite the carping of the critics, it was success—would stimulate other women to cultivate a comparatively new field. The White City of 1893 marked for many "the first great artistic triumph of the American people. After 1893 it would be known the world over that there was an American school of architecture." The Woman's Building, designed by Sophia Hayden, had been part of that White City of 1893—among the smallest, but far from the least significant part.

The architect herself, despite her breakdown, was able in 1894 to prepare plans for a Memorial Building projected by the women's clubs of the country, and was able later on to marry an artist, William B. Bennett. Although she lived to the great age of more than eighty, however, she built no further buildings. Within a few years of her death in 1953, there were 308 registered women architects in the country, nearly one third of them members of the American Institute of Architects. The building she had designed had stood, indeed, for an idea. "Substantial, spacious, symmetrical," it had been, in its own special way, "the 'bright particular star' in the crown of the Exposition" that had pioneered a pathway for women. Harriet Irwin, who presented a book to the library of that building, Louise Bethune, who opposed the competition that led to its construction, and Sophia Hayden who created it—all stood for an idea—the idea that architecture was yet another avenue along which women could walk, an avenue lined with lyrics if not epics in stone.

Science & Technology

4

America's First
Woman Telegrapher

SARAH G. BAGLEY

1846

A CHARMING little story is told of the first days of the telegraph
in this country. The scene is a hotel room in Washington;
the time, March 4, 1843; the dramatis personae, Samuel F.B. Morse
and the sixteen-year-old Annie Ellsworth, daughter of the inventor's old friend, the Commissioner of Patents. Morse—so the story
goes—had sat all the preceding day in the Senate gallery waiting
in vain for his telegraph bill to be reached by the lawmakers. After
dark he had retired to his hotel thoroughly discouraged, having
been assured by the Senators that the bill could not possibly be
reached before midnight, when the Congressional session would
end. The following morning, Miss Annie Ellsworth appeared at
Morse's hotel, exclaiming, "I have come to congratulate you."
"Indeed, for what?" "On the passage of your bill. . . . Father was
there at the adjournment at midnight, and saw the President put
his name to your bill, and I asked father if I might come and tell
you, . . . Am I the first to tell you?" Morse, overcome with the
news, at last replied, "Yes, Annie, you are the first to inform me,
and now I am going to make you a promise; the first dispatch
on the completed line from Washington to Baltimore shall be
yours."

Scene Two, therefore, is the United States Supreme Court, where
Morse's telegraph had been installed; the time, over a year later:
May 24, 1844; the dramatis personae, Morse, Miss Ellsworth, her
mother, and sundry visitors; the occasion, the historic formal opening of the first completed electro-magnetic telegraph line in the

United States, that between Washington and Baltimore, where
Morse's assistant Vail was ready to receive the first telegraph message. Morse was true to his promise, asking Annie Ellsworth to
choose the words for the first message, and, after consultation with
her mother, the words were selected: "What hath God wrought!"
Morse ticked off the message, Vail received it in Baltimore, and
the strip of paper upon which it was indented was claimed by
Representative Seymour of Connecticut because Annie Ellsworth
was a native of that State.

Although the source of the story is none other than Morse himself, who recounted it to Bishop Stevens of Philadelphia in a letter
of November 1866, the hotel room scene has since been discounted
as apocryphal since Morse's bill was passed early on the morning
of March 3, laid before the President, and signed several hours
before adjournment. None the less, it has, like most fables, not
only a kernel of truth, but a larger all-round significance, for it
links the early days of the American telegraph with a woman—
an association of fact and idea that was prophetic. The invention
of the telegraph was to open to women an important means of
livelihood long before the days of the telephone and the typewriter,
long before the Civil War. If Miss Annie Ellsworth points the way
toward this association in a dramatic little fable, it is another
woman who actually made the first step, serving as America's first
woman telegrapher and hence as a pioneer in a field that would
attract more and more women as the years passed.

She was rather older than Annie Ellsworth, and her background
was far less distinguished. Yet the lowliness of her origins, the
vigor and determination of her personality, the forcefulness of her
principles all had an indirect part in her almost accidental appointment to a post that may now be recognized as historic.

Sarah G. Bagley's story properly begins ten years before that
appointment, when, in 1836, smitten with what was known as
"Lowell fever," she appeared in the City of Spindles to work as
a piece weaver in Mill B of the Hamilton Manufacturing Company. She was—along with most of the "acres of girlhood" who
came by stage or baggage wagon and formed a large part of
Lowell's population—a New Englander, a native of Meredith, New
Hampshire. Like most of them, too, she had had a common school
education. Her origins are obscure, but it is not unlikely that,

like the heroine of a tale she was soon to write, she may have seen service as a domestic before she decided to seek her fortune in the factory town of Lowell, Massachusetts. This was the young woman who, during the decade between 1836 and 1846, was to make her name known, first as one of the earliest of New England's labor reformers, and finally as the country's first woman telegrapher.

In the exciting and revolutionary 1840's there was much to inspire her, much to oppress her, for Lowell was a city of paradox—a model industrial town to some, to others a seed-bed for rebellion. It was primarily a city of newness, and as Sarah G. Bagley walked through its streets, she saw that newness reflected in its unpainted wooden churches, its bright red brick mills, the fresh signposts of its stores. She saw many beginnings in Lowell, from the establishment of its Museum and City School Library to its manufacture of "Cherry Pectoral." But especially she found the newness reflected in the words of the reformers who came to look at Lowell and to speak there. The city attracted them all, abolitionists and agrarians, associationists and Millerites, and Sarah G. Bagley, unknown piece weaver in the Hamilton Mills, heard them all and saw them all. When Ripley, the high priest of Brook Farm, came to elucidate the mysteries of "association," Sarah Bagley was on hand to listen, or when Horace Greeley, the white-haired oracle of the *New-York Tribune,* lectured on reform, or when Garrison discoursed on anti-slavery, or when Charles Dana expounded the new social order. She listened to them all—the Fourierists, the phrenologists, the hobby riders of every reform that dazzled New England in the vibrant 1840's. And she saw them all—all who came to inspect the model City of Spindles—from Catherine Beecher to Dickens, from Robert Owen to Whittier.

They did not always see in Lowell what Sarah G. Bagley saw there. They knew, as she did, that the town had been planned as a model industrial community and named in honor of Francis Cabot Lowell, and they saw, as she did, those "acres of girlhood" dressed in bonnets and shawls, clogs and pattens. They happily observed that the textile mill operatives were thrifty depositors in the Lowell Savings Bank, and that after about three years of work they were able to return to their New England farms with enough money for their wedding outfits. Meanwhile, as they saw it, the girls worked pleasantly in well ordered rooms with plants in the windows, and they slept comfortably in boarding houses that boasted a joint-stock piano. They subscribed to the circulating libraries, heard lectures at the Lyceum or the Institute, and evinced to the complacent world at large that there was "mind among the spindles" and that all was for the best in this best of all possible factory towns.

Sarah Bagley did not quite agree. She had arrived in Lowell in 1836, shortly after an unsuccessful "turnout" or strike for higher wages. At the Hamilton Corporation, where she remained for six and one half years, and at the Middlesex Factory, where she was to continue her labors, she earned about $1.75 a week clear of board. The board itself came to about $1.25 a week, and the boarding houses were controlled by the corporations. In order to enter such a boarding house, Sarah Bagley had to agree to the observance of certain regulations. She was to be answerable for any "improper conduct." If she were habitually absent from public worship on the Sabbath, she could not be employed by the company. The doors of the corporation establishment were locked at ten at night. It was supervised by a respectable widow whose daughters doubtless worked in the mills, and the house was crowded with fifty or sixty young women who ate in a large communal dining-room.

Although circulating libraries were encouraged, reading was strictly forbidden in the mills themselves. Dickens—and at first Sarah herself—might have been pleased by the green plants trained on the windows, but in time she was more impressed by the badly ventilated high narrow building in which she worked, weaving cassimeres and broadcloth. The light was so poor that she was forced to depend upon a "petticoat lamp" fastened to her loom and filled with whale oil. She needed the light, for she worked over twelve hours a day, starting before seven in the winter mornings, before five in the summer, and continuing until seven at night, with a half-hour off for breakfast and another half-hour free for mid-day dinner.

It was the long hours that most disturbed Sarah Bagley. She was awakened by the bells that called the operatives to the mills, dressed hurriedly, and began her weaving by lamplight, working at the loom hour after hour after hour. She began to consider—

as Ripley was to do—that "the screeching of the bell before light on a cold winter's morning is apt to suggest the inquiry whether there is no other way of supplying the world with bleached cotton and calico."

She began to wonder. She would soon seize the opportunity to share that wonder and, by speaking and by writing for what came to be called the Ten-Hour Movement, to make of a lowly and unknown New England mill operative one of the earliest and most vital forces in labor reform.

Her opportunity came in a strange and unlikely way. Ever eager to improve not only others but herself, Sarah Bagley joined one of the "Improvement Circles" held fortnightly in the session-rooms of Lowell's Universalist Churches. Its particular "improvement" was directed primarily to the art of composition and, with the other young operatives who attended, Sarah Bagley submitted original articles which were corrected by the pastors, read aloud at the meetings, and finally presented to the public in a magazine known as *The Lowell Offering*. What set it apart from its many rivals was the fact that it was entirely written by women employed in the Lowell mills. What eventually gave Sarah Bagley an opportunity for speaking her mind was the fact that it insisted upon neutrality and, ostrich-like, buried its sentimental and literary head in sands already sprinkled with the controversial seeds of labor reform.

Signing herself "S.G.B.," Sarah contributed several articles to the *Offering*. Those that were accepted—including one entitled "Pleasures Of Factory Life"—were innocuous, affording an almost roseate glimpse into the Lowell mills. Those that were rejected were more controversial and hence, it soon appeared, unacceptable to a magazine that was controlled less by the operatives who wrote for it than by the corporations that employed them. For Sarah Bagley, the die was cast.

On July 4, 1845, she celebrated an Independence Day of her own by rising to address a convention of New England's workingmen and women in a "beautiful grove" at Woburn. In a speech marked by "thrilling power" of language she combined her appeal for a ten-hour workday with her condemnation of *The Lowell Offering* and so gave an impetus to labor reform and at the same time plunged headlong into the career from which she would emerge as a pioneer agitator for labor's rights. The *Offering,* she stated, was not the voice of the operatives, but rather gave a false representation to the truth. It was controlled by the manufacturing interest to give a gloss to their inhumanity, and anything calling in question the factory system was neglected. Her own articles of that nature had been rejected. Moreover, notwithstanding the present lengthened time of labor, the proprietors of the mills were striving to add two hours to the working day. But, she concluded triumphantly, "the girls have united against this measure, and formed a society to repel this movement." Sarah Bagley took her seat amid "the loud and unanimous huzzas of the deep moved throng," a seat from which she was to rise time and again to demand for workers the right of a ten-hour day. Sarah Bagley, who was soon to slip quietly and without fanfare into the position of America's first woman telegrapher, had found a sounding-board for her beliefs and her purposes. The mill operative of Lowell, Massachusetts, labor reformer and telegrapher-to-be, had just begun to be heard.

The society to which Miss Bagley referred in her revolutionary speech at Woburn was known as the Lowell Female Labor Reform Association. By January of 1845, she had joined with a few other women operatives to organize a society that would fight for a ten-hour day and show the "*driveling* cotton lords," the "mushroom aristocracy of New England," that "our rights cannot be trampled upon with impunity." In January the Society, of which Sarah G. Bagley was elected president, consisted of two members and thirteen officers; by April it boasted a membership of 304 operatives. Revolution, it appeared, was contagious. As an adjunct of the New England Workingmen's Association, the Female Labor Reformers held social gatherings to increase funds for their cause —festivals and picnics, May parties and meetings in the reading room at 76 Central Street. As President of the union, Sarah Bagley prepared reports which announced the increasing membership of the society and exalted "the laboring part of the community" as "the true nobility of the land." She was pleased to interpret the ridicule of the press as an indication that her influence had been felt and feared. "We mean to fight on till a complete victory crowns our efforts."

Fight on she did, with every means at her disposal, from the circulation of *Factory Tracts* to control of a reform newspaper,

H. M. Irwin.

Construction of Buildings.

Nº 94,110.   Patented Aug. 24, 1869.

Fig: 1.

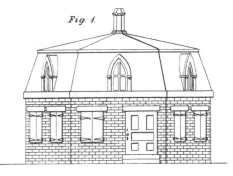

Fig: 2.

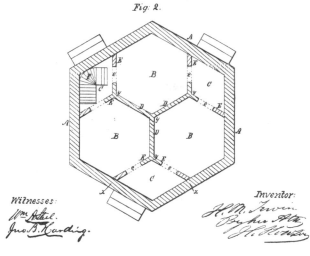

Witnesses: Inventor:

H. M. IRWIN'S PLAN FOR A HEXAGONAL BUILDING (1869)
—United States Patent Office

Louise Bethune

R. A. Bethune

LOUISE BETHUNE AND R. A. BETHUNE
—*The National Cyclopædia of American Biography*

from vehement public speeches to acerbic journalistic letters. Having signed and circulated a petition for the Ten-Hour Day, Sarah Bagley was invited to appear with other operatives at the Boston State House for legislature committee hearings. There she reported that the health of the operatives suffered because of the length of time they were employed in the mills. Moreover, they had too little time "to cultivate their minds." She herself had taught a few girls during the winter evenings in her room, instructing them in the simplest branches of composition, and, after eight and one half years in the mills, her own health had begun to fail. This was distorted by the committee into a statement that the extra labor of keeping evening school for four years had injured Miss Bagley's health. The petition failed, perhaps because the reactionary William Schouler, who published *The Lowell Offering,* was chairman of the legislative committee, perhaps because the mills of God grind more slowly than the mills of Lowell, Massachusetts.

The motto of the Female Labor Reform Association was "Try Again." It was Sarah Bagley's motto, too. There were few reform meetings held between 1845 and 1846 which she did not attend as delegate. In the illustrious company of Robert Owen, Charles Dana, Wendell Phillips, Albert Brisbane, Greeley and Ripley and Garrison, she appeared in Boston at the first convention of the New England Workingmen's Association to speak for Lowell's labor group and present a banner made by her society. On home ground she served as secretary of the Lowell Industrial Reform Lyceum which sponsored lectures on the laboring classes, the organization of society, and human progress. To the papers she sent her letters correcting the impressions of those who viewed the Lowell mills through rose-colored glasses, until finally she found a newspaper that her Female Labor Reform Association could actually control.

In March 1846, the Association bought, with a first payment of $100, the type and press of the *Voice of Industry,* a weekly that labored for "the abolition of idleness, want and oppression; the prevalence of industry, virtue and intelligence," and Sarah G. Bagley served on its publishing committee, becoming editor—one of the first women labor editors in the country—for a short time. At 76 Central Street in Lowell, close to the Bank Building where Abram French dealt in cassimeres and vestings, and not far from the daguerreotype rooms of A. W. Van Alstin, Sarah Bagley helped to issue a sheet that strove for the ten-hour system, the rights of women, and the reform of labor conditions. The organ of the New England Workingmen's Association, the paper published articles on Capital and Labor, reported on the Association's conventions, ran a Female Department, and flourished for a time as the "uncompromising foe to all the oppressions of the age." Apologizing for the fact that its columns were "under the Editorial control of a common schooled New England female factory operative," Sarah Bagley pledged herself to the improvement of the condition of the laboring masses, devoted her Female Department to the defense of woman's rights, and minced no words in her own contributions to the weekly. Of an agent who threatened to discharge an operative for participation in the ten-hour movement she wrote, "We will make the name of him who dares the act, stink with every wind, from all points of the compass." In a report of her visit to the State Prison of New Hampshire, she mused about a handsome inmate: "What a pity, . . . that you did not make a more judicious selection for the practice of rascality. You might have selected some game equally dishonest, that would not have exposed you, but have made you looked up to, as a man of wealth, . . . You might have performed some 'hocus pocus' means of robbery, . . . and passed as an Appleton, a Lawrence, or an Astor in society."

Sarah Bagley had found a sounding-board and a crusade to champion. In meeting, in speech, and especially in newsprint she echoed and re-echoed her demands for labor's rights. Yet both her medium and her cause were destined to short lives. The Ten-Hour Movement, despite Sarah Bagley's vigorous and vociferous attempts, was to end in failure, primarily because of the control that the corporations exerted over the Massachusetts Legislature. Its time had not yet come. And the *Voice of Industry,* converted into *The New Era of Industry,* would turn to other ringing causes of the day—co-operation and land reform.

Meanwhile, the apparently unconquerable Sarah Bagley had found an opportunity for an altogether new career, new not only to herself, but to the world at large. As mill operative she had taken her place in the vanguard of women who strove for the reform of labor. As telegrapher she would take an even more historic place as the first woman who ever operated that strange new "inanimate messenger" whose invention was to improve the conditions not only of labor, but of all the world.

In the *Voice of Industry* itself, on February 13, 1846, her appointment was announced:

The Magnetic Telegraph is now completed from this city to Boston, and will be in successful operation in a few days. This enterprise has been prosecuted under the direction of Mr. Paul R. George, whose democracy in selecting a superintendent in Lowell is truly commendable; having appointed to that office Miss Sarah G. Bagley, one of our publishing committee. This is what we call *"the people's"* democracy, Miss Bagley having served ten years in the factories, is now entitled to the situation she has received, and for which she is eminently qualified.

What the *Voice of Industry* failed to indicate was the fact that in this simple appointment an underlying drama was implicit, a drama that would change the face of the country and offer unprecedented opportunity to half its population. To the world at large the opening of a telegraph office in a New England factory town would ultimately mean that a successful advance in technology had been made which would in time annihilate distance and draw the outlying areas of the nation closer together in a network of communicating wires. To the women of the country Sarah Bagley's appointment as superintendent of the Lowell Depot would signify that a new profession had been inaugurated for all women who wished to follow it. In 1846, when women's industrial opportunities were restricted by and large to the sewing table, the schoolroom, the mill, the opening of a new field of labor heralded economic emancipation and personal independence, and hinted at the possibility that "man's" work might be woman's, too. By 1863, fifty women would be employed by one telegraph line alone and the fact that a new "source of employment" had been opened to them would become patent. By 1953, forty-four per cent of the personnel of the world's largest telegraph company would consist of women. An instrument had been invented that would change the nature of communication and by the rapid transmission of ideas give wings to space. An instrument had been invented that would give birth to a new industry in which women would find undreamed-of opportunity, a new place in a new world.

Of this, nothing was mentioned in the Lowell press, for of this no one in 1846 was as yet aware. A new office had simply been opened on the commercial street of a mill town, and a woman had been chosen to superintend it. That was all. Yet, when, on February 21, 1846, Sarah G. Bagley entered the Lowell Telegraph Depot at 122 Merrimack Street (north side) and placed her hand on the signal-key of her instrument, a drama was enacted without audience, without applause and without fanfare—a drama that was to revolutionize the country and emblazon for its women a new declaration of independence.

Many people, many events, and no little courage had been involved in the pioneer step taken by Sarah G. Bagley. Without the high-handed activities of the colorful and aggressive "Fog Smith"—more formally known as Francis O.J. Smith—the New York and Boston Magnetic Telegraph Association would not have been organized and its intermediate line between Lowell and Boston would not have been built. Without the forthright, democratic principles of "Apostle Paul"—officially known as Paul R. George —Sarah Bagley would not have been appointed superintendent of the Lowell office. "Fog Smith" was aggressive, however, and enterprising enough to resign his post as Congressman from Maine when he became Morse's partner and set about building a line whose wires, leaving New York over the route of Governor Lovelace's seventeenth-century post, entered Boston to result in the first successful electric telegraph between the two cities. "Apostle Paul"—Yankee trader who had swapped horses, carriages, and an entire circus before he was twenty-one—had also, somehow, been marked out for his place in Sarah Bagley's history. Like Sarah, a native of New Hampshire, he had moved to Lowell where he opened a dry goods store and had moved on to a variety of speculative ventures, including a journey up the Mississippi into wilderness country, all of which no doubt had shaped him into a man of business energy eager not only to experiment with the new, but to advance that " 'people's' democracy" which Miss Bagley represented.

Courage, too, was involved in that first historic step: the courage of "Fog Smith" in expanding his New York and Boston Magnetic Telegraph line with an intermediate connection to Lowell; the courage of "Apostle Paul" in selecting as superintendent a woman who had agitated so violently for the rights of labor; and especially the courage of Sarah Bagley herself to leave the security of the mills for the precarious uncertainty of an untried, unknown field in the days when the telegraph was still an experiment.

Drama and courage were both inherent in the unacclaimed preliminaries that laid the groundwork for what would become a new profession. Events, as "Fog Smith" planned and "Apostle Paul" speculated and Sarah Bagley prepared, moved swiftly. By October of 1845 the wires for the Boston and Lowell Magnetic Telegraph had been purchased, and negotiations were under way for obtaining a right of way from the railroad corporation. By February of 1846 the wires were up, "nearly, if not quite the whole distance," and on Friday, the thirteenth of the month, Sarah Bagley's appointment as superintendent of the Lowell Depot was announced. Meanwhile, she had made her own preliminaries by spending between three and six weeks in a study of Morse's "inanimate messenger" and Morse's telegraphic alphabet. A new vocabulary, along with a new technique, required mastery. The mysteries of the galvanic battery must be elucidated; the method of transmitting messages through the signal-key must be learned, as well as the method of receiving and interpreting messages that appeared in the form of dots and dashes on a strip of paper that passed from the register. Otherwise, the new appointee was well equipped with the "fair knowledge of orthography, arithmetic, geography, and ordinary mechanical ability" that were to become general requirements for all telegraphers. She possessed, moreover, an interest—unusual to women in 1846—in scientific advances, an interest she had evinced six years before when, among the "Pleasures Of Factory Life" which she had described for *The Lowell Offering,* she had included the "complicated, curious machinery" of the mills that reflected the boundless possibilities of the mind.

The ground had been broken, the stage set. On February 21, 1846, the line was completed, and Sarah G. Bagley, walking into No. 122 Merrimack Street· in Lowell, Massachusetts, to seat herself before a telegraph with a battery at her feet and a signal-key beneath her hand, walked into a new career that would at the same time shrink the expanses of a continent and enlarge the vistas of the women who followed after her. An event had occurred breathtaking in its implications, but of their neither the world, nor the press, nor perhaps Sarah Bagley herself was as yet aware.

The press found the event amusing rather than significant, and used the vagaries of the new instrument as a butt for its rather feeble attempts at humor: "The terminus of the line of communication between this city and Boston," *Vox Populi* reported, "is *now* at 122, Merrimack st., (north side). The wires were first placed at the brick ten-footer, on Merrimack, corner of Kirk st., they were, in the next place, removed and fastened to a young elm on the opposite . . . side of the street. The young elm being very much shocked with such a procedure, they were next hitched to a couple of stone posts a little removed from it, and subsequently to the station first mentioned.

"The next remove will be to the steeple of the Free Will Baptist Church, and the final one to the stump of the hickory pole in front of the Advertiser office. The last two removes will be made in obedience to the well known magnetic rule, 'The maximum of the magnetic attraction [of humbug] is always at the centre [of humbug].' "

If the press found a target in the building of the line, it discovered a bull's eye in its caprices after completion. The soft copper wires, made to cross and recross the road, swung against each other whenever a storm set in, broke in numerous places, and frequently fell hazardously in the way of passing trains. "Fog Smith," who exhibited a lofty indifference to the need for insulation, was compelled to report at the end of the first year's business that half the time the wires had not worked. *Vox Populi* simply reported, "The Magnetic Telegraph is said to be *'lying still.'* " When lightning coursed along the wires, the phenomenon was interpreted as news of a battle with Mexico, and when a gray squirrel "mysteriously disappeared" from the telegraph office, it was hinted that he had taken passage, by lightning on the wires, for the Rio Grande. As for the lady superintendent herself, the *Boston Journal* was moved to ponder, "The long mooted question 'Can a woman keep a secret?' will now become more interesting than ever," while the *Lowell Courier* simpered, "We presume that the young bachelors in Boston, . . . will be sending Valentines . . . over the wires all the time."

There is no record that Sarah Bagley, decoding the dots and dashes on the marked strip of paper that passed from the register into her hands, ever found a Valentine message from a Boston beau. The messages she did receive concerned primarily the arrivals of steamships in Boston—the *Hibernia,* the *Britannia* bringing intelligence fifteen days later, the *Cambria* sixteen days from England, the *Caledonia* fourteen and a half days from Liverpool bringing reports of the upward tendency of the corn market and the decline in the price of breadstuffs. For a world in which news had traveled slowly, through news sheets often carried by post-riders along the muddy roads of outlying communities, the information that Sarah Bagley received by magnetic telegraph and transmitted to the local press had already begun to shatter distance and to reveal in her unique instrument a "wonderful invention *ticking* its intelligence from point to point with a speed which makes former fables appear like prophecy." Since she was limited to communication with the Boston office in the Merchants' Exchange, and since the Boston office was in its turn limited to the few cities with which it had connecting wires, it was well nigh impossible for Miss Bagley to have received telegraphic information of a more imposing nature. The way was being pointed, however, the way to the flashing of vital news from the far-flung reaches of the globe, as Sarah Bagley sat with her left hand on a signal-key and a battery at her feet.

In addition to receiving messages, and transmitting them at the rate of forty-five cents for every ten words and four cents for each additional word, Miss Bagley superintended the Lowell office, served as battery man removing the zinc cups from the acid cups and cleansing them every night, and incidentally acted as information headquarters if a new school were opened in town or as ticket agent if a Fourth of July celebration were planned. In return for her labors, which consumed at least ten hours a day, she received a salary of between $300 and $500 a year. In return for the part she had taken in courageously making the pioneer step in a new profession for women, she received neither money, nor commendation, nor acclaim of any kind. The country was almost as unaware of the enormous possibilities of the telegraph as it was of the invention's first woman operator.

To correct that apathy and indifference, Sarah Bagley in August of 1846 took part in an exhibition designed to make the local citizenry at least alive to the wonders of the new instrument. Again a drama was to be enacted in the history of the telegraph—a scene as theatrical perhaps as the dispatch of the first message over the first line in the country. Again the dramatis personae would be headed by a man and a woman, a man as colorful a personality as the inventor himself, the woman a figure of far greater stature than the young Annie Ellsworth.

The setting of Lowell's telegraphic drama was the town's City Hall; the time, Monday evening, August 24, 1846, at eight o'clock; the price of admission, twelve and a half cents. The male lead in the performance was Gardner Quincy Colton, whose name would be remembered for all time as one of America's first anaesthetists. The female lead was Sarah G. Bagley, whose deeds as one of America's first women labor reformers and as the country's first woman telegrapher would deserve far more acclaim than would ever be accorded them.

Like nearly all the men associated at one time or another with the telegraph, G. Q. Colton had enjoyed a strikingly varied and fascinating career. The son of a poverty-stricken weaver of Vermont, he had been apprenticed to a chairmaker at five dollars a year before he had ventured to New York and studied medicine under Dr. Willard Parker. In the course of his studies, he learned of the exhilarating effects exerted by nitrous oxide when inhaled, and in 1844 he had begun giving public demonstrations of those effects. One of his demonstrations happened to occur in Hartford, where it attracted the attention of a dentist named Horace Wells, who permitted Colton to extract one of his teeth while he was under the influence of the gas. The end result of Colton's Hartford demonstration was anaesthesia—but at the moment the Yankee lecturer on natural philosophy and laughing gas had turned to a somewhat different field that would destine him for a leading part in the drama which he would perform with Miss Sarah G. Bagley of Lowell, Massachusetts.

Colton, who had been instructed in the working of the magnetic telegraph by none other than Morse himself, had given a lecture on the instrument at New York's Broadway Tabernacle, where he read the first telegraphic message to reach the city: "Canst thou send lightnings, that they may go, and say unto thee, Here we are"—a message which evoked "thunders of applause" from the audience. Pleased with the results, Morse had given to Colton a "letter of unqualified recommendation" with which he traveled and lectured all over the country.

Armed with his letter, Colton appeared at Lowell's City Hall on Monday evening, August 24, 1846, to exhibit, with Sarah Bagley, Professor Morse's electro-magnetic telegraph. At one end of the hall, a telegraph in front of him, stood G. Q. Colton, one of the country's first anaesthetists. At the other end of the hall, a telegraph in front of her, stood Sarah G. Bagley, the country's first woman telegrapher. Between the two telegraphs and between the two pioneers, the wires were extended. The audience was invited to write messages which Colton ticked to Miss Bagley, who read them aloud from the tape of her register. The exhibition was followed by a detailed explanation of the operation. Then, to amuse the audience of nearly one thousand, a variety of philosophical experiments was offered, from the exhibition of a newly invented air pump to the hanging of a piece of iron in the air by electrical current. The experiment of the five-dollar gold piece followed, the coin being offered to any who could take it from a dish of water connected with a magnetic machine. Finally, a balloon inflated with hydrogen was sent up with a car filled with dolls, and the "wonderful power of galvanism" was demonstrated on the body of a rat. The audience was satisfied that it had received twelve and a half cents worth of "rational attractions" and "brilliant Experiments," for the exhibition was repeated two evenings later and again on September fourteenth. There is no indication at all, however, that the audience was aware of the significance of what had been a most portentous meeting of two pioneers. Yet history had been made in Lowell, and a drama unfolded, and the bright beginnings of a new science laid bare.

G. Q. Colton left Lowell and went his way, a way that would lead him to California and back to New York, where he would open a "Dental Association" in Cooper Institute, extracting the first tooth for two dollars and each subsequent tooth for one dollar. Sarah Bagley's way ends in the mists of uncertainty and the speculations of unrecorded history. How long she remained in the Lowell Telegraph office, what she did after she left, when she died, where she is buried are all mysteries that evade the grasp of the biographer. Her name disappears from the local press, and she herself becomes elusive, her future—if she had a future— untraceable and unknown.

Late in September 1846, Sarah Bagley, signing herself "S.G.B.," sent a letter to the *Voice of Industry* from Boston, where she had gone as a delegate to the American Union of Associationists. Ever interested in the communal efforts of Brook Farm, she had recently been elected Vice-President of the Lowell Union of Association-ists. Yet there is no record that Sarah Bagley ever visited or belonged to the Brook Farm Association. Her name appears among the delegates to a National Reform Convention at Worcester planned for October 8 and 9 of 1846; yet there is no proof that she ever arrived in Worcester or attended the Convention. The notice of a special meeting of the Female Labor Reform Associa-tion, dated October 16, 1846, is signed "S.G. Bagley, Pres." Yet by February of the following year her place had been taken by Mary Emerson, and it was the society's secretary, Huldah Stone, who presented its report. By 1847, Sarah G. Bagley's name dis-appears from the local press. Did she return to her home in Meredith, New Hampshire? Did she, after her many labors, suffer a breakdown? No record offers proof, and her history is further complicated by the fact that both Sarah and Bagley were common New England names. There were other Sarah Bagleys in the Lowell mills, and there was a Sarah O. Bagley of Amesbury who became interested in Christian Science. Finally, to complicate the compli-cations, there was yet another S.G.B., author of one volume of a *Biography of Self-Taught Men,* who was incorrectly identified as Sarah G. Bagley, but who actually was Stephen Greenleaf Bul-finch, minister and author of religious poetry.

After her tremendously vital activities, Sarah Bagley is lost in shadow. After her forceful utterances, she subsides into silence. And nothing is left, nothing but a name and a fact. Yet, wherever she wandered, however she ended, she had compressed into ten short years the struggles and the achievements of a lifetime. She had been among the first of the country's women to speak out loudly and unhesitatingly for the rights of labor and the rights of women who labored. In the untrodden field of telegraphy, during America's earliest technological awakenings, she had taken her place, not among the first, but as the first woman telegrapher in the country, and so she had given an impetus and a new oppor-tunity to all the women who followed after her. If no inscription marks her unfound grave, she made her imprint upon history. And if no monument has been raised to her memory, her accom-plishments are her monument to all time.

5

The First American
Woman Doctor of Dental Surgery

LUCY HOBBS TAYLOR

1866

IN THE four-story building on Cincinnati's College Street that housed the Ohio College of Dental Surgery, a little ceremony took place on the evening of February 21, 1866, that was to make history. The lecture room was "filled to overflowing" for the annual College Commencement. The President of the Board of Trustees gave an extemporaneous speech, offering "good counsel and practical advice upon professional matters," and the Degree of Doctor of Dental Surgery was conferred upon nineteen graduates. To each member of the class a Bible was presented, while the exercises were "interspersed with most soul stirring music by Menter's celebrated Band." In his Valedictory Address, Professor Spalding announced in conventional fashion: "Gentlemen Graduates:— . . . You . . . are prepared . . . to take your places in society as professional men"—remarks to which one of the graduates responded "most beautifully, and impressively." "Thus closed the most interesting session, with the largest class, ever held in this institution."

Upon each diploma the grave Latin words were inscribed, beginning "Lectori Salutem In Domino," and upon each diploma five professors had indited their names and titles. Each of the nineteen diplomas was doubtless to be framed and hung on the wall of some dental office in the mid-west, but only one of the diplomas was to find its way to the archives of a State library. That diploma had been earned by a "Gentleman Graduate" with a firm, expressive mouth, a flaring nose and hazel eyes, whose name was Lucy B. Hobbs. For the first time in history the Degree of Doctor of Dental Surgery had been conferred upon a woman. Lucy B. Hobbs, not quite thirty-three, had, after years of struggle and rebuffs, been accepted as one of the members of that "most interesting session" of 1866. When she carried off her diploma from the lecture room of the Ohio College of Dental Surgery, she carried off more than a parchment in Latin. She carried off more even than the testimony to a personal triumph for which she had labored for years. She carried off, in that parchment roll, an historical document that recorded a professional first for women and pointed the way to a new field for those who would follow her.

Although Lucy Hobbs was unaware of the fact, a few other women had practiced dentistry before her. Emeline Roberts Jones of Connecticut had assisted her husband in his practice and carried on independently after his death, and one periodical had advertised as early as 1858 that an English dentist in New York planned to teach dentistry to "females." None of the "females," however, who dared to plug or pull teeth, could boast the Degree of Doctor of Dental Surgery, and the patients were few and far between who believed that "it would be more agreeable to most ladies to have their teeth cleaned and plugged by a lady. They would not feel the same hesitancy in going alone at any time to a dentist of their own sex." Dentistry might "humorously" be called "a 'woman's profession,' " in which she would "have a fair opportunity to foil her enemies and accusers; and her children's *teeth* would not be set on edge without the possibility of instant relief. There is no mystery in the dental structure, which the turnkey, in her magic hand, could not *unlock;* and no terrible pain in tooth extraction, which her mystic power could not exceedingly mitigate." The fact remained that neither the "magic hand" nor the "mystic power" of a woman had ever received official recognition in dentistry before the eventful Commencement exercises of 1866 at the Ohio College of Dental Surgery.

Indeed, as Lucy Hobbs was fully cognizant, dentistry itself had but recently emerged from the primitive days when "the dentist was on the same platform with the traveling tinker," when "the knight of the torturing turnkey" shared the honors of extractions with quacks and charlatans and medical confidence-men, or with the jewelers, itinerant preachers, singing school teachers and photographers who practiced the "profession" as a side show.

Dentists had been little more than "tooth carpenters" who used the silver filed from a coin to plug the teeth of their victims, when the first woman Doctor of Dental Surgery was born on March 14, 1833, in northern New York State. Itinerant practitioners, whose outfit consisted of a Spanish quarter and a vial of mercury, a file and two or three excavators, may well have found their way to the Hobbs home in Franklin or Clinton County, New York. In Ellenburg, Benjamin and Lucy (Beaman) Hobbs lived with their ten children in a log cabin, squared by axe and adze, and as a child Lucy learned to know the uplands, mountainous in the South, rolling in the North, of a community whose first road had been laid out only a short time before her birth in what was then a dense wilderness. The church, the saw-mill and the grist-mill may have marked the confines of her wanderings, but surely they set no limit to her visions. When Lucy was only ten, in 1843, her mother died, and her father married his sister-in-law, Hannah Beaman. Death continued to pursue the family, for Lucy's step-mother died less than two years later, in 1845. At the age of twelve, Lucy Hobbs, the seventh of ten motherless children, depended upon her eldest sister Hannah for such strength and comfort as she could not find in her own undeveloped resources and her own unfocused dreams.

Both the resources and the dreams were given some channeling at the Franklin Academy in Malone, where Lucy and her brother Thomas were sent to school in the fall of 1845. Only a generation before, bounties for wolves and panthers had been offered in Malone, but the three-story stone building of Franklin Academy pointed the way for young Lucy Hobbs to the future rather than the past. There, she and her brother lodged and boarded while they studied in the recitation and classrooms. She would recall later that at thirteen she had taught school, instructing "pupils older than myself, . . . who knew about as much as I did." After four years in Malone, Lucy Hobbs, age sixteen, was better equipped to embark upon a teaching career. In the same year of 1849 when she completed her studies at Franklin Academy, another young woman completed more advanced studies in a different school in New York State. Whether or not Lucy Hobbs had ever heard of Elizabeth Blackwell and her graduation from the Geneva Medical School, her own ambitions and her own pursuits were to parallel in many ways the career of the lady Doctor of Medicine. Sixteen long years were to pass before she would enter an advanced institution of learning, but during that time she would not cease her studies, nor find fulfillment in teaching, nor lose hope for a larger quest.

When a teaching assignment was finally offered in Brooklyn, Michigan, the schoolmistress was quick to accept it. The village in Michigan's Jackson County, with its dam, its blacksmith shops, its saw- and grist-mill, was not unlike the country she had known as a child. In what had been the wilderness of Michigan, she found many York Staters who had come on foot, westerly over an Indian trail, buying oxen and breaking the soil. When she was not teaching in the schoolhouse, she could join the spelling bees, the debating societies, the holiday celebrations, the singing schools to which each family brought a tallow candle and a collection of music—the social life of the young community of which she was a part. She could also "read" and study medicine with a local physician, gaining enough details of anatomy and physiology from her "preceptor" to focus her ambitions at last. After ten years of teaching, Lucy Hobbs decided to make medicine her career. At the suggestion of her "preceptor," she decided also to venture to Cincinnati and enroll in the Eclectic College of Medicine, where, it was reported, women were admitted for study and for graduation. Dominated by a desire for independence, her interests focused now in a medical profession, Lucy Hobbs in 1859 moved on to Cincinnati, and a twenty-six-year-old woman from upstate New York, as determined as she was dauntless, prepared to fling a gage at fortune.

Fortune, however, for her invested in Cincinnati's august Eclectic faculty, declined to take up the gage. Although she would soon have fulfilled the requirements for graduation, that the candidate "possess a good moral character; must have read medicine three years, and have attended two courses of lectures," the institution had "yielded to the prejudices of the profession and closed the doors against women." If those doors were closed to her, Lucy was successful in opening another, smaller door. In Charles A. Cleaveland, Professor of Materia Medica and Therapeutics, she found a preceptor willing to give her private instruction. She discovered almost as much to interest her in Prof. Cleaveland as she did in his subject. The Professor, she learned, had started his medical career as agent for the New York State manufacturer of Semour's Galvanic Abdominal Supporter, and although himself of the "Allopathic persuasion," he had been invited to take the chair of Materia Medica and Medical Botany at the Eclectic Institute in Cincinnati. A turbulent controversialist, "ever ready for a disturbance," he had stirred up such an imbroglio that he had been expelled and had organized the College of Eclectic Medicine. Lucy, glancing at his dark hair and sideburns, his bright, penetrating eyes, shared his "vast knowledge and solid achievements," and enjoyed a taste of both the Allopathic and the Eclectic approaches to medicine. Far more significant than his teaching, however, was the almost casual suggestion that he offered her to drop medicine and pursue dentistry instead. A dentist need not "make calls away from his office in all kinds of weather. . . . an office practice would be more suitable for a woman." Moreover, the vulcanite denture had recently all but revolutionized the science of dentistry. Finally, Lucy Hobbs could study dentistry, as the average dentist did, under an apprenticeship system rather than at a formal institution of learning. Lucy Hobbs was convinced. Prof. Cleaveland, late agent for Seymour's Galvanic Abdominal Supporter, had planted the seed. Whether or not it would bear fruit was dependent entirely now upon Lucy Hobbs.

Although Dr. Charles Bonsall, president of the Cincinnati Dental Association, wrote a letter on her behalf to his friend, Dr. George Watt, practicing dentistry in Xenia, Ohio, to receive her as a student, "for reasons beyond . . . control," Dr. Watt was forced "regretfully" to decline. As Lucy Hobbs made the rounds of the Cincinnati dentists, walking up and down 4th Street, wandering between Race and Elm, the regrets mounted with the declinations. As she herself would dramatically recall years later, when the drama had turned into history, "in the fall of 1859, there appeared in the western horizon a cloud 'not as big as a man's hand', for it was the hand of a young girl, risen in appeal to man, . . . for the opportunity to enter a profession where she could earn her bread, not alone by the sweat of her brow, but by the use of her brain also."

"The cloud though small was portentous [sic]. It struck terror into the hearts of the community, especially the male portion of it. All innovations cause commotion. This was no exception. People were amazed when they learned that a young girl had so far forgotten her womanhood as to want to study dentistry." With the "bitter opposition," the "foolish objections," her determination proudly vied. The expressive mouth grew firmer, the hazel eyes more defiant. "The main objection was that her place was at home, taking care of the house. They forgot, . . . that she had no home, . . . Some were afraid their characters would be ruined if it was known that they had a lady student, . . . One was kind enough to propose to let her come and clean his office and look on while he worked, if she would not let any one know that she was learning. . . . Nothing daunted, she kept on until nearly every office in the City of Cincinnati, . . . was beseiged [sic]."

At one office the siege was successful. Dr. Jonathan Taft, physician, surgeon, and Doctor of Dental Surgery, would accept the young woman temporarily as a student in his office until she succeeded in finding a preceptor. Lucy Hobbs soon realized that she had found in Dr. Taft not only "an earnest advocate of the right of women to study and pursue his profession," but "probably the most distinguished dentist who . . . ever practiced in Cincinnati." A graduate of the Ohio College of Dental Surgery, the bearded, mustachioed Dr. Taft had been appointed Dean and Professor of Operative Dentistry of that institution, had just completed a treatise on his subject, and had recently helped organize the American Dental Association. For three months in his office, Lucy Hobbs observed the practice of operative dentistry at first hand. The period ended quickly, but fruitfully, for at the end of it Lucy Hobbs had found on Cincinnati's 4th Street a dentist who was willing to take on a woman apprentice and initiate her into all the new, strange mysteries of mechanical and operative dentistry. "The woman that pulls teeth" was on her way at last.

Dr. Samuel Wardle, a graduate of Prof. Taft's institution, the Ohio College of Dental Surgery, Class of 1859, had opened an office at 142 West 4th Street, between Race and Elm. There, Lucy Hobbs appeared daily, walking from the little attic room she had rented, to plunge into an arduous apprenticeship. Under Dr. Wardle's watchful eye, she took care of the office, cleaned the spittoons, polished the plates, and learned extracting, making impressions, filling teeth, and making teeth from rocks. In addition, she continued her studies in anatomy, physiology and hygiene. Since her preceptor advertised "Teeth extracted without pain by the application of Electricity," Lucy Hobbs learned the "method of producing local anaesthesia by passing an electro-galvanic current through the teeth at the moment of removal," observing how the negative pole of the machine was attached to one handle of the forceps while the patient grasped its metallic handle. Despite his use of electricity, Dr. Wardle was not averse to trying nitrous oxide for dental operations. Under his tutelage, Lucy also became familiar with the manufacture of artificial porcelain teeth—that "French invention" which had been "greatly improved by American dentists." As the weeks and the months passed, as Dr. Wardle took on an associate, Dr. Joseph Doughty, Lucy Hobbs was also privileged to attend discussions on filling teeth when the Cincinnati Dental Association met at the 4th Street office. Most of her evenings, however, she spent in her attic room "with the needle, earning a few pennies for the morning meal" that would begin the days of incessant labor "at a new and strange task." "No pen," she was to recall, "can portray the toil and privation of the next few months. . . . A previous study of medicine made the *study* easy, but there was much other *hard work* connected with an office experience. It required all her Yankee perseverence [sic] and pluck not to give up." Lucy Hobbs was endowed with enough of both to push on, mastering the manual assignments, gaining skill in dental technique. In her eyes, the "large hearted" Dr. Wardle was "making it possible for women to enter the profession. He was to us what Queen Isabella was to Columbus."

In September of 1860, the Columbus of dentistry savored some reward for her labors. In the new building of the Catholic Institute at the corner of Vine and 6th Streets, the Ohio Mechanics' Institute opened its 18th Exhibition to the throngs of visitors who were daily "entertained by music from Menter's unrivaled band" as they examined the "grand display of the products of the Ohio valley." Among those products was a collection of dental and surgical instruments and appliances. Drs. Wardle and Doughty had, of course, contributed a set of artificial teeth that carried off a small silver medal since it showed "a marked degree of superiority over the others." Lot 45 of the collection in mechanical dentistry, "although inferior to its competitors," was "yet, as being the work of a student, worthy of a high degree of commendation." Lot 45 was, therefore, awarded a diploma. Lot 45 happened to consist of a set of artificial teeth made by a woman apprentice named Lucy B. Hobbs.

That woman apprentice, however, still longed for a diploma of a different kind, a diploma that would qualify her officially as a dental surgeon. In March of 1861, her studies under Dr. Wardle completed, Lucy applied for admission to the Ohio College of Dental Surgery, the pioneer dental school of the West. At the same time, "a gentleman, a native of Liberia," had made a similar request. At a faculty meeting, Dr. George Watt made application to admit the two unconventional students to the College. The reaction was swift. "By a vote of four against two," a resolution was passed that "neither women nor men of African descent would be received." For Lucy Hobbs the outlook was bleak. "There was not a college in the United States," she found, "that would admit me, and no amount of persuasion could change their minds. So far as I know, I was the first woman who had ever taken instruction of a private tutor." She was the first, too, who had attempted to break down the barrier in which dental institutions were immured. She had failed, but the Yankee perseverance and pluck were still at work. She would not rest "until Dental Colleges were open to women."

Meanwhile, Dr. Wardle offered apparently sound and practical advice. There were few gentlemen dentists who could boast a Degree in dentistry. Lucy Hobbs was perfectly capable of joining the "large majority of . . . male practitioners" who were not graduates, and of opening her own dental office without benefit of a diploma. On March 14, 1861, celebrating her twenty-eighth birthday, Lucy Hobbs began the practice of dentistry "in a little plain building on 4th Street, Cincinnati, Ohio." The woman apprentice had embarked upon her years as journeyman.

Lucy Hobbs' first dental venture was destined to be brief. She must face the competition of all the well established dentists on 4th Street, From Dr. Davenport to Dr. Francis, from Taft and Hendrick to Wardle and Doughty. The customary fees, a quarter for an extraction, $50 for a denture on a gold base, were slow to materialize. Lucy Hobbs kept on. "She was of good courage even though the pittance left after rent was paid was very meager—

only twenty five cents per week at times, kept her from starvation." The weeks were few, however, for both the lady dentist and Dr. Wardle had reckoned without reference to a fort in Charleston Harbor. In April, Sumter was fired, and the guns reverberated in far-off Cincinnati. Amid the excitement and confusion, Lucy Hobbs learned that four of her brothers were enlisting in New York regiments, Prof. Cleaveland was off to the war, and in Cincinnati itself, so near the border, business was paralyzed and "old practitioners failed." The little office on 4th Street was closed, and Lucy Hobbs, lady dentist, moved westward on her journey.

Borrowing money for her fare, she ventured to Bellevue in northern Iowa, and the site of Black Hawk's camping ground became the site of Lucy Hobbs' second dental office. In Jackson County, where "dogs, wolves, and wildcats were the main perpetrators of illegal acts" and bounties were still paid on wolf scalps, the "woman that pulls teeth" aroused sufficient curiosity to make her expenses and in addition to save $100 that could be metamorphosed into a dental chair. The beginning of her second year in Iowa "found her equipped for her business."

Not content with the resources of Bellevue, however, Lucy moved on that second year to McGregor, in Iowa's Clayton County. There, in 1862, in the thriving river town with its steam ferry, its gambling houses, its saloons, she set up her office. Through streets crowded with heavily laden wagons, four abreast, carrying grain and produce to market, she wandered. She found a main street filled with teams; she heard talk of the rafting and the logs racing down the Mississippi. She watched the pontoon bridge stretching across the river to Prairie du Chien, and she reveled in the spirit of McGregor where, in spite of floods or war, everyone believed in the promise of the future. If not everyone, at least a goodly proportion of the population seemed to believe, too, in the promise of the "woman that pulls teeth." Her lancet in hand, Lucy Hobbs performed enough root extractions during her first year in McGregor to earn "a $3000.00 balance on the other side of the ledger." As the war months, the war years passed, "a confidence born of success took the place of sadness," and she earned a reward far more significant than dental fees. Lucy Hobbs' "reputation widened until all Iowa knew of the *woman that pulled teeth.*"

Especially a recently formed organization known as the Iowa State Dental Society knew of the "woman that pulled teeth." To its July meeting of 1865 an invitation was extended to Lucy Hobbs, an invitation that was eventually to revolutionize her life and open officially a new profession to women. Through Dr. Luman Church Ingersoll of Keokuk, president of the Iowa Dental Society, a man who was to become the "first dental educator of Iowa," an authority on dental histology and a pioneer of dental nomenclature, the invitation to attend the meeting at Dubuque had been sent. "With many misgivings," Lucy donned her "best frock," closed her office and journeyed to Dubuque. "One grasp of the hand of the president" dispelled her fears. Lucy Hobbs looked at Dr. Ingersoll's piercing eyes and aquiline nose and knew that she had found a champion of her cause. In the rooms of the Board of Education she seated herself with the members of the Iowa Dental Society who had ridden long distances by stagecoach to attend the meeting. With them she listened to essays on mechanical dentistry and dental etiquette, heard the discussions of the use of rubber for a cheap base and the "wholesale destruction of . . . natural teeth," and examined the exhibitions of curiosities, the casts of mouths, the "instruments of peculiar construction." After Dr. Chase had read an essay on "Lancing the gums in extraction of teeth," Lucy Hobbs felt sufficient assurance to respond to the request for a comment:

My experience has not been very large, as compared with that of old practitioners. I came to hear, and not to be heard; I did not expect to teach, but to learn. I certainly find the lancet very necessary. I may have to use it more than you gentlemen, who have stronger hands. I find pulling teeth more than I have strength to perform, unless I take every advantage possible. Three-fourths of my operations are the extraction of roots, and I have, of course, to use the lancet. I find my patients complain less when I use the lancet than when I do not. I use the lancet in almost every case.

The woman that pulls teeth, the woman who had been denied admission to dental college because she was a woman, had spoken before her colleagues and been attended. After a six-years' struggle, she had received professional recognition; she had felt the "balm for many old wounds." Moreover, she had received that recognition in a tangible and material form, for, among the nine

new members admitted to the Society, Miss L. B. Hobbs of Mc-
Gregor was one, the first woman in the history of the profession
to be accepted by a state dental society.

On the afternoon of the second day of meetings, July 20th,
1865, Lucy Hobbs sat listening as the Iowa State Dental Society
passed several resolutions, thanking the Northern Line Packet
Company for carrying members at half fare rates, thanking their
host at the Julian House, and the Board of Education for the free
use of their rooms. She watched as Dr. Ingersoll, with his mustache
and sideburns, his spare body and eagle look, arose to offer yet
another resolution that would transpose the narrative of her life
into the documentary history of a profession:

Whereas, The Iowa State Dental Society has, without a precedent,
elected to membership a lady practitioner of dentistry, and

Whereas, It is due to her to know that the unanimous vote by which
she was elected was not simply a formal vote, and

Whereas, It is due to the profession at large, that we make a formal
declaration concerning the position we have assumed in our action,
therefore,

Resolved, That we most cordially welcome Miss Lucy B. Hobbs, of
McGregor, to our number, and to our professional pursuits, trials,
aims and successes.

Resolved, That the profession of dentistry, involving, as it does, the
vital interests of humanity, in the relief of human suffering, and the
perpetuation of the comforts and enjoyments of life in civilized and
refined society, has nothing in its pursuits foreign to the instincts of
women, and, on the other hand, presents in almost every applicant for
operations, a subject requiring a kind and benevolent consideration
of the most refined womanly nature.

"In a very brief and very neat speech," the lady member of the
Iowa State Dental Society "thanked the Society for all the kindness manifested towards her. She deemed the reception she had
met with among them, an ample recompense for all the rebuffs
and discouragements she had received during the past four years,
while fighting her way into and in the profession, and expressed
her determination to make her mark in the profession, so that
they should never regret the step they had taken."

The honors did not come singly. Lucy Hobbs had not only been admitted to membership in a dental society that was to champion reform, fight for formal dental education, and attack all kinds of malpractice from defects in artificial teeth to the use of chloroform, she had also been appointed essayist at the next meeting and had been invited to attend the American Dentists' convention in Chicago. Moreover, Prof. Jonathan Taft, of Cincinnati, who had been elected an honorary member of the Iowa State Dental Society, was urged to use his influence to have Miss Lucy B. Hobbs, practicing dentist of McGregor, admitted to the Ohio College of Dental Surgery.

In Chicago, during that same eventful month of July 1865, the American Dental Association sat in session, its "most interesting meeting" attended by a young woman member of the Iowa State Dental Society who heard the lectures and enjoyed the "sumptuous entertainments." She surely enjoyed even more a private conversation with Dr. George Watt, who took the opportunity to report to Miss Hobbs that when she had originally applied for admission to the Ohio College of Dental Surgery, "not one who had voted against her" had been "a member of the faculty, and that the present authorities would receive her." Did Dr. Watt know that, or did he only hope it was true, she wondered. Dr. Watt was apparently well informed. "The woman dentist and her well filled purse and the State of Iowa to back her was a different person from the penniless girl with an over-weening ambition to do men's work." A majority of the Ohio College of Dental Surgery faculty was on hand at the meeting, and after the influence of the State of Iowa had made itself felt, they "got together and formally voted to receive her if she should renew her application." The six-year struggle to batter down the doors of a dental college was all but over. No "knight of the torturing turnkey," but a woman armed with forceps and with lancet had marched onto a professional battlefield, and would not leave it till her spurs were won.

"As a practitioner of years," the thirty-two-year-old woman applicant with the steady hazel eyes was examined and admitted to the senior class of the Ohio College of Dental Surgery. She would not find it difficult to fulfill the requirements for graduation—the thesis on dental science, the manufacture of a full set of teeth, the examination in all the branches taught. On the first of November, 1865, the session began, and with a class of eighteen men, Lucy Hobbs plunged into the delights of formal dental education at last.

From anatomy and physiology to pathology and therapeutics, from operative dentistry to mechanical dentistry, from the institutes of dental science to the vagaries of Lord Oxygen, she followed the lectures of Professors Taft and Watt and Spalding, observed the clinical demonstrations, studied the textbooks of Wilson or Carpenter or Williams. Especially she studied *The Principles and Practice of Dental Surgery* by Dr. Harris, late of the Baltimore College of Dental Surgery, mastering the organs of prehension and of mastication, reviewing the diseases of the teeth from necrosis to exostosis, from salivary calculus to alveolar abscess. The time required to fill a tooth, she read, should be from thirty minutes to two and one half hours or longer. To point his own excavators, a dentist needed a lamp, a small anvil and hammer, a set of fine cut files, and steel rods. It was often more desirable to promote bleeding after extraction by rinsing the mouth with warm water than to attempt its suppression. In the fashioning of artificial teeth, a variety of substances might be employed, from human teeth to the teeth of cattle, from porcelain to teeth carved from the ivory of the elephant's tusk and from the teeth of the hippopotamus. If anaesthesia were used, several possibilities offered themselves, from sulphuric ether and chloroform to the electro-galvanic current and congelation or freezing, a local anaesthesia first used in Paris. With interest, she perused Prof. Harris' conclusions on the subject of anaesthesia:

As the use of anaesthetic agents of any kind in the extraction of teeth is attended with inconvenience, nearly always delaying the operation, the author is of opinion that their employment, as a general thing, should be dispensed with. In the case of females with a highly nervous organization, it may now and then be advisable to give a temporary courage to endure pain by the administration of a teaspoonful of brandy. But we have found less trouble with delicate females than with stalwart men; and to the latter we certainly would never advise this use of stimulants.

Miss Hobbs turned from her books to infirmary operations, where teeth were extracted and nerves were destroyed. From Prof. Taft she received the accolade, "As an operator she was not surpassed by her associates. Her opinion was asked and her assistance sought in difficult cases almost daily by her fellow-students." In the laboratory and infirmary of the Ohio College of Dental Surgery there was opportunity indeed for a variety of opinion. The extraction of teeth was "more frequently required than . . . all other surgical operations combined." While Prof. Harris shied away from anaesthesia, Prof. Watt held that "thousands of teeth are daily sacrificed on the altars of avarice and ignorance. . . . But as long as any mutilation is necessary, let that be painless whenever practicable." With scientific detachment, Lucy Hobbs studied all opinions and approaches to her profession. As Prof. Taft would recall, "She was a woman of great energy and perseverance. Studious in her habits, modest and unassuming, she had the respect and kind regard of every member of the class and faculty. . . . Though the class of which she was a member was one of the largest ever in attendance, it excelled all previous ones in good order and decorum —a condition due largely to the presence of a lady." Prof. Watt was to add, "She is a credit to the profession and an honor to her Alma Mater. A better combination of modesty, perseverance and pluck is seldom, if ever, seen."

For Lucy Hobbs the months rolled swiftly by. In her final examination "she was second to none." The $30 diploma fee was paid. And on the evening of February 21, 1866, a woman appeared in the lecture room of the Ohio College of Dental Surgery with eighteen gentlemen to receive a copy of the Sacred Scriptures and the Degree of Doctor of Dental Surgery. In the first building in the country especially erected for dental education, the first woman had been graduated. In 1865 there had been only sixty-five graduates of dental schools in the entire United States. At 29 College Street in Cincinnati, a significant event had taken place. As Lucy herself was to put it, "I graduated from the Ohio Dental College . . . in . . . 1866—the first woman in the world to take a diploma from a dental college. I am a New-Yorker by birth, but I love my adopted country—the West. To it belongs the credit of making it possible for women to be recognized in the dental profession on equal terms with men."

The terms were not yet precisely equal. To Lucy Hobbs' admission to the Iowa State Dental Society, and to her graduation from the Ohio College of Dental Surgery, there were mixed reactions.

The battle lines were clearly drawn, and while Lucy Hobbs herself went quietly about her business, practicing the profession she had studied, the guns were fired from the opposing camps. In his Valedictory at the tenth annual Commencement of the Pennsylvania College of Dental Surgery, Dr. James Truman boldly championed her cause. "I rejoice," he announced, "that dentistry has, though the youngest of the professions, welcomed woman, in two of our State organizations, to full membership, and have [sic] recognized her as a co-laborer in a field full of interest, and one in my judgment, to which she is well adapted." In the April 1866 issue of *The Dental Times,* Lucy Hobbs could read the answer to Dr. Truman's tocsin. Dr. George T. Barker, Professor of the Principles of Dental Surgery and Therapeutics in the Pennsylvania College of Dental Surgery, differed from his colleague. "Should females be encouraged to enter the dental profession?" For Dr. Barker the question was almost rhetorical. "I contend they should not, . . . The very form and structure of woman unfit her for its duties. . . . its performance would, under certain circumstances, be attended with great danger." If Lucy Hobbs smiled at Dr. Barker's conception of the delicate female in dentistry, the smile must have broadened to a grin when she read in the August 1866 issue of *The Dental Register,* edited by Jonathan Taft, a reply entitled "Ho! Every One To The Breeches!!":

The "G.T.B." editor of the *Dental Times* . . . since the day that his mother spanked him . . . has not had such misgivings in reference to the encroachments of woman upon the rights of man. And the primary cause of this turmoil is a little girl out west who has gone and made a dentist of herself; and the finishing stroke is that she has been admitted to membership in a first class State Society; and, as if adding insult to injury, she has graduated in the Ohio College of Dental Surgery, and is, therefore, Lucy B. Hobbs, Doctor of Dental Surgery, which is something not provided for by the customs of society nor even laid down in the books.

"G.T.B." [proposes] . . . "to offer an amendment to the constitution of the American Dental Association, at its next meeting in Boston, to allow none but males to be eligible as delegates from the local societies."

G(o) T(o), B(rother)! . . . If Doctor Lucy should be at Boston as a delegate, before you offer your amendment, get her to fill a tooth for you, (if you have no decayed ones let her drill a hole in a sound one) and your objections to lady dentists will vanish into thin air. The doctor will do it well. The Ohio College will go her security; and it will appear so perfectly natural and proper to the patient that his amendment will never be thought of again. When there is but one lady graduate in the whole dental profession of the world, it looks like taking time by the fore-lock to shut her out.

While the gentlemen engaged in the battle of the pens, Lucy Hobbs was battling with forceps and lancet. Armed with her diploma, she had journeyed from Cincinnati to Chicago and there, in Room 3 at 93 Washington Street, near the rooms of Lewis and Todd and of E.F. Wilson, supplier of "Dental Materials," Lucy Hobbs, D.D.S., had opened her office. Like herself, the dental profession looked to the future. The dentists of Ohio were forming a State dental society and working for a Bill that would regulate the practice of dentistry. Dr. Atkinson of New York had gone to Iowa to demonstrate his invention of the malleted gold filling, and Dr. Hobbs studied the use of the mallet with intense interest. In May of 1866, "the first lady dentist of record here, Miss Dr. Lucy Hobbs," was presented to and elected a member of the Illinois State Dental Society when it met at Tremont House. Taking time off from her practice, Lucy journeyed to Burlington, Iowa, in July, to address the members of the Iowa State Dental Society on "The Use Of The Mallet."

The thirty-three-year-old woman Doctor of Dental Surgery with her expressive mouth and intent hazel eyes stood before her colleagues now as their peer. "Although among the later professions," she began, "yet there is none, to my knowledge, that has made more rapid progress, or attained a higher degree of perfection than dentistry, in its various branches." Mechanical dentistry, she continued, had "occupied nearly, if not all the time, and talent of the gifted in the profession, each vieing with the others to see who should make the greatest change in the prevailing system, till we had almost as many different ways of inserting, or preparing artificial dentures as we had dentists. That department . . . brought out all the talent of the profession, so that . . . any *ordinary* dentist could make teeth to excell even nature itself, as we were often informed." It had not been so, she pursued, with operative dentistry. Here, "they did not even seek a change; but each operator followed on the well beaten track of his illustrious predecessor, year after year. . . . each followed on in the old system of hand pressure in its various forms, till Dr. W.H. Atkinson . . . conceived the idea of the use of the mallet in condensing gold fillings." With the mallet, she revealed, "I have known the patient to sleep, . . . Let the operator hold the instrument in such a manner that every blow will drive the mass to the walls of the cavity, so that a fine solid margin is made to the filling, thus protecting the edges of the enamel, from the fluids of the mouth." After her detailed description of the use of the instrument, Dr. Hobbs closed on a humble, retiring note. "Feeling that what little I may be able to say upon the subject is so much better understood by the profession than I can possibly be expected to understand it, I feel like asking pardon for attempting it, and consuming so much valuable time and not rendering a just equivalent for it."

She had rendered a just equivalent, none the less, and when she returned to her Chicago practice, Lucy Hobbs carried with her the knowledge that she had battered down yet another five-barred gate that had stood between women and a new profession. The first woman who had been admitted to a state dental association, the first woman graduate of a dental school, had been the first woman to address a dental society. She returned to a Chicago that offered more than a dental practice, for there, on April 24, 1867, Lucy Hobbs was married to James Myrtle Taylor, a thirty-seven-year-old painter in the car shops of the Wisconsin Division of the Chicago and Northwestern Railway, who like herself had been born in New York State, and who had served as a private in the Eleventh Illinois Infantry during the Civil War. "Miss Dr. Lucy Hobbs" had been metamorphosed into Dr. Lucy Hobbs Taylor. Moreover, she who had studied under so many different preceptors was transformed herself into a preceptress, for Lucy proceeded to teach to her husband the science of dentistry. For the rest of their life together they would be not only husband and wife, but colleagues in a young profession. On November 1, 1867, Dr. Taylor sold her Chicago office to Edmund Noyes and, in search of a more healthful climate, the young couple moved on to Lawrence, Kansas. Lucy Hobbs Taylor had served a long apprenticeship and had wandered far as journeyman. Now, as master of her profession, she had found her place at last.

Kansas was bright with the newness of the times. In spite of Indian wars and the trials of frontier settlers, immigrants poured in and with them came new fields and orchards, new towns, new houses, new faces. The new year of 1868 had opened fairly. On the first of the year, the Kansas Pacific reached the 335th milepost in Western Kansas. Work was progressing rapidly on the railroads. Peace had come to the borders. There was room in Lawrence for a young couple from Chicago who were ready to practice dentistry.

At 98 Massachusetts Street, their office was opened. The excavators, the drills, the plugging and cutting instruments, the gold foil, the files, the mallet, were assembled, the plush dental chair was installed, the anaesthesia apparatus, the gasometer and inhaling bag were placed in readiness. The practice was built up. There might, in time, be competition from one or two local practitioners who were open from 7 A.M. to 6 P.M., and who provided the "Best Artificial Teeth, upper or lower" for $9 and gold fillings at "half the usual price." Some sufferers might prefer "Straffon's toothache jelly" and similar elixirs to a session at a dental office, but, as the years passed, there were enough potential patients in Lawrence to fill the days of the lady that pulls teeth, from Mrs. Orme, the milliner, to Mrs. West, the dressmaker, from Mrs. Hubbell, the tonsorial artist, to Dr. Anderson, the homeopathic but "popular M.D." A.L. Selig, who dealt in insurance, and Alfred Whitman, who had sat for Louisa Alcott's portrait of "Laurie," and now ran a rental agency in Lawrence, were all possible candidates for toothache and its cure in the office of J.M. and L.H. Taylor, dentists. For the children, little Bessie Anderson and Frank Banks, a gift of candy would alleviate the terrors of drill or extractions and, in time, the Drs. Taylor developed one of the most lucrative practices in Kansas.

In time, too, Dr. Lucy Hobbs Taylor was gratified to learn that other women were following the path that she had cleared. Henriette Hirschfeld had come from Germany, she heard, had attended the Pennsylvania College of Dental Surgery, and had sought out her predecessor in Chicago after her graduation. And there were others, too, as the years passed—Mrs. Grubert of Berlin, who completed the course at the Ohio Dental College; Countess Vongl de Swiderska of Russia, who was graduated from the New York College of Dentistry; Annie D. Ramborger, who attended the Pennsylvania College of Dental Surgery. The struggle for a professional education for women that Lucy Hobbs had begun, was being fought out by those who came after her. Dr. Truman still championed their cause. In 1869, when the American Dental Association met in Saratoga, he had introduced a resolution "That in view of the successful results obtained in the education of women as dentists, we recommend to subordinate associations to admit to full membership any woman duly qualified. . . . That in consultations, considerations of sex should be avoided; ability and moral character alone being the standard of judgment in all cases." The resolution was tabled, but it had at least been voiced. By 1870, twenty-four women were practicing dentistry in the United States. By 1880, there would be sixty-one. Lucy Hobbs Taylor, standard bearer, was accompanied now by an advance guard.

Oblivious to the attacks that continued to be launched by dentists who held that "women should not be encouraged to undertake man's work," Dr. Lucy Taylor found ample compensations in the pursuit of her profession. With the statement in *The Woman's Journal* she was in full accord. "Among the various occupations opening to women, there are few which promise more profitable or certain employment than that of the dental profession. Though few have yet chosen it, owing to its novelty and the various obstacles to be overcome, yet those who have done so have met with a degree of success, which, once recognized, will certainly stimulate others to make a similar effort with an equal chance of success." There were enough patients who agreed that "the presence of a gentle woman operator promises to detract something" from the terrors of the dentist's chair, to fill the office of at least one woman operator in the mid-west. She could compete with the dentists who offered bargains—"three extractions for a dollar, free with a denture." For Americans had begun to "take much pride in the appearance of their teeth" and it had become a "mark of social inferiority and want of cultivation to be the possessor of teeth not clean, and innocent of the dentist's care. . . . Even the servant girls of America spend money freely for dental operations, and it is not uncommon for them willingly to pay a fee of ten or fifteen dollars for the preservation of a single tooth."

Moreover, Lucy Taylor could find intense interest in following the progress of her science, a science that was advancing as she herself was advancing in its practice. As the gold shell crown appeared, and gutta percha was used in filling root canals, as sterilization slowly began to be employed, and the "germ theory" invited discussion, and orthodontia evolved in its modern application, she grasped the signs of the changing times in dentistry, developing as her profession developed. She fully agreed that

The making of False Teeth is not a mere mechanical operation— . . . They must be made to appear to be part of yourself. They should correspond in size to the anatomy of your person, especially to the features of the face; they should harmonize in color with the complexion, hair and eyes; they should have such an artistic arrangement as to disguise their falseness, and such general adjustment as to restore to the mouth and face their natural expression. This is the study of an artist; and a dentist, so far as it is required of him to imitate nature, should be as *truly* an Artist as if he were a sculptor carving the features in marble.

The artist-scientist who was Lucy Hobbs Taylor could look back now upon the days when the "tinker" had "developed into a traveling dentist, he to a resident dentist, he to a seeker, . . . a dental student, he to an imparter, . . . dental teacher, he to a co-operator with other men of science." The "knight of the torturing turnkey" had been disarmed. His place had been taken by the man of science, by the man of an advancing profession, by the woman of that profession, too.

Practicing on Massachusetts Street and later on Vermont Street, at the first door north of Lawrence House, Dr. Lucy Hobbs Taylor, of medium height, growing rather stout, her hair worn short and parted in the middle, was a striking and familiar figure in the Kansas town. Confining her work for the most part to women and children, she established a reputation for dignity, gentleness and kindness, and even the bewhiskered pioneers gave her their accolade, "By Krout She can pull a tooth as good as a man."

The woman that pulls teeth did more, however, than pull teeth, for her interests broadened as the years passed by. She might wander to Bismarck Grove for a camp meeting or a fair, or to Mount Oread for a fine view of the Kansas landscape. As early as 1871, she had joined the Rebekah Lodge of the Independent Order of Odd Fellows, and five years later had become a charter member of the Adah Chapter of the Order of the Eastern Star.

"Firsts" pursued her even here, for Dr. Taylor became the first woman Noble Grand of Degree in the Rebekahs, as well as Worthy Matron of the Adah Chapter. While her husband attended meetings of the Halcyon Lodge or the Washington Post of the G.A.R., Lucy served as treasurer of the local Woman's Relief Corps and as president of the Ladies' Republican Club of Lawrence. The first woman Doctor of Dental Surgery, who had once subsisted on twenty-five cents a week, had become a substantial citizen of Lawrence, the owner of valuable property, who provided baskets of food and clothing for the poor. Her interests extended, too, to woman suffrage, and for Elizabeth Cady Stanton she collected the names of Lawrence "ladies who are praying that our cause may prosper," while for Susan Anthony she was not above playing the hand organ as part of the entertainment at a social affair that honored the sufragette.

Varied only by a nine months' pleasure trip to California to restore her husband's declining health, the Lawrence years passed fruitfully. In 1886, Drs. J.M. and Lucy H. Taylor took "pleasure in announcing to their many friends, and patrons in Lawrence," that they had "associated with them, in the dental profession, Dr. L.M. Mathews, of Ft. Scott," who was "widely known to the profession, as one of the finest operators in the west. . . . equalled by few, and excelled by none in gold work, both operative and mechanical." The "pleasure" was not altogether unadulterated. The "long illness" of her husband had apparently necessitated the association with Dr. Mathews, and on December 14, 1886, James Taylor died.

Mrs. Dr. Taylor continued her dental practice in a desultory way, indulging in a semi-retirement, accepting only enough patients "to keep herself out of mischief." She expended more of her "mental force" now upon civic affairs than upon professional pursuits, and the chair of the Independent Order of Odd Fellows attracted her as much if not more than the dental chair. She took pleasure in her large brick house, which she had planned herself, in her conservatory and rose garden. The years slipped by. Lawrence, too, was changing. On its Massachusetts Street, where she had first set up practice, the Nickel Theatre offered Moving Pictures and Vaudeville, and near Vermont Street's livery stable a "Model Steam Laundry" was available.

The profession that she had practiced for so many decades was metamorphosed, too. It was becoming self-conscious. The recorders were already at work. As early as 1886, when Elizabeth Cady Stanton, Susan B. Anthony and Matilda Joslyn Gage were editing their *History of Woman Suffrage,* Prof. Jonathan Taft was invited to contribute his recollections of the first woman graduate of the Ohio College of Dental Surgery, and Lucy herself was asked for a brief autobiography. "I am grateful to you," she wrote, "for giving me the opportunity to place in history the fact of my study of dentistry," and the "fact" was published, for Lucy herself to read, in the dental periodicals—*The Odontographic Journal, The Ohio State Journal of Dental Science.* While she lived, her story was finding its "place in history." By 1890, 337 women had joined the ranks that she had opened, and two years later the Woman's Dental Association of the United States was organized. By 1893, women dentists were often averaging an income of $5000 a year and the doors of dental colleges which Lucy Hobbs had once battered down were opening quietly and without fanfare to female applicants.

For the Kansas Branch of the Medical Department of the Queen Isabella Association, Dr. Lucy Hobbs Taylor contributed a paper entitled "The Early Women in Dentistry," recalling the battle she had "commenced in earnest," recalling Dr. Samuel Wardle who had been "to us what Queen Isabella was to Columbus," recalling her own "toil and privation" and the long corridor of doors she had forced open through the years. The girl who had clamored for a preceptor on Cincinnati's 4th Street was now a member of the Woman's Advisory Council of the World's Dental Congress. In August of 1893 that Congress opened in Chicago, and Dr. Jonathan Taft—once of 4th Street, Cincinnati—appeared on the platform to announce, "Our sisters, our lady friends, have had a door opened to them through which they have entered into this profession." Although she was not named, Lucy Hobbs Taylor could know that she had been the instrument by which that door had opened.

By the turn of the century, the door had opened wide enough to admit nearly one thousand women to the new profession. Lucy Hobbs Taylor, who had already indited her Will, was soon to turn over to a young Lawrence dentist with an historical frame of mind,

THE WOMAN'S BUILDING OF THE WORLD'S COLUMBIAN EXPOSITION
(1893) DESIGNED BY SOPHIA G. HAYDEN, ARCHITECT
—John J. Flinn,
Official Guide to the World's Columbian Exposition

LUCY HOBBS IN 1866 AT THE TIME OF HER GRADUATION
—Courtesy Dr. Wilbur G. Adair, Vero Beach, Florida

THE FIRST DENTAL DIPLOMA GRANTED TO A WOMAN, LUCY HOBBS,
1866, BY THE OHIO COLLEGE OF DENTAL SURGERY
—Courtesy Kansas State Historical Society

the parchment that had been at once the signal of her own official entrance into dentistry and the herald for those who would come after her. On October 3, 1910, at the age of seventy-seven, Lucy Hobbs Taylor, D.D.S., died in Lawrence. The diploma that had given her her title was presented to the State Historical Society of Kansas. If not the Columbus of a new profession, she had been to the science of dentistry what Dr. Elizabeth Blackwell had been to the science of medicine. The drama she had lived had ended. But the history into which it was transmuted had begun.

6

The First Woman Graduate of M. I. T.

ELLEN H. RICHARDS
Chemist

1873

PROFESSOR Charles Farrar, late of Elmira, now in 1869 a member of the Department of Natural Philosophy and Chemistry at Vassar Female College, stood in front of his lecture room, holding in each hand a small vial. The young ladies assembled to hear his explanation of the contents and the chemical effect when they should be poured together agreed that Professor Farrar's special experiments were extremely stimulating. Even the English ivy seemed to take kindly to the "intellectual atmosphere" of Poughkeepsie's three-story building designed in imitation of the Tuileries, and the Venus of Milo herself might have cocked a ready eye to the Professor's manipulations could she have been moved from the gymnasium to the chemical laboratories. For one of the students at Vassar Female College, however, his words and his demonstrations meant more than a momentary fascination between hymn singing in the chapel and lessons in horsemanship from the German nobleman in charge of the riding school. Ellen Henrietta Swallow, age twenty-six, slight, quick in motion and in speech, a steadfast look in her large, gray, thoughtful eyes, watched Professor Farrar with rapt awareness and, as she listened to his conclusions that science could help in the solution of practical problems, she was consumed with an enthusiasm that would never leave her.

She had come to Poughkeepsie on the Albany Express with $300 in her purse, and in her mind ambitions that were as yet unchanneled. Now, as she sat before a practice table in the students' laboratory of Vassar Female College, surrounded by reagents and apparatus for qualitative analysis, she examined everything that came her way, "from shoe-blacking to baking powder," from bread to coal tar, from leather to poisons. In the laboratory she saw a complete cabinet of the elements and compounds. Paracelsus had taught, as Professor Farrar was hinting, that "the object of chemistry was not to make gold, but to prepare medicines." From the cabinet of elements and compounds, Ellen Swallow was to select, for a lifetime's analysis, life's three most important "medicines,"— air, without which none could breathe, water, the great common carrier, and food, without which none could live. Out of these three "elements" she would build her life. With crucible and retort, test tube and vial, she would analyze the triangle upon which all life was built. But she would do more than that. With her deft manipulations and her overpowering enthusiasm she would apply the chemistry of the laboratory to the world outside the laboratory. She would help make the science of chemistry an indispensable guardian of public health, industry, and the home. In many fields she would rank a woman first, but in the applications of chemistry to the towns in which men gathered, the factories in which they worked, the houses in which they lived, she would cut a way that could not be ignored. The way, and even the ambitions to clear that way, all lay ahead of her. Now, in 1869, she was still a student seated at a practice table and watching a professor of chemistry hold a small vial in either hand.

Ellen Swallow had been older than most applicants when, in 1868, she had sought entrance into the junior class of Vassar College. Although she had been "born with a desire to go to college," "the world" seemed to have been "full of persons born to prevent her." Her world certainly had been full of hampering exigencies. The daughter of Peter and Fanny Taylor Swallow, she had been born on December 3, 1842, at Dunstable, Massachusetts, and had grown up on her father's farm, driving the cows to pasture, pitching hay, riding the horses, following the plow, making the candles. Neither the farm near the New Hampshire border, nor the schoolteaching which her father combined with farming brought any great prosperity, and in 1859, when Ellen was sixteen, Peter Swallow moved to Westford, where he opened a village store. Between selling tobacco and molasses, saleratus and baking soda, keeping accounts and buying merchandise for her father, and caring for her mother, who was frequently ill, Ellen attended Westford Academy, studying a little mathematics, some French and more Latin. A few years later, the family moved to Littleton, and already Ellen Swallow seemed to have embarked upon the art of living several lives in one. When she was not weighing sugar in her father's new store, she was helping her mother keep house, papering the walls and laying the carpets; when she was not attending lectures in Worcester, she was teaching forty-one pupils, "calling out over thirty classes each day," with "a few large scholars who study the higher branches, which makes it more pleasant for me." The girl who had been "born with a desire to go to college," was, however, not doing what she wished to do. For over two years she "lived . . . in *Purgatory* . . . . thwarted and hedged in on every side."

On September 10, 1868, Ellen Swallow's "Purgatory" was over. On that day, having passed the preliminary examinations, she was admitted by the President of Vassar College to "a special course. . . . and everything promised fair." The slight, dynamic Nellie Swallow was on her way. On the fifteenth of the month, she made her "Farewell to Littleton; met Father at Waldo House and took the Albany express," arriving at Vassar the next day. Everything promised fair indeed, from Thomas, the man of all work, who brought up her bags and lit the gas, to Miss Lyman, the stately lady principal in her streamered lace cap and black silk dress. Now, she was hedged in no longer. The world was opening up before her oval study table. With zealous enthusiasm, she explored that world.

The bell strikes at six. At quarter of seven we have breakfast. . . . I get time to make my bed, . . . In chapel we sing, and Miss Lyman offers prayer. We have ten minutes then for arranging our rooms, or . . . for study, then we have twenty minutes alone for devotion and meditation. . . . Study hours do not begin until nine. At quarter of ten I go down to philosophy [physics]. I like Professor Farrar very much. There is an intellectual power about him. All recitations are forty minutes. At twelve we have Trigonometry, at one comes dinner, . . . then I go out of doors for an hour, write an hour, and . . . go into the Library directly after French, and perhaps read or study a little before dressing for tea, which is at six. Then chapel and another twenty minutes as silent time, from 7.30 to 9.45 for writing, reading, or study. . . .

The only trouble . . . is they won't let us study enough. They are so afraid we shall break down and . . . the reputation of the College is at stake, for the question is, can girls get a college degree without injuring their health?

From the chiming of bells for rising to the chiming the hour for rest, while the parlors grew dim as the gas was turned off, Ellen Swallow tirelessly proved that a woman could learn as much as a man, that a woman could learn all there was to be taught at Vassar College. Translating anecdotes into German, re-reading Wayland's *Moral Science,* delving into political economy and physiology, donning her gray flannel gymnastic suit for a geological excursion, tutoring in Latin or arithmetic for $1.50 a day, she followed *"ad libitum"* the courses offered by the bearded Professor Orton or the whiskered Professor Farrar.

Her enthusiasms were divided between the Observatory and the laboratory. The Observatory at Vassar happened to be in charge of "an American lady-observer, who enjoys a well-earned celebrity at home and abroad," and whose name was Maria Mitchell. From Miss Mitchell, Ellen Swallow learned that "a mathematical formula is a hymn of the universe" and that ignoring one one-hundredth of a second in an astronomical calculation was tantamount to failure. With Miss Mitchell she looked "through the telescope, an entrancing instrument." "We have been making the universe today by a large globe of oil in alcohol and water, throwing off planets." Ellen Swallow made the universe and beheld its meteors, found its nebulae and its star clusters, and heard Miss Mitchell say, "You will make valuable discoveries in the course of your life."

Yet the life of the laboratory seemed more urgent to Nellie Swallow than the life of the Observatory. "Prof. Farrar encourages us to be very thorough there, as the profession of an analytical chemist is very profitable and means very nice and delicate work fitted for ladies' hands." The profession seemed fitted to one lady's hands at least. Through Professor Farrar's eyes, Ellen Swallow began to see that there was a connection between "the facts . . . of science and the . . . problems of common life," a connection that she could observe in the retorts and test tubes on her practice table. From the chemistry of bread-making to toxicology, from the products of coal tar to the curing of leather, she analyzed and experimented and pondered. Professor Farrar cautioned that bu-

tyric acid, formed in strong butter, was one of the "worst poisons."
The *why* of life's processes unfolded before her—why fresh bread
was indigestible, why the whites of eggs could be beaten into foam.
"The chemistry class went to the gas house and Prof. Farrar explained gas making." "Professor Farrar has been telling us some
interesting and startling facts with reference to air and . . . ventilation." Between life at a Dunstable farm or a Westford store
and life in the test tube of a chemical laboratory, a bridge was
building. Ellen Swallow was learning to cross it.

During her years at Vassar she "kept in her corner," emerging
to deliver an essay in her "black silk with lace sleeves and her
class pin." She preferred "surveying for a week to spending a week
in fashionable society." Indeed, fashionable society showed no
inclination to tempt her to its narrow fold. There was little that
suggested fashion in her hat that was "a soup dish of white straw,"
or in her principle that clothing was "a net to catch air." It was
not considered orthodox at Vassar "to be found outside the grounds
except in parties of three, so that if one is hurt, one can stay by
to see that she does not elope and one can run to get help." None
the less, Ellen Swallow did "not trouble herself to stay within
the red fence when she saw something she wanted the other side."
She could be accused of orthodoxy no more than she could be
accused of leanings to fashion. She had started vaulting over the
red fence already, and had begun to see what she wanted on the
other side. Professor Orton had had a hand in making her see it.
"Last night, after our natural history meeting, where Prof. Orton
told us . . . what we might do for science, thinking of that and
of my astronomy and chemistry and of the world whose door is
now wide open to me, I felt as though I . . . could be useful and
contented in learning, any where that I might be. I feel as though
I was fast on my way to the third heaven, . . ." "I ask nothing
more, only longer days or quicker memory. There is so much to
do." Ellen Henrietta Swallow, A.B., Vassar 1870, was on her way
to doing it.

Even for a Vassar Baccalaureate, however, the doors were not
swift to open. Between June and December, Ellen Swallow knocked
futilely at several. An appointment to teach in South America fell
through. Letters to Merrick & Gray, Boston commercial chemists,
and to Booth & Garrett of Philadelphia, applying for an appren-

ticeship, bore no results except the pregnant suggestion that she attempt to enter the Institute of Technology in Boston. The attempt, in the form of another letter, was made. "I have quite made up my mind to try Chemistry for a life study and have been trying to find a suitable opportunity to attempt it. . . . but everything seems to stop short at some blank wall."

At Boston's Institute of Technology, in December of 1870, the wall gave signs of cracking. On December third, the Faculty met to consider, among other topics, "An application . . . received from Ellen H. Swallow, . . . to enter the school as a special student in Chemistry. The question of the admission of female students was postponed till the next meeting." On December tenth, the Faculty assembled again, resuming "The question of the admission of Miss Swallow . . . and after some discussion it was

Voted—That the Faculty recommend to the Corporation the admission of Miss Swallow as a special student in Chemistry."

Professor Rockwell was quick to offer a cautionary resolution, "That the Faculty are of opinion that the admission of women as special students is as yet in the nature of an experiment, that each application should be acted on upon its own merits, and that no general action or change of the former policy of the Institute is at present expedient."

Ellen Swallow knew nothing of the timid resolution. She knew only that she had received from President Runkle a letter congratulating her "and every earnest woman upon the result. Can you come to Boston before many days and see me? I will say now that you shall have any and all advantages which the Institute has to offer without charge of any kind." Ellen Swallow was unaware that, as no fee would be charged, no precedent would be established. She was aware only that the first woman in the world had been admitted to the Massachusetts Institute of Technology. "One of my delights is to do something that no one else ever did. I have the chance of doing what no woman ever did. . . . To be the first woman to enter the Massachusetts Institute of Technology, and so far as I know, *any scientific* school." After an interview with Dr. Runkle, the special woman student was introduced to Mrs. Stinson, assistant in charge of the chemical storeroom, who commented later, "She looks rather frail to take such a difficult course," a comment to which Dr. Runkle replied, "But did you notice her eyes? They are steadfast and they are courageous. She will not fail."

From Mrs. Blodgett's boarding house in Boston, Ellen Swallow, late of Vassar, now of Massachusetts Institute of Technology, made her way up the granite steps of the brownstone Rogers Building on Boylston Street with its Corinthian columns, and entered the laboratory of "the people's university of science." In its smells and its stains she would find her life's milieu. Among its balances and microscopes and spectroscopes she would find her individual appurtenances. Through her laboratory exercises she would learn to apply the sign language that the chemist had constructed, the symbols that were the chemist's alphabet. Wherever there was life, there was chemical change. That change she followed now, devotedly. "The true scientific spirit" that was "the careful, constant search for truth," the suspension of speculation until evidence had been amassed, this she was learning, and this she would apply to public health, to industry, and to her country's homes.

Now the third heaven opened wide before her. She learned of Professor Storer's examinations of air for carbon dioxide, of Professor Nichols' investigations of the presence of lead in water, of Professor Richards and his chemical manipulations. Under Professor Ordway, consulting expert in technical chemistry, she observed how laboratory techniques could be applied to industry. She was crossing many bridges now, the bridge that spanned the laboratory and the world, the bridge that was built out of water and out of air. In her corner of the laboratory, the "quiet little" Nellie Swallow made herself useful. When there was no mineralogy to be learned from Professor Richards, and no State Board of Health work to be done for Professor Nichols, she could always mend another professor's suspenders or sweep the laboratory. When a small piece of the rare mineral, samarskite, came into her possession, she analyzed it until she concluded that it contained elements as yet unknown. When a small bottle of water from Bitlis, Turkey, was given her to analyze, she entered into a fruitful experiment "On the Occurrence of Boracic Acid in Mineral Waters." With hammer, chisel and botany press she spent her summer, returning to the laboratory for more experiments and more analyses. Only her father's sudden and accidental death in 1871 marred the years and checked, temporarily, her plans. Even for this, there were compensations. She was developing in the laboratory not only the crystallization of her scientific spirit, but a warm friendship with Professor "Bobby" Richards of the metallurgical department, who had seen Donati's comet and made chemical tests for Alexander Agassiz, and whose life she would one day share.

Meanwhile, in 1873, the first woman Bachelor of Science of the Institute of Technology received her Degree in chemistry. At the same time she was granted a Master of Arts Degree from Vassar after submitting a dissertation "on the estimation of vanadium in an iron ore from Cold Spring N.Y." She hoped now for a Doctorate as well, but "the heads of the department did not wish a woman to receive the first D.S. in chemistry." Despite her intense disappointment, Ellen Swallow kept her "feathers well oiled" so that "the waters of criticism would run off as from a duck's back." If she could not be granted a Doctorate, there was no reluctance about granting an "Artium Omnium Magistra" to the little woman who cleaned and dusted the chemical laboratory of the Institute when she was not analyzing a rare mineral or performing an experiment on water. In the masculine world of the Institute of Technology, Ellen Swallow could make up in labor what she lacked in title.

As resident graduate, Miss Swallow continued her assistance to Professors Nichols and Ordway, besides supervising, later on, "a private class" of eight "in chemistry in our little Laboratory." In 1876, "our little Laboratory" would be converted into the more ambitious Woman's Laboratory. Before that, on June 4, 1875, Miss Ellen Swallow was herself converted into Mrs. Robert Hallowell Richards. In his slow and deliberate manner, the professor had put the question to the special woman student shortly after her graduation. "I admired her pioneer spirit, as I think she respected me for the hard work which I was doing." At all events, the metallurgist, who was a bit younger than the lady chemist, was accepted, and while Ellen translated German technical books for the professor's lectures, "Cupid . . . appeared among the retorts and receivers." Cupid's guise was somewhat unorthodox, for the wedding journey to Nova Scotia was graced not only by a bride in a short skirt and heavy boots, but by Professor Richards' entire class in mining engineering. The scientific union took for its domestic backdrop a home in Jamaica Plain, and Ellen Richards plunged enthusiastically into the development at Massachusetts Institute of Technology of a Woman's Laboratory.

The Woman's Education Association had promised money for instruments, apparatus and books. The Institute had offered space for a laboratory in a small brick annex intended as a gymnasium. In May, Technology's government had voted "that hereafter Special Students in Chemistry should be admitted without *regard to sex.*" Early in June, the Richards's went abroad, visiting twenty-five cities in twenty-four days, visiting principally mining schools, smelting works and laboratories. At Jena, Mrs. Richards saw Carl Zeiss, inspected his apparatus, and chose the instruments she needed for the Woman's Laboratory.

In November of 1876, the Woman's Laboratory was opened at Massachusetts Institute of Technology, Professor John M. Ordway in charge, Mrs. Ellen Richards, assistant. In the one-story building that had been erected on a sand lot and that was known to students as the "dump," Mrs. Richards, small, compactly built, "absolutely unafraid," lent her extraordinary and inexhaustible energy to the task of training women in the sciences. The need was great. "Women of twenty-five . . . have missed the scientific education of the present day, yet they . . . must have the knowledge of the present." That knowledge Ellen Richards gave for the next seven years without financial compensation, developing a new course in chemistry for her students, and finding professional work for them. At the Woman's Laboratory, whether she was devising a new method for determining nickel in ore or adapting formulas for the determination of tannic acid, Ellen Richards constantly imparted her own principles of efficiency. If a student's hand made two trips instead of one between a balance and a box of weights, Mrs. Richards was sure to mark and check the waste of motions. From her Woman's Laboratory teachers went forth, better equipped than they had ever been before, to the colleges and seminaries of the country. She was "seeing the realization of her hopes and wishes in all directions. . . . At the Institute women have now their position and can take a degree. This is the great step which I have been waiting for." Even she herself received, in 1878, a title—that of instructor in chemistry. Many men were and would be promoted over her head. But Ellen Richards, Fellow of the American Association for the Advancement of Science, first woman member of the American Institute of Mining Engineers, and only woman on the instructing staff of Massachusetts Institute of Technology, continued to confine her ambitions to essentials, to substance, not to form.

By 1884, her title was altered to that of instructor in sanitary chemistry, and her laboratory, too, underwent a metamorphosis. In July of 1883, when she knew that the Woman's Laboratory would be torn down, she felt "like a woman whose children are all about to be married and leave her alone, . . . We women have raised ten thousand dollars and given to the Institute to make suitable provision for women students in all departments. The new building, . . . is to be ready in October. In that are to be the chemical laboratories, the ladies' parlor and reading room, etc. Our present women's laboratory will be torn down and my duties will be gone, . . . I do not know that I shall have anything to do or anywhere to work. Professor Richards is to have a new mining laboratory and Professor Ordway a new industrial chemical laboratory. . . .

Everything seems to fall flat and I have a sense of impending fate which is paralyzing."

Impending fate was kinder than she had anticipated. In the plain, utilitarian new building of Massachusetts Institute of Technology, a separate laboratory for sanitary chemistry—the first of its kind in the country—was opened, and there, as assistant to Professor Nichols, expert in water analysis, Ellen Richards found her place. As instructor in sanitary chemistry, a title that she would hold without promotion until her death more than twenty-five years later, she would radiate an unforgettable influence upon the public health, the industry, and the domestic life of America. Up the long flights of stairs that led to the third floor—"those Judgment Stairs"—she climbed to her corner in Room 34 of the Kidder Laboratories for new work, new experiments, new plans. She was surrounded by her apparatus—glass-stoppered gallon bottles for samples of water, filter paper, flasks and condensers, Bunsen burners and Nessler tubes, pipettes and chemicals. She was fenced in by books and charts and papers that would come to be "a contemporaneous biography, as the topic once foremost in her mind and on the shelves was gradually pushed by its successors into a less and less conspicuous place." From her little cell, glassed off from the rest of the laboratory, she turned to give a brief preliminary greeting to her students, a keen glance, and then she swept forward to the vital issue, transporting them to larger worlds with a transfiguring touch.

Before her lecture or laboratory period, Mrs. Richards took care of time-saving details, seeing that the stoppers of her reagent bottles could be easily removed, arranging her apparatus in a logical manner. With systematic method, with studied technique and experimental skill, she approached the problem of the day with her students. There was nothing too small for her attention, nothing too large for the rich fertilities of her thought. Here in the Kidder Laboratories, she developed "the elementary school where the sanitary engineer learns the ABC and the simple language needed. Here he learns to understand the signs of the trail, the broken twig, the plucked leaf, the flower bent by the moccasin," whether the signs led to polluted water or inadequate ventilation or adulterated food. The sciences, she taught, were "no longer in watertight compartments, but flowed freely from one to the other." And these were golden days of the sciences at Massachusetts Institute of Technology, when no tradition or precedent hampered the freshness of her subject, when a new era demanded a new training. William Thompson Sedgwick, the "father of the modern public health movement in America," had recently been called to the Institute. Mrs. Richards and all the faculty were stirred when, after Professor Nichols died abroad in 1886, some tubes of Koch's strange new gelatin medium were brought back to the Institute with his personal effects. Two years later, the first course in bacteriology was given at Massachusetts Institute of Technology. The sciences were indeed flowing together, and Mrs. Richards' science, sanitary chemistry, was designed to prevent the beginnings of illness, to inform the people of what had been learned in the laboratory.

In the laboratory itself, the woman instructor was teaching her students to do the impossible. She was teaching them, too, the chemical examination of air and of water and of food, the "three essentials for healthful human life." She was teaching them that the leaders in technological movements "must not betray the rank and file," that they must not be "browbeaten by any combination of capital" or tempted by shrewd promoters to make the worse appear the better food, or to perfect a filter which would "pass the credulous multitude but which adds a danger rather than lessens a risk." No taint of work done for advertising purposes that would defraud the public or endanger men's lives must bear the stamp of her institution or of herself or of her students. Beneath all her experiments, whether she tested air for carbon dioxide or water for free ammonia and nitrites, or milk and butter for adulterants or poisons, this was her underlying motif. To this end she applied all her resources, from her "experienced nose" to her passion for efficiency, from her detective skills to her powers of interpretation.

Rising at half past five in the morning, walking, or cycling around Jamaica Pond, she went briskly through the long day's work. "I have helped five men to positions they would not have held without me," she wrote in 1889, "but I am content."

. . . Beside my housekeeping, my plants and my garden, helping my husband with his lectures, keeping up with all the German and French, mining and metallurgical periodicals (some twenty papers a week come into our house) . . . [I have] my classes in sanitary chemistry.

Through the years she was up and out early every morning, "rain or snow or sunshine . . . —wheels or shanks mare."

What am I doing? I think it would be easier to say what I am not doing.

Books and articles had begun flowing from her pen—notes on antimony tannate, a book on minerals in which she ventured the prophetic suggestion that aluminum, "the most abundant metal in the earth, . . . would be valuable if it could be obtained cheaply." When she had time, she could enjoy a ride on her little chestnut mare, Duchess. Time was a resource that only her efficiency could extend, an efficiency that was adopted as conscientiously to her person as to her laboratory. Long after chatelaine bags had gone out of fashion, Mrs. Richards wore one if she could not have a pocket in her dress. "Don't you *ever* get tired?" she was asked. "Yes, every night, and then I go to bed." Between sessions at the Institute, she manufactured both the time and the energy to act as chemist on her husband's expeditions to the copper regions of northern Michigan, or to climb a rope, hand over hand, to a freshly opened cave in Virginia. Things fixed, she taught, were dead. But the chemical change of all living things consumed her.

Especially over the years she had been and would continue to be consumed by the properties of water, the great carrier and solvent that "extracted something from each obstacle in its flow." Her laboratory in the Massachusetts Institute of Technology was not only a teaching medium, but an analysis station for the benefit of the public health. While Mrs. Richards preached the science of sanitary chemistry to her students, she practised it, too, applying to the domain of public health the chemistry of the laboratory.

As early as 1872, when she was still a student at Massasachutts Institute of Technology, the recently organized Massasachusetts State Board of Health had asked Professor William R. Nichols to undertake a chemical study of the State's water supply, and Professor Nichols had selected Miss Swallow as his assistant. "A new work" had been placed in her hands—a work through which the chemistry of the laboratory would be applied to public health, a work that would develop her conviction that "practical problems offer the greatest stimulus to research in pure science." There were practical problems indeed in the last quarter of the nineteenth century, scourges of typhoid fever, a death rate nearly double the necessary estimate. Water, the carrier of life, could also be the carrier of death. From cedar swamp to limestone quarry, from factory to farm, from village to city, a stream might run, and with it ran pollution. The nineteenth century itself, with its inventions, its cities, its "civilization," was polluting the sources upon which it depended for life. "Water rightly read is the interpreter of its own history." "If it encounters a jam of logs, a pile of sawdust, a dead deer or fox, a barnyard or chicken farm, a paper mill, a village, each will leave its mark. He who knows will read." Ellen Richards knew, and read.

With "the art of . . . [an early] Sherlock Holmes," she drew out the facts of water pollution, examining the samples sent in by the State, recording her observations, setting aside the racks of tubes, analyzing for organic matter and mineral substances, testing for ammonia, nitrites and chlorine. Among the tools of her trade—the filter paper, the flasks, the condensers—she lived, while Professor

Nichols, reporting to the State Board of Health of Massachusetts, took "pleasure in acknowledging his indebtedness to her valuable assistance, and in expressing his confidence in the accuracy of the results obtained." As she analyzed, she experimented, serving from 1872 to 1875 as chemist to the Massachusetts Board of Health. Long after the student, Ellen Swallow, had become the instructor in sanitary chemistry, Ellen Richards, in 1887, the State of Massachusetts began an extensive sanitary survey of its waters. Professor Nichols had died and had been succeeded by Dr. Thomas M. Drown. Mrs. Richards remained the assistant in a work that would mark an epoch in public health. Between Dr. Drown's phrase, "What is desired in a drinking water is innocence, not repentance," and Mrs. Richards' dictum, "Chlorine once in the water always in the water," a method was developed that would not only "protect the purity of inland waters," but that would become a classic in the field.

Now, in Room 36 of the Institute's new building, Ellen Richards was truly *"under water."* There, a laboratory for water analysis had been equipped, and for a decade Mrs. Richards conducted the analyses and supervised her corps of assistants. In 1872 she had written, "I have made about 100 water analyses." In 1893, the 10,000th sample was analyzed, an event signalized by a celebration and a dinner at Mrs. Richards' home. There was already much to celebrate. Through the work of her laboratory, a new fact would be established, a new method developed that would become a model for all later surveys. Water normally contained chlorine, a condition caused by two factors only, its nearness to the sea, "that great repository of chlorine," or sewage disposal. Ellen Richards' tests were designed to prove primarily whether the chlorine content of a water was occasioned by its nearness to the sea or by pollution. The great Normal Chlorine Map of the State of Massachusetts, charted through her pioneer work, proved that the normal chlorine content of unpolluted water remained constant at certain distances from the sea. But if a water contained a higher content of chlorine than was consistent with its distance from the sea, then the cause lay in pollution. This was, as she put it, "our one new fact." Like most significant new facts, it was simple, once it had been discovered.

The discovery had not been easy. Ellen Richards was "on constant duty from 8 o'clock to 5.30 or 6 every day, Saturday included." At times, she worked fourteen hours a day, and if the day was too hot for analyzing water, the work was done at night. The work was done until some 40,000 water samples had been analyzed and until "drinking water, concerning which there has been hitherto but imperfect knowledge," had been subjected to a scientific study that helped make possible the entire public health movement in the United States.

Ellen Richards was water analyst not for the State of Massachusetts alone. For physicians recommended by other physicians, she examined samples of well water. At Vassar College, of which she was elected Alumna Trustee in 1894, she might appear among the "gay parterre of hats which blossoms at a meeting of the Vassar Alumnae Association," but she appeared primarily to urge an irrigation plant for the college's sewage disposal. Through the years, the work of water analysis for the State suggested other analyses, other experiments—a prolonged series of determinations on the oscillaria of Jamaica Pond, investigations on the coloring matter of natural waters for the American Chemical Society, a study of the hardness of water which she prepared for the State Board of Health, a paper on nitrites in streams which she reported to the American Public Health Association. With the studies, came the books—her *Laboratory Notes* on water analysis which she prepared for the use of her students in the sanitary chemistry laboratory, *Conservation By Sanitation* which included a laboratory guide for sanitary engineers.

When she left her laboratory, Ellen Richards did not abandon her work in water analysis for the public health. With two carriages and mules supplied by the Boston Fruit Company to transport her apparatus and luggage, she journeyed to Jamaica in the West Indies, circling the island, bottling samples of water that would be analyzed at the Institute's laboratory until a Normal Chlorine Chart of Jamaica could be mapped. With a portable laboratory consisting of two boxes strapped together and containing movable racks, bottles for reagents, pipettes and tubes, the slight, indomitable Ellen Richards took to the field. In Mexico, where the American Institute of Mining Engineers met in 1901, she analyzed samples of water from Ajusco on the divide, from Cuernavaca on the Pacific side, from Pachuca on the East. In between a bull fight and a dip in the Gulf of Mexico, she recorded her notes on the country's potable waters, a woman Sherlock Holmes abroad with her kit. In the Black Hills of South Dakota, at Deadwood and Lead, she continued her analyses and her note-taking. In 1903, Ellen Richards ventured to Alaska with her husband, and with her went her portable laboratory, for she believed that "a record of the condition of the available waters in this early stage of the development of the country must have a certain value in the future." Between her observations of the salmon fishing at Ketchikan, the totem poles at Fort Wrangel, the dug-out boats, the Russian churches at Killisnoo, she collected the waters from mountain streams and Indian pools, from rivers and melted snows, a woman chemist in the field, a prospector for pure water armed with a portable kit and the conviction that the chemical laboratory existed primarily for the public health.

Not water alone, but food, too, commanded her attention. The inventions of the nineteenth century—canning and cold storage—benefited the public, but because of what she called "the sophistications of unscrupulous dealers," tainted meats were disguised with sauces and French names, streptococci lurked in ice cream, and the word *ptomaine* became familiar through headlines in the newspapers. In 1878, Ellen Richards embarked upon another course of detection to advance the public health, the examination of staple groceries for the State of Massachusetts. The next year, she wrote to a friend, "I am to prepare a paper on the ingredients of food liable to adulteration this winter." Now her chemical analyses were directed to the starch in mustard, "a proof of adulteration," or to alum in bread and baking powders, and her microscope revealed the adulterations in pepper. "Twelve specimens of cinnamon were examined. Only three of these contained any cinnamon at all. Even these were mixed with cassia and sawdust. The other nine were chiefly cassia and sawdust, mahogany sawdust being distinctly identified in some of them." In 1879, Mrs. Richards' report, "Adulteration of Some Staple Groceries," made its appearance. In 1885, as a result of her years of laboratory examination of food materials, she prepared a book, *Food Materials and Their Adulterations.* In between those years, from 1882 to 1884, the State of Massachusetts passed the first of its Food and Drug Acts. They had been passed not without reference to the work of a slight, but inexhaustible woman working in the laboratories of the Massachusetts Institute of Technology.

Through the years she continued to work for the public health. In the Bulletins of the Department of Agriculture's Office of Experiment Stations her experiments were summarized. For Boston's Health-Education League she prepared booklets on *Meat and Drink* or *The Plague of Mosquitoes and Flies*. For safe water and safe food she crusaded, cautioning the public against flies hatched in stable manure, and from water and food she moved on to the third great element of life, air. Air, too, was a food, and in her laboratories exercises were performed in the inspection of ventilation, while she herself served as a member of the American Public Health Association's Committee on Standard Methods for the Examination of Air. The nineteenth century had already become the twentieth when she wrote:

The day is not far distant when a city will be held as responsible for the purity of the air in its school-houses, the cleanliness of the water in its reservoirs, and the reliability of the food sold in its markets as it now is for the condition of its streets and bridges.

That not far distant day had been brought nearer by a small, dynamic woman in a laboratory, who believed that chemistry was dedicated to the public health.

There were other services, too, to which her chemistry was dedicated as the years passed. As she applied her science to public health, she applied it also to industry, whose manufactures and patents so closely affected the people. A chemist, she believed, must leave the laboratory to visit manufactories and to study new processes. As always, she lived her preachments, developing an active private practice as expert chemist-consultant to industry. From industrial water analysis for the Mutual Boiler Insurance Company to gas analysis, from the testing of fabrics and wallpapers for arsenic to the testing of soap solutions, from the study of flour manufacture in modern milling to suggestions to manufacturers that the right-sided lip on saucepans was inconvenient for right-handed people, she applied her knowledge to the world of industry. Experimenting on a "purified gluten" prepared by the New York Health Food Company, she devised an artificial gastric juice with pepsin and hydrochloric acid, and subjected wafers of gluten to artificial digestion. Nothing that lived or was pertinent to life was alien to her, and little escaped her experienced eye.

Nor did her own activities at the Institute of Technology escape the interested attention of one of Boston's great industrialists. The massive, imposing Edward Atkinson was himself one of the nineteenth century's more extraordinary products. He was part and parcel of an age that had witnessed so many technological beginnings—the age of oil and steel and electricity, the era when the Massachusetts Institute of Technology itself had been born. Atkinson had argued for a grant of land for the Institute in 1861, and later was to offer a plan for its textile laboratory. Although he seemed larger than he was, he was large enough, and his interests ranged from economics to statistics, from finance to free trade. In 1878 he had become president of the Boston Manufacturers Mutual Fire Insurance Company. Faced with the problem of widespread loss by fire, Atkinson, always insistent that he be fortified by facts, always eager to "close the door *before* the horse was stolen," left his office in Boston's Rialto Building to present his questions to Professor Ordway of the Massachusetts Institute of Technology. Through Professor Ordway, Ellen Richards became involved in yet another application of chemistry to industry.

The questions concerned the spontaneous combustion of oils, the fires that smoldered in piles of dyed goods, questions that deeply affected not only the New England Cotton Manufacturers Association and the Boston Manufacturers Mutual Fire Insurance Company, but the consumers. Again the laboratory went into action, testing the oxidation of oils and dye-stuffs in contact with inflammable materials. With Professor Ordway's apparatus, the experiments continued, experiments on shavings and leather and skeins of dyed yarn, to determine the cause of fires and the degree of safety of oils used in manufacture. Of four samples of kerosene burning oil, only one was shown to be safe. The claims made for so-called safe oils, transformed by "special and secret processes of refining," were exposed. Mineral oils, it was determined, had no affinity for oxygen. By the simple substitution of such oils in place of animal oils for lubrication, the danger of spontaneous combustion was almost entirely eliminated, and lubrication itself was elevated into an important applied science.

During those investigations, the oils used for smearing wool were examined, and Ellen H. Richards, who in 1884 would be appointed chemist for the Boston Manufacturers Mutual Fire Insurance Company, turned inventor, devising a method for cleansing wool that eliminated waste and "stimulated research the world over." She tested wools from Uruguay and the Cape of Good Hope, from Vermont and West Virginia. What she called "a little investigation of cleaning wool by means of Naphtha," resulted in an important new method adopted by the wool industry and reduced the cost by the use of "a quality of naphtha called 'gasoline,' " then merely a waste product of petroleum refining. At the Insurance Engineering Experimental Station set up by Atkinson, Ellen Richards' investigations were followed by a host of other investigations that eventually inaugurated in the country the use of indirect illumination and the development of " 'factory-ribbed' glass."

The impressive Mr. Atkinson had literally many irons in his fire, among them an invention of his own known as the Aladdin Oven. "In the preparation of food," he stipulated, "the single rule is this: Take one part of gumption and one part of food; mix them together . . . put the compound into the oven and keep it there long enough for the heat to do the work." The oven he had in mind was his own Aladdin Oven that eliminated the waste of heat and permitted the slow cooking of foods at low and controlled temperatures. When he wanted his oven tested, he quite naturally turned to the woman chemist who had detected adulterations in food and made scientific studies of so many food materials.

Mrs. Richards doubtless agreed with Edward Atkinson that "The Lord sends the meat and the Devil sends the stoves," the old iron cooking ranges, the frying pans that promoted nineteenth-century American dyspepsia. In 1890, a perfect opportunity arose for testing the Aladdin Oven. With a gift of money from Mrs. Quincy Shaw for the purpose of "making a thorough study of the food and nutrition of working men," and a grant from the trustees of the Elizabeth Thompson Fund, the New England Kitchen was opened on Boston's Pleasant Street. Mrs. Mary Abel, winner of the Lomb Prize for the best essay on sanitary and economic cooking, took charge, while Mrs. Ellen Richards served as adviser. At the New England Kitchen, standard dishes were prepared according to scientific formulas before the customers' eyes, and food was offered for sale. In the Aladdin Ovens, which could be ordered at the New England Kitchen, huge quantities of beef broth and pea soup were cooked daily, according to recipes perfected after chemical analyses at the Institute. Later a restaurant was opened. Somehow, Boston's poor found the delights of scientifically prepared cornmeal mush and fish chowder, oatmeal cakes and Indian pudding, dubious. Although it gave rise to later, more fruitful experiments, the New England Kitchen was a failure. Neither Mrs. Richards nor Edward Atkinson nor the Aladdin Oven could dissuade the public from the unscientific point of view epitomized by the woman who commented, "I don't want to eat what's good for me; I'd ruther eat what I'd ruther."

Failure pursued another interesting and provocative experiment whereby Mrs. Richards and her progressive peers hoped to serve the public. The Household Aid Company, organized under the auspices of the Woman's Education Association of Boston, was an attempt to provide private families with skilled help and to study the problems of household labor. Injustices in the demands for service were mediated by the Company, which also gave tests and training to employees. Although it was the first well planned experiment in household service, the Company failed financially and was abandoned.

Both the New England Kitchen and the Household Aid Company were services not only to industry, but to the home life of the country. Ellen Richards, who had applied her chemistry to public health and to industry, spent much of her indefatigable enthusiasm upon applying it also to the household. ". . . Of what use is it," she asked,

to lay pipes carrying water to a community which still drinks at the well in the stable yard? or what use to build model tenement houses on clean soil, when in a year or two the occupants will have soaked it through and through with refuse which it is too much trouble to carry away?

The death rate was being lowered in all cases under state control, but it was rising in the sphere of individual responsibility. The individual was at liberty to drop dead from heart disease and to suffocate in close rooms until the white plague claimed him. The state had applied science to engineering problems, drained swamps, furnished good water; but the people in their apathy failed to take advantage of the technological advances of their century.

The parlor maid is duly instructed in her duties, and everything is quite right in the dining-room, but what an expression of amazement would come over many a housewife's face did you ask her what was the condition of her cellar, or if 300 cubic feet of air a minute passed through every room. . . .

The child poring over his book in the evening, with his head close to a student lamp, complains of a headache. "Those lessons," says the mother, not stopping to think that it is the close air and the heat from the lamp, no matter how many laws of chemistry she has studied.

The knowledge gained from the test tubes of the laboratory must be carried into the home.

The home itself had undergone a metamorphosis. "The time was when there was always something to *do* in the home. Now there is only something *to be done*." Spinning, weaving and soap-making had left the home for the factory. The large mill had replaced the family mortar. Home life had lost its industries, but had gained in their stead the mechanical appliances of a technological age. In place of the punkah man and the buzz-wheel fan, heating and cooling apparatus could be controlled by motors. The electric light and the gas stove were familiar objects. The inventions were there, but what woman understood them?

Can the cotton manufacturer know too much about cotton fiber? Can a cook know too much about the composition and nutritive value of the meats and vegetables which she uses? Can a housekeeper know too much of the effect of fresh air on the human system, of the danger of sewer gas, of foul water?

All the fruits of chemical science—the self-rising flour, the bread powders, the washing powders—could be bought, but if the lady of the household wished to avoid the palpable frauds that were practised by unscrupulous manufacturers, she must learn something of the chemistry of daily life, for the "running of a household was a no less responsible task than the running of a steamboat or an engine."

Ellen Richards was applying chemistry to the home, and evolving from the application the science of domestic economy. She had evolved it first of all in her own home. 32 Eliot Street in Jamaica Plain was filled with books and plants and sunshine—"never mind the carpets." Nor did the parrot and the cats interfere with its hygienic arrangements. At the Richards home, rugs were substituted for carpets and gas for coal. A vacuum cleaner replaced the feather duster and a ventilator topped the gas chandelier in the study. Curtains, except short washable ones, were eliminated. Here was no bric-a-brac shop or upholsterer's establishment. On the altar of the goddess of health, superfluous draperies had been sacrificed. The dust of non-essentials had been swept away. And although the food served at Mrs. Richards' table was served with reference to its effect upon efficiency in work, the creamed chicken and scalloped oysters titillated the taste of students who dropped in for an exhibition of Professor Richards' glass-blowing after an old-fashioned company supper. Mrs. Richards had a servant to whom she gave typewritten directions, but Mrs. Richards was her own housekeeper, and her home was an expression of herself.

What she practised, Mrs. Richards preached for the homes of America, and especially for the women of the country. The doctrines formulated in her chemistry laboratory she applied to life. Nothing in the home escaped her insistent urgings. For the kitchen, the "center and source of political economy," she made dietary studies and developed a *Dietary Computer*, bills of fare based upon food values and cost, claiming at the end of the century that "sufficient raw food material for health and production of energy may be secured anywhere in America within reach of a railroad for nine to ten cents per day per person." In *First Lessons in Food And Diet*, published by Whitcomb & Barrows, a Boston firm whose existence was "due to her belief in the need for specialized service in the literature of Home Economics," Ellen Richards expounded her philosophy of dinners—a first course designed to stimulate the appetite, relishes to remove the flavor of the last dish and cleanse the tongue and palate for the next, the sweet (a very little of it) to clear the traces of the oily matter of the salad or the fat of the meat. A meal of lettuce dressed with oil and eaten with bread and cheese, she held, fulfilled all the requirements of nutrition and might cost five cents. The same food value from sweetbreads and grapefruit might cost a dollar. A cheap food was not necessarily a poor food, nor an expensive food a good food. Plain living, in Mrs. Richards' doxology, went with high thinking. The soldier took his ration of bread, bacon, beans or stewed meat and coffee without the frills of strawberry shortcake, ice cream or coffee-jelly

which a Harvard boat crew required. The one cost fifteen to twenty
cents, the other eighty cents to a dollar. The usual American breakfast of flesh or fish or fowl and hot bread would, she declared,
never fit a man for his best work. And it was food that was converted into work by the human machine, whether the work was
thinking or weight lifting. The food question was "ever present . . .
in spite of the Phillipines [sic] or Cuba." Against the inventions
of diabolical cooks of past ages she crusaded, the rich gravies and
sauces with which meats were dressed, against quack foods and
the dyspepsia that gave the nation the habit of ill health, and
against costly prepared material shrewdly advertised. Advertising
she saw as the "science of creating wants," until it was "no longer
respectable to save" and waste was encouraged, for "swell swill"
had come to signify "swell people."

From the kitchen, the chemist turned crusader invaded every
other room of the house, from cellar to attic, championing scientific ventilation, plumbing, heating and lighting. "Economy of
labor," she declared, "has not been thought of in the construction
of houses. In what other business would the coal-supply be dumped
on the sidewalk to be shovelled and wheeled into the cellar, only
to be brought up again; the ashes carried down, only to be again
brought up and carted away." Against matter in the wrong place
she struggled, experimenting on dust and concluding that "to remove dust and tracked-in dirt in an ordinary eight-room house
costs 18 hours a week, 50 weeks in a year, or 900 hours." The
experiments continued while the books rolled from the press, experiments on washing soda and bluing, books on *The Chemistry
of Cooking and Cleaning, The Cost of Food, The Cost of Shelter,
The Cost of Cleanness*. The ideal home she championed was dry
and easily aired, with windows that opened smoothly at the top,
with washable walls, perfect plumbing, and the indispensable vacuum cleaner to replace the ubiquitous feather duster that stirred
up dust. In it must be united all the physics and chemistry of air
and fire and water, fully understood and carried out not only by
the builder, but by the occupants.

It was not through books alone that Ellen Richards carried her
message to the world. As head of the Science Section of the Society
to Encourage Studies at Home, she taught the sciences by correspondence to students on western ranches and in isolated mountain

regions, sending microscopes and laboratory material and apparatus through the mail. Under the auspices of the Association of Collegiate Alumnae, which she helped found, she organized a Sanitary Science Club. She became a charter member of the Naples Table Association for promoting laboratory research by women. In lectures and addresses she urged the scientific education of women, who "have lacked respect for nature and her laws," who have "feared the thunder and ignored the microbe," who "expect hot, foul air to come down from the top of the room and obediently go out of the window," who have "allowed the sink drain to feed the well and the dark, damp cellar to furnish air to the house," who "need the influence of the scientific spirit, which tests all things and *suspends judgment.*" Ellen Richards left the laboratory not only for the homes of the country, but for its institutions, crusading for healthful schoolhouses, penny lunches and domestic science courses, serving as dietary consultant to insane asylums and to the Massachusetts General Hospital, creating a new profession for women, the profession of dietitian and home economist.

At the time of the Columbian Exposition, she left the laboratory not only to address the World's Congress of Chemists on "Carbon Dioxide as a Measure of the Efficiency of Ventilation," but to supervise a model kitchen set up by the State of Massachusetts in a tiny frame building south of the Fair grounds. At the Rumford Kitchen, named in honor of Count Rumford, visitors might have their choice of ten standard luncheons while they could study menus that informed them of the calories and food values in proteid, fat and carbohydrates, as well as the cost of raw materials, of the food they were about to consume. As they glanced up from their baked beans, brown bread and apple sauce, they could examine the wall mottoes that assured them, "A man is what he eats," or "The fate of nations depends on how they are fed." They could wander about the room, seeing models of Count Rumford's oven and the Aladdin Oven, and apparatus from the New England Kitchen, or they could pick up the Rumford Kitchen Leaflets on "King Palate" or "Comparative Nutrition." This dramatic attempt to demonstrate the scientific principles underlying nutrition had practical results, for the University of Chicago purchased much of the equipment of the Rumford Kitchen when its Women's Halls were opened.

Six years after the Exposition, in September of 1899, the ubiquitous Mrs. Richards appeared in a room over the boathouse at Lake Placid, New York, to chair a conference on home economics with Melvil Dewey as secretary. Eleven people were present. They caught the enthusiasm of their leader. As one gentleman put it, "I always like to see that little woman conduct a meeting. It is an education in itself." In 1908, the Lake Placid Conference on Home Economics was transformed into the American Home Economics Association with Mrs. Richards as president. A half century after eleven people had met in a room over a boathouse in the Adirondacks, 20,000 members, with an office building of their own in Washington, were disseminating the views of a woman chemist who had served as consulting engineer to the home economics movement.

Her views had progressed as she herself progressed. Her views, toward the end of her life, were crystallized into a single word that she had coined, *Euthenics,* the science of controllable environment. To this single word her applications of chemistry to public health, to industry, and to the home, had brought her—to the belief that man, by the right application of scientific principles to living, could conquer his own environment. Euthenics preceded eugenics, and better men could be developed now. She had come a long way since she had watched Professor Farrar hold a vial in each hand during an experiment at Vassar Female College. The "contemporaneous biography" reflected by the changing books and charts and papers in her office at Massachusetts Institute of Technology had undergone several metamorphoses. Yet the purpose had remained the same. She had been assayer of ores and water analyst, industrial expert and investigator of foods, instructor in sanitary chemistry and "super-engineer." What had she not pointed out to benefit the public, from the futility of violent boiling that did not increase the temperature but did waste gas, to the desirability of a study of the distance traveled by droplets in a mild or explosive cough? The laboratory had been grist to her mill, a mill that continuously ground out the applications of chemistry and the science of controllable environment. In the exact science of the laboratory she had found a basis for the art of "right living."

Although Ellen Richards never rose above the rank of instructor at Massachusetts Institute of Technology, now, at the end of her life, she was crowned with laurel. The Doctorate in science she had never achieved at the Institute came to her, in honorary form, in 1910, when Smith College made its citation:

Ellen Henrietta Richards, Bachelor and master of arts of Vassar College, bachelor of science of the Massachusetts Institute of Technology, and there for over a quarter of a century instructor in sanitary chemistry. By investigations into the explosive properties of oils and in the analysis of water, and by expert knowledge relating to air, food, water, sanitation and the cost of food and shelter, set forth in numerous publications and addresses, she has largely contributed to promote in the community the serviceable arts of safe, healthful and economic living.

"Doctor" Ellen Richards was still a slight woman filled with drive and energy. On her sixty-eighth birthday, in December 1910, she rose at 5:30 and by 7:30 had taken a brisk walk around Jamaica Pond, had had her breakfast, watered the plants, and was off to her laboratory. Yet, as the new year rolled on, her face seemed thin and pallid, her hair was white, and the three flights of stairs that led to her office at the Institute had somehow lengthened. Between research and its applications, between laboratory and lectures, between the cottage she had built at Randolph, New Hampshire, and named "The Balsams," and her home in Jamaica Plain, she vibrated, still leading many lives.

In 1911, those lives were honored when the Naples Table Association for promoting laboratory research by women named its $1000 prize for an original paper embodying the results of scientific research, the Ellen Richards Research Prize. Two years later, the Ellen H. Richards Research Fund was presented to the Massachusetts Institute of Technology for research in sanitary chemistry. At Vassar College, the *Ellen S. Richards Monographs* were published, including an address on the discovery of radium by Madame Curie, and a division of euthenics was established. In Building Four, at Massachusetts Institute of Technology, a bronze tablet was unveiled in her honor, and at Pennsylvania State College the Ellen H. Richards Institute was founded to study the improvement of standards of living in the fields of food, clothing and shelter.

These honors were memorial. On March 30, 1911, Ellen Richards died, at the age of sixty-eight, at her home in Jamaica Plain, after a week's struggle with angina pectoris. During that week she characteristically gave the final touches to a paper on "The Elevation of Applied Science to an Equal Rank with the So-Called Learned Professions," which she had planned to read at the fiftieth anniversary of the granting of a charter to Massachusetts Institute of Technology. "The technologist," she had written, "is one who can both think and act—who can translate his reasoning into results." The essential element in technological education, she wrote, was "the creative spirit." To applied science she had given all her technological skills and all her creative spirit, until, by her own life, she had helped to raise that science to an equal rank with the learned professions.

For women's part in the drama of scientific advance she had done still more. Once she had written, "We may discount all the scare-heads about what will happen if women do thus and so. They have done nearly everything and the heavens have not fallen." As early as the turn of the century, one woman in five in the United States had already ventured outside the "historic mission" of women. Ellen Richards had certainly ventured. The air she breathed had ever been "full of projects." "We have hardly dreamed," she wrote, "of the possibilities of the human being." But she had dreamed of those possibilities, and through applied science she had helped to realize them. From the test tubes and condensers that had been the appurtenances of her life, she had taken the formulas that would develop the public health, improve the products of industry, and advance the American home. The tiny woman chemist with sparkling eyes and dynamic energy had distilled in the laboratory an elixir of life for the world.

The Professions
and Trades

7

America's First Woman College Professor

REBECCA PENNELL DEAN

1852

A T HORACE MANN'S small white frame house in West Newton, Massachusetts, where, not long before, Hawthorne had completed his *Blithedale Romance,* another romance had just begun. In November of 1852, Horace Mann, Congressman from Massachusetts, had called a meeting that would write a prelude to history. The tall, silver-haired educator who had reorganized the public school system of his State and had been offered the presidency of a new college in the West, looked at the small group he had assembled with penetrating eyes behind gold-bowed spectacles, and raised his resonant voice to outline a nineteenth-century dream.

The dream had been named Antioch College in honor of the Syrian city where "the disciples were first called Christians." While the dream had as yet little substance, it had a site, midway between Xenia and Springfield in the Buckeye State, in a town on the Little Miami Railroad named Yellow Springs. The College had been projected by a group of the "Christian" denomination, who had promised that it would be non-sectarian and that it would offer equal opportunities to students of both sexes. Horace Mann had been unable to resist "the two great ideas" that had won him toward the "plan." To realize that "plan" he had called his first faculty meeting.

Horace Mann's cast of characters at that historic November meeting included a group of interesting gentlemen who would occupy the professorial chairs of Antioch College, along with the building agent who would design its ambitious brick towers, and one who would, before the dream was ended, attempt to destroy it with a scathing vituperation. If the garden of an educational Eden was being sown at West Newton, the garden boasted not only its serpent, but its Eve.

At that fruitful meeting a woman was present, the first in the country to bear the title of college professor, a woman whose name would "always be indissolubly associated" with the success or failure of Horace Mann's "new enterprise." If, as at least one observer would believe, "the history of America began with the foundation of Antioch College," then a woman had a hand in that beginning. Miss Rebecca Pennell, niece of Horace Mann, aged thirty-one, was a handsome woman, filled with lightning, whose charm was not obscured by her elaborate title of Professor of Physical Geography, Drawing, Natural History, Civil History and Didactics. If the title revealed anything at all, it revealed her comprehensive capabilities and her extraordinary powers as a teacher.

She had received her appointment two months before when, with her brother, Calvin Pennell, she had been "duly elected" a member "of the College Faculty." Now, at the first faculty meeting, she listened while the educational "newness" of the nineteenth century was bandied about by the dreamers of reform. "We were all teetotalers; all anti-tobacco men; all antislavery men; a majority of us believers in phrenology; all anti-emulation men,—that is, all against any system of rewards and prizes designed to withdraw the mind from a comparison of itself with a standard of excellence, and to substitute a rival for that standard." The standard of excellence waved bravely in the breeze while professorships were projected, courses outlined, a circular planned, ideals adumbrated. The College would breathe the non-sectarian spirit. A "Joint Stock Company" would be formed by the union of science and humanity. The College would recognize the "claims of women to equal opportunities of education with men."

It would recognize, too, the claims of women to equal professorial opportunities with men. In her own keen, lovely presence, Miss Rebecca Pennell embodied both that claim and its recognition. If she lent herself to the subtle intrigues of college politics and family quarrels, she would do so with an air of fascinating femininity. She would carry more than her charm, more than her

ANTIOCH COLLEGE.

FACULTY.

Hon. HORACE MANN, LL. D., President,
and Professor of Political Economy, Intellectual and Moral Philosophy, Constitutional Law and Natural Theology.

Rev. W. H. DOHERTY, A. M.,
Professor of Rhetoric, Logic and Belles-Lettres.

IRA W. ALLEN, A. M.,
Professor of Mathematics, Astronomy and Civil Engineering.

Rev. THOMAS HOLMES, A. M.,
Professor of Greek Language and Literature.

C. S. PENNELL, A. M.,
Professor of Latin Language and Literature.

Miss R. M. PENNELL,
Professor of Physical Geography, Drawing, Natural History, Civil History and Didactics.

Professor of Chemistry, and Theory and Practice of Agriculture.

Professor of Mineralogy and Geology.

Professor of Modern Languages.

Rev. A. L. McKINNEY,
Principal of Preparatory School.

THE FIRST ANTIOCH COLLEGE FACULTY INCLUDING THE FIRST AMERICAN WOMAN COLLEGE PROFESSOR
—*Dedication of Antioch College, and Inaugural Address of its President, Hon. Horace Mann*

MRS. ISABEL C. BARROWS.

Fac-simile of the Reporting Notes of Mrs. Isabel C. Barrows, Boston, Mass.

ISABEL C. BARROWS AND A FAC-SIMILE OF HER REPORTING NOTES —*The Student's Journal. Devoted to Graham's Standard Phonography* (July 1891) title, on the long road from West Newton to Yellow Springs. She would carry the capabilities of a past-mistress of the didactic art, capabilities developed in the course of a long and exciting apprenticeship that had paralleled the bright newness of the times in which she lived.

Two fortuitous events dominated Rebecca Pennell's life—her father's early death and her mother's relationship to Horace Mann. From this combination of factors her destiny was determined before she was aware that she had a destiny. Her mother, Rebecca Mann, the sister of Horace Mann, had married Calvin Pennell of Colrain, Massachusetts, in 1815. There a son was born—Calvin Smith Pennell—the following year. By the time their daughter Rebecca was born, on March 12, 1821, the Pennells had moved to Deerfield, New York, a small town about two miles from Utica. Both her father and her mother were "adepts in the teaching profession," and by 1824, when the family had been augmented by two more daughters, Eliza and Marcia, they may well have looked forward to a little schoolhouse in the home where new ideas of education could be inculcated and heretical reforms in pedagogy could be established as orthodoxy. But in 1824 Rebecca's father died and her mother, a widow now with four children, returned to her home in Franklin, Massachusetts.

While young Calvin Pennell studied at Franklin Academy, his sister Rebecca studied the life that gradually unfolded about her. The life of the past was there in Franklin, embodied by the Rev. Dr. Nathaniel Emmons, whose Sunday sermons graphically described the eternal torments of the damned. To the child, Rebecca Pennell, his antique dress, his hair powdered and in a queue, his three-cornered hat and knee-breeches made him look "so much unlike everybody else, that it never occurred to her that he was a man, but some other sort of a contrivance." If Rebecca's "certain old Orthodox minister" symbolized the past, surely her uncle represented the future.

There was not even a hint of powdered hair or knee-breeches in the decorous attire of Horace Mann. In his long-skirted black coat he peered at his young niece through his gold-rimmed spectacles, a tall, thin man with a high forehead and a firm mouth, and Rebecca, peering back, knew that here was no "contrivance" but a man, even, perhaps, a father. Whether he was practising law

at Dedham or Boston, or serving in the Massachusetts State Legislature, Uncle Horace Mann seemed always to have time and love
for his young niece. To some he might appear a chronic sufferer
from headaches and dyspepsia; to some his boast that he "was
never intoxicated in his life; . . . never swore: . . . never used the
'vile weed' in any form" might seem gratuitous. To Rebecca Pennell, the tall spare man who championed free soil and free men,
free air and the free use of cold water, was a transfigured being.
She may not yet have heard the word *phrenology,* but she knew
that his "organ of benevolence" was "prominently developed."
"My mother," she wrote,

who was eight years his senior, has often spoken of his jests, telling
how they were always tempered by his kindness; and also how they
vanished at the calling of duty or when a new book came in sight.
I remember, . . . how it was always running over (as he caught me
in his arms and swung me around his head, or made some witticism
of every word I uttered), . . .

In 1830, when Rebecca was nine, her uncle married Charlotte
Messer, daughter of the President of Brown University. Two years
later his young wife died, the Mann house in Dedham was dis-
mantled, and Aunt Charlotte's bonnets and dresses were packed
for the Pennells to wear. But whatever pleasure there might have
been in seeing that array of pretty clothes was dispelled by the
sight of Uncle Horace after his "great bereavement." "That stroke,"
Rebecca remembered,

paralyzed everything of him but his moral nature. Glee was hushed;
ambition for what the world covets, *killed.* We children, when he came
among us, stood aside silent, and almost awe-struck at the change.

And so, though he almost never spoke of her whom he mourned, we
knew where his thoughts were, and felt no power to draw them away.
I used then to comb his hair, . . . and hours and hours while thus
employed, have I heard him half articulate snatches of poems, . . .
passages of Holy Writ,—and some resolves of self consecration.

The young girl combing her uncle's hair to give him relief from
pain did not know that she would one day have a part in his
"self consecration." She knew only that here was a man who
loved her as he would have loved a daughter, who set his imprint
upon her mind and character.

Especially he set his imprint upon her education. In 1837, when Rebecca was sixteen, frail and slender, oval-faced, black-eyed, her uncle became the first secretary of the Massachusetts Board of Education, a task that would consume him for twelve years and transform not only the State's educational system, but her own development. Now she beheld, if she did not share, his "self consecration."

When expostulated with for taking upon himself terribly arduous labors, as he did all through his Secretaryship of the Board of Education, he once said, 'never mind this shattered hulk, if it goes down in a good cause, what matter, whether a few years sooner or later?'

. . . Experience of the difficulty of bringing things right by legislation, of which he had enough in his attempts at carrying forward these reforms, must necessarily force a man with causality to look for other means; he saw in education that means. Education not as it was then generally administered, but education broadened so as to include the physical relations of man, and deepened so as to touch the secret springs of moral action.

That education, broadened, deepened, Horace Mann tried to give his country and his niece. As Theodore Parker would say of him, "He took up the common schools of Massachusetts in his arms and blessed them." Against incompetent teachers with low salaries, against public apathy and appalling educational statistics, he waged his war. His sword was drawn against "the desultory, irregular, and very superficial course of education now so common in all parts of our country," against a course of study for females that was varied to suit "the notions of parents, or the whims of children, or the convenience of teachers," against schools that might be at the "height of prosperity one week, and the next week entirely extinct." For the dependence upon the rod, Horace Mann would substitute Pestalozzi's doctrine of intuition and sense perception, while he upheld the idea that practice was more important than theory and that the development of man's innate capacities was the true responsibility of the teacher. The sword he used in his crusade was part of the newness of the times, one with phrenology and non-resistance, temperance and transcendentalism. It was called the Normal School. For he believed that "Neither the art of printing, nor the trial by jury, nor a free press, nor free suffrage, can long exist, . . . without schools for the training of teachers." In such a school, whose innovations and reforms Horace Mann and Rebecca Pennell would eventually carry to the West, the Secretary of the Massachusetts Board of Education enrolled his nieces, Rebecca and Eliza, in October of 1839.

The battle against ignorance and bad teaching had been begun on the plains of Lexington, just a few months before, when the Lexington Normal School, the first State normal school in the country, had opened its doors to three pupils. On the northeast corner of Lexington Common, overlooking the first battleground of the Revolution, Rebecca Pennell saw the two-story building where she would learn to be a teacher. She observed with even greater interest the principal, Cyrus Peirce, with his slightly stooping figure, his long hair parted in the middle and brushed smooth behind his ears, who had come from Nantucket to launch the new experiment and who not only did all the teaching, but rose at three in the morning to build the fires, shovel the paths and fetch the water.

"Father Peirce's" methods were fascinating to Rebecca Pennell. Education to him was "the *drawing out*" of all man's powers, "physical, intellectual, and moral," "in their just harmony and proportion." He would teach reading, not beginning with letters, but with words. He would state the principle and then apply it to the facts, for it was "the principle which gives character to the fact." With her slate and pencil, her blank book and Bible, her copy of Worcester's *Comprehensive Dictionary* and Morse's *Geography,* Rebecca Pennell was armed for the work at hand. Through conversation and analyses, through the mingling of theory and example, she studied the art of teaching, learning, if she had not learned it before, that education was "the drawing forth of ideas," that excellence, not competition must be emphasized, that learning by rote was as useless for the most part as corporal punishment.

To the Normal School a Model Department was attached where the village children were taught by the Normal pupils, where the art of teaching was made to grow out of the science of teaching. In between visits to "Normal Grove" and walks on the Lincoln, Concord and Burlington roads, in between squash pies and coffee pots of cider, Rebecca Pennell studied the science of teaching under "Father Peirce" and practised the art of teaching in the model school. With her classmates, Mary Swift and Hannah Damon, Almira Locke and Lydia Stow, she rose at six and followed the routine of a school whose aim was to make better teachers. From discussions of "Is the Reading of the works of Fiction injurious?" and "Are Capital Punishments ever Justifiable," she turned to the subject of gravity and attraction or an explanation of the air pump. From recitations in "Combe's Constitution of Man" or Colburn's analysis of the method of extracting the square root, she tried experiments in galvanism and pneumatics or inspected an apparatus in hydrostatics. Especially she studied "the art of teaching and its modes," learning from Jacob Abbott's *The Teacher: or Moral Influences employed in the Instruction and government of The Young,* how to take care of "the untidy desk," mending pens, or whispering and leaving seats. From Jacob Abbott's text she learned, too, that "the teacher . . . . has human nature to deal with, most directly. His whole work is experimenting upon mind."

The eighteen-year-old, black-eyed Rebecca Pennell experimented upon mind indeed, whether she was reciting "A voice from Mt. Auburn," reading "Brigham on Mental Excitement," or enjoying school visits from her brother, now at Waterville College, or from Bronson Alcott, who "spent the morning defining" Transcendentalism, or from Mr. Felch, who lectured on phrenology. Even the indefatigable Horace Mann was a little disturbed about his niece's intellectual activity, cautioning her, when he enclosed money for her bills, "If you are reading 'Brigham on Mental Excitement,' you must take care of your own excitement."

The excitements of the day were crystallized in Lexington Normal School, not only by the visiting lecturers who dilated on reform, but by the attacks upon the Normal School leveled by "Ignorance, bigotry and economy." Despite, or perhaps because of those excitements, Rebecca Pennell was developing. Cyrus Peirce, to whom she was "my Jewell," would "never forget, but always kindly remember, the good influence she exerted throughout Normaldom, and the substantial aid she rendered me thereby, in the dark and somewhat discouraging times through which we passed at Lexington." He could not praise sufficiently "Your industry, your attention to order, your success in lessons and general improvement, your constant cheerful regard to all my wishes, the salutary influence which your exemplary conduct shed upon others and the deep concern you felt and manifested for the character and prosperity of the Institution." Cyrus Peirce's "Jewell" may well have been not only a teacher learned and skillful in her art, but a teacher born. By the new year of 1841, the twenty-year-old member of the first class of the first State Normal School in America would have an opportunity to prove it.

The apprentice had become, quite literally, the journeyman. While her brother Calvin, after his graduation from Waterville, headed Wrentham Academy, Rebecca Pennell took the State of Massachusetts for her province, and for the next decade amplified her teaching art in a succession of posts throughout the Commonwealth. In New Bedford, where she served as principal of the Bush Street School, in Franklin, in Mansfield, and at Walpole's Centre School, she learned while she taught that her "great business was to convince children that knowledge is within their reach,— that they can attain it, and have a sufficient motive to strive for its attainment." With enthusiasm she excited "a new life and activity" in her scholars' minds, never resorting "to corporal punishment, *but in one instance.*"

Her services were appreciated, and in their annual reports the school committees of the towns of Massachusetts sounded their plaudits. After four months during which she had been keeping a school of fifty-two children under eight years of age in Walpole, the school committee concluded,

. . . we have seen what no words of ours can adequately describe, viz., the superiority of a good instructer over a poor, or an indifferent one. . . .

. . . we have seen what learning and aptness to teach, and entire devotion to the work, can do in the business of elementary instruction. Such a teacher is cheap at almost any price.

From New Bedford, where she had taught with her sister Eliza, the praises reverberated.

Miss Rebecca M. Pennell, and her sister Miss Eliza Pennell, were employed in one of the largest and most important public schools in this town, for about two years; and as teachers, they exhibited a tact in governing and an aptness in teaching, which caused them to be looked upon as among the best teachers in our service. Their school was orderly, quiet and attentive; and we believe that none have ever succeeded better in gaining the love of their pupils, or the esteem of the parents. . . . Miss R.M. Pennell subsequently filled the place of assistant in our high school. In that station, also, . . . she acquitted herself to the entire satisfaction of the committee. If the Normal Schools can furnish such teachers for the children of the Commonwealth, they deserve, and will receive the support of every friend of popular education.

In 1843, the year in which, according to the Millerites, the world was to end, Rebecca's world was altered somewhat by two family events. Toward the end of the year, her sister Eliza married Gardiner Blake. On May Day of that year, her Uncle Horace Mann married for the second time. He had met Mary Peabody at Mrs. Clarke's boarding house in Boston, and although a driving rain prevented Rebecca from attending the wedding at Elizabeth Peabody's West Street Bookstore, a new and not altogether felicitous influence had come into her life. Mary Mann, only fifteen years older than Rebecca, would now take over as confidante and hair-comber to the prince of educators. Yet Mary must share her husband, not only with his dead first wife, but with his very much alive niece, Rebecca Pennell. Even during his honeymoon abroad, the heart of Horace Mann, according to his wife, turned to the "rising generation at home" too often. Whether she had in mind the "rising generation" of the Commonwealth of Massachusetts, or the "rising generation" of his sister's household, she did not specify. The seeds of turmoil and of jealousy seem, however, to have been early planted. They would be watered in time not only by Mary Mann, but by her sister, Sophia Hawthorne. At Antioch College, where Rebecca and Mary would be in close association, they would bear ugly fruit. Meanwhile, Mary Mann's own "rising generation" would make their bows—Horace, the baby who "must have opened its mouth the moment it was born, and pronounced a School Report," then George Combe, and finally Benjamin, who, after a strict phrenological examination, Mann declared was "not worth bringing up."

Meanwhile, too, Rebecca Pennell continued her work. At Westfield Normal School, a co-educational institution housed in a "noble Grecian edifice," she assisted the principal, David S. Rowe, and enjoyed stimulating lectures by Guyot, "the peerless geographer," who "gave new, comprehensive and profound views of the earth," and by Agassiz, who, "with inexpressible charm, led the students to discover wonders in the structure of some tiny insect, or . . . presented his . . . vision of the massive changes wrought during the glacial age." From Westfield she turned to West Newton, where the old Lexington School had been moved, and while she lived with Mary Mann, served as assistant in the State Normal School. To Horace Mann, who in 1848 resigned his secretaryship of the Massachusetts Board of Education to serve in the United States House of Representatives, his wife confided, "I . . . left the beloved chamber, consecrated anew by your divine presence,—in Rebecca's keeping again—who has set her house in order and planted herself there in the holy places."

Perhaps as difficult for Mary Mann to bear were the solicitous inquiries, the affectionate observations about his niece which Horace Mann had expressed and would continue to express throughout the years. As she was to put it, "She [Rebecca] is more influenced by you than by any one, and will do that which she thinks in her innermost mind will make you approve & admire her the most, that being her weak point. . . . She is rather too much inclined to think the world depends upon her, valuable as she is to the good cause of education." To Rebecca her uncle wrote, urging her to attend the teachers' institutes in Massachusetts, adding, "You can teach better than any who will be there, tho some of them have been to college." Refusing most of her payment for her stay with Mary, he declared that "it is probably I should be brought in your debtor!" When female teachers were sent from Mt. Holyoke Seminary to the Cherokees, he wondered "what wicked deed the Cherokee people have done, that teachers should be sent to them from Mt. Holyoke and you kept away," but "What a missionary spirit did flare up in you when you proposed to go!" To his wife he confided both his anxieties and his admiration for his niece:

I am sorry to hear that Rebecca is laying out for so much work. Her brain will have no time to rest and grow. Two lessons a week with what you can help her I should think would be sufficient; but she is somewhat like Sir Walter, who, when he was told to remit the forced action of his brain, said that Molly might as well put the teakettle on and tell it not to boil.

Rebecca Pennell's intellectual teakettle boiled over in West Newton. At Horace Mann's small frame house, painted white with green blinds, she might find Catherine Beecher or Elizabeth Peabody, Theodore Parker or the Hawthornes, Celia Thaxter or Nathaniel T. Allen, whose house was a station on the underground railroad and who was in charge of the model school at West Newton. If the educational newness erupted at West Newton, between Elizabeth Peabody's date charts and her own views on pedagogical reform, Rebecca could leave the village and enjoy a walk to Brook Farm. Always, however, she was fascinated by the processes and the effects of good teaching, writing to her uncle of newly trained instructors:

I do believe they will help a little in carrying forward good measures, both by their teaching & their influence out of school; & so will they aid in a quiet but sure way to bring those better times which seem to be so clearly visioned to you, but which the less clear sighted, & pure minded, regard as the fancies of a dream.

. . . I have not read much in quantity but I cannot say that I have not read *much*; now that I have finished your Report; so full of gratification to the intellect, & of quickening power to the best affections of the heart.

Her ties with the Manns persisted through the years, and were strengthened when, in July of 1850, her mother died, and she turned to her uncle "more than ever as a father now." At West Newton Normal School, Rebecca continued her teaching, taking time off for reunions with the members of the first class of the Lexington Normal School, for a party, for painting in oils.

Her abilities extended now in three directions. She was, first and foremost, a teacher. Governor Briggs of Massachusetts, a man who championed "that democracy which elevates man," had said of her that she was "the best teacher in the world." Her uncle recognized her "large attainments." Although there was little doubt that she could teach any subject at all, her particular propensities seemed to be concentrated in the two fields of science and of art. When Horace Mann came to write his *Few Thoughts on the Powers and Duties of Woman,* he may well have been thinking of his niece Rebecca when he urged, "Let woman, . . . be educated to the highest practicable point; not only because it is her right, but because it is essential to the world's progress."

Fresh from Congress, where he had opposed Daniel Webster's temporizing on the issue of slavery, Horace Mann seemed by 1852 to believe that Antioch College, where woman could be educated to the "highest practicable point," was also "essential to the world's progress." To her niece Rebecca, Mary Mann wrote in May of that year, "If your uncle will be president of a male and female college, will you be Professoress . . .?" On September 15th, at a meeting of the sub-committee at the college office in Yellow Springs, it was reported, "Mr. and Miss Pennell . . . were . . . duly elected members of the College Faculty." At the November meeting of the faculty in West Newton, Rebecca Pennell had been present, and the next month she could have read in *The Gospel Herald*:

Perhaps the most important fact in the election is the appointment of an eminent and accomplished lady as Professor in the College. Miss Pennell has been . . . at the head of the female department of the State Normal School in West Newton . . . and is perhaps the most accomplished instructress in this country. . . .

. . . She is . . . well qualified for the novel position which she has been called to fill.

Now the opportunity opened before her. Because she was a woman and a teacher who had drunk from the very fountainhead of the new education, she in her own person embodied that newness. Dignified by the title of professor, she could carry to the West the educational reform of the East. The first so-called woman professor in the country had been fortified for the work at hand.

Only her health, whose poor state may have been combined at this time with the renunciation or disappointments of a mysterious love, seemed to trouble Horace Mann. In January of 1853 he wrote to her from Toledo, a letter brimful of caution and concern:

. . . I want you to leave that school and dedicate yourself, till we go West, to the confirmation of your health. I know, or at least can guess, what you will say in reply to this; viz., that you are well now, and do not need any reprieve from labor. To all this, I feel bound in conscience to give a flat contradiction. That you seem to yourself to have activity enough to go through with all your proposed labor, that your assertion is prompted by your feelings, I have no doubt. But it is judgment, not feeling, that should guide, and there are cases where your friends are a truer guide than your own sensations.

. . . Indeed, that state of mental excitement, in which you are so sure you are well, and feel equal physically to any task, and protest that you need no repose, is just as obvious to me, as a looker-on, as is the condition of a man who has taken champagne. . . . Now, on the eve of a new enterprise, with whose success or failure your name will always be indissolubly associated, are you not bound to enter upon it with all attainable advantages? . . .

Now, I mean by all this, not simply that you should leave your school. You should leave hard work of all kinds and consecrate yourself to the renovation and confirmation of health alone. Your future pupils will have the benefit of it, and what is more, the new and momentous experiment we are to try, will have that benefit in a still higher degree.

. . . You are most dear to me at any rate, but the stronger and better and more superior you are, the more there will be of you for me and others to admire and love. Do not try to compass everything in this life, but leave something for eternity.

Both eternity and her own health seemed less important to Rebecca Pennell than Antioch College and her own immediate future. Like her uncle, she was consumed with plans for the College. There must be sufficient blackboards, she urged. Could there be cooking arrangements at Yellow Springs like those at the North American Phalanx? Although Horace Mann wished his Ohio home to resemble the one in West Newton, Rebecca hoped for a better proportioned building. While he did not take his niece's architectural advice, he came to rely upon her more and more for her pedagogical influence. "Our whole force at Antioch will have to be educated anew, and Calvin and R—will have to do it. . . ."

. . . I look upon the Normal-school girls as part of my thunder, though they have R—'s lightning in them to make them shine.

In September 1853, taking the northern route via Portland, Mann and his faculty journeyed to Yellow Springs, Ohio, the town on the Little Miami Railroad connecting Cincinnati and Sandusky, "easily accessible by railroad and steamboat" from all the "great towns and cities" of the Western States. Calvin Pennell with his family, Horace and Mary Mann with their boys now aged five, seven, and nine, and Rebecca Pennell inspected the site of the great experiment that had been named Antioch College. It had been built, appropriately, on the highest land in the State, and its ambitious brick towers would have been more impressive had not the whole area consisted of "one vast quagmire of clayey soil, in which plank walls sank below the surface, and in rainy weather floated upon it." The great brick towers on the one hand, and on the other the miry soil upon which huge tree stumps were lying symbolized both the strength and the frailty of Antioch. The towers aspired as the educational experiment about to be tried aspired, but the unfinished aspect of the place, its mud, its stumps of trees at the very threshold of the College, suggested perhaps a weakness underlying the greatness.

On October 5th, Antioch College was dedicated, and Rebecca Pennell—Professor Rebecca Pennell—with the rest of the faculty, looked on as the inauguration ceremonies progressed. In a letter to her father, Mary Mann described the scene:

Three thousand people were upon the ground. They arrived the night before in such numbers that they had to sleep in their carriages! . . . At half past nine people assembled on the ground before the grand entrance, over which was erected a temporary platform from which Mr. Phillips, the prime agent, addressed the multitude. . . . he presented the college with three splendid Bibles, and Mr. Mann accepted them in a few appropriate words. We all had seats on the platform. After the presentation, Mr. Phillips begged money in the most impressive and witty manner.

At twelve o'clock, the procession moved to the College Chapel, and after a hymn by the choir and a prayer, the charter and keys of the institution were delivered to the President elect, who replied in noble terms: "This youthful Western world is gigantic youth, and therefore its education must be such as befits a giant. . . . Wherever the capital of the United States may be, this valley will be its seat of empire." With the "immense concourse of spectators," the black-eyed lady professor listened to her uncle, the President, deliver an inaugural address that would occupy over a hundred pages in print. On the American Bible Society and steam navigation, on the "abominable weed" and the Sermon on the Mount he discoursed, giving special attention to Antioch's co-educational scheme. With rapt attention Rebecca listened to his words:

Mankind at large are to be educated, not a few beloved Benjamins, but all the sons,—AND ALL THE DAUGHTERS TOO,—and all inconceivably above our present standards. . . .

I am aware that, in proposing to educate males and females together, and to confer equal opportunities for culture upon both, we encounter some objections.

These objections Horace Mann proceeded to answer. Female education must "be rescued from its present reproach of inferiority, and advanced to an equality with that of males." Separate but equal institutions for the different sexes would not only double expenditures, but result "in bringing male education down to the present level of female education." Both the architecture of the College, which guaranteed "the incommunicable separation of our dormitory buildings," and a stringent "code of regulations" would militate against "that epidemic of incongruous matches which now afflicts society both in city and country."

Horace Mann may have answered the objections to co-education; indeed the thousands who came to the dedication ceremonies, bringing comforters and provisions, groaned out their Amens and "swayed before the great orator as a forest yields to a mighty storm." But he could not prevent the prejudices and jealousies that the presence of women, especially of women from the East, would arouse. Horace Mann may have lauded the non-sectarian character of a College that would not "inculcate creeds, articles, or confessions of faith," but he could not stem the bigotry of the so-called non-sectarian "Christians" against the Unitarians of the East. He might point with joy to the lofty towers of Antioch, but he did not know that the scholarship system that had built them would swiftly lead to bankruptcy. Beneath those lofty towers the earth was soft.

On the morning after the dedication, Rebecca and the faculty supervised the entrance examinations. They were obliged to clear off the breakfast dishes from the dining hall tables, and at noon to clear away pens, ink and papers for dinner. After dinner the dishes were cleared again for the examinations, so that "at first, over the dining-tables of our commons' hall, the cook and the professor held divided empire." Of the one hundred fifty applicants examined, only eight passed and were enrolled as College students. The remainder, "old and young, married and unmarried, some of them ministers who had given up their parishes," were assigned to the preparatory school connected with the College.

Faced with the low state of learning of the applicants, Horace

Mann and Rebecca may have recalled certain warnings they had heard in the East. Miss Beecher had prayed to Horace Mann, "if I want any more comfort in this life, that I will not try to build up a college at the West, and says Mr. Stowe held up his hands in deprecation at the thought." Yet, if Tecumseh and his warriors had drunk the salubrious waters of Yellow Springs, perhaps others would find in Antioch a fountainhead for intellectual vigor. In the little straggling village, with its Water Cure Hotel, its blacksmith shop, its "Surveyor and Daguerrian" establishment, there were signs of the vitality that coursed through Ohio in the 1850's, when the frontier had passed its borders, and canals and railroads were abuilding.

As Rebecca and the Manns settled into the unfinished College, they had need of all the vitality they could muster. The President's house had not yet been built. There were no fences around the campus, no doors in the halls. "A room had been set apart for a library, but there was not a book in it, nor a shelf on which to put one. . . . We had not a black-board, nor a school-chair, nor a school-desk for any student, nor any habitable school-room, or recitation-room." There were neither stoves for heat nor provisions for fresh water. "The students, . . . were obliged to walk a quarter of a mile with their pitchers to procure a draught. . . . all the water furnished being brought from a distance, and poured into a huge vat . . . which stood upon a raised platform near the door of the Ladies' Hall." In the dining room "tables were furnished, not with chairs, but with stools, . . . Napkins could be had only by special arrangement, and it was by the greatest diplomacy that a change of plates could be secured . . . when dessert was to be served." Cockroaches were cooked in the dried applesauce, and Ohio pigs walked in the corridors.

But the still undaunted enthusiasm of the East and the rude vitality of the West combined to transmute Antioch into a workable medium for a great experiment. In time, both the cistern and the pump from the spring were in operation, although "the state of unfinick and incompleteness in which we buckeyes, consent to live are truly amazing, when viewed from a Yankee point of view." In time, the dormitories offered rooms furnished with stove and bedstead—a Gentlemen's Hall and a Ladies' Hall—while students aired and made their beds, and swept their rooms before eight in the morning. Just outside the College fence rose the President's house and the professors' houses, and the ring of the mason's trowel and the tap of the carpenter's hammer testified to the new world abuilding. In the President's study Horace Mann's black walnut bookcases lined the walls, presided over by a portrait of Dr. Channing. Rebecca's room was "furnished with a darker set, . . . brilliantly flowered, with . . . curtains to favor her eyes & the secretary . . . for her books & writing table. She has a beautiful view of the College lawn, & beyond it a reach of the ravine, with woods & something like hills in an opening beyond."

The College that was gradually taking physical shape had had its intellectual and moral shape ordained long before by its President and its faculty. Here, where one of the great educational experiments of the nineteenth century would be tried out, there would be no bars for race or sex or creed. Justice would be done to the Negro and to woman. Unlike Oberlin, where "most of the women took a course that was two years shorter than the regular one," Antioch would encourage women to meet men as students on an equal footing. Such association as took place between the sexes would, of course, be under strict supervision. Students were forbidden to permit any person of the other sex to enter their rooms, and any violation of the rule would be followed by immediate and unconditional expulsion. The sexes would visit the Glen on alternate days—gentlemen on Wednesdays, ladies on Thursdays. If co-education marked one foundation stone of Antioch, non-sectarianism marked the other, in theory at least. Moral standards were high. Tobacco and intoxicating liquors were prohibited, for tobacco was held stultifying and alcohol corrosive in its effects. The use of tea and coffee was discouraged. Firearms, gunpowder and fireworks were forbidden. "Emulation" was discarded as a motive to study. Physiology was a required course. Indeed, Mrs. Mann would one day write a physiological cook book entitled *Christianity in the Kitchen*. Group gymnastics were encouraged. At the ringing of a bell the teachers would meet the scholars for exercise as they met them in the recitation room for lessons. In the Mann code of honor, every student must be his brother's keeper.

The experiment that had taken theoretical shape in the mind of Horace Mann was put to its practical test when Professor Rebecca

Pennell and her colleagues took up the work that had drawn them
to Yellow Springs. As Professor of Physical Geography, Drawing,
Natural History, Civil History and Didactics, Miss Pennell divided
her time between the small College proper and the far larger
preparatory school. The students were separated "into twenty nine
classes, of which Rebecca, being the most accomplished teacher,
takes *seven,* besides having them by platoons at odd hours to
teach them how to study their lessons." Her routine was as arduous
as that of her pupils, who rose with the six o'clock morning bell,
took breakfast and attended chapel exercises before studies and
recitations commenced at eight. As Mary Mann reported to Cyrus
Peirce:

You know Rebecca's style of working, so you may conceive the life
she leads. I have not sat down with her one hour since she has been
here, except when I have been present at the Faculty meetings. . . .
Rebecca & Calvin—Rebecca particularly, have already made a great
impression with their teaching—the students come to the President to
know if they cannot have R. to teach them in other things, "for then
we can learn." She has put all the other Professors' noses out of joint
already. And she lives through all her labours because she *will.* There
is nothing so powerful as a good strong will.

To the teaching of science she gave most of her "will," using
manikins for demonstrations in anatomy, and upholding Horace
Mann's novel and important conviction that "the sciences are not
only constantly enlarging their respective spheres of action and
discovery, but they are, . . . entering into copartnerships with each
other, . . . so that a man is bound not only to know more in regard
to any one science, but more sciences." Physical Geography was
itself an integration of many sciences, and Professor Rebecca Pennell, introducing her students to the "mutual relations" of the
"material body of the globe," "the myriads of plants and animal
forms living upon it, and man himself, as a part of the life-system,"
revealed with stimulating enthusiasm the mysteries of earth and
land, of waters and atmosphere, and the whole life that spawned
upon the earth. As for the human body, she understood it "as
well as tho' she had made it." She was teacher of geology and
physiology, zoology and botany, as she explained lucidly, fasci-
natingly, the forces that had raised the continents, the distribution
of birds and insects, the future prospects of the human race. Vary-

ing her lessons in the texts of Arnold Guyot or Mary Somerville with field excursions, she took her students to the wooded Glen along Yellow Springs Creek which served as a laboratory for her classes in botany and geology. There, too, her troop of pupils armed with books and botanical boxes, the handsome Miss Pennell exposed the phenomena of life and the laws that governed them.

As "the most accomplished teacher," Rebecca Pennell was naturally assigned the important task of teaching didactics, or the theory and practice of teaching. In her own person she embodied the principles expounded in her text, David Page's *Theory and Practice of Teaching*: "The teacher should go to his duty full of his work. He should be impressed with its overwhelming importance." Not the pouring-in process, but the drawing-out process was to be employed, for education did not consist in knowledge. Its object rather, as Potter and Emerson agreed, was "to form a perfect character," "to draw out, naturally and fully, every faculty of the body, mind, and soul." To "the thorough education of the whole person" Rebecca Pennell applied herself, emphasizing the physical health of her students, stressing the importance of their character development, minimizing grades and prizes as "dissocial" motives, advancing the idea of the perfectibility of man. Although she taught from textbooks, using Gray's *Botanical Text-Book* or Agassiz and Gould's *Zoölogy,* she gave extensive oral instruction, for "teaching from text-books alone was like administering the same prescription to all the patients in a hospital ward; but oral instruction was mingling the cup of healing for each individual case." With classroom conversations and scientific apparatus, she applied Pestalozzi's methods, brought the skills of the East to the West, championed Horace Mann's educational crusade, and helped make of Antioch College "the little Harvard of the West."

Rebecca Pennell's work was varied by levees at the President's house, where the faculty appeared in white gloves for dramatic readings or music on the guitar, by prayer meetings in the chapel, by the May Walk to the Little Miami Gorge, and by lectures from distinguished visitors—Greeley or Bayard Taylor or Theodore Parker, who came to observe the great experiment in the "barbarous West."

In return for her services Miss Pennell had been promised, it was said, $1000 a year, although the general salary level had been set at only $800 for male professors and $500 for female. Shortly after the new year of 1854 had begun, on January 13th, Rebecca Pennell wrote a letter to the Trustees of Antioch College, informing them that

When I accepted the position to which you elected me, it was with the hope, among others, of being instrumental in assisting you to carry out juster ideas, than had previously been embodied in any educational establishment, with regard to the powers, the duties & the rewards of woman.

Under the circumstances which a vote of yours, passed today, places a Female Professor in the Institution I feel that she would be false to the interests to which I have referred by continuing in a situation, where her labors are awarded less recompense,—just because she is a woman.

Another consideration, of less weight however, influences me. The Department of Study entrusted to my direction, has risen of late to a great importance in the minds of the best Educators; & I should regret to have Antioch College degrade it in the eyes of the world as it must of necessity do, by leaving it in the hands of "an officer upon half pay["] in obedience to my convictions of duty. I hereby resign the place I had had the honor to hold.

Although Rebecca Pennell's offer of resignation was not carried out, salaries at Antioch were in arrears almost from the start, a state of affairs that shadowed disasters to come.

If her relations with the trustees left something to be desired, her relations with her students seemed, at first at least, to want for nothing. While Horace Mann pleaded with his pupils or melted them to tears, turned upon them "all his old lawyer's logic," or "poured out his wrath in fiery sarcasm," Rebecca Pennell moved among them, a fascinating presence, sharing with them her "mental excitement." The bewhiskered gentlemen scholars—Henry Clay Badger and Eli Jay and James De Normandie—, the young ladies —Adelaide Churchill, Achsah Waite, who had left Oberlin because of the "discrimination which did not permit women to graduate on equal terms with men," Ada Shepard, who would become governess to the Hawthorne children and sit for the portrait of Hilda in *The Marble Faun*—all felt the charm of her personality, the stimulation of her intellect. To one, she was "the best teacher and the finest woman whom I have ever known." To another, Olympia Brown, she was "a woman of the finest culture."

Yet, as Mary Somerville had remarked in her *Physical Geography,* "the individuality of man modifies his opinions and belief; it is a part of that variety which is a universal law of nature." Not everyone at Antioch shared exalted views of Rebecca Pennell. To Mary Mann the lady professor was showing signs of increasing egotism. As she would one day confess, "R had never been a favorite of mine." Her elevation to a professorial post "lashed her vanity into a passion." Storm clouds were gathering over Antioch, rumblings of thunder still distant. Horace Mann was cautious and although, according to Rebecca, "He saw the 'exceeding sinfulness of sin' more clearly than any person I ever knew," still "he loved the calm and peaceful everywhere." At Antioch there was little that was calm or peaceful. To some his impassioned pleas were "venomed javelins" and his peculiar code of honor led to spying at keyholes. There would be murmurs of unjust dismissals and of cruel treatment. The seeds of dissension had been sown in "the little Harvard of the West."

In the relations of the staff dissension manifested itself also. The faculty was divided, some of the "Christian connection" and of the West appearing inferior to the Unitarians from the East. The man selected to teach bookkeeping, it was said, had never studied it a day in his life. Mann relatives seemed in time to spring up everywhere, Eliza Blake's husband serving as deputy treasurer, and their presence appeared to weight the odds too heavily in favor of the forces of the East. Rebecca's presence still fascinated, however, whether she conversed with that "extraordinary young" minister, Austin Craig, whom Mann had persuaded to come to Antioch, or worked with her "right hand man," Professor Warriner, whether she consulted the "mercurial" trustee, Eli Fay, or observed the teaching of Mr. Zachos, who was to invent a "method of teaching reading by the signs of sound." If she found the Rev. W.H. Doherty, who had appealed against "the unholy alliance of Fanaticism, Rumism, Rowdyism, Infidelity And Pride" that had excluded him from his pulpit, a peculiar incumbent for the chair of mathematics, astronomy and civil engineering at Antioch, she made no noticeable signs of disapproval. With other women who had been appointed to the faculty—Julia Hitchcock and Lucretia Crocker—her relations gave rise to no recorded volcanic eruptions.

With one member of the Antioch staff, however, Rebecca Pennell was to enter upon a more enduring relationship. Austin S. Dean, assistant treasurer of Antioch and agent for collecting College funds, ran a boarding house for students from Cincinnati and Dayton, New York and Massachusetts, and was a member of the committee on printing. More than two years younger than Rebecca, he had been born in Canada, studied at the theological school in Meadville, Pennsylvania, and served as pastor of the Christian Church at Union Springs, New York, before he ventured west. As elder of the Christian denomination, he had taken the New York agency to raise money for the building of Antioch and now, at Yellow Springs, he turned his attention as much upon the charms of the College's lady professor, Rebecca Pennell, as upon the charms of its treasury. Whether or not his round chin and fair complexion, his dark brown hair and light blue eyes appealed to Rebecca, the idea of marriage assuredly did. She probably did not share Mary Mann's belief that "the higher the state of civilization and refinement, the more unmarried women there are." At the age of thirty-four, Rebecca Pennell was more than ready for marriage. To her father, Mary Mann confided, "What should you think if I tell you that we think . . . Mr. Dean will carry off Rebecca? . . . He is the last person we should ever have imagined her marrying, but there is no accounting for tastes." Sophia Hawthorne offered her opinion in a letter to her sister, "I think it must be . . . [Rebecca's] peculiar fancy to rule her husband or she would not unite herself to an inferior person."

Whether or not Austin Dean was weak and inferior, he was Rebecca's choice. At six in the morning, on June 16, 1855, they were married by the Rev. W.H. Doherty. Rebecca appeared "lively and cheerful as ever" in her "brown and white plaid silk dress," with a white straw ribboned bonnet wreathed with flowers. Mary Mann provided the wedding breakfast, and Ada Shepard, who sat next to the bride, took notes of the occasion, remarking that "Mr. Dean, . . . was much agitated all the time" and that she had never seen "more distress pictured on anyone's face than on Mr. Mann's during the sacrificial ceremony. He feels her loss more than any other person." Perhaps, as Rebecca would suggest, "he never wished her to be married to any one." At all events, for better or worse, Professor Rebecca Pennell had become Mrs. Austin S. Dean.

The couple started at once for New York and Liverpool, then a few months in England, Scotland and the Continent. On board ship, Rebecca sent a charming note to the three Mann boys, revealing nothing of her emotions but much of her extraordinary teaching technique:

Cousin Rebecca has had a plenty of time to think of the little folks left behind, in the two weeks she has been sailing on the ocean. She thinks a great vessel a wonderful contrivance when it skims like a bird along the surface of the water, carrying in its bosom thirty thousand bushels of corn, as much wheat, a great deal of tobacco, . . . & oil; five hundred clocks, as many great boxes of India rubber shoes, & about two hundred people. I do not know how you would like being at sea, far, far out of sight of land, but there are some children on board who seem to enjoy it very much. I think Horace or Georgie would like to learn to guide the ship, or "star," as the sailors call it; but how should you like to stand at the wheel two hours without speaking a word, . . . Then Horace would like to learn to use the quadrant by which Cap. Bretton every day at noon, ascertains where abouts on the broad ocean we are. . . .

At Grasmere, the Deans met the Hawthornes. Sophia soon sent a report to Mary Mann:

I was pierced to the heart to see such a shadow as she was, & I took her in my arms & kissed & embraced her over & over as a sort of solace—Her voice too was so low & sweet & far off that it seemed to me it was vanishing away. She never seemed so interesting to me. I thought Mr Dean looked goodnatured & honest, but I could not endure him as Rebecca's husband. He looked terribly rude & heavy— . . .

By the time the "married Rebecca" returned to Yellow Springs, she looked less "shadowy" than "elegant," even "somewhat showy," for, as Mary Mann put it, "The rest of us in Yellow Springs cannot dress up to her mark. She seems very well & is very agreeable & affectionate. Mr. Dean rather cold & distant & depressed. He feels very dignified now."

Rebecca Dean had returned to Antioch at a time when change was mounting and crisis was imminent. Even in the village she found much excitement, for Thomas Nichols and his wife, Mary Gove Nichols, had proposed establishing a community, Memnonia, in Yellow Springs, which Horace Mann, fearing a free love taint, denounced as "the superfoetation of diabolism upon polygamy." At the College itself, she heard the "sound of disintegration" although she continued her professorial duties. In October of 1856, her brother, Calvin Pennell, left Antioch for a post at the St. Louis high school. The following year, the trustees voted to reorganize. Throughout the turmoil Rebecca Dean held her classes in physical geography and didactics and led her field excursions to the Glen.

Against a background of increasing chaos, Rebecca attended Antioch's first commencement exercises, in honor of which she had designed a seal for the diplomas depicting Horace Mann facing a young man and woman who themselves faced the rising sun. To the President, if not his chief teacher, it was "a glorious Commencement" graced by the presence of Ezra Gannett, the Unitarian minister from Boston, and of Governor Chase. For Rebecca Dean, the commencement heralded a time of sorrow and of strife. In October 1857, her sister, Eliza Pennell Blake, with whom she had attended Normal School, died, and Rebecca "adopted" her sister's son, Henry G. Blake, who roomed at the Dean boarding house. Between her teaching and the supervision of her nephew, she faced the discords and dissensions that threatened to annihilate the great experiment at Yellow Springs.

She realized now that financial embarrassments, religious and personal differences had formed a triangle whose apex pointed to disaster. When her husband was accused of standing "with one hand in the College treasury and the other in his pocket," of being a "notorious falsifier" who indulged in *"misrepresentation and deception,"* she rallied to his defense. When his plea to exonerate himself by his own statement in a *Rejoinder* to the attack was rejected, she was roused to frenzy. On a "terrible night" she held an "interview" with Horace Mann, accusing him of sacrificing "justice to expediency," and in consequence of that violent episode she suffered a temporary "paralytic shock."

Not Horace Mann alone, but Rebecca Dean, too, found she was a victim of the plots and counterplots at Yellow Springs. At the College where, somehow, she still imparted her enthusiasm for the sciences to her students, she found the lines sharply drawn—

Christians set against Unitarians, Westerners distrusting Eastern-ers, differences ripening into suspicions, and suspicions enlarged into accusations. The College had turned into a battleground and the fascinating Rebecca Dean was a prime target. She was guilty, it was said, of slander and misrepresentation. She was "false and cunning," looking "very like a snake." Not Horace Mann, but she was "President of the College." Her control over her uncle was "almost unlimited." She was "a determined woman" who be-lieved herself "an Aspasia, or Cleopatra."

She believed herself, above all, a teacher who wished to foster a great experiment in education. As such, Rebecca left the havoc of Yellow Springs to collect funds in the East for the bankrupt College, while agents, traveling with horse and buggy, solicited help. "If the young people only realised what Antioch costs, & what is expected of them," she wrote to her husband, "they would make Antioch by their fidelity a pattern to the world." Surely the "desperate fight at Thermopylae" had been nothing compared with the struggle to save Antioch. "Debts," Rebecca wrote, "continue to come in; the total now is above 88m I think." The publication of Professor Ira Allen's lengthy and vituperative *History of the Rise, Difficulties & Suspension of Antioch College* and the expul-sion of the editors of a scurrilous satire on the College called *The Probe* in which Rebecca had been assigned the role of "Poll Par-rot," had exaggerated a situation fast becoming desperate. In April 1859, Antioch College was auctioned off for some $40,000 to a New York banker who turned it over, free of debt, to the friends of the institution. Under a new board of trustees, the Col-lege would now be reorganized and Rebecca Dean, like her uncle, could face the June commencement exercises with something ap-proaching equanimity.

Though she had helped stay the threat of disaster, she could not stay the onslaught of time which was fast running out. As she looked at Horace Mann standing at the high desk reading his baccalaureate address to the guests who crowded the chapel, she heard his resonant phrases, "I beseech you to treasure up in your hearts these my parting words: *Be ashamed to die until you have won some victory for humanity.*" They had been, almost literally, his parting words.

On August 2, 1859, Rebecca's uncle died at Yellow Springs after a prolonged and "glorious" deathbed scene which his niece recorded. To his family, his students and his friends he made his farewells. To Austin Dean he said, "Your wife is a treasure; take care of her for my sake." To Rebecca herself he said, "You have been to me the loveliest, dearest, gentlest, faithfulest daughter, sister, friend, almost wife." The chapel was draped in black and Horace Mann was buried in the College grounds. His great experiment was over. Less than a week later, America's first woman college professor replied to a committee of the senior class who had entreated her to remain with them:

Since I received your communication, my heart has been too full to permit me to reply.

I thank you for your expressions of confidence & affection, & it pains me that I must deny your request.

I cannot be willing, that you should feel for a moment, that this denial is from personal considerations; the pain I experience at sundering the ties which bind me to you & your Associates, is all that my bereaved heart can bear. I would most gladly make any possible sacrifice of ease, interest, or inclination, to promote your reasonable pleasure, or the prosperity of Antioch College. But I have been here already six years,—just twice the time I proposed remaining when I came among you. The desire of him whom we mourn has induced me to stay. For him I came,—for him I staid, ever happy with him & with you, & your companions,—with him it is wisest that I should go away.

Your action of Wednesday, has rejoiced me. "Stand by the College" for the sake of the principles upon which it is founded,—for the sake of the departed friend, who sacrificed so much for them,—for the sake of the good you will gain thereby.

. . . A place is vacant in the ranks of the good men. But that work that good men do, must go on. It will soon devolve upon you, & such as you, to take up the weapons of Light—& Love which have fallen from his hands. . . .

Mary Mann left Antioch for Concord, Massachusetts, where she would read and reread her husband's old letters, mull over the past, exalt his memory, and exchange with her sister, Sophia Hawthorne, notes on the malice of Rebecca Dean, whom she "never wished to look upon" again. The Rev. Thomas Hill would succeed Horace Mann as President of Antioch. By the fall of

1859, the College buildings looked neglected. Their panes were cracked, their doors unhinged, their locks broken off. The College would rise again, though never exactly as it had been when the spare, majestic New Englander had dedicated himself to its principles with the help of his stimulating, black-eyed niece. Through their combined teachings, Antioch had crystallized the most progressive pedagogical ideas of the day, had championed the importance of the sciences, had planted in the West a citadel of free thought with educational equality for every class, race, religion and sex. If the history of America had not begun with the foundation of Antioch College, that history had surely been extended and enriched at Yellow Springs. By conferring upon a woman for the first time in the country the title of professor, it had dignified women everywhere in the land. Now that woman was thirty-eight years old. Her life work of transplanting in the West the educational convictions and techniques she had learned in America's first State Normal School, was not yet over. While Mary Mann returned to Concord, Rebecca Dean moved farther westward to carry on the work she had begun two decades before near the battleground of Lexington, Massachusetts.

A few months before Horace Mann's death, a school had been established in St. Louis, where Rebecca's brother, Calvin Pennell, had settled, a school that was in its way also a pioneer experiment. Under the auspices of Washington University, Mary Institute had been opened as a non-sectarian girls' school for the growing frontier community. Its founders had discarded the old belief that "To cultivate virtue is the science of men; to renounce science is the virtue of women," and held that woman's education was no longer "*finished*" when she had learned to work a fire-screen or dance a polka or "drum a sentimental tune upon an unhappy piano." Rebecca Dean now joined the staff of the school on Lucas Place to which students came on muledrawn streetcars, and settled with her husband in St. Louis, "a growing place," in a West that had "a large hand and a strong grasp."

In the eight-room schoolhouse on Lucas Place, Rebecca Dean took up her new work as teacher of physiology and natural history under principal Edwin D. Sanborn from Dartmouth, "a courtly gentleman" on whose dark blue suit the polished brass buttons gleamed. Instructing her pupils in Hitchcock's *Physiology* or Agassiz and Gould's *Zoölogy,* at the rate of $1200 a year, she imparted to them her understanding of the human body, its cells and membranes and fibers, and instilled in them her enthusiasm for the sciences as she had done at Antioch. Later, to a curriculum that offered Fasquelle's French Course and the delights of Solfeggio Singing, she added her services as teacher of drawing, giving instruction in the composition of figures by a combination of lines, the study of form, light and shade, the theory of perspective. By 1862, her brother took Edwin Sanborn's place as principal of Mary Institute, and under the orderly and unperturbed regime of Calvin Pennell the school's graded course of study was perfected, its academic standards raised, and calisthenics emphasized to advance the "development of the whole child." Yet, as one visitor to Mary Institute remarked, "its real management is in the hands of a brother and sister who were both formerly Professors at Antioch College, Ohio, and who are 'teachers born.' "

While Mrs. Dean continued her educational reforms in St. Louis, working with the preparatory, academic or advanced departments, attending rehearsals of "The Alpine Shepherd" or the "Flower Queen," discussing the problems of her pupils with Captain Hammersley, master of calisthenics, Dr. Tafel of the German Department, or Etienne Boileau, teacher of writing, she found time, too, for the world outside the classroom. At the wharves of St. Louis she could see thousands of steamers loading and unloading, and in the city itself she could meet the German intellectuals, hear Carl Schurz speak on "The Doom of Slavery," or catch a sight of the Chicago Zouaves on a visit. Soon, she saw a St. Louis fortified and large columbiads mounted a short distance from the city. She saw soldiers encamped in their tents, heard of Union meetings and of secessionists drilling at the Tobacco Warehouse. War had come to the nation, had come to St. Louis, had intruded even at Mary Institute.

Less than a month after the fall of Sumter, Camp Jackson was taken. In a slave State, the act of the people had arrested secession. The next day, the students of Mary Institute drove in a horse-drawn bus to a picnic, and Rebecca Dean saw mothers arriving at the grounds with rumors of shots that had been fired and soldiers slain. While her husband served as captain and additional aide-de-camp to Brigadier General Strong, Rebecca joined the executive committee of ladies of the Mississippi Valley Sanitary Fair. On July 19, 1863, Captain Dean died in St. Louis. The following June, his widow, still teaching at Mary Institute, attended the school's first graduation, hearing her pupils read their essays and sing their choral selections.

The war years passed in St. Louis, until Rebecca Dean saw steamboats at the levee with flags dressed in crape, saw churches with decorations bordered in crape. The Thanksgiving services planned for April 1865 had been converted into mourning services with news of Lincoln's assassination. Rebecca Dean stayed on in St. Louis, the years punctuated by later graduations, when addresses on "Crises in History" gave way to discourses on "Nature's Library" or "Being a Woman, What Shall I do?" On June 8, 1868, she resigned her position at Mary Institute. She had taught for more than twenty-five years. She had studied in a school that was America's first experiment in "Normal" education; she had made her own impress upon the great experiment at Antioch; she had carried the experiment farther westward to St. Louis. She had dealt with human nature and experimented always upon mind. Now, in the North, at St. Paul, Minnesota, where her nephew, Henry Blake, had settled, America's first woman college professor would round out the years that her work had so fully enriched.

In her nephew's large, charming house, built on a hill overlooking Lake Owasso, Rebecca Dean made her home. She could come into town to hear Horace Greeley or Henry Ward Beecher lecture at the Opera House and, in the midst of her western retreat enjoy through them reminders of the East. In 1874 she journeyed to Boston to attend a reunion of the first class of America's first State Normal School, and three years later Rebecca Dean gathered together a "class of young ladies" including her niece, Marcia Hersey's daughter Rebecca, for an educational trip abroad. Now, on the upper story of the Blake house, the narrow parlor was filled with souvenirs from Europe—a Watteau plate of Saxon ware, an oil painting of Titian's daughter as a flower girl, a small Murillo in pastel, engravings, statuettes and photographs.

Between enjoying the brilliant parade, the streaming banners and triumphal arches in St. Paul that celebrated the uniting of two sections of the Northern Pacific Railroad, and a visit to the city's new ice palace when "gorgeous pageants and unique displays" heralded the winter carnival, she took time to return to Boston in 1884 for yet another class reunion. Her hair had grayed. On the second story of the Blake home her lares and penates were gathered—collections that mirrored the life she had led. She was surrounded now by tangible reflections of her past. She could pick up a seal that had been her father's, a lace flounce that had been her mother's, and be transported back to the early days in Franklin, Massachusetts. She could turn to an ivory paper holder that had once belonged to her Uncle Horace Mann, or the pearl handled fruit knife that had been her husband's, and the turbulent days of Yellow Springs would flood back in memory. Her photographs from *The Marble Faun* recaptured a family association that still evoked some bitterness. Europe crowded into her mind as she thumbed through her pictures of the Albert Memorial. Seated at her mahogany writing desk, she could reflect upon objects that were testimony to her life work—her geological collection, her solar microscope, her magnifying glasses, her anatomical drawings, her books.

Rebecca Dean left her family and her relics in the summer of 1889 to attend her fiftieth class reunion at Framingham, Massachusetts. There she was "one of the most honored guests," a "gracious hostess," as she planned meetings during the weeks she would remain in New England. Going on to Walpole, where she had taught almost fifty years before, she was stricken with a "severe illness." She rallied, rested for a time with friends in Providence, and then journeyed to New York, where her sister, Marcia Pennell Hersey, lived. There, in February 1890, she was able to indite a seven-page Will, bequeathing to her friends and family the curios and relics that crystallized her life. On March 5, a week before her sixty-ninth birthday, she died. Two days later she was buried in Green-Wood Cemetery.

At Antioch College a dormitory hall was named in honor of "that remarkable, redoubtable woman" who had been America's first woman college professor. Her title had been significant, but less significant perhaps than the work which it had honored. Rebecca Pennell Dean had carried to the West the educational reforms of the East, had embodied in her teaching the pedagogical newness of the times, had made practical applications of the theories that had been adumbrated in the mind of Horace Mann.

He had been fond of quoting those words of Paul—"thirdly, teachers; *after that*, miracles." Perhaps he had had his fascinating, black-eyed niece in mind.

8

The First American Woman
Stenographic Reporter for
Congressional Committees

ISABEL C. BARROWS

1871

IN THE office of the sergeant-at-arms the employees of the National Capitol assembled to take the "iron clad oath." One after another they raised their right hands and swore that they had never borne arms against their country and that they never would. Coming as it did, a few years after the Civil War had ended, the new law aroused little comment. Both the matter and the scene, as the employees filed by, were routine—except for one fact. It was a fact that caused a flutter among the chiefs of office and that raised the eyebrows of the sergeant-at-arms. For among the men who pronounced their loyalty oaths was a "Benjamin," a "Benjamin" in the form of a woman, the only woman in the National Capitol who raised her right hand and swore that she had never and would never bear arms against her country. If she turned the heads of the gentlemen present, it was not because of anything extraordinary in her appearance. Extremely slight, in her late twenties, she would have passed unnoticed elsewhere. But at this time and place, in the political hub of the nation, she embodied a revolutionary portent of things to come. She had joined the ranks of men to swear the "iron clad oath" and to demonstrate by her otherwise unremarkable presence that the National Capitol had for the first time been invaded by a woman.

The slight, unassuming woman who filed past the sergeant-at-arms had already lived several lives and would live several more. Against a background that shifted from Vermont to Washington, from New York to Boston, from India to Russia, she had and would live out those lives. And in the course of them she would prove to an astonished world that a woman could work in the National Capitol as stenographer, could perform competently as an ophthalmologist, could attempt the rescue of a prisoner in Czarist Russia, and still remain a woman. Quietly, effectively, Isabel C. Barrows lived out her varied lives, a woman in whom the fires of life were never banked.

By the time she swore the "iron clad oath" she had been twice married and had already pioneered in two professions—ophthalmology and stenography—when both professions were themselves part of the newness of the day, bound up with a world in quest of panaceas and reforms.

She had been born on April 17, 1845, in Irasburg, Vermont, the daughter of Henry and Anna Hayes, emigrants from Scotland. Her father had been a Grahamite physician, her mother a school teacher who inclined toward the doctrines of Mrs. Amelia Bloomer. From Irasburg to Hartland, from Hartland to Derry, New Hampshire, the family moved, while Isabel learned to milk cows and harness a horse, to husk corn and pare apples, to churn butter and keep accounts. Between skating and coasting, chestnutting and sleighing, donation parties and private theatricals, she pursued her studies at home and later at the village school in Candia. After a brief session at the Pinkerton Academy, she was enrolled at Adams Academy, where she earned her tuition by sweeping the floors, making the fires, and ringing the bell for the opening of school.

She learned more, however, than Andrews and Stoddard's Latin Grammar and translations from Nepos and Virgil. The little New England girl, with her turned-up nose, red cheeks and curls and her Scottish burr, was early initiated into the two professions in which she was to pioneer. Driving with her father, sitting on his medicine box in the little two-wheeled sulky, she learned also to roll pills for Papa's colander at the rate of one cent for every one hundred forty-four, to skin a calf with a scalpel (albeit unwillingly), to dress the hands of a boy whose fingertips had been cut off in a straw-cutter, to watch with the patients and hold their heads while, for fifty cents a tooth, Dr. Hayes performed extractions. The mysteries of wet sheet packs, fomentations and "dripping sheets" were revealed to her as she grew up in the valley of the Connecticut beneath the New Hampshire hills. And still another mystery was laid bare to the little girl in the new China silk bonnet. When she was only nine, "a copy of a Webster shorthand book, which her sister used, fell into her hands and she learned the alphabet"—a brief and early initiation into a skill that was to serve her all her life, introduce her to the varied reforms of the day, and admit her to the ranks of women firsts.

Her head crammed with Butler's *Analogy* and Upham's *Philosophy,* Shakespeare and Racine, "a smithereen of German, a breath of Greek," the seventeen-year-old Isabel Hayes rang the bell that summoned her friends and neighbors to her graduation. Within a year she was to trade her Latin for Marathi and the New England hills for the plains of Ahmednagar. As the bride of a missionary to India, the eighteen-year-old Isabel Hayes Chapin had begun her courageous march through a life that was to be as many-faceted as it was colorful.

Isabel had met William Wilberforce Chapin during a visit to Andover, where the dignified, full-bearded twenty-six-year-old student was attending divinity school. Her interest in him was at first based solely upon the fact that he was the brother of the head of Mt. Holyoke Seminary, where she had hopes of studying or teaching. But Chapin's tales of his home at Somers, Connecticut, and his expedition to a mission island in Labrador vied with his plans for missionary work in India to broaden that interest, and a quiet wooing followed the quiet meeting. On September 26, 1863, two days after he was ordained, Isabel Hayes became Mrs. William W. Chapin. Only her mother's death, little more than two weeks later, tinged the occasion with sorrow but could not impede the swift advance of events. Her father and brother were going to war. She must pass a test before the august American Board of Commissioners for Foreign Missions, buy jaconet muslins, checked silks and traveling dresses at Hovey's, and pack her books and linens in four strong chests for what promised to be a ten years' stay in India.

With her cat in her arms, the eighteen-year-old Isabel and her reverend husband boarded the *Sydenham* in January of 1864. Loaded with ice for Bombay, the ship set sail from Boston Harbor, its masts and spars and ropes coated with ice. Marathi lessons were begun on deck and continued for nearly five months until the *Sydenham* anchored off Bombay, and a strange new world of

turbaned Hindoos and Mussulmen in flowing trousers unfolded before the girl from the Vermont hills. From Bombay she journeyed
with her husband by rail and bullock cart to Ahmednagar on the
tableland far above sea level, where Isabel learned at first hand
the nature of heat and rain and mirages. Their bungalow stood in
a large compound, at its back door a huge banyan tree where the
crows roosted. In the schoolhouse on the compound they were
welcomed, garlands of jessamine flowers twined round their necks
as they sat cross-legged on the floor. For over six months Isabel and
William Chapin remained at Ahmednagar, studying five hours a
day with a Brahman pundit, walking about the fort and visiting
the old Mohammedan palace in the country. Before proceeding to
their assigned station at Pimplus, they joined a tenting tour, riding
astride to the mud-walled villages to visit the schools and watch
the work of native teachers, pitching their tents in mango groves
infested with monkeys and parrots and black crows. Before Isabel's eyes rushed the Indian kaleidoscope—the oxen drawn up at
the well, the women, their faces veiled, their ear- and nose-rings
flashing, their ankle bangles tinkling.

At length, mounted in their bullock carts, the Chapins journeyed
to Pimplus, where they were assigned their home in the mission
house—a far cry from Derry, New Hampshire—with its mud
walls and thatched roofs where parrots made their nests. From
the dining room Isabel could look out on the Pimplus River
through a grove of tamarind and peepul trees. Studies with the
pundit continued, along with visits to catechists and schools and
Sunday services in a life of isolation for a nineteen-year-old girl
from New England. Her life at Pimplus was brief, but her sense
of isolation sharpened, for in less than three months William
Chapin succumbed to diphtheria. Taken in a bullock cart to
Ahmednagar, he died on March 22, 1865, leaving a nineteen-
year-old widow in the loneliness of a strange and far-off country.
Undaunted even in this grief, Isabel sent again for the doctor,
who had the case reported, wrote to the commander of the place
who arranged for the burial, and returned to Pimplus to dismantle
her home. Although the Board refused her permission to adopt
Hindoo dress and live in the zenana with the women, she was
allowed to gather together a little school of Hindoo girls in the
suburbs of Ahmednagar and spend her mornings teaching them.
From March to September she stayed on, teaching, studying medi-

cal "Theory and Practice," working with native patients. Gradually her plans and purposes crystallized. She would return to America to equip herself as a medical missionary and go again to India. Aboard the *Gunga,* she sailed via Arabia toward the West, boarding the *Pennsylvania* at Liverpool. On the last day of November in 1865, the twenty-year-old widow landed at Castle Garden and sat on her trunk to wait for the customs officer. Her father had died at Memphis in the War. She had returned with no one to meet her, no home to go to, "not a dollar in the world, with all she loved best in the grave." But she had returned to a life far richer than the life she had lost despite the bitter loneliness of that November day at Castle Garden.

Dansville, New York, bore little resemblance to the gaudy interior of India, but its Sanatorium seemed as good a training ground as any other for a medical missionary. Indeed, to Isabel, with her Grahamite background, "Our Home on the Hillside" which Dr. James Caleb Jackson had founded only eight years before, was a welcome part of the newness of the day in medical experiment. As bath assistant, she quickly learned the object of the Sanatorium—to treat invalids "suffering from diseases more or less chronic, by a system peculiarly its own, and yet strictly scientific in every respect." Accompanying the bearded, long-haired Dr. Jackson on his morning rounds, Isabel studied the effects of water treatment, the advantages of ministering to the sick without medicine, and the beneficence of "esthetic gymnastics" and "psycho hygiene." Dr. Jackson, abolitionist, Grahamite and hydropathist, who believed that "cohabitation with the design to have a child should never take place in darkness, or by any other than solar light," and who invented the health food known as Granula, elucidated his trainee in a host of "scientific" ideas that were "peculiarly" his own. Carrying out his prescriptions, giving footbaths, douches and dry rubs, preparing trays and assisting in the "fomentations" of the bath, Isabel quickly shared in every aspect of life at the "Cure," from its efforts at hydopathic health reform to its weekly dances in "Liberty Hall." In her "American Costume" with short dress and trousers, she attended lectures, spoke on life in India, and laid plans for medical studies in New York that would bring her closer to the missionary field.

One incident only was destined to alter those plans. Isabel Chapin was introduced to Dr. Jackson's stenographer, a young man just her age who hailed from New York. At the same time she was re-introduced to the mysteries of phonography or shorthand which she had first glimpsed as a child. A cabalistic sign signifying "Our Home" written in a note from Samuel June Barrows was to open to the twenty-one-year-old widow a new way of life and yet another aspect of the newness of the times. As Barrows himself was to put it, phonography "secured me an inestimable wife." It secured for Isabel an equally inestimable husband, and the course of her history, too, was soon to turn "on the shorthand pivot." Samuel June Barrows had studied stenography so that he could use it as a "ladder to the ministry." It was to lead him and his "inestimable wife" to other ministries as well, from the State Department of the national capital to the counsel tables of international commissions.

The young stenographer soon laid bare his brief but colorful history for the receptive young widow. The pale, beardless young man had been born in 1845 on New York's lower East side, where, after his father's untimely death, his mother had made a living by manufacturing shoe blacking after an old English recipe. When not yet nine, Samuel had been engaged as errand boy in the printing works of a cousin, "Colonel" Richard Hoe, where he exchanged ten hours of his day for one dollar a week. Later he learned to operate the first private telegraph service in the world, strung to the Hoe factory. He devised his own system of shorthand and, having seen an advertisement that deceptively promised, "Short-Hand learned in fifteen minutes," began at the age of sixteen to study Graham's revision of Webster's phonography. Going through handbook and reader, he studied on a bale of hay at half-past four in the morning at the foot of New York's Broome Street until he was able to record his pastor's sermons for posterity every Sunday. The pothooks, curves and angles became keys that opened for the young student "the doorway into a new realm of thought and occupation." After nine years with the Hoe printing works, young Barrows applied for a position with the publishing concern of Fowler and Wells—the Golgotha of Broadway—a place of skulls where phrenology and phonography went hand in hand. There, Isabel learned, he had been trained under the resident examiner, Dr. Nelson Sizer, to report in a phrenological cabinet where "Characters" were taken down from dictation.

Exchanging tales of "the frosty air of New England" and "the table-land of the Deccan" for stories of a more rugged youth, Isabel listened, enchanted, to the autobiography of the young man whose life she would soon share. During the recent War he had volunteered in the Navy, but because of ill health had not been mustered in. Instead, he had found his way to Dr. Jackson's Dansville Sanatorium to earn his living while he recovered his health. The two lives that had been so divergent had at last come parallel. Soon they would merge. Barrows' ambition was still the ministry, Isabel's medicine. In both pursuits the pothooks that had brought them together could serve a purpose. Phonography could be, and to a large extent would be, the fulcrum of their history.

Having agreed to postpone their marriage until one had finished her medical course and the other his theological studies, Isabel moved to New York with a Dansville colleague, Hattie Knight. At 129 Waverly Place they found "a little room with a big sunny window" and a tiny coal grate, along with the privilege of using "Madame Bertrand's little kitchen in the story above." With the modicum of money left by her father, lectures on "Life among the Hindoos" and rewritten items for the newspapers, Isabel eked out her income and pursued her medical studies. In her "American Costume" she attended lectures through the winter, working at Gray's *Anatomy* and Dalton's *Physiology,* dissections and surgery, and incidentally causing a minor revolution among the male population of Bellevue.

Surgery was the most attractive part of the work to me, but I did not enjoy the "spitballs" which the dignified medical students of Bellevue used to fling at us. The professor laughed at their insults to us, for he had a sneaking desire to do the same, not approving of petticoats coming to his clinics, as he frankly said. . . . This was long before the day of trained nurses and I wonder now that anyone ever recovered at Bellevue.

By the end of the "spitball" winter, the young woman medical student and her beloved stenographer experienced a change of mind if not of heart. They had missed each other so much that they decided "it was better to marry while we could and then go on with our studies alternately." In a modified "American Costume" of alpaca Isabel appeared with the prospective groom at the home of the Reverend Henry Ward Beecher where, on June 28, 1867, they were married. Each was twenty-two, with nothing to bring to their union but their love, their inflexible purposes and their ambitions.

Back at 129 Waverly Place they settled, Barrows working as stenographer first for the *Sun* and later for *The World,* Isabel following his example by the assiduous study of Graham's handbook and her husband's shorthand. In 1867, phonography was not unlike the other reforms of the day in which Isabel had shared. It had much in common with hydropathy and phrenology, "psycho hygiene" and dress reform, for it, too, was part of the newness of the times. It was, to Isabel as to most practitioners, an idealistic pursuit, "the art of writing brought into close proximity with that of speaking," an art that "emancipates mind and gives full scope to the out-reach of never-ending thought." With Messrs. Fowler and Wells, she agreed that "Shorthand straightens and shortens the road to learning and gives a new impulse and a freer and wider range to thought." What the steam engine had done in locomotion and commerce, phonography could do in fastening thought upon paper. This harmonious art of writing by sound could, according to Andrew Graham, "ennoble the most degraded . . . . its sweet beauties refine the tastes . . . . it develops beautiful friendships among its thousands of lovers" who formed a "Phonographic Fraternity," a great "Brotherhood, by means of a fraternal correspondence." It was a fraternity in which women could share as "lady amanuenses" and in "the phonographic republic" equal rights for women seemed not unattainable.

During the early months of her marriage, Isabel Barrows laid the groundwork to enter the "reportorial profession" and join the high-minded "Phonographic Fraternity." Shorthand, she discovered, was no easy taskmaster. Had not Dickens written that "a perfect and entire command of the mystery of shorthand writing and reading—was about equal in difficulty to the mastery of six languages." Like David Copperfield, Isabel plunged into its "sea of perplexity," studying "the changes that were rung upon dots, . . . the wonderful vagaries that were played by circles; the unaccountable consequences that resulted from marks like flies' legs; the tremendous effects of a curve in a wrong place." It was a study, Barrows explained, which required "an agile mind, deft fingers, and unremitting application." The good shorthand writer must have a phrenological temperament in which "the Mental ought to be active and abundant to give the thoughtful and studious spirit; there should be enough of the Motive to give endurance and industrial energy, and enough of the Vital to give zeal and health." He—or she—must be endowed not only with good grammar, spelling and penmanship, but with an "excellent memory" and "large perceptive organs."

After three months, in the course of which Isabel developed her "perceptive organs" by alternating between Dalton's *Physiology* and Graham's standard phonography, a telegram arrived at 129 Waverly Place which was eventually to alter her life, give her the opportunity of joining the "Phonographic Fraternity" in her own right and make of her a woman first.

The telegram was addressed to her husband, offering him the position of stenographic secretary to William H. Seward, Secretary of State, at a salary of $1600 a year. Together they had not earned more than $1200. Within forty-eight hours they were in Washington. Isabel found the national capital a "great country village" where cows and geese and pigs fed about the streets, where markets offered sassafras bark and wild flowers. In two rooms she set up house, building up a Hindoo oven and preparing her Graham bread. Between teaching an infant class in a mission school, studying anatomy from borrowed bones, and pursuing Graham's shorthand, she spent the winter, while Barrows worked as stenographer in the State Department.

It was strange to think that, had not an assassin attempted Seward's life, a young woman from Vermont would have lived an altered history. As it was, the Secretary of State had suffered such injuries to his right hand at the time of the assault that it was painful for him to write a letter. He needed the services of a stenographer to whom he could dictate his diplomatic dispatches. From October 1867 until the summer of 1868, Samuel Barrows acted as Seward's secretary, bringing home to his wife tales of Reconstruction politics and Mexican revolutions, the Johnson impeachment proceedings and the "Alabama Claims." He brought home, too, stories of the State Department library, of the dispatch box on the Secretary's table, and of the Secretary himself, the "simplicity of his republican manners," his impassive reserve and his kindness of heart.

Then, during the summer of 1868, Isabel Barrows came to know the Secretary of State herself, witnessed the proceedings of the State Department at first hand, and shared not only in the "Phonographic Fraternity," but in American diplomatic history. Barrows was stricken with a long and severe illness. His wife took his place. By so simple a procedure, the first woman in history was employed in the State Department, and Isabel Barrows was on her way to becoming the first woman stenographic reporter for Congressional committees.

On a hot August morning in 1868, she entered the brick building on Fourteenth Street that housed the State Department and approached Secretary Seward. The "mark of the assassin's knife" was still upon him, the muscles of one side of his face were contracted, and his speech was thick as he welcomed her with "impassive courtesy." Isabel delivered her message.

"I am sorry for your husband, madam," Seward replied, "but I am also sorry for myself, for I have never had such an accumulation of work since the war."

"Perhaps I can find some one to take his place," Isabel suggested.

"I do not want any one else. The advantage to me of your husband and his predecessor, . . . is that they bring head as well as hand to their work."

Since she knew that none of the clerks in the Department could write shorthand, Isabel remarked,

"If I only knew a little more of stenography, I would gladly do my husband's work till he is better."

Seward grasped the suggestion.

"Go right up in the library, and we will see how we get on together."

In the little alcove in the library at the head of a private staircase that led to Seward's room, Isabel was provided with notebook and pencils and told to wait until she heard the "little bell," the famous bell that would summon her to the counsels of diplomacy. At its ring she appeared below.

"Be seated, madam," said the Secretary, pointing to a comfortable chair with a footstool, . . . "To the minister at St. Petersburg."

Then followed "a long diplomatic dispatch, full of technical terms,
. . . names of Russians, instructions for procedure . . . with cor-
rections" preceded by "Strike that out, madam," until Seward
remarked, "That is all at present. You may now read to me what
you have written."

That sudden power of speech was given to Balaam's ass was not more
wonderful than that by some hocus-pocus of magic or inspiration
Isabel was able to read off, without break or stumble, the long and
involved dispatch.

It sealed her fate not only for the remainder of the summer, but
almost for all time.

"That will do perfectly, madam. You may act as my private secretary
till your husband's return."

Isabel did so act, receiving from the disbursing agent the full
amount of salary for the full amount of work—a woman member
of the "Phonographic Fraternity" who was bringing equal rights
to her sex and making history in the State Department.

Every morning during the hot summer of 1868, Isabel watched
Seward's arrival, saw him enter the large room on Fourteenth
Street, observed him as he read dispatches and official communi-
cations or glanced up at the large maps mounted on rollers at
one side of the room. She observed him also as he thought aloud,
pacing up and down with his hands behind his back and his
eyes fixed steadily upon the floor, and she listened to the stories
he told her, following his slow dictations and revisions. After
Isabel read to Seward a dispatch from stenographic notes, she
transcribed it on every other line of wide-ruled dispatch paper
which was sent to the diplomatic division where it belonged to be
re-copied for his signature. She learned, as her husband had
learned, that it was necessary for the Secretary's amanuensis to be
"something more than a phonograph echoing all his utterances."

The tinkling of the bell summoned her not only to labor but
to history. "It was a time of wars and rumors of wars. There were
revolutions in South America, excited times in Japan, trouble in
Russia, and complications in Brazil." Isabel listened as Seward
told her about the purchase of Alaska, which had recently been
effected, hearing his astute observation that she would probably
live long enough to have its value appreciated, though he never

would. For her benefit he described a heated Cabinet meeting at which he hoped he had warded off a war with Brazil, interrupting himself to exclaim, "Here I am telling you *state secrets!*"

The notes accumulated, the reading of dictations from the notes, the transcriptions for the engrossing clerks, while the tinkling of Seward's bell summoned Isabel to the unfolding of American history and to the unfolding of Seward's history. She took down from dictation a difficult dispatch to Japan immediately followed by a charming letter to his grandchild Nellie, smiling as she followed his voice with her pencil. Over hot chocolate she listened to his discussions of a Canal across the Isthmus of Panama and over her notebook she listened to his "Cross that all out, madam." Upon one occasion, when she had returned to her alcove to transcribe an important dispatch on the Canal, she was "sure that the words did not say what he meant them to imply."

I tripped down the stairs, . . . read the notes aloud slowly and asked if they were right. "Yes, madam, that is quite right." A little chagrined, I went back to my desk. The more I studied the passage, the more convinced I was that it wholly misrepresented the Secretary's meaning. I plucked up my courage and went down again, . . . He glanced hastily through it, and said, "Why, yes, that is right; of course it is." My humiliation increased. But . . . . I *knew* it was wrong.

I re-wrote the entire dispatch in longhand, went down-stairs, asked for audience with Mr. Seward, and . . . asked the privilege of telling him where I thought the dispatch was wrong. . . . I read it as it was written.

"Now what would you have me say instead?" he asked.

. . . I told him what I supposed the meaning ought to be, but that the involution of the sentence made it read just the contrary. He paused a moment, and wrinkled his brow. . . . "You are right, madam," he cried, and instantly changed the entire passage, and re-dictated it, . . . "Let me thank you; and if in addition it is any satisfaction to you to know it, let me tell you that you are the first woman in the United States to know of these proceedings, and you may have the further satisfaction of knowing that you have saved the Secretary of State from a serious mistake."

She had the satisfaction, too, of knowing that she had been the first woman ever employed by the State Department and probably the only one who drew the same pay as a man. She had the satis-

faction of knowing that "that little woman," as they called her in
the Department, had observed history at first hand and made it, too.

Relieved by a Congressional reporter who was able to take her
place as Seward's secretary, Isabel took a vacation with her husband before deciding to return to New York to continue her
medical studies. Reporting to "eke out her means," she attended
lectures, worked at the New York Dispensary, and in the spring
of 1869 completed her term at Woman's Medical College of New
York. The first woman stenographer of the Department of State
was on her way to becoming another first in a different field.

In 1869 the medical school of the University of Vienna was for
American students a mecca of advanced learning. When, through
a friend, Mary Safford, the suggestion was made that Isabel spend
a year there, her husband, still working as a government stenographer with an annual salary of $1600, had exclaimed, "You must
go, if I have to live on pea soup and sleep in a coal box." In
September of 1869, less than six years since her passage to India,
Isabel sailed aboard the *Ethiopia,* entrained for Vienna, and drove
straight to the hospital. With Mary Safford she

went over to the office of the University and they were so dazed at
the idea of two young women wanting to matriculate that before they
fully recovered consciousness after the stunning effect of our un-
heard-of demand, we had signed the papers, paid the insignificant fee,
and were students in the great university of Vienna, the first women
ever admitted, and as *B* comes before *S* (Safford), I suppose I may
claim that I was the first.

As *The Revolution* was to put it, "both are now taking leading
positions in the medical classes of Vienna, and upon equal terms,
and with the same privileges, as the gentlemen there studying."

From their large sunny room with its porcelain stove and
couches and writing-desk, the two women firsts of Vienna walked
to the hospital and took their place in the ancient University.
Taking all her notes in shorthand, translating into English as the
professors lectured, Isabel applied her phonographic skill to her
medical studies, as she would apply it to so many varied enterprises in the course of her colorful career. In practical surgery,
where she was the only woman in a class of thirty men, in nose
and throat, obstetrics and dermatology, she attended lectures and
walked the wards, studying under Oppolzer and Schroter, Gruber

and Politzer, Zeissel and Braun. But Dr. Bella C. Barrows had already begun to specialize, finding in ophthalmology her particular forte.

My *"Fach"* was the eye. That to me was of absorbing interest, and during much of the winter I put in eighteen hours of the twenty-four in that department, largely in reading, and three or four in the clinics. No one in Vienna ever had such a chance, I veritably believe. I was young, strong, enthusiastic, industrious, friendly, appreciative of kindness, and realizing the rare chance I was having, and the professors, who had never had women as students before, were surprised and evidently pleased, and so helped us as they did not the men.

In her black dress, the slight young woman student only five feet tall attended the rival eye clinics, Arlt's and Jaeger's, manipulating hundreds of pigs' eyes in the mask, until at last she was informed by Professor Jaeger,

"Frau Doctor, tomorrow you are to operate on a living eye." The students standing about us were amazed. No student was allowed to do such a thing, still less a foreigner and least of all a mere woman! It was simply incredible, and even I thought I must have misheard.

The next day I took my seat in the semicircle about Professor Jaeger, who sat with his towel across his knee as usual. A patient was led in and put on the stool facing him. He always prided himself on operating with the patient sitting before him and in not giving choloroform, which was the only anaesthetic used. He examined the eye, stood up, looked at me, and pointed to his stool. I obeyed the mute order, sat down in his place, and he took my stool. I too glanced at the eye. It was a cataract, and a left-handed operation. The tall assistant handed me the instruments and held the eye open. I poised my left hand as I had been taught, and without a tremor drove it into the eye, and in less time than it takes to tell it, the cataract was removed, the eye carefully bandaged, the woman laid upon a stretcher and carried away. The Professor stood up, I did the same, and we again changed seats in silence. He laid his towel across his knee as before and looked thoughtfully at it as if wondering what to say. I was on thorns. It seemed to me as if everything had gone off all right, but what did he? Then he broke the silence and all listened. "Frau Doctor! Heute haben Sie Ihre Knechten Sporne [sic] gewonnen." The students broke out in applause and the next patient was brought in.

One by one, Dr. Barrows earned her spurs in the various eye operations—iridectomy and enucleation, plastic operations, operations for strabismus and glaucoma and the tear tube, until she was completely "at home with a knife." Following up her cases in the wards, she took charge of them there, and in Dr. Arlt's eye clinic she studied the cases and kept records of her observations. The little "Frau Doctor" worked on pigs' eyes by the bowlful and on human eyes as well, both in socket and in mask. She studied in the laboratory, imbedding specimens in wax, slicing off her sections, coloring them with carmine and examining them under the microscopic lens. Interrupted only by an attack of smallpox or by brief botanic excursions into the country and briefer visits to the opera, she continued her initiation into the mysteries of the eye, meeting the great oculists of Europe at the world university where she had "heroically struck out a new path for her sex . . . in thoroughly fitting herself for the profession" of ophthalmologist. As she was to put it, "My one success in Vienna was with the knife. Nothing gives me the pleasure of my successful operations on human eyes. Do you wonder when even one of my professors said, after the first one made, with the left-hand, too, 'You have to-day won your Ritterspoon.' "

The Franco-Prussian War put an end to Dr. Barrows' studies at Vienna, and to her "Ritterspoons" as well. Her husband had written, begging her to "keep away from the smell of gunpowder," and the small woman in the quiet black dress moved on to London, where she attended eye courses at Moorfields Hospital before embarking on the *Ethiopia* for home. "A tall, straight figure was standing on the pier, and the year of absence was forgotten." "After the manner of government clerks who must save daylight for duty," Dr. Bella C. Barrows and her husband "went to Washington by night." Her education had been completed. Now the time had come for her to apply what she had learned both in ophthalmology and phonography so that her husband's studies could proceed.

Taking a floor in a sunny house on Massachusetts Avenue, Isabel set up her penates once again and in addition had a sign painted "to tell the world that here was an oculist." With the hundred dollars' worth of eye instruments which she had brought home, she opened her office to the public. Moreover, Dr. Robert Reyburn, surgeon in charge of Freedmen's Hospital and professor of surgery at Howard University, who would one day be one of the six physicians in charge at the time of Garfield's assassination, offered her his office at 628 F Street for half the rent, he to occupy it part of the day and she the other. In the *Daily Morning Chronicle* of May 29, 1871, Dr. Barrows inserted her professional card: "Oculist," "Office hours 10 A.M. to 1 P.M.," and at F Street she received her patients—the protégé of Ben Butler for whom she prescribed glasses, the gentleman from the Patent Office, the many patients recommended by the District physicians. The first woman stenographer in the State Department had become the first woman, regularly educated, to undertake the practice of ophthalmology in Washington.

She became also lecturer in diseases of the eye at the School of Medicine of Howard University, taking charge of the eye department at Freedmen's Hospital for $100 a month. Giving clinical instruction in eye disorders—the nature of amaurosis or cataract or night blindness—she taught the junior and senior medical students, lecturing in Freedmen's Hospital, in the clinics and in the wards, "the little woman from Vienna who looked after the eyes of poverty-stricken Negroes" in the national capital.

The ophthalmologist had not, however, forgotten that she was also a phonographer. When she was not lecturing at Howard University, attending clinics at Freedmen's Hospital and prescribing for patients on F Street, she was pursuing another profession as the first woman stenographer for the Congressional committees of the United States.

"The offer of work at the capitol while Congress was in session" brought to Isabel the unprecedented opportunity for a woman to report hearings before committees on finance and commerce, public lands and Indian matters. Since "all the really important consideration and action on every matter before the national legislature" took place in committee, she found her work not only varied but highly responsible. In the House committees the discussions were so spirited and rapid that a verbatim report required all the stenographic skill she could muster. Her work was an education in itself, for she found that as a reporter she must be a specialist in many a branch of learning, from coinage to weights and measures, from rivers and harbors to insular affairs. As the committee members moved about the room, hurled questions at witnesses and opened cross-table colloquies, Isabel followed the rapid-fire discussions with her pen, recording in pothooks the deliberations of committees on every conceivable branch of legislation. Senate committees were usually more sedate and formal in procedure and hence comparatively easier to report. Actually there was little that was easy for the first woman assistant stenographer at the United States Capitol.

When she began her work her chiefs, Frank Smith, the first official reporter of House committees, and Andrew Devine, who became his successor, cautioned Isabel to sign only her initials to the vouchers, "for as no woman had ever been employed in the capacity of shorthand writer they might turn her out." The next year, she joined with her male colleagues to take the "iron clad oath" before the sergeant-at-arms. With amanuensis work for such prominent reporters as James Clephane and Henry Hayes, Smith and Devine, Isabel Barrows found that she could command —from all sources—the munificent sum of $400 a month. She earned her pay, as her long day testified.

I rose at five and . . . prepared breakfast. . . . At nine I was in the classroom of the university. Then from there I flew to F Street to my office, where I had an hour only a day that winter. Then to the Capitol where from twelve till four, sometimes longer, I had not a moment to call my own. Indeed later, . . . I did not even stand up once from my chair from one at noon till one in the middle of the night. . . . I have had a call from . . . the second woman to be employed in the capital, . . . and she . . . said, "I remember hearing Mr. Devine once say, 'My, but Mrs. Barrows does get out a lot of copy!' " I did, I am sure of it. I earned all that I had and never felt guilty when I received and kept my share of the back-pay bill that made so much talk. . . .

That winter, from all sources combined, I earned $400 a month.

She was earning enough not only to keep "the kettle boiling," but to fulfill her share of the marriage bargain and send her husband to school. As Barrows had insisted that his wife study in Vienna, now Isabel insisted that he attend Harvard Divinity School. She "cut and made with her own hands all his shirts and underclothes and got a tailor to cut his trousers and waistcoats, . . . and a thin alpaca coat. She put them all together and finished them. . . . even knitted all of his stockings." What was more, she wrote to Professor Louis Agassiz, asking if he had work for a good stenographer named Samuel J. Barrows, who would report his scientific lectures for the *Tribune,* and rented a room in Divinity Hall for her husband. Barrows, who had become a Unitarian and had studied during his own "leisure" hours at Columbian University, exchanging shorthand for Latin and Greek, resigned his position in the State Department, and with satchel in hand and phonographic pencils in his pocket was at last enrolled at Harvard Divinity School where he would complete his own professional education for the ministry. "Three more years of separation looked pretty long, but at least the ocean would not be between us."

During the summers of 1873 and 1874, however, the continent lay between them, for Samuel Barrows spent those months with General Custer, first on the Yellowstone and then in the Black Hills as correspondent for the *Tribune.* What Isabel did not learn from his letters, she could learn from the reports spread on page one of the *Tribune* and sent in by the paper's "Special Correspondent"—reports of General Stanley's expedition and the Yellowstone War, of the battles of Tongue River and the Big Horn, of Sioux decoys and adventurers in buckskin. The first report of the discovery of gold in the Black Hills was recorded by Barrows in a dispatch carried by Indian couriers from Custer Gulch in Dakota Territory. The young divinity student, however, who was also stenographer, correspondent and pioneer, "found that no good report of an Indian rifle could be made in shorthand, and came back with his scalp." He came back, too, with a memento of his adventures in the form of a Henry rifle bullet which he kept in his vest pocket and sharpened into a pencil to report a theological lecture—not the last spear which Samuel J. Barrows would turn into a pruning hook.

Only two years later, when Custer and all his men were slaughtered by the Indians, Barrows would not have returned at all. As it was, by that time the Barrowses were a united family with a daughter, Mabel, and the head of the family was an ordained minister settled in the First Parish Church of Dorchester.

Isabel had burned her Washington bridges, performed her last cataract operation in the hospital, and resigned from government work. Her daughter was born in 1873. Two years later, Barrows was graduated from Harvard Divinity School. In September of 1875, the family sailed abroad for a year at Leipzig, where Barrows studied music and political economy and his wife Italian,

French and German. The day they received their last check of $300 from New York, their bank announced its suspension. When Barrows returned home and learned that his money was lost, his only comment was, "The worst of it is that a poor theologian is not permitted to swear." A stranger who overheard the remark next day left a check of $300 for him. It was fitting that his first sermon as an ordained minister was delivered on the theme that "God is Love."

For four years, from 1876 to 1880, Isabel Barrows, first woman stenographer of the nation's Congressional committees, adapted her versatility to the demands laid upon a minister's wife. As pastor of Boston's oldest Unitarian Church, Meeting House Hill in Dorchester, Samuel Barrows naturally wrote all his sermons in shorthand so that he could "take up a bundle of words in his eye and fling them at his audience." His wife naturally assisted him. Between superintending their home on Dorchester's High Street and no doubt serving as a sounding-board for his sermons, she was not idle. Nor were her fingers empty whether they wielded a skillet or a pencil.

Then, with the new year of 1881, Isabel Barrows, who had turned her many-faceted skills to such varied enterprises to launch her husband on his way, found that she could assist him even more closely. Appointed editor of *The Christian Register,* the weekly organ of the Unitarian Church, Barrows resigned his ministry. His wife became his secretary or associate editor, and the pencil that had traced in pothooks the deliberations of Congressional committees now recorded in curves and angles the deliberations of Samuel June Barrows and of the editorial contributor who happened to be his wife.

At 141 Franklin Street in Boston they worked on the journal, whose pages reflected not only the concerns of the Unitarian Church, but their own ever widening interests as well—Indian education, science and immortality, education for the blind. One article, surely contributed by Isabel Barrows, was entitled "Short-Hand For Women" and elucidated women's initiation into "the mysteries of the hooks and curves."

As amanuenses, they are becoming invaluable. One publishing house in Boston employs three or four. Merchants, insurance officers, and manufacturers depend upon them for letter-writing. Even the grocer and the baker dictate their orders, which are received in short-hand.

From the position of private secretary, the amanuensis advances to that of reporter, taking notes of lectures and essays, doing work for the press, and even entering the court-room in some States. . . . only the exceptional ones go on to the speed of one hundred and fifty or sixty words, necessary for the verbatim reporter.

. . . The quick ear, the trained eye, the rapid perception, the hand of the ready writer, must be accompanied by a fair education and good judgment.

These abilities Isabel concentrated now upon *The Christian Register,* with her husband making the first verbatim phonographic report of Phillips Brooks' rapid sermons for the weekly, contributing articles on "The Disappearance of Birds" or "Gymnastics In Sweden," and reading proofs—her hands "never free from pen, pencil, or editorial scissors." The editorial office became headquarters not only for the reforms of the day, but for the reformers, too, who gathered at Franklin Street for the daily luncheon of cheese, fruit and chocolate. While the presses thundered overhead and the wagons rumbled along the stony street, they talked—a Negro from Alabama who had just organized a school, William Lloyd Garrison, Alice Stone Blackwell, the daughter of Lucy Stone, to whom Isabel eventually introduced a brilliant young Armenian along with the problems of Armenian oppression. "It was a communistic feast. One sliced the bread while another buttered it. One raised the literal board, which was hinged to a writing-desk, to serve as a side table. Another removed the pile of exchanges from a movable table, drew it up, spread the cloth and set on the cups and plates, while I made the chocolate."

For a time, during the early 1880's, Isabel alternated between the office of *The Christian Register* and her own medical office in Dorchester where she worked as an affiliate of the New England Hospital Medical Society. But whether her fingers held scalpel or editorial scissors, whether she worked in Boston or at the summer camp in Canada, she compressed into twenty-four hours the work of forty-eight. In 1885 her immediate family was augmented by the adoption of a nephew, William Burnet Barrows, but in a larger sense the human family she gathered about her seemed limitless.

On the shores of Lake Memphremagog in lower Quebec, the Barrowses' summer camp was a refuge for the members of the human race—a prisoner's family, children white and yellow, red, brown and black, Greeks and Germans, Frenchmen and Spaniards, a brilliant young "Russian Armenian." For them, Isabel prepared breakfast of cereal, johnnycake and Postum coffee, and sounded reveille on the bugle to awaken the campers. She awakened them to the joys of fishing for lunge or journeying to Brome Lake in the interior, and she awakened them, too, to reform that had been raised from theory to practice, to the living, all-embracing humanity that she herself personified.

Through the years, Isabel Barrows practised that humanity, lived that reform, and through the years she naturally shared her husband's work and versatile interests whether he immersed himself in the temperance movement or the "young science of social psychology," whether he dipped into the Greek poets or studied Hungarian, whether he set his lyrics to music or served as department editor of *Charities*. Did he plan a book describing life in the Barrows summer home in Canada—Isabel collaborated with him on *The Shaybacks In Camp*. Did he compile a volume of Theodore Parker's sermons—Isabel carefully compared each line with the original manuscript to insure an accurate transcription. Was he the only American who accompanied Wilhelm Dörpfeld on his historic excavation of Troy in 1893—Isabel joined him when he entered "Greece by the portals of the Odyssey" and left it "through the Trojan gates of the Iliad." And when he came to write his *Isles And Shrines of Greece,* she lent him her "eyes," her "memory," and her "literary taste."

The wife of the minister, the wife of the editor, became in 1897 the wife of the Congressman, for Samuel June Barrows was elected to the Fifty-fifth Congress from the Tenth Massachusetts District. Then, too, her shadow was upon him, for he introduced bills and joint resolutions to "provide permanent buildings for Freedman's Hospital," and secured from Congress permission to send ships to India loaded with grain for sufferers from famine. Whether the Honorable Samuel June Barrows sent articles signed "Floor Correspondent" to *The Independent* or served as the American member of the Interparliamentary Union for Arbitration, arranging a tour of the delegates at the time of the St. Louis Exposition, his wife was a force behind him, the unobtrusive spur that aided as it drew him on.

By the time of that St. Louis Exposition in 1904, Samuel June

Barrows had added to his many-sided career yet another preoccupation that was to win him his greatest achievements and dominate the remainder of his life. The stenographer, clergyman, editor, traveler and Member of Congress had become a circuit rider in penology, and in this work also his wife would share. As Secretary of the United States delegation to the International Prison Congress, Barrows journeyed to Paris in 1895, to Brussels in 1900, and to Budapest in 1905, advancing, whether he spoke in French or English or Hungarian, the cause of the indeterminate sentence and the probation system. Often he journeyed with his wife, who also served as delegate to the Budapest Congress and who visited with him the juvenile reformatory of Kassa. When Barrows was appointed Corresponding Secretary of the Prison Association of New York, Isabel moved with him to the old rooms over the office on East 15th Street in "thundering lower Manhattan." There, "simply dressed, writing and casting up accounts" before the long table, she sat, aide-de-camp to the penologist who was her husband. As Barrows traveled abroad to inspect prisons, she, too, wandered over the country, a member of the Women's Committee inspecting women's institutions, from the House of Refuge for Women at Hudson and the prison at Auburn to the jails in the western part of the State. On the Pacific Coast she visited the prisons of Oakland and San Quentin, and on Barrows' biennial trips to Europe as prison commissioner, she became, like him, an "informal ambassador to all nations in the cause of enlightened justice."

Yet, throughout her life, Isabel Barrows was never merely the shadow of her husband. If she lent him her eyes and her brain and her pencil, she used them also in her own right. Especially those stenographic skills which she had first employed to free him for study, she adapted in the course of the years to the multitudinous reforms of the day. Phonography, which had been itself a reform, a phase of the newness, became in the hands of Isabel Barrows the clay to shape a brave new world.

The first woman stenographer of Congressional committees had been on hand to report the Belknap impeachment proceedings when Grant's Secretary of War had been charged with "malfeasance in office," and the first woman phonographer who had served William H. Seward later served Garfield in a similar capacity. Isabel Barrows reported the sermons of Reverend Minot J. Savage of Boston and the political addresses of Carl Schurz, performing the remarkable feat of hearing Schurz's speech in German and recording it in English, "between the ear and the fingers, translating into what the speaker . . . called 'capital English.' "

In most of her stenographic work, however, Isabel Barrows displayed more than "a marvel of reportorial . . . expertness." She worked for the causes whose sessions she recorded, for the prisoner and the Indian, the Negro and international peace. For half a century, "the courageous missionary, the skilful oculist, the indefatigable editor" "made the world her own for service." As official reporter and editor of the National Conference of Charities and Correction, she not only reported the sessions and edited the *Proceedings,* but participated actively in the conferences from the St. Louis meeting of 1884 to the Portland meeting of 1904. Isabel brought more than her stenographic pencil to the sessions that considered the care of the insane or the problems of pauperism, the prevention of crime or juvenile delinquents. From St. Louis to Washington, from St. Paul to Omaha, from Buffalo to San Francisco she traveled, hearing addresses by Julian Hawthorne or Frank Sanborn, Ex-President Hayes or Felix Adler, Seth Low or Clara Barton, hearing and joining in the discussions on the care of imbeciles or manual training for the feeble-minded, leaving her mark not only upon the volumes of *Proceedings* which she edited, but upon the sociological progress that they represented.

Isabel coupled her work for the National Conference of Charities and Correction with her stenographic reporting of the Lake Mohonk Conferences for which she also acted as secretary and historian. In the low-studded parlor at Lake Mohonk, with its open fireplaces and rock crystals heaped high between the pillars, she sat, following with her pencil the discussions at the Lake Mohonk Indian Conferences, Negro Conferences and Conferences on International Arbitration. Whether the sessions considered industrial schools for Negroes or the administration of Indian affairs, Apache prisoners of war or cattle-herding, the reindeer experiment in Alaska or the development of peace, Isabel was on hand to listen and record the nation's experiments in reform. The sessions themselves reflected the metamorphoses of the times, the "new days" that brought "new duties"—the problems of Hawaii and

Puerto Rico, of the Philippines and the whole "Path of Empire." The unobtrusive phonographer joined with Garrison and Edward Everett Hale, with the Hindoo leader, Protap Chunder Mozoomdar, and John Burroughs in that "Moral Citadel" that was Lake Mohonk, whose spirit was reflected in one instant when a hymn by Luther, set to music by a Jew, was played by a Catholic priest in a Quaker house.

Her own all-encompassing humanity was reflected, too, in the work she did for the National Prison Association. Isabel served as official reporter of its Congresses, traveling "the length and breadth of the United States," to Texas and Nebraska and to Mexico, to edit the *Proceedings* and to add her voice to discussions on the need for a Federal probation law. Reporting her investigation of jails in Indian Territory, journeying to London to open a discussion of "Women in Prison" before the Women's Congress, Isabel Barrows brought not only her pencil but her human sympathy to service.

For conferences on manual training and physical training, for Indian Commissioners' meetings, for the Association of Superintendents of Training Schools for Nurses and the Association of Superintendents of Institutions for the Feeble Minded, Isabel plied that tireless phonographic pencil. Even she concurred that she had "done an immense amount of shorthand work. I report entire sessions of conferences, get out the notes myself, edit the volumes and put them through the press." Yet it was characteristic that she added, "I do not, however, consider myself a *professional reporter*. All the shorthand work that I do is as an aside to an otherwise busy life." It was an "aside" with which she had made history.

Even in the cause of Russian freedom, Isabel Barrows found occasion to use her phonographic skill. As she had once visited abroad the "Armenian revolutionary leaders" who had escaped from a "Turkish hell," now, in 1909, Isabel Barrows at the age of almost sixty-four journeyed alone to Russia to free a woman who for two years had been imprisoned in the Fortress of St. Peter and St. Paul. She had met the woman in the office of the New York Prison Association a few years before, had taught her English pronunciation, had translated her writings from French into English, and had introduced her to the lecture platform. Now the woman, officially known as Catherine Breshkovsky, unofficially as

Babushka, the little grandmother of the Russian Revolution, had
been betrayed and cast into the fortress without trial.

Isabel was aware that imprisonment was no stranger to Madame
Breshkovsky. Arrested years before for the crime of teaching the
peasants on her estates, she had been kept in solitary confinement
and subsequently exiled to Siberia for twenty-one years. Then,
through the machinations of the traitor Azeff, she had been imprisoned again. While the Friends of Russian Freedom had succeeded in releasing another revolutionary—Nicholas Tchaykovsky
—on bail, every effort to liberate Madame Breshkovsky had failed.
For Isabel Barrows there was no reason to hesitate. The eighteen-
year-old missionary to India would simply become the sixty-four-
year-old missionary to Russia. Only the country and the mission
had changed, not the missionary.

She sailed in March at the suggestion of her husband, who
planned to join her in time for the Paris meeting of the International Prison Commission. Unlike most of his plans and purposes, this one was not destined for fulfillment. His missionary
wife needed all the fortitude that her dauntless years could summon. She had barely arrived in Petrograd when a cablegram informed her of her husband's illness. The fastest steamers could
not bring her back in time. She returned to New York after his
death on April twenty-first. The world had lost a minister-at-large,
a "circuit rider in the humanities." Isabel Barrows had lost the
companion of more than forty years. The loss had postponed, but
had not altered her purpose. The mission still remained and with
it the missionary. A month later she started again for Russia.

David had a sling and five smooth stones to meet his giant. I had . . .
nothing but smooth words. A simple petition setting forth the fact
that the undersigned would count it an act of friendliness on the part
of Russia if she could deal leniently with the woman they honored—
now aged and frail—signed by about three hundred well-known citizens of Boston, New York, and Chicago . . . was my chief reliance. . . .

It is a far cry from New York to St. Petersburg—five thousand miles
as the crow flies, and farther yet by Russian trains. . . . Russian ways
are slow. . . . One must prepare for a long siege. . . . It was lonely . . .
sitting waiting, waiting, in the dreary hotel.

At long last, "Madame Barrows" received official word that she
would be given an audience by Stolypin, Minister of the Interior

at St. Petersburg. Armed with her petition, her letters and her passport, she drove past the Admiralty buildings, the Winter Palace and the Hermitage, over the bridge that spanned the Neva, past the Fortress of St. Peter and St. Paul where her prisoner waited, unaware of her presence, on to the island palace.

I went alone. My driver and horse had been carefully chosen by the hotel people, . . . Three sets of sentinels were subdued . . . by the order from Mr. Stolypin which I held. . . . we swung up the circular driveway to the palace door.

. . . a series of gendarmes passed me from hand to hand till I was seated in the long room with twelve windows and almost as many mirrors, . . . a little old lady.

The interview was brief. The case of Madame Breshkovsky was, it appeared, "a much more difficult question" than the case of Nicholas Tchaykovsky. It involved, Stolypin explained, "a fanatical old woman" known as the "grandmother of the Revolution," "a dangerous woman" who advocated "fire and sword and bomb." "What she advocates when she speaks Russian," Isabel replied, "I do not know, but when she speaks French or English she advocates none of those things; at least *I* have never heard her." It was, she explained, "simply one old woman pleading for another." Madame Breshkovsky asked only for "such things as seem to us every land should have. . . . no other Russian has ever made us feel how great are the problems with which your country has to deal. . . . I did not come as politician, but to plead for my friend."

Isabel handed Stolypin her letters and credentials and arose. She "ran the gauntlet of . . . officers, gendarmes, servants, messengers, dropping a ruble into this and that waiting palm, and so back to the city, past the grim fortress where . . . Catherine Breshkovsky was sitting."

Isabel had failed in her immediate mission. Her petition was pigeon-holed, her entreaty to see Madame Breshkovsky refused. The last night she was in St. Petersburg, however, "there came unexpectedly into my hands for an hour five letters" which the prisoner had been permitted to send her son. "There was present at the time one who understood both Russian and English, and in hot haste these letters were translated *vive* [sic] *voce*." Now, to her missionary zeal, Isabel added her phonographic skill, taking the translation in shorthand, a translation that included a sentence of thanks to Isabel Barrows for twelve rubles received by the grandmother of the revolution. Even in Czarist Russia the pothooks and curves traced by Isabel Barrows' pencil were brought to the service of humanity.

From Russia Isabel journeyed on to Paris to take her husband's place at the International Prison Congress where she was sent as a delegate by the United States government to lay before the meeting the plans that he had formulated. They were plans for the quinquennial congress in Washington in 1910 at which Barrows was to have been president. Not only at international congresses did she take his place. As he had served as department editor of *Charities,* Isabel became contributing editor of *The Survey,* assembling articles on reformatories for women or crime and its cure. She more than took his place. In her own right the woman who had been a leader in so many varied pursuits of her time became in the few years remaining to her a leader in prison reform.

On October 25, 1913, Isabel Barrows died. She had traveled far in the course of her sixty-eight years, from a Vermont homestead to a Vienna university, from the National Capitol to crossroad jails, from international gatherings to the prison fortress of an empire. She had been many things in the course of that lifetime: missionary and oculist, editor and champion of human rights. She had been, too, the first woman stenographic reporter of Congressional committees, and in her little "aside to an otherwise busy life" she had carried an ever-present phonographic pencil. "In her place," Madame Breshkovsky wrote, "a man would be a celebrity known all the world over. . . . It would be . . . well . . . to have a full description of her life, which has been an uninterrupted course of reasonable labor and noble actions. . . . She has never been tired, . . . and all she could give away she has given." She gave the gifts of mind and heart and fortitude in the cause of the only race she recognized—the human one. And as she gave, the gifts and the giver, too, were indelibly recorded with a phonographic pencil that traced in pothooks the progress of mankind.

9

The First Woman Admitted to Practice Before the United States Supreme Court

BELVA ANN LOCKWOOD

1879

O N MONDAY, February 2, 1880, Belva A. Lockwood, a forty-nine-year-old Washington attorney, appeared before the Supreme Court of the United States, faced Chief Justice Morrison I. Waite, and in a terse phrase made history. Her phrase was simple indeed, for it was couched in the form of a motion that would admit to practice Mr. Samuel R. Lowery, principal of the Huntsville Industrial University in Alabama. Yet, despite the simplicity of the words that were spoken, in that impressive courtroom no more impressive scene had ever been enacted. If ever a subject had been fitted for a historical painting, this was the subject. For Mr. Lowery was a Negro, and Belva Lockwood was a woman. Moreover, she was the first woman who had been admitted to practice before the Supreme Court of the United States. Mr. Lowery would be the first Southern Negro. And in the scene that had unfolded before the black-robed justices of the Court on that historic Monday, the Fourteenth Amendment had been brought to life, the word "citizenship" had been invested with a fuller meaning, and the opportunities of the new world had taken on properties that were more than verbal. Another door had been opened in the corridors of American history.

Mrs. Lockwood was accustomed to opening such doors. Just a year before she had been the first woman admitted to the federal courts of the country, and no doubt the remembrance of that other historic "first" stirred strongly as she made her way to the court-house from her home on Washington's F Street. Yet in reality she had come a longer way by a more circuitous route to batter down the barriers of ignorance and indifference. In all the long way no door had opened easily to her, yet in the end all doors had opened. The first had been the door of a farmhouse in upstate New York, a small door that had opened on her world.

She was born Belva Ann Bennett on October 24, 1830, on Griswold Street in Royalton, New York, the daughter of Lewis and Hannah Bennett. She was born to a farming family in poor or moderate circumstances, with nothing to indicate that she would ever rise beyond the background of the Niagara frontier with its plank roads and stone fences, its whittled shingles and the routine of milking cows. Nothing but an occasional hickory raising or a visit to Lockport for a cattle show or a purchase from the Fashionable Clothing Emporium altered the birthright that seemed also to be her destiny—a combination of country crossroads and rural four corners, of gristmill, tavern and blacksmith shop, of hominy, hog and venison. Yet it was from such a strong but simple background that she was to rise to become the first woman lawyer admitted to the highest court of the land. The impulse to open doors was early upon her.

By the time she was fifteen, Belva Bennett, having completed her lessons in grammar and geography, arithmetic, algebra and philosophy at the country schools near Royalton, became a teacher at the district school during the summer months and continued her studies during the winter at Royalton Academy. On the Niagara frontier the years passed swiftly. Her father's apparent opposition to her scholastic ambitions, her monetary need persisted, but did not thwart her. In 1848, when she was eighteen years old, she married Uriah McNall, a young farmer, moving with him to the country near Gasport, New York. A daughter, Lura, was born to her the next year, but the marriage itself was to terminate tragically. As the result of a sawmill accident which had occurred a few years before, and a "lingering consumption," Uriah McNall died in 1853, leaving Belva a twenty-two-year-old widow with a child to support.

Belva McNall acted—as she would always act—decisively. Selling the farm and stock, she entered Gasport Academy, boarding near McNall's sawmill. Only by completing her own education could she equip herself to educate others, and teaching seemed at the time the only avenue open to her. Between writing prose and verse for the village papers, studying geometry and bookkeeping, anatomy and physiology, and teaching, Belva prepared herself to enter college and almost accidentally laid the groundwork for a career as yet undreamed of. When she had been offered half the salary granted to men teachers, she had complained to the school trustees and approached the wife of the Methodist minister. The answer she had received planted a seed of revolt that was to flower in the years to come. "I can't help you; you cannot help yourself, . . . it is the way of the world." Belva McNall early determined to alter the way of the world by every means within her power.

"After much mending and turning of a scanty wardrobe," her trunk was packed and the sixty-mile journey made to Lima, New York. Leaving Lura with her parents who had moved west, Belva entered Genesee.

There, for tuition of $8.50 a term, she followed the "Scientific Course," studying, in addition to the mysteries of electricity and magnetism, electro-chemistry and geometry, the law of nations, political economy, and the Constitution of the United States. With all the students, Belva furnished her "own lights, pails, wash-bowls, towels and mirrors," and with the lady students she was charged "$1.25 per term for sawing and carrying wood" to her room. The College was only eighteen miles from Rochester, to which it was connected by a "good plank road," but Mrs. McNall was more intent upon the lessons imparted by James L. Alverson, Professor of Mathematics Pure and Mixed, and by William Hopkins, Professor of Chemistry and Natural History, than upon the more worldly pursuits of the town of Rochester. On June 27, 1857, she received her reward in the form of a Bachelor of Science degree from the College that was to become Syracuse University. Belva McNall had prepared herself for a career. She had also prepared herself for a credo that she would one day formulate: Women "will be educated so that they can be members of Congress, United States consuls and ministers, justices of the Supreme Court, Cabinet officers, and possibly, some day, one of them may be President of the United States."

In 1857 she was apparently content with becoming merely preceptress of Lockport Union School—the first in a succession of teaching posts that would occupy her for a decade. Lockport, where her daughter studied at the same time as Belva taught the girls to declaim and introduced athletics in their curriculum, was followed by the Gainesville Female Seminary, operated under the Mount Holyoke plan of combining study with housekeeping, and Gainesville gave way to the Hornellsville Seminary before Mrs. McNall became proprietor of the Female Seminary in Owego, New York, on the banks of the Susquehanna. Besides teaching in the seminaries of upstate New York, she shared in the conflict of the times by joining the Lockport Ladies Aid, cutting, basting and stitching to equip the 28th Regiment of New York Volunteers— a most appropriate gesture for one who had indited an ode on the freeing of the Russian serfs. By the time the Civil War had emancipated the American "serfs," Mrs. McNall was ready to emancipate herself. In her middle thirties, a slender woman of medium height, with piercing blue-gray eyes, broad forehead and soft brown hair, she determined to pull up her roots and strike out for the national capital. Her profession was still teaching, but her ambitions were wider than the classroom. Those studies in the Constitution and the law of nations at Genesee had somehow planted a desire for deeper, more particular knowledge.

In 1866, with her daughter Lura, she abandoned the climate of Niagara County with its Mountain Ridge and Erie Canal for the more bustling climate of the nation's capital—"this great political centre,—this seething pot," where she could "learn something of the practical workings of the machinery of government, and . . . see what the great men and women of the country felt and thought." Uncertain as yet where her still vague ambitions would carry her, she had arrived at her setting-off place. She had arrived at the podium of the world, where wrongs could be cried out and crusades championed. She had arrived at a place of many doors not all of which were open to her. But she had come—a battering ram from upstate New York—prepared to force an entry with her will.

By 1867, after a brief session assisting at Miss Harrover's Boarding and Day School, Belva McNall had established herself at the Union League Hall on 9th Street, where she opened her own school for young ladies. She would have preferred a broader sphere of activity, such as the consulship at Ghent, but despite her readings in international law and the Consular Manual, her application was ignored. Belva simply decided to study more intensively in international law, Spanish and German. Besides, Washington itself seemed, superficially at least, a seed place of opportunity. Certainly it was a city of many voices, and gradually the Union League Hall became a sounding board that echoed those voices. Belva rented a few other halls, using one for her school, where her daughter soon took charge of the French and Latin classes, and leased the others to temperance, religious and political organizations.

Washington was already a convention center that bristled with the newness of the times. The Universal Franchise Association, organized by James and Julia Holmes, a bloomer girl who had been the first white woman to climb Pike's Peak, was created in 1867 with Belva as vice-president. The Union League Hall was soon given over to peace and suffrage meetings. Everywhere voices were raised in protest or demand. By the end of 1868, George W. Julian had submitted to Congress the first proposal that the right of suffrage be based only upon citizenship without regard to race, color or sex. Belva's voice joined his—joined the voices of the Universal Franchise Association, and, despite the heckling that interrupted the meetings, she held forth vociferously for equal rights as she took the chair. But Belva was no bloomer girl. Arrayed in a brown silk trimmed with white fringe and bugles, her hair ornamented with artificial white flowers, she confined her demands to equal political rather than sartorial rights.

By the time the equal rights meetings were in full swing, Belva had changed her name to the one by which she would be known for the remainder of her long life. Dr. Ezekiel Lockwood, a local dentist who advertised that he would "perform all Dental Operations at reduced prices," and that teeth could be "extracted without pain by the use of nitrous oxide gas," had also served as chaplain of the Second District of Columbia Volunteer Infantry during the war. Spare and tall, spry despite his sixty-five years of age, he had been attracted not only by Belva's charms, but by her advanced views with which he agreed. On March 11, 1868, they were married. The dentist gave up his quarters in the Washington Building to set up his office at the Union League Hall. Belva gave up the name of McNall and took on the name of Lockwood, a name that would soon become memorable.

The demands of domestic life seemed merely to increase Mrs. Lockwood's extra-curricular activities. Even the birth of a second daughter in 1869—even the child's death eighteen months later—served only to extend rather than diminish her multitudinous interests. To the United States Senate she presented in January of 1871 a memorial on "The Right of Women to Vote." The following year she worked as special correspondent for *The Golden Age,* traveling through North Carolina, Georgia and Tennessee, campaigning for Horace Greeley, and sending reports on "Southern Immigration" or the "Wants of the South" to Theodore Tilton's paper. She journeyed to New York to obtain signatures in support of "A bill to do justice to the female employees of the Government," a bill that would give women government workers equal pay with men for equal work. Later on, she would petition Congress "to confer the right of suffrage without regard to sex."

Meanwhile, however, Mrs. Belva Lockwood had entered the preliminaries in what was to become the greatest struggle of her life and the most enduring achievement of her career. For Belva Lockwood, a married woman almost forty years old, had made up her mind to study law not as an amateur but as a professional. A few other women had preceded her in the field, but only a few. In college she had studied "the Constitution of the United States, the law of nations, political economy." Shortly after her graduation from Genesee in 1857, "a law class was opened in the village by a young law professor, and a goodly number of college and seminary students, myself among the number, commenced attendance thereon. . . . this was the beginning of my study of the law." In Washington she had "listened to the debates in Congress and the arguments in the United States Supreme Court, investigated the local government of the District," and become fortified in her conviction that law was "the stepping-stone to greatness." On October 23, 1869, she therefore made formal application for admission to the law class of Columbian College and received the following reply from its President, the Rev. G. W. Samson:

I have consulted the Professors as to the attendance on their classes of others than young men. . . . They think the attendance of ladies would be an injurious diversion of the attention of the students. Both of them, therefor object to receive others than gentlemen into their class-room. My own lectures given on Tuesday and Thursday evening have never been attended by other than gentlemen.

Undeterred by the possibility of proving a distractive influence to gentlemen of the law, Belva applied to Georgetown University Law School, where she was refused with no reasons given except that she was a woman. Not long after, however, an opportunity arose which she was quick to grasp. William B. Wedgwood of New Hampshire agreed to open the National University Law School to women. Of the fifteen women who matriculated during the first quarter, Belva was one. Of the two women who followed the course to completion in May 1873, Belva was also one, although she had been cautioned to use only her initials so that the records would not disclose the presence of a distracting influence. Between the completion of the course, however, and the awarding of degrees, the gap was wide. Although she had been granted a Masters Degree by Syracuse University in 1872, the granting of a Bachelor of Law Degree seemed as remote as ever. Since some gentlemen of National University Law School did not choose to graduate with women, she was refused her diploma. To Ulysses S. Grant, President of the United States, who was also by virtue of his office President of the National University Law School, she addressed a letter on September 3, 1873:

You are, or you are not the President of The National University Law School. If you are its President I wish to say to you that I have been passed through the curriculum of study of that school, and am entitled to, and demand my Diploma. If you are not its President then I ask you to take your name from its papers, and not hold out to the world to be what you are not.

Mrs. Lockwood received no direct reply to her demand. A week or so later, however, she was granted the Degree of LL. B. from National University Law School, the diploma signed by the faculty and President Grant, and in all likelihood handed to her without ceremony by Vice-Chancellor Wedgwood. At the age of forty-three, Mrs. Belva Lockwood had at long last embarked upon her career. She had opened the first of a long series of doors that stretched before her.

On September 24, 1873, Mrs. Belva A. Lockwood was admitted to the Bar of the Supreme Court of the District of Columbia, an event which occasioned one of the justices to remark, "Bring on as many women lawyers as you choose. I do not believe they will be a success." Chief Justice Cartter's reaction was more constructive. His leonine face marked with smallpox, a noticeable impediment in his speech, which, according to the more astute, was purposely designed to give him time to think, he assured the new member that if she came into his court she would be treated "like a man." Under the circumstances, Mrs. Lockwood had no objections whatsoever.

On September 29, 1873, she filed the papers in her first case before the District Bar: a bill of divorce by Mary Ann Folker against her husband, Frederick Folker. Charging the defendant with drunkenness, cruel treatment, desertion and refusal to support, Mrs. Lockwood entered her client's "prayer" for divorce. She would enter many another such plea in the course of her long legal career, pleas for women, pleas for the oppressed. This was merely the first. Yet even in this, Mrs. Lockwood exhibited a legal acumen that justified the Chief Justice's decision to treat her "like a man." Having filed the testimony of witnesses, she won the case for her client, obtaining the decree of divorce and alimony with costs. The defendant, however, refused to pay. As Belva put it, "The judge told me there was no law to make him pay. . . . I told him there was, and I showed him I could issue a *ne exeat*. I issued the writ, and the man was clapped into prison until he agreed to pay the alimony." Mrs. Lockwood had had a long apprenticeship in challenging denials. She would put it to good use in the years that lay ahead.

The cases, and gradually the legends accumulated. So, too, did the skill and the disenchantment. Through them all, Mrs. Lockwood emerged invincible. There were cases in equity and cases in law, divorce cases, contract or account cases, settlements, injunctions, and especially claims, of which Belva was beginning to make a specialty, a circumstance that was shortly to impel her into the most significant fight of her career. Meanwhile she was learning that, despite her admission before the District Bar, the law was still an unequal contest. She might draft and secure passage through Congress of the Soldiers and Sailors Bonus Bill. She might be admitted to the United States Court of Western Texas. She might save herself by her wit when a woman client on the witness stand described in detail how she had committed the crime of shooting a constable for which she stood accused. Belva, as defending attorney, arose before the court and declared, "Gentle-

BELVA LOCKWOOD, FIRST AMERICAN WOMAN LAWYER ADMITTED TO PLEAD BEFORE THE UNITED STATES SUPREME COURT, AND SAMUEL R. LOWERY, FIRST SOUTHERN NEGRO ADMITTED

—Collection of Mrs. Dorothy Thomas, New York City

REBECCA W. LUKENS
—Courtesy Mr. Stewart Huston, Coatesville, Pennsylvania

men of the jury, the laws must be enforced. My client has committed the double offense of resisting an officer of the law and shooting a man. The District is under the common law. That law says a woman must obey her husband. Her husband told her to load a gun and shoot the first officer that tried to force his way into the house. She obeyed him. Gentlemen, I claim that that husband loaded the gun and shot the officer, . . . I claim you are not trying the right prisoner. You would not have a woman resist her husband?" The jury brought in the verdict of "Not guilty." Yet, despite such successes, despite even the appellation of "Judge" Lockwood with which male reporters dubbed her, Belva sensed keenly the chilliness and uncongeniality that characterized the unequal practice of men and women lawyers. Assisted by her daughter Lura and by her husband, who had abandoned dentistry to become a notary and claim agent, she gradually built up both a practice and a credo. The judiciary wrongly lent itself to party politics. Many a legal wrong cried out to be righted. She saw "colored men and women . . . who had lain in jail for years because they had no money." The criminal code, the police courts, the prisons—all needed reforming. Especially the inequality of the contest must be righted when men and women lawyers pleaded before the courts. In one case in particular, that inequality led Belva into a five-year fight that culminated with her admission as the first woman attorney before the Bar of the Supreme Court of the United States.

The case was a simple government claims case—one of many that were now "being sent to her from various parts of the country"—the case of Charlotte von Cort against the government for use of and infringement of a patent for a torpedo boat invented by her husband and used by the government. The case had been carried before a federal court—the United States Court of Claims —and, as Mrs. von Cort's attorney, Belva Lockwood applied for admission to that Court. Her application was denied.

At precisely twelve o'clock the five justices of that dignified court marched in, made their solemn bows, and sat down. . . . after the formal opening of the court by the clerk, and the reading of the minutes . . . my gracious attorney moved my admission. There was a painful pause. Every eye in the court-room was fixed first upon me, and then upon the court; when Justice Drake, in measured words, announced, *"Mistress Lockwood, you are a woman,"* . . . I at once pleaded guilty to the charge. . . . Then the chief justice announced, "This cause will be continued for one week." . . .

On the following week, . . . I again marched into the court-room, . . . When the case of Lockwood was reached, and I again stood up before that august body, the solemn tones of the chief justice announced, "Mistress Lockwood, you are a *married woman!"* . . .

Mrs. Lockwood was a woman, and a married woman. For those reasons she could not defend any client whose case was carried into a federal court. As a woman she could not appear with her men colleagues before the Supreme Court of the United States or the United States Court of Claims. Mrs. Lockwood, so practiced in refusing to accept denials, refused once again, and entered upon the most important struggle of her life—a struggle that would open to her and to all the women lawyers who followed after her the doors of the federal courts of the United States.

In the December 1873 term of the Court of Claims, the case of Lockwood versus the United States was brought to trial. The motion was simple. "A married woman, domiciled in the District of Columbia, and admitted to practice as an attorney in the highest court of the District, applies for admission to the bar of this court," an application which she considered no favor, but the recognition of a legal right. The opinion of the Court was equally simple. There was no statutory law and no precedent for the plea. A married woman attorney might conceivably misapply the funds of a client, and under the common law her husband might be sued for the wrong which she had committed as an attorney. Justice Charles C. Nott, Lincoln's appointee to the Court of Claims, a man who abhorred technicalities and who doubted the merits of permitting women to "enter the fierce battle of modern competition," delivered the opinion of the Court. "Under the Constitution and laws of the United States a court is without power to grant such an application, . . . a woman is without legal capacity to take the office of attorney." If the Court erred, he conceded, the Supreme Court might review the error. In "breathless suspense like a man about to be convicted of murder," Belva Lockwood had heard Judge Nott's denial of her application. She was "crestfallen but not crushed." Nor did she mean "to be defeated." She would carry her case before the Supreme Court, applying for admission to the highest tribunal of the land, and to the Congress of the United States if necessary.

"To the Honorable the Senate and House of Representatives in Congress assembled," Mrs. Belva A. Lockwood, "Attorney at Law of Washington D.C. . . . duly licensed to practice before the bar of the Supreme Court of the District of Columbia," presented her petition that those "Honorable Bodies" "speedily pass a Declaratory Act, or Joint Resolution to the effect:—That, no *woman otherwise qualified,* shall be debarred from practice before any United States Court on account of sex." With the petition she submitted a brief, announcing that she had been debarred from the Court of Claims because she was a married woman, referring to such precedents as Ann, Countess of Pembroke, and Queen Victoria, and asserting that "the right to practice law" was "one of the privileges of citizenship." On May 25, 1874, the petition, with the brief, was referred to the Senate Committee on the Judiciary.

The arduous work, the preparations, the struggles continued until, at the October 1876 term of the Supreme Court of the United States, Mrs. Lockwood applied for admission to that Court. The "nine gowned judges looked at her in amazement and dismay." Morrison I. Waite, who had been appointed Chief Justice succeeding Salmon P. Chase in 1874, announced the decision. "By the uniform practice of the Court from its organization to the present time, . . . none but men are admitted to practice before it as attorneys and counselors. This is in accordance with immemorial usage in England, and the law and practice in all the States, until within a recent period; and the Court does not feel called upon to make a change until such a change is required by statute." Congressional legislation would be necessary before Mrs. Lockwood could be admitted to practice before the Supreme Court.

Belva's reaction was characteristic. She was fully capable of coping with the sagacity of the "nine wise men on the bench." In an address before the Washington Convention of women suffragists she reviewed the decision of the Court. "To arrive at the same conclusion with these judges," she announced, "it is not necessary to understand constitutional law, nor the history of English jurisprudence, nor the inductive or deductive modes of reasoning, as no such profound learning or processes of thought were involved in that decision, which was simply . . . 'There is no precedent for admitting a woman to practice in the Supreme Court of the United States.' " Mrs. Lockwood considered that it was "the glory of each generation to make its own precedents." There had been no precedents for Eve in the Garden of Eden. Even Blackstone, of whose works she was forced to infer that the judges were ignorant, had, none the less, given several precedents for women in the English courts. In her velvet dress and train, her eyes blazing with indignation, she marched up and down the platform, a Portia of the Venetian bar transposed to Washington, rounding out "her glowing periods."

Words, however effective, were still words. Action, in the form of a bill lobbied through Congress, would be necessary before Mrs. Lockwood or any woman could be admitted to practice law before the Supreme Court of the United States. Without hesitation, therefore, she drafted a bill "that any woman who shall have been a member of the bar of the highest court of any State or Territory or of the supreme court of the District of Columbia for the space of three years, and shall have maintained a good standing before such court, and who shall be a person of good moral character, shall, on motion and the production of such record, be admitted to practice before the Supreme Court of the United States." The bill became known as H. R. No. 1077. Its passage was to involve months of labor, speeches, resolutions, public meetings, newspaper articles, and canvasses of Congress. Mrs. Lockwood had determined to continue to bring the bill up every year as long as she lived, until it became the law of the land.

The history of H. R. 1077 was Mrs. Lockwood's history, too. Neither the death of her husband in April 1877, nor her fight for entrance into the Maryland courts before a judge who proclaimed that "in the statutes of the States the pronouns were masculine," deflected Belva Lockwood from her prime purpose. In November 1877 her bill was introduced into the House of Representatives. Entitled "a bill to relieve the legal disabilities of women," it was read twice and referred to the Committee on the Judiciary. In February of the following year, Representative Ben Butler—known to some as the "Beast of New Orleans" but to others as an advocate of the rights of labor and of women—reported the bill favorably and asked that it "be put upon its passage." After three readings, the bill was passed in the House with 169 yeas, 87 nays, and 36 not voting. Its title amended, so that the bill would be construed to remove "certain" but not "all" of the legal disabilities of women, House Bill 1077 was again referred to the Committee on the Judiciary, which, in March, returned an adverse report to the Senate. Under the law, the Supreme Court of the United States was authorized to make its own rules regulating the admission of persons to practice. Since no legal obstacle actually prohibited the admission of women to practice in that Court, it was up to the discretion of the Court itself to admit them or not. Women suffered no legal disabilities. Hence no legislation to remove such disabilities was required. The Committee recommended the indefinite postponement of the bill. At the insistence of one who was to emerge as one of Mrs. Lockwood's most forceful champions, however, the bill was placed—along with the adverse report—on the calendar.

Senator Aaron A. Sargent of California, aggressive, untiring, a masterful machine politician, had decided that Mrs. Belva A. Lockwood was within her legal rights. It was he who asked that the bill be placed upon the calendar, and it was he who, in April 1878, presented her petition, signed by 155 lawyers of the District of Columbia, to the Senate. Listening from the gallery, her hair graying, a bit of lace about her neck, Mrs. Lockwood heard Senator Sargent in her defense—heard him fire the cannon that she herself had molded. "Where," he asked in his rapid, persuasive speech, "is the propriety in opening our colleges, our higher institutions of learning, or any institutions of learning to women, and then when they have acquired in the race with men the cultivation for higher employments to shut them out? . . . Some excellent lady lawyers in the United States are now practicing at the bar, . . . and when they have conducted their cases . . . in any court below, why should the United States courts to which an appeal may be taken and where their adversary of the male sex may follow the case up, why should they be debarred from appearing before those tribunals?" As for the lack of English precedent referred to by the Chief Justice, "Elizabeth herself sat in *aula regina* and administered the law." "I glory," he concluded, "in the fact that the House of Representatives passed this bill." If the laws now existing were properly construed, women would be admitted to the courts of the United States.

"There is no reason because a citizen of the United States is a woman that she should be deprived of her rights as a citizen, and these are rights of a citizen. She has the same right to life, liberty, and the pursuit of happiness and employment, commensurate with her capacities, as a man has; and, as to the question of capacity, the history of the world shows, from Queen Elizabeth . . . to . . . Mrs. Stowe, that capacity is not a question of sex." As a result of Senator Sargent's gallant oratory, Bill H. R. 1077, now amended to provide that "no person shall be excluded from practicing as an attorney and counselor at law from any court of the United States on account of sex," was referred back to the Committee on the Judiciary.

The struggle was not yet over. On May 20, 1878, the second adverse report was delivered. It echoed the first. Since there was no law prohibiting a court from admitting a woman to practice law, there was no necessity for the bill. Hence, the committee again recommended indefinite postponement. And yet again Senator Sargent asked that the bill be placed upon the calendar. His attempt to ascertain, later in the month, "whether the bill has any more friends" than the one he knew it had, was unsuccessful, for the Senate denied the motion to consider. It was not until February of 1879 that Bill H. R. 1077 was at last brought to debate on the floor of the Senate of the United States. As Senator Sargent put it, "It is a bill that has been rather a foot-ball during this whole Congress. It is very important to the class named in it, and we desire that there shall be a vote of the Senate upon it." After an interruption from Senator Cockrell, who confused the bill with one about the Birdsell clover patent, Mr. Sargent was able to present once again a petition requesting its passage. And once again, from the gallery, Mrs. Lockwood listened to his impassioned defense. The issue, he declared, was "merely a measure of justice, . . . It is generally recognized that women are taking to themselves a wider sphere of action and filling it well. . . . No man has a right to put a limit to the exertions or the sphere of woman. . . . In this land man has ceased to dominate over his fellow—let him cease to dominate over his sister; . . . Believing that the effect of the defeat of bills like this would be to prevent women from entering an honorable profession in which they are qualified to be useful to society . . . I am in favor of its passage, and I trust the Senate will give us a vote upon it to-day, and pass this bill as it came from the House."

Senator George F. Hoar of Massachusetts, an advocate of woman's rights, rose before the Senate, his bland blue eyes sparkling behind his spectacles, a quizzical expression on his round, cherubic face. The bill, he announced, was not a bill merely to admit women to the privilege of engaging in a particular profession; it was a bill to secure to the citizen of the United States the right to select his counsel. That was all. "The greatest master of human manners," he concluded, "who read the human heart and who understood better than any man who ever lived the varieties of human character, when he desired to solve the knot which had puzzled the lawyers and doctors placed a woman upon the judgment-seat; and yet under the present existing law if Portia herself were alive, she could not defend the opinion she had given before the Supreme Court of the United States." The forty-eight-year-old Portia in the Senate gallery had won at last. She had succeeded in "the strongest lobbying" she had ever performed. "Nothing was too daring for me to attempt. I addressed Senators as though they were old familiar friends, and with an earnestness that carried with it conviction. Before the shadows of night had gathered, the victory had been won." On February 7, 1879, more than five years after the case of Lockwood versus the United States had been lost, the bill was passed in the Senate with 39 yeas, 20 nays, and 17 absent. To the Senators who had advocated her bill, Belva sent bouquets of flowers, with grander floral offerings for those who had more grandly championed it. In the evening she paid a visit to the wife of President Hayes, who complimented her upon her achievement —a fitting exchange between the first lady of the land and the first woman of the federal courts. On February 12, 1879, the bill was signed by the Vice-President and three days later by the President of the United States. Bill H. R. No. 1077 had become an Act. Mrs. Lockwood's five-year struggle was over.

On March 3, 1879, Belva donned her black velvet dress with satin vest and cloth coat, a white ruffle round her neck, picked up her black kid gloves, pinned a bouquet on her lapel, and sallied forth to the Supreme Court of the United States. Between Judge Samuel Shellabarger and the Hon. Jeremiah Wilson she sat, waiting to be presented under the new law. At length, by motion of the Honorable Albert Gallatin Riddle, Mrs. Lockwood was admitted to the Bar of the United States Supreme Court, Chief Justice Morrison I. Waite administering the oath. Surely, as she took that oath, a slender woman of forty-eight in a black velvet dress, she sensed not only the personal triumph that crowned her long struggle, but the far-reaching implications of that triumph for all women throughout the land. Three days later when, on motion of the Honorable Thomas J. Durant, she was admitted to the United States Court of Claims, that triumph was complete. Despite Justice Nott's decision, a woman was no longer "without legal capacity to take the office of attorney."

The reaction of the newspapers to the event was mixed. John W. Forney's *Progress* concluded that, despite the occurrence, "the country was still safe and the home was not in peril," while the *Public Ledger* mused about "the status of women citizens" under the headline, "Enter Portia." She had indeed entered. And what was more, she had opened the door through which would enter the hosts of women who followed after her, to whom this legal right of citizenship could never more be denied. She had fought and she had won. And the victory was not for her alone, for it had brought into active life a freedom of opportunity that had before her been a phrase.

A few days after the President had signed the "Lockwood" Bill, Belva purchased the twenty-room house at 619 F Street, N.W., which was to serve as her home and office and as the center of her multitudinous activities for more than thirty years. On its ground floor, Belva A. Lockwood, Attorney and Solicitor, practicing in the Court of Claims and the United States Supreme Court, opened her office. And thither her clients came, bringing their problems to the sharp-eyed woman behind the desk on F Street.

She welcomed any case, from land and patent to customs matters, from divorce to probate, "from a common assault to a murder." She rebelled against the English common law under which the District lived, a law that could compel a man to support his illegitimate child but could not compel him to support his wife and his legitimate children, a law that held a wife to be "her husband's slave." With sorrow she informed a weeping widow with seven infant children, whose husband had been killed by the railroad cars, that she could not recover for the loss of that husband. She settled estates, sometimes after years in the courts, during which the heirs received no benefit from them. She determined, therefore, to work for the reform of probate law and the recognition of the rights of widows and orphans. Marriage, she concluded, should be a civil contract in which property rights were equal.

Although all cases were grist to her mill, Mrs. Lockwood made a specialty of back pay claims and pension cases, bringing to light the "oppressions, inconsistencies and often erroneous rulings of pension officials, as well as defects in law." Her speech animated, her bright intelligent features glowing, she worked often from early morning until ten or eleven at night, preparing her briefs. Assisted sometimes by Mrs. Lavinia Dundore and by Mrs. Marilla Ricker of New Hampshire who was to become known as "the prisoners' friend" and also as one who "fears neither God, man nor the devil, because she does not believe particularly in any of them," Mrs. Belva Lockwood soon became one of "the three graces" of Washington's legal mythology, a "grace" whose dicta were recorded by Miss Lillie Sadler, the "young woman typewriter" in her office. The acumen of those dicta gradually increased, until Belva could feel the very pulse of the law courts. "In a court case," she decided, "it is never wise to get a public opinion in advance." Her oratorical ability and talent for elaboration she attributed to the fact that "she could at the moment tell all she knew." She was developing a reputation as a lawyer who was "on friendly terms with all political parties, . . . esteemed throughout the Nation for her sterling integrity and fine abilities."

Before the Court of Claims especially, Mrs. Lockwood demonstrated those abilities. Seated on "Challenge No. 2," an English tricycle which she introduced to the amazed capital, along with her own dashboard that kept her skirts down when the wind blew, revealing her red stockings, she pedaled away from F Street, where business houses and professional offices vied with old residences for ascendancy, threading along, her head erect, her feet working energetically. She rode wherever her business called, to the Departments, the Capitol or the Courts, setting her own fashions, a determined whirl with a bundle of briefs who soon became a familiar sight on Pennsylvania Avenue.

Especially she was a familiar sight at the United States Court of Claims, the only court in which a citizen of the country could prosecute his claim against the government. On the lower floor of the Freedman's Bank Building on Pennsylvania Avenue, opposite the Treasury Building, Belva walked, presenting her evidence in the form of public documents and depositions, filing petitions and briefs, submitting her questions to the five justices of the court, of whom her onetime opponent, Judge Nott, was one. While the Attorney-General reviewed the case for the government—the claims for salvage or bounty or royalties or Southern war claims—Belva Lockwood presented her case for the citizen toward whom the government of the United States had duties as well as rights.

Somehow, during her long day, she found time, too, to appear before Congressional committees to urge reforms in legislation, or to work for the appointment of a matron in the District jail and police stations or to speak in Buffalo—"The Portia of the Republic"—on "Women and the Law." She had found the time and the will in 1880 to move the admission of the Negro, Samuel R. Lowery, to the United States Supreme Court. Now, in 1884, she found time to write a letter to a magazine known as the *Woman's Herald of Industry*—a letter that would start her off on the most publicized event of her career. The first woman admitted to the Federal Courts of the country was about to become the first formal woman candidate actually to run for the Presidency of the United States.

Although the event was colorful and highly publicized, it was comparatively unimportant. Yet Mrs. Lockwood believed that she was cutting the opening wedge in the battle for the enfranchisement of women. For that reason she allied herself with a cause that was doomed to failure and to a campaign that lent itself to mockery and ridicule.

The *Woman's Herald of Industry* was the organ of the Woman's Republic, founded in California by Mrs. Marietta L.B. Stow, a female "Electrician" who claimed to cure the lame, the halt and the blind by the use of electricity. Mrs. Stow had also invented the "Tripple S. Costume" consisting of trousers and kilt skirt, had founded a new dietetic order known as "Cold Food," and had been reduced "to a state of beggary" because of "the innumerable abominations practiced by the Probate Court." After a "Trinity of Calamities," including accidental poisoning by a male practitioner and imprisonment for the "crime" of owning a home in San Francisco, she had founded the Woman's Republic to create "an independent center of thought and action for women."

To its organ, *Woman's Herald of Industry,* Belva Lockwood, on August 10, 1884, addressed a letter on "Women Rulers." She had been impelled to write the letter after a visit to the Chicago Republican Convention that had nominated Blaine for the Presidency. Her plea to the resolutions committee to adopt a plank that would give some recognition to women had been futile. Yet, such renowned suffragists as Elizabeth Cady Stanton and Susan B. Anthony were urging the women of the country to support Blaine and the republican party. Why not, instead, urge them to support women rulers? "Why not," she asked, "nominate women for important places? Is not Victoria Empress of India? . . . *If,*" she pursued, *"women in the States are not permitted to vote, there is no law against their being voted for, . . .* We shall never have rights until we take them, nor respect until we command it. Reforms are slow, but they never go backwards."

To Mrs. Marietta L.B. Stow, who had herself run as "Independent Candidate" for the Governorship of California, the answer was obvious. "Bravo! . . . Behold our Deborah!" At a meeting of the Equal Rights Party of the Pacific Slope in San Francisco, "our Deborah" was in short order nominated for President of the United States. She would, according to her constituents, "bring no blush or barnacles of youthful, or *mature,* 'wild oats sowing' into the White House—to smirch the Nation's escutcheon. . . . She sits at the gate of the temple and the Nation's heart beats in unison with the Equal-Rights party." To the prospective candidate Mrs. Stow dispatched the news of the nomination, adding, "We await your letter of acceptance with breathless interest."

Mrs. Lockwood's answer was, perhaps, the most effective weapon in the campaign, for it not only accepted the nomination, but formulated her platform and the platform of her party. She would "seek to insure a fair distribution of the public offices to women as well as to men." She would "protect and foster American industries." She would work for "the soldier's widow" and orphan. She would oppose "wholesale monopoly of the judiciary of the country by the male voters," and would appoint a competent woman to any vacancy that might occur on the United States Supreme Bench.

She would strive for temperance, a uniform system of laws for all the States, the extension of commerce with foreign countries, and the citizenship of Indians. With her party's "unanimous and cordial support," she believed—or she said she believed—that "we shall not only be able to carry the election, but to guide the Ship of State safely into port."

As the *Woman's Herald of Industry* put it, Mrs. Lockwood had "climbed Capitol Hill . . . and faced the bearded lions in their marble stronghold." She faced also the mockery of reporters, the amusement of interviewers, and the general humors of a campaign that tickled the ribs of a nation trying to decide between James G. Blaine and Grover Cleveland. Not all the papers believed, with *National Equal Rights,* that the candidate was "our white plumed Lady" and "the greatest living woman." Even the suffragists—Mrs. Stanton, Miss Anthony, and Lillie Devereux Blake—were opposed, announcing that they had not made the nomination and that therefore it was not "regular." According to *The New Northwest,* Belva Lockwood's candidacy was "one of the sad features of the Presidential campaign." She was obtaining "a great amount of notice and notoriety," increasing her law practice through the advertising which the press was giving her, but she was bringing upon woman suffrage "an abundance of odium and contempt at a time when it was commanding respect and enlisting help. The damage done by her and a little band of eccentric zealots in San Francisco cannot be estimated." Belva, of course, disagreed, for she sincerely believed that "the establishment of the principles that a woman may be nominated and elected President of the United States" was calculated "to do a vast amount of good." If her party could get one elector on the electoral college, the campaign would become "the entering wedge—the first practical movement in the history of Woman Suffrage."

Many of the women of Washington concurred. They determined on a grand ratification meeting, but since no Washingtonian had a vote, an electoral ticket was prepared for Maryland, where Mrs. Amanda Best, who owned a country home in Prince Georges County, offered to act as hostess. Under the spreading apple trees that surrounded the rambling old farmhouse, the militant ladies held their reception, long tables of lemonade and sandwiches, pies and cakes vying with the oratory of the candidate, who counseled the women to rise up, while a large white streamer waved the stars and stripes along with Belva's portrait in the breeze. "Who," she demanded, "are the people of these United States? . . . Are women persons? Are they citizens? May they be freeholders, and can they contract, sue and be sued? . . . The full fledged American woman stands before you to-day, ready for the workshop, ready for the pulpit, the forum or the political arena, demanding equal political rights under the Constitution and equal rights before the law."

With engagements to speak on "The Political Situation" in New York, Philadelphia, Chicago, Cincinnati and Cleveland, the "Plumed Lady" carried on her campaign to the intense enjoyment of the country. The Belva Lockwood Club of Rahway, New Jersey —an all-male organization—joined the bandwagon by donning uniforms that included poke bonnets, Mother Hubbard dresses, and striped stockings. In full array, the members sported Japanese parasols and flourished silk banners embroidered with such appropriate mottoes as "Belva and Reform" and "No Night-keys." While the Mother Hubbard Clubs sang songs and made speeches, and the Broom Brigades paraded, "causing great merriment along the line," Belva campaigned against the background of masquerades and burlesques. Lecturing in Michigan on "Women and Money," she announced that her "campaign fund" consisted of her "lecture receipts." The lectures mounted up. From Cleveland's Opera House to New York's Academy of Music she carried her message, while banners billowed with the portrait of Belva Lockwood: Our Next President. In her black velvet gown, roses in her corsage, her hair in the Japanese fashion, the candidate stepped briskly onto the stage to decry the wrongs of womankind and to proclaim that "In this free Republic, contrary to the Bill of Rights, we are governed without our own consent."

With the organ of the Equal Rights Party turned into her campaign sheet, pictures of the candidate struck off to "have a wholesome effect upon the male voters," and a Lockwood button ready for those who would wear it, the campaign of the first formal woman nominee for president drew to a close. From an all-male America at the ballot box, Mrs. Lockwood, and her running-mate, Mrs. Stow, polled 4,149 votes plus the entire electoral vote of Indiana, a State which, Belva claimed in a petition to Congress, had first cast its vote for Cleveland but had changed its mind in favor of herself. The nation, whose heart had, after all, not beaten "in unison with the Equal-Rights party," elected Grover Cleveland to the White House and, after a brief but colorful episode in its political history, returned to its usual routine. A few were unkind enough to suggest that Mrs. Lockwood had simply "cleared $1,500 by her lectures and had her business gratuitously advertised to the value of $2,000." Others, including Belva herself, were more idealistic. The white plumed lady had run "to make America conscious of women's right to political equality." And the Equal Rights Party had elected—if not a president—at least a precedent.

In 1888, Mrs. Lockwood, who had apparently developed a taste for electioneering, acted once again upon the precedent she had established. Nominated by the Equal Rights Party meeting in Iowa, she campaigned once more, her running-mate the pacifist, Alfred H. Love, "one of the darkest horses" ever named for the Vice-Presidency. The combination of Lockwood and Love was one that no newspaper could resist. As *The World* put it, "Though Love Deserts the Ticket, Cupid Will Lend His Aid." Despite the aid lent by Cupid, and even by that redoubtable woman reporter, Nellie Bly, who interviewed Mrs. Lockwood for her paper, the White House was not "swept and garnished for a woman's entrée in '88," but rather for Benjamin Harrison's. Although Mrs. Lockwood had accomplished little by her unprecedented forays into public life, she had savored the piquancies of that life. In the three decades that remained to her she would never lose her taste for meetings and conventions, for lecture halls and banquets. The first lady of the Washington law courts was also to become living proof of her own belief that "women in politics have come to stay."

The Belva Lockwood of public life flourished a banner inscribed on one side with the words "Women's Rights" and on the other with the word "Peace." She flourished other banners, too—the banners of temperance and labor reform—but woman suffrage and arbitration were her special causes, the double-faced standard she carried high throughout her life. She had been a signer of the *Declaration of Rights of the Women of the United States* prepared for Independence Day of the Centennial year 1876. She would continue to sign petitions, to serve on committees, to live and to work for equal rights as long as she could hold a pen or speak upon a podium. The house on F Street became a meeting place for those who would advance the cause of women, and Mrs. Lockwood became a patron of that cause. She was—despite her work in the courts—always available. At suffrage bazaars, on the lecture platform, at conventions and banquets, Belva was present, in her black satin or blue silk—a compact intensity of dedication to a cause. In crowded tents and in soldiers' homes, from covered band stands or grand opera houses, her voice, tersely chopping off her phrases, was heard throughout the land. And when her voice was silent, her pen moved swiftly, drafting bills to Congress and memorials to the Senate, endorsing the property rights of married women, pleading for suffrage. She was a joiner of joiners—committeewoman, chairman, president of any and all associations that carried her standard, from the District Federation of Women's Clubs to the Woman's National Press Association, from the Woman's Federal Equality Suffrage Association to the District of Columbia Woman Suffrage Association. By 1900 she could say, "I have attended every convention . . . in Washington for the last thirty-two years."

And outside of Washington, too, she was a familiar figure. When the Congress of Charities and Correction was held at Geneva, Mrs. Lockwood was appointed delegate by the government, and when the American Woman's Republic was organized in Missouri by the publisher and promoter, E.G. Lewis, she became its attorney general and dean of ambassadors at a salary of $200 a month. She was an ambassador *par excellence.* Neither blizzards nor trans-Atlantic journeys deterred her. From the Chicago Exposition to the Atlanta Exposition, from the Triennial Council of Women to the Woman's Convention in Budapest, she wandered—a determined envoy with banner emblazoned. In 1913, when she was eighty-two years old, she could report that she had attended meetings of the National Council of Women, the Federation of Women's Clubs, the International Law Congress, and all the woman suffrage meetings including pageant, inauguration and march to the Capitol! The busiest woman in a city that bristled with busy women, Belva Lockwood was indefatigable in the championship of her cause.

Especially she was indefatigable in the cause of international arbitration. Member of the Universal Peace Union, president of the National Arbitration Society, and secretary of the American

Branch of the International Peace Bureau, Belva Lockwood attended nearly every international peace congress from the first, held in 1889 during the Paris Exposition, to her last held in 1911 at Rome. At London's Westminster Hall, at the Villa Reale in Milan, at Antwerp and Berne, at Budapest and The Hague, she appeared as delegate, upholding the view that "No one can be called a Christian who gives money for the building of war ships or for carrying on a conflict." Whether the delegates discussed the massacres in Turkey or the Armenian question, the woman lawyer from the United States was present to add her words to the pleas for peace, even speaking on board ship to promote the cause of international arbitration. And in that crusade also her pen was busy, writing for *The Peacemaker,* compiling a "List of Treaties and Arbitrations Concluded between the United States and Foreign Powers," preparing an "American View" of *Peace and the Outlook* after the Spanish-American War. For the American Branch of the Peace Bureau, Belva opened a large room on the main floor of 619 F Street, replete with a peace flag, a small library, and an attendant in waiting. Since a strike was nothing but a small war, she directed her talents toward helping to settle the shirtwaist strike in Philadelphia. Since the Nobel Prize was a prize for peace, she joined its nominating committee. For her work and her words, many a toastmaster called cheers for Belva Lockwood, many an audience rose to its feet to give an ovation to the woman whose day had no end. In 1912, when Washington was full of "Conventions and Moving Picture shows" and Ringling's circus was preparing an airplane for exhibition, when Belva Lockwood, still enthusiastic, still vigorously aggressive, had become a gray-haired woman of eighty-two, this eloquent advocate of many causes could write, "It is hard for me to leave at this time of year . . . . Congress meets to-morrow."

Neither Congress, nor the law courts, nor the committee rooms of the national capital would have been quite the same devoid of her familiar figure. For, with all her public activities, her professional career had kept pace. In 1887, she had joined with her daughter, now Lura Ormes, to form the firm of Belva A. Lockwood & Company, Attorneys at Law, a firm that would continue to flourish until Lura's untimely death in 1894. With the aid of her "two young women clerks," Lura and Clara B. Harrison, she had kept up her law business even during her lecture seasons, "gathering up and sending home as many claims against the Government" as she could find. "In this day and age of the World," she held,

when so many avenues of trade, and so many professions are opening to women, the ground principles of the laws of each State . . . should be taught to the girls of the public schools. Women have always been the chief sufferers of bad legislation, and if being the weaker physically it is harder for them to acquire a fortune, the more need of the legal knowledge of how to keep it. There is plenty of room to-day for women who are willing to apply themselves in the law.

It was an old maxim in England that every gentleman's son should know the law. We ought to reverse that in our Country and expect every lady's daughter to be versed in the law, that she may be early schooled to a necessary protection of herself and children.

At the age of fifty-nine, this particular "lady's daughter" could boast, "For 16 consecutive years I have practiced law and 13 of them have been passed in court every day, in which I have defended several hundreds of criminals." The cases had mounted up, and would continue to mount up after Lura's death, when Belva Lockwood & Company reverted to Belva A. Lockwood, Lawyer—the Winton case, cases before the Government Departments and Congressional committees, the Myra Gaines Will case, especially the pension and claims cases against the government. By 1890, Belva had "collected about 1000 pension and other claims" and it was this specialty that was to lead her to the most celebrated suit of her life and the greatest legal triumph of her career.

Early in her practice before the United States Court of Claims, Mrs. Lockwood had met the North Carolina Cherokee Indian, Jim Taylor, for whom she had conducted several cases and through whom the members of his tribe had been persuaded to entrust her with their long-standing claim against the government. The claim had actually arisen in 1835 with the Treaty of New Echota, a treaty that had called for the removal of the Cherokee Indians from North Carolina and the purchase of their land by the government, a treaty that had been followed by innumerable disputes and differences between the United States and the Cherokees. In 1891 a new treaty had been signed, involving the sale and purchase of over eight million acres of land known as the Cherokee Outlet. The government made no objection to the payment of the amount originally agreed upon. The quarrel arose over the interest on the as yet unpaid principal which, in the course of so many decades, amounted to far more than the capital. Moreover, the Cherokees maintained that "to make them pay for their removal from homes which they did not wish to leave to a country to which they did not wish to go was a monstrous abuse of the obscure provisions of a treaty which they had not read, which they had not signed, and to which they had not in fact been parties." It was Belva A. Lockwood, first woman attorney admitted to the Court of Claims, who pleaded the case of the Eastern and Emigrant Cherokee Indians before that very judge who had first denied her entrance to that court—Judge Charles C. Nott, now Chief Justice of the United States Court of Claims. On neither of the principals was the irony lost.

For Belva Lockwood, the work and the details involved in the case were all but incalculable. In the interest of her Cherokee clients she traveled to Muskogee in Indian Territory, trying some seventeen land cases. She had between three and four thousand families or from twelve to fifteen thousand persons on the Cherokee Roll to defend, all of whom looked to her for justice. She must, above all, review the numerous treaties and statutes that governed the long history of the Cherokees, filing briefs and motions and petitions to uphold the claim of her Indian clients.

On March 20, 1905, the case of the Eastern and Emigrant Cherokees against the United States was decided before the Court of Claims. With zealous passion Belva Lockwood arose to argue the cause of her clients, presenting their rights to a claim so long overdue, Assistant Attorney General Louis A. Pradt elaborating the case for the government. After her impassioned defense, Chief Justice Nott, delivering the opinion of the court, was constrained to agree that "The Cherokee Nation has parted with the land, has lost the time within which it might have appealed to the courts, . . . and the United States are placed in the position of having broken and evaded the letter and spirit of their agreement." None the less, although he decreed that the Cherokees recover certain amounts due in the account rendered by the government, he could not bring himself to allow the full interest on those amounts. The case was therefore promptly appealed to the Supreme Court of the United States.

There, on April 30, 1906, the case was adjudged. Pleading once again for the Eastern and Emigrant Cherokees, Belva Lockwood rose up before the court to which she had been admitted a generation before. The seventy-five-year-old gray-haired woman attorney faced the nine blackrobed justices on the bench. She who had fought for her own right to be heard now fought for the rights of the claimants she represented. In those august chambers a circle was completed. As she spoke, with more zeal than ever before, she rose to inspired heights. The justices themselves agreed that she had made "the most eloquent argument of any of the attorneys before the Court." Questions and answers followed swiftly. Why, the court demanded, did she claim interest for her clients. The answer was terse and to the point. "Because it was an interest bearing fund." The court had heard a woman's impassioned defense of the Indian and his rights. The court now expressed itself, Chief Justice Fuller delivering the opinion. "We agree," he declared, "that the United States were liable, . . . the moneys awarded should be paid directly to the equitable owners." Mrs. Lockwood had won her case—had won $5,000,000 for her clients, of which about $4,000,000 was interest—but her triumph was greater than that. She had disproved eloquently and irrefutably Justice Nott's decision of nearly thirty-three years before that "a woman is without legal capacity to take the office of attorney." Justice Nott himself was aware of her triumph. Meeting Mrs. Lockwood on the day of the final decree on the steps to the court room, he shook her hand warmly, congratulating her upon her success. In *The Woman's Tribune* Belva Lockwood had read the story of "A Woman Lawyer's Triumph"—the story of one who had "won the most important case, as far as amount of money is involved which has ever been brought before the United States Court of Claims, . . . Her share of the fees will probably be $50,000, so she will be regarded as a 'success' and as vindicating the power of woman to take a high place in the legal profession."

That high place she continued to take. Battling, not always with success, to plead before the New York and Virginia Bars, she had persisted with her memorials to Congress, urging reforms in legislation, working for the establishment of a House of Detention for women, arguing in the Marble Room before the Senate Committee on woman suffrage. And still the clients came and the cases accumulated—the settlement of a car strike, a Choctaw case, a lottery case, an insanity case, the Sevier estate case. By 1912, when she was eighty-one, she could write, "I have 3 heavy law cases on hand, one in Court of Claims . . . and in District Supreme Court . . . and am . . . tried with details not settled." Yet even for the apparently untiring woman attorney, time must make a stop.

On her eighty-sixth birthday she announced to her interviewers that, although she had retired from active practice of the law, she was still active in public matters. In token of the fullness of her life she had been crowned with many laurels. She had received the honorary degree of Doctor of Laws from Syracuse University; she had sat for her portrait. In the Congressional Union demonstration of 1914, she stood at the head of the Capitol steps and joined the leaders of a deputation that presented resolutions to Congress. Yet the honors had not always proved substantial. In the same eventful year of 1914, Mrs. Lockwood, despite the high retainer she was reported to have earned for her part in the Cherokee case, suffered financial reverses, possibly through her vulnerability to an "unscrupulous admirer." Later she was dispossessed from the home where she had lived and worked for thirty-five years. Moving to smaller quarters on Indiana Avenue, she continued, in the short time allotted to her, to work for woman suffrage and for peace, and at the end for the re-election of Woodrow Wilson.

Washington, with its "Conventions and Moving Picture shows," was a different city from the one that Belva McNall had first seen at the close of the Civil War. And now, as the country faced another war on a distant battleground, it was obvious that her efforts toward international arbitration had failed. It was somehow appropriate that, as the United States prepared to enter World War One, Belva Lockwood should relinquish the field. On May 19, 1917, she died at George Washington University Hospital. The funeral service held in the Wesley Chapel of the Methodist Episcopalian Church recalled the triumphs of her life, and the newspapers recorded her history. She had been, they said, "one of the last of that generation still living to see some of the hopes of those forerunners of freedom for women working out into practice in this." That woman suffrage would become the law of the land she had prophesied, for in 1915 she had said, "Suffrage is no longer an issue . . . It is an accomplished fact." That a scholarship would be established in her name and that a bust of Belva Lockwood would be unveiled by the Women's Bar Association of the District of Columbia to commemorate the seventy-fifth anniversary of her admission to the Supreme Court, she could not know. Yet she herself had been aware of her accomplishments, for she knew that it had been through her own unrelenting struggle that the "law schools and the courts had been opened" to all women. As early as 1897, in answer to an inquiry whether she considered herself "a 'New Woman,'" she had tersely, almost matter-of-factly, summed up her achievements and her beliefs:

As a rule I do not consider myself at all. I am, and always have been a progressive woman, and while never directly attacking the conventionalities of society, have always done, or attempted to do those things which I have considered conducive to my health, convenience or emolument, as for instance: Attended college and graduated when the general sentiment of the people was against it, and this after I had been a married woman.

Entered a law school and graduated, at a time when there was much opposition to such a course.

Applied for, and was admitted ultimately to the United States Supreme Court. Such a course had been previously unknown in our history. I was the first woman to ride a wheel in the District of Columbia, which I persisted in doing notwithstanding newspaper comments.

I accepted a nomination to the Presidency by the Equal Rights Party, and my letter of acceptance was published throughout the length and breadth of 2 worlds.

I do not believe in sex distinction in literature, law, politics, or trade; or that modesty and virtue are more becoming to women than to men; but wish we had more of it everywhere.

I was new about 60 years ago, but did not then appreciate my privileges.

She had said, too, "I have never stopped fighting. My cause was the cause of thousands of women." In those words she had written her own obituary. The farm girl from upstate New York had journeyed a long and arduous way to climb the steps of the highest court of the land. And as she climbed, she cast behind her the shadows of the thousands upon thousands of women who would follow a road that she had cleared and enter a door that she had opened.

Business & Industry

The First American Woman in the Iron Plate Rolling Industry

REBECCA W. LUKENS

1825

NEITHER flags nor bunting decked the small neat houses of Coatesville, Pennsylvania, and no parade of workmen marched through the streets of the little town on the Brandywine. No tablet was erected in Chester County to mark a day in 1859 which quietly made history. Simply, without fanfare, the name of a plant had been changed, and Brandywine Iron Works had become the Lukens Iron Works. The change had been made, ostensibly, to avoid confusion with a competitor at the "West Brandywine Iron Works." But the new name did more than serve expediency. It honored a man whose perspicacity had produced the first iron boiler plate in the country. But it honored even more a woman whose courage had built and expanded an industry, whose vision had helped develop America's iron age. She herself had been dead for five years when her mill was renamed, and even in her lifetime she would have been more interested in substance than in title. A "Quakeress," born on the banks of the Brandywine in Chester County, Pennsylvania, had taken as her province a world of charcoal blooms and forge fires and plate rolls. In 1825, at the age of thirty-one, she had become the first woman in the country to run an iron plate rolling mill. Rebecca Lukens, "Quakeress" and mistress of Brandywine, had manufactured the iron that sped through the country by rail, that plowed through its waters in the hulls of ships, that gave strength to a nation and a name to an age. Now, in the plant she had expanded with her own iron fortitude, her name would endure as long as iron itself endured.

Rebecca Webb Pennock had been born in 1794 in Pennsylvania's Chester County, the daughter of Isaac and Martha Pennock. And she had been born to a rich and varied heritage. In her eyes surely, the Brandywine was a romantic stream that by tradition took its name from a vessel laden with brandy and wine and lost at its entrance. Along its banks she rambled as a child, "as wild, happy and joyous as youth could make me," delighting in gristmills and waterfalls, oaks and rolling hills. In the saddle or on foot she rejoiced in the country she was born to, and in Primitive Hall, which had been built by her great-grandfather, she found romance of another kind, the romance of a "feudal castle," whose latchstring was always left hanging out, whose kitchen floor had sometimes been covered with sleeping Indians, whose great fireplace held the Yule-log dragged in by oxen. In the books she read she discovered romance, too,—"The wild Dramatic stories of Hotsebin and Lewis" that she "eagerly devoured." "Shakespeare awoke the noblest feelings of my heart, . . . I read with avidity *all* that fell in my way."

There was perhaps less of romance in the duties assigned her at home, for her "mother's rule was strict," and Rebecca, the eldest child, must care for her younger brothers and sisters when she was not learning to cook and sew and quilt or spending "long hours at the spinning-wheel." Her family were members of the Society of Friends, and that, too, imposed restrictions, albeit they were "gay Friends" who could give an elastic interpretation to the rules of "plainness of speech, behavior and apparel." Her mother's reserve, which "rather repelled than claimed my confidence," might have dampened the spirits but could not clip the wings of the warm and strong-willed girl whose courage and intellectual curiosity would make her iron-master on the Brandywine.

Iron flowed in her veins. Eagerly she heard how her father had abandoned farming and malting for the manufacture of iron—a business which his own father had regarded as decidedly hazardous "when wheat was selling at $3 a bushel and the influence of Great Britain was [still] detrimental to the success of the iron industry." Shortly before Rebecca was born, Isaac Pennock had started a slitting mill on Buck Run in Chester County, and his daughter, who delighted in literary romance, doubtless discovered a more realistic variety in his tales of the Federal Slitting Mill. There, she learned, iron slabs supplied from nearby forges were heated in an open charcoal fire, rolled out into sheets and slit into rods for blacksmiths' use. One day the Federal Slitting Mill would be known as the Rokeby Works, named after Scott's *Rokeby,* and the romance of poetry to young Rebecca Pennock was not a far cry from the romance of iron. There was a fascination in seeing the sheets slit into rods for use in blacksmith shops, hoops for barrels, and iron tires. There was a peculiar beauty in the mill dam and in the "Bank" of workmen's houses. There was adventure in transmuting iron into gold.

By 1810, when Isaac Pennock extended his interests to the Brandywine Mill, his eldest daughter had advanced her learning along more conventional lines as well. When she was twelve she had been placed in a boarding school, resuming her studies later at a "different seminary." Joshua Maule, a "very worthy member" of the Society of Friends, and Eli Hilles of Chester County had taken over the Boarding School for Young Ladies opened in Wilmington by Mrs. Capron of Philadelphia, and there, Rebecca Pennock could join the "females" from the various States and the West Indies in her eager pursuit of ornamental drawing and French, English literature and higher mathematics, botany and static electricity—the "branches of a plain English education."

Now it was that life began to open new charms for me. I was rapidly improving, a favorite with my teachers and at the head of all my classes, . . .

I was young, ardent and happy. My preceptor was the best of men.

Later, when her "respected teacher had . . . engaged in a larger school . . . . Chemistry and the French language claimed my attention and I devoted myself with untiring zeal to their acquirement."

Although Rebecca left Wilmington "with regret," she had merely exchanged one intellectual adventure for another. In 1810, Isaac Pennock had purchased a sawmill property on the Brandywine Creek and reconstructed it for the manufacture of iron. With local labor he had installed his mill and the overshot water wheel that was its prime mover. With deep interest his daughter learned now the workings of the new mill named the Brandywine. She watched while, on horseback or in carts, through rough hilly paths or over dirt roads, deliveries were made—deliveries of the imperial metal that would shape the backbone of a nation. For the metal ran in her veins, and Brandywine would one day be hers.

Meanwhile, there were other adventures. During a visit to Philadelphia with her father, Rebecca Pennock met Dr. Charles Lukens, a member of the Society of Friends and a physician who had recently begun practice in Abington. To Rebecca, however, he was far more than Friend and physician. "He bowed with a peculiar grace," his face was "interesting," his figure "tall and commanding."

An air of grace and dignity were blended in his form. His hair was of the deepest shade of black, his eyes haze[l], and his other features manly and remarkably handsome. . . . the expression of his countenance . . . . spoke of lofty unbending principle, of a mind exalted and that felt its own power, while the benevolence which beamed from his eye and the suavity of his manner won their way to the heart, and fixed his empire there.

Young as she was, she "had heard the language of love in its most witching form."

Later, after she had returned home, Dr. Lukens pursued his courtship. "From the beauties of the view he turned to the charms of poetry," quoting "some of the witching stanzas of 'Marmion,' " expatiating "on the beauties and order of the Heavenly bodies," culling "the sweetest flowers of fancy" for her and giving "freely of the stores of his highly cultivated mind."

There was a thrilling sound in his tone as he spoke, and such a purity of thought, such a grace of expression, that I felt allmost [sic] as though I were listening to a being of another sphere.

The question was asked. "Say then, dear R.[ebecca], . . . may I hope to win thy love? . . . I can offer thee a heart that has never before felt the witchery of female power, a heart that would love and cherish thee as the first, best gift of heaven. Our tastes are alike, our minds assimilate, and may I hope for a reciprocal interest?" The question was answered. Rebecca, "agitated with powerful emmotion [sic] . . . . replied to his impassioned request. . . . A long and interesting discourse followed and . . . our plighted faith freely exchanged."

In 1813, when Rebecca was nineteen and Dr. Lukens twenty-seven, they were married. Rebecca Lukens donned the thin muslin cap she would henceforth wear on all formal occasions, and the couple settled near the old Federal Slitting Mill—later the Rokeby Works—for Dr. Lukens had decided to abandon medicine for the iron industry, becoming a partner of Isaac Pennock in the Federal Slitting Mill under the name of Pennock and Lukens. After some three or four years on Buck Run, they moved to the Brandywine, Charles Lukens leasing the iron works from his father-in-law for $420 a year. At his death, Isaac Pennock assured Rebecca, the mill would be hers.

Now, as mistress of Brandywine, Rebecca Lukens turned her hand to improving her mansion and rearing her children. Of the six she would bear, only three would survive. She heard the heavy stagecoach lumbering through the village and saw the Conestoga covered wagons transporting goods along the turnpike, onward over the Alleghenies. She sat to Edward Hicks for her portrait, donning her peach-colored dress for the occasion. She planted weeping willows near Brandywine House, holding the trees while the earth was filled in. And in her husband's life she lived vicariously, seeing through his eyes and hearing from his lips the struggles and the adventures of the ironmaster.

The Brandywine Iron Works and Nail Factory, Rebecca realized, needed "an owner's care. Everything was in a very delapidated [sic] state about the Mill, house and farm. . . . The mill had been hastily built and the harness on which the weight of heavy castings were placed, was in such a state, that . . . the mill could not be kept in center, which caused tremenduous [sic] breakage. . . . We were continually repairing." One winter, "the whole dam was carried away in a freshet." It must be rebuilt. A new large water wheel and a new head must be installed. New pinion housings and other castings must be put in.

If Rebecca shared the hardships with her husband, she shared his triumphs, too. Through him she learned now how the nails were cut from the ends of the sheets. From him she heard of his purchase of nail making machines. But especially she rejoiced in his plans for expansion of the mill which he decided to convert for new and larger purposes. As Dr. Lukens explained to Rebecca, steam boilers were destined for enormously extended use in a power age. Moreover, the charcoal iron which he would manufacture into sheets was admirably suited to bear high pressure strains. He would, therefore, adapt the Brandywine Mill for the work of rolling charcoal iron boiler plates. At Brandywine, the first such plate in America would be rolled. Iron rods and nails were well enough, but iron plates that would gird ships and locomotives expanded the vision, enlarged the mind.

Rebecca watched, as workmen were engaged to commence the boiler plate business. She joined in the adventure of producing in the little mill on the Brandywine plates that would be used in the boilers and hulls of ships, plates that would become part of wood-burning locomotives, plates that would help bring to reality the new age of steam and of power.

In 1825, Rebecca shared with her husband in the fruition of his vision. A note, dated March 31st of that year and addressed to Dr. Charles Lukens by John Elgar, acknowledged his letter which

states that thou wilt deliver sheet iron to me at York at $140 per ton rolled 2 feet wide and from 7 to 10 feet long.

. . . The money will await thy order in York Bank on the delivery of the iron.

The letter was historic. For John Elgar, associated with the firm of Davis, Gartner and Webb, was building the first metal hull vessel in the United States, the *Codorus,* in York, Pennsylvania, a vessel that would be girded with iron plates rolled by Charles Lukens at the Brandywine Mill.

The hull of the first American ironclad steamship was not completed until November of 1825. By the time it was launched on the Susquehanna, the Erie Canal had been opened and there were high hopes for the progress of the new age of steam. But by that time, hope had dimmed for Rebecca Lukens on the Brandywine, and her husband's visions of that progress had become a memory.

By the summer of 1825, when the citizens of Chester County streamed in carriages and on horseback and on foot to watch the arrival of Lafayette in his barouche, Rebecca Lukens had taken part in a procession of a different kind. Dr. Charles Lukens, who had just succeeded in rolling the boiler plate that was to take so important a role in the development of the country, died after a short illness. "I am as one bound on a pleasant journey," he had said. He had also said that his wife should carry on the mill, the mill that was all but bankrupt from the expenses that had been incurred in expanding it. A year and a half before, in February of 1824, Rebecca's father had died. There were claims upon her husband. Payments must be made to her mother. Dr. Charles Lukens had died intestate with a personal estate "insufficient for the payment of his debts." His widow was alone now with her children, one of them still to be born. With a mill that faced ruin, the mistress of Brandywine must become the ironmaster of Brandywine. The life she had lived vicariously she must live now in her own right. The iron hulls of America's ships, the iron of her locomotives must be manufactured now at a mill whose ironmaster was a woman.

Rebecca Lukens donned no rose-colored spectacles when she examined the situation before her.

In the summer of 1825, I lost my dear and excellent Husband, and then commenced my hard and weary struggle with life. . . . it was utterly impossible there should be a support left for the young and helpless family now dependent solely on me. Dr. Lukens had just commenced the Boiler Plant Business, . . . a new branch in Pennsylvania, and he was sanguine in his hopes of success, and this was his dying request—he wished me to continue and I promised him to comply. Indeed I well knew I must do something for the children around me. The estate shewed an alarming deficiency when the books were examined. I will not dwell on my feelings, when I began to look around me. There was difficulty and danger on every side. . . . Mother wanted me to leave Brandywine, and said it would be folly for me to remain. Necessity is a stern taskmistress, and my every want gave me courage.

She needed courage. She needed courage to oppose her family and her mother, who offered her "no assistance" if she left, "but thought as a female I was not fit to carry on such a concern." Her father's Will was ambiguous. Brandywine would not be hers "in a little while," for her mother could claim it "during her life, if she choose [sic] to hold it" and demand payment of "the whole of the claim my Father had held against my husband." This, Rebecca determined, "should be done as soon as practicable, with every other debt my husband owed."

In the *Village Record,* Rebecca W. Lukens, Administratrix, placed notice that "All persons indebted to the Estate of Dr.

Charles Lukens, late of Brandywine Iron Works, . . . are requested to make immediate payment—and those having demands against said estate will present them for settlement." The demands flowed in—for coal and castings, for cutting nails and nail kegs. In December, Rebecca's last child was born. She must be not only ironmaster, but mother and mistress of Brandywine. Some friends there were who rallied to her side. Her husband's brother, Solomon Lukens, would assist in managing the business. Charles Brooke would supply iron on credit "for a reasonable time." James Sproul would furnish charcoal blooms on credit. "The workmen were tried and faithful, and so with some fear but more courage I began to struggle for a livelihood. I think at this period I must have possessed some energy of character, for now I look back and wonder at my daring. I had such strong, such powerful incentives for exertion, that I felt I must succeed."

Her feelings were still prophetic. At the moment, she must sustain heavy losses on contracts. She must meet payments for repairing a factory wheel, for smith work, for iron. She must fill a contract for boiler plates made by Dr. Lukens with a firm of New York merchants who refused to free her from the obligation. The mistress of Brandywine found that she, too, was made of an imperial metal. Rebecca Lukens reviewed the multiplication tables and embarked upon a career as the first woman in the country to operate an iron rolling mill.

At seven in the morning she appeared at the mill office, directing and overseeing its affairs until late afternoon. She must supervise the manufacture of plates and sheets, rods and nails. She must be responsible for a mill operated by water power from the Brandywine, whose blooms were brought white-hot from the furnaces and run through a pair of heavy rolls. From its chimneys flame spouted forth. Its gong, itself made of boiler plate, summoned her men to work or a change of shifts. While Solomon Lukens took charge of the mill, Rebecca managed and controlled its commercial end.

Seated in the mill office, Rebecca Lukens of Brandywine bought supplies for her establishment—"100 Tons of sound Boiler plates trimmed square at the ends suitable to Roll into Boiler plate Iron," flat bars for sheet iron, hundreds of bushels of charcoal, tons of "first quality Blooms," bituminous coal. She set prices shrewdly but justly, mastering the mysteries of profit and cost. If she spent

THE EVENING TELEGRAM.

VOL. III.–NO. 816.   NEW YORK, FRIDAY, FEBRUARY 18, 1870.   TWO CENTS.

THE WALL STREET HIPPODROME.

HOW TO MANAGE A BALKY TEAM.

VICTORIA WOODHULL AND TENNESSEE CLAFLIN MANAGE A BALKY
TEAM IN THE WALL STREET HIPPODROME
—*The Evening Telegram* [New York] (February 18, 1870)

THE DESIGNING-ROOM.

THE DESIGNING ROOM OF ASSOCIATED ARTISTS
—*Harper's New Monthly Magazine* (August 1884)

$153.40 for slabs and labor, coal and hauling, she believed a price of $176.50 a fair one for plates and trimmings, yielding her a profit of $23.10. She made sales contracts for boiler plates, agreeing to furnish "Boiler and Sheet Iron . . . rolled in a Superior Style, . . . as heretofore." The mistress of Brandywine met prospective customers and studied any legislation that might affect her business. With her dozen millhands she signed agreements. Jacob Appleton was to "cut and head nails . . . agreeably to Re. W. Lukens' orders—at eighty-five cents per hundred pounds." He was "to attend strictly to the business from five in the Morning until seven in the evening if it be required of him and his work to be done in the best manner—excepting out of his day two hours and one half for meals also unavoidable detention by sickness." Morris Clarke was "to cut nails on the Machine . . . agreeably to R. W. Lukens orders" and was to "pay . . . twenty-five cents per hour for each and any hour he is absent from his business provided the Factory is capable of doing business, sickness and unavoidable accidents excepted." She took more than a contractual interest in her mill-hands, who lived on the "Bank" in a cluster of stone houses and who helped store away the winter vegetables of Brandywine farm or slaughter beeves and hogs when they were not working at the mill.

Rebecca Lukens' workday was long. She faced not only contracts and customers, but difficulties and delays. The roads were rough and teaming expensive. When she did not ship by water, her market was confined to an area of from fifty to seventy-five miles. The coal she used must be hauled from Columbia. Her plates must be teamed by wagon through toll-gates to Philadelphia or Wilmington. In the spring the roads were impassable. When she shipped by schooner, she shipped "subject to the dangers of the seas," the delays of vessels, the opening of navigation.

The Brandywine itself was a problem. Rebecca depended upon the dammed up stream for her water power, and when it ran low she was forced to shut down the mill. A mill race carried the stream to the overshot water wheel that turned the machinery. Repairs were ruinous, causing delays and increasing expenses. Castings broke and stacks fell. When the mill threatened to stall, Rebecca Lukens' millhands rushed for the water wheel, climbed up on its rim and by their combined weight helped the "pass" through the rolls to prevent a "sticker" which would mean fire-cracked rolls.

Immediately upstream, competitors began to build their mills, one firm bringing suit against her for having raised the level and backed the water when she repaired her mill dam. Although Rebecca was ordered by a Committee of the Orthodox Branch of the Society of Friends to lower her mill dam six inches, she had the satisfaction of admonishing the plaintiffs with a prophetic warning: "Men, I have something to say to you. You have started out in business taking unfair advantage of your neighbor, and, mark my words, you will never prosper."

After her mother's death in 1844, Rebecca Lukens faced more prolonged litigation closer home. It took several law suits carried by the Pennock heirs to a variety of law courts to determine the meanings of ambiguous words in her father's Will and to evoke the final decree, rendered on January 27, 1853, that his property had been given to his widow—a decision that forced Rebecca Lukens to make heavy payments to the estate before Brandywine could legally be hers. She herself felt that she "held Brandywine by a stronger tenure."

Through the years, Rebecca Lukens sustained the onslaughts of family jealousy and litigation, of price declines and underselling, of complaints that "Blooms were not well refined" or that plates had "raw spots." The slings and arrows of outrageous fortune were shot not only by her family and her business, but by the times in which she lived. She faced and surmounted the Panic of 1837, when

The difficulties of the times throws a gloom over everything. All is paralyzed—business at a stand. I have as yet lost nothing but am in constant fear, and have even forbidden my agents to sell not knowing who would be safe to trust. . . .

I have stopped rolling for a few weeks, and set my men to repairing the race dam, &, having a heavy stock manufactured already, I do not wish to encrease it until times are more settled, but shall take advantage of the first gleam of sunshine to resume.

We do not know how to do without a circulating medium. Every one that has a dollar in silver hoards it up as though they never expected to see another and our cautious country people as yet are affraid [sic] of your small notes.

After the Panic, Rebecca was confronted by the tariff reductions of the '40's, when her employees could work only half-time. In the campaign of 1840 she took an active part with the ladies of Coatesville, who made a silk banner to carry in parade, a banner bearing an inscription written by Rebecca Lukens:

> Let patriots from each wooded height,
> And freemen, from our fair vale, come
> To rear this banner broad and bright,
> And rally round brave Harrison.

For the next election, when the men of Brandywine marched in procession with their banner—a large sheet of iron on a pole—the ironmistress composed the inscription that would be painted upon it in white letters:

> We fondly hope for better days,
> When every furnace fire shall blaze,
> And streaming to the midnight sky
> Proclaim to all 'prosperity.'

Poetry could not forestall reductions of revenues on foreign merchandise and a crisis in the domestic iron industry that called for the revision of revenue laws, and Rebecca was quick to dispatch her representative to a meeting of iron manufacturers and dealers in Philadelphia in 1849.

By that time, Solomon Lukens had been followed by Dr. Lukens' brother-in-law, Joseph Bailey, as her manager, and he in turn by Abraham Gibbons, Jr., who had married Rebecca's eldest daughter. By that time, Rebecca Lukens could look about her and be gratified not only by the storms she had weathered, but by the progress she had made. Through her work at the mill she had been enabled to sustain her position as mistress of Brandywine. She had repaired the mansion house, and enlarged its grounds. She walked in her apple orchard and her garden, seeing the hills in the distance, the rolling mill chimney to the right, the sweep of the Great Valley to the left. By her old willow trees she planted ivies. In front of her hickory wood fire she sat, telling stories to her children of the past and of the future, or in summer evenings on her piazza she chatted with the passers-by. She was mistress of a comfortable domain, the lady of Brandywine, of a home built on a hillside whose kitchen had its wide hearth, whose farm yielded its harvest of hay and wheat, whose rooms were filled with rush-bottomed side chairs and sideboards, swell-front bureau and sewing stand. From the end of her upper porch she could see all who passed by, and seated there she gave orders for the day to the hired man who stood below her in the garden. In her receipt book she recorded the secrets of her table—the ingredients of pickle green tomatoes or of soda cake, potato pudding or Indian griddle cakes. Reading still consumed her, and from her centre table she could pick up the novels of Richardson or Scott which she read by the light of an astral lamp as the night came on. She found time, somehow, for travel, too. In her high-swung coach, upholstered in cream-colored brocade, she drove to West Chester to meet Squire Everhart when he returned from London with her commissions for the "priceless wares of India House," or, tucked in her buffalo robe, she might ride on to Pottsville "and view their mining operations." The mistress of Brandywine was a "Quaker," but a "gay" one.

The mistress of Brandywine was also a successful ironmaster, whose achievements had mounted with the years, whose progress had been identified with the progress of her times. Standing in her doorway and looking across the Chester Valley, she had years before remarked to her uncle, "I should not be surprised to see a railroad running along the face of those hills some day." To his objection that the chasm could not be crossed, she had replied, ". . . they could easily span that with a bridge." The chasm of the Brandywine Valley that cut into the Chester Valley from the north was spanned in 1834. The Housatonic Railroad brought supplies from Boston. The railroad expanded the country while it enlarged the market for Rebecca Lukens' iron. "The opening of the Pennsylvania Railroad gave our iron ready access to market." The ironmaster of the Brandywine seized every opportunity for enlarging that market until her boiler plates were known to all engineers. To Boston and to Baltimore, to Albany and New York her products were transported. And her mill rolled plates for New Orleans—plates that found their way into the boilers of Mississippi River steamboats. In the different cities she placed her agents, William Kemble accepting the New York agency since he classed "the iron from Gardner—Parke & yourselves as the best iron made in Penna." In some cities Rebecca Lukens established almost a monopoly in the boiler plate industry. For steamboats and for locomotives she produced plates, while the manufacture of rails themselves gave puddling a leading position in iron manufacture.

In her preoccupation with quality, Rebecca Lukens had not forgotten the needs of her millhands. She built "good and substantial tenant houses" for them on the "Bank," and offered them premiums for increasing the mill's yearly output to five hundred tons. In her "long and weary struggle to gain a living" she had emerged triumphant. By 1844 she was worth over $60,000 and by the time of her death her estate would be valued at over $100,000. She had settled her husband's debts, paid the balance due the Pennock estate, and rebuilt her mill. "The mill has been entirely remodeled and rebuilt from the very foundation. Dam entirely newly built, Wheels put in, castings, furnaces, mill head, mill house much larger, all were built anew." She had indeed built anew, and she had built a firm and sure foundation. At the last she could boast, "I had built a very superior mill, though a plain one and our character for making boiler iron stood first in the market."

On October 1, 1847, Rebecca Lukens signed Articles of Co-partnership with her son-in-law, Abraham Gibbons, Jr., agreeing that they were to become "copartners in the business of manufacturing boiler and flue iron at the mills and works of the said Rebecca." Under the name of A. Gibbons Jr. & Co., the firm would be managed and conducted by Abraham Gibbons, "subject always to the advisement and concurring judgment of . . . Rebecca W. Lukens." Rebecca would supply a capital of $16,000, Gibbons of $8,000. The firm would pay Gibbons $1,000 a year for his services, and to Rebecca $1,400 a year "as rent for the use of her rolling mill, warehouse and the machinery and fixtures thereof." The profits would be divided, two-thirds to go to Rebecca, one-third to Abraham.

The Articles, signed, sealed and delivered, brought a semi-retirement to Rebecca Lukens, whose partnership would henceforth be a fairly silent one. Two years later, in 1849, her second son-in-law, Charles Huston, was admitted to the firm. Grown stout and heavy and asthmatic with the years, she was all but ready to relinquish her role as ironmaster of the Brandywine. In that same year of 1849, Rebecca lost the daughter who had been born after Dr. Lukens' death. "The blow was stunning." "I think," she wrote, "I will keep a diary from this time of the events of each day— My time hangs heavily on my hands. . . . I believe that having

passed so many years in constant excitement has had a very delete-
rious effect on me—It was a stimulant to my existence and now—
I feel the want of something to give an impetus." Even business
seemed "dull enough," the "market . . . much depressed."

Yet, by 1850, surely Rebecca Lukens could be gratified, for her
Brandywine Works, managed by her two sons-in-law, boasted two
heating furnaces and a train roll and consumed 21,000 bushels of
bituminous coal, fifty tons of anthracite coal, and nine hundred
forty-four tons of Bloom. It employed seventeen men and boys,
along with four oxen, horses and mules. It was growing with the
country it served. And it would continue its growth. On December
10, 1854, its ironmaster died in the sixty-first year of her age,
saying, "I have a work to do that none can do for me."

She had already done her work. The industry she had developed
would be carried on unto the third and fourth and fifth generation.
The town would grow into a borough, and the borough into a city.
In 1870 a modern steam plate mill would rise near the old water
power mill. In 1890 the firm would be incorporated as the Lukens
Iron and Steel Company, and in 1910 its centennial would be
celebrated by a parade of some 1,500 workmen of the plant. From
its plate mill, its open hearth and electric steel plants would come
steel for bridges and for ships, for the chemical, petroleum, marine,
machinery and construction industries, for the parts of atomic
reactors. As the Lukens Steel Company, it would produce in 1929
nearly 400,000 tons of steel plates, in 1957, nearly 600,000 tons.
The largest plate mill in the world would be built for the firm
that a woman member of the Society of Friends had developed
on the banks of the Brandywine.

Her vision was far-reaching, but this it could not have foreseen.
To Rebecca Lukens the greatest blessing which Providence had
bestowed upon her was "the power of being useful." She had
been useful indeed. She had built up an industry almost from its
infancy. Throughout her struggle and her success she had been
aware that "the manufacture of iron is not a mere local or individual interest, but is of national importance, . . . affording a
supply of a chief element of progress in time of peace, and an
important engine of defence in time of war." This element she
had provided. The mistress of Brandywine had supplied to an
expanding country the imperial metal that formed its backbone,
and her own.

II

America's First
Woman Stockbroker

VICTORIA C. WOODHULL
The Fascinating Financier

1870

NOT SINCE Black Friday had there been such a sensation on that "pandemoniac thoroughfare" known as Wall Street. Against the plate glass windows of 44 Broad, gentlemen on exchange flattened their inquisitive noses. Crowds of investors and members of the Boards flocked from the Stock Exchange and the Gold Room to mill about the quarters recently vacated by the notorious William Gray, but not to meditate about his gigantic frauds. The Bulls and the Bears abandoned the stock ticker to stream in a steady line toward the premises. Jay Cooke and Charles Lamont, John Bloodgood and the portly, mustachioed "Uncle" Rufus Hatch edged their august way through the throngs past the "wary Ethiopian stationed as a scout on the outskirts of the *sanctum sanctorum*." Even the bootblacks could not resist dashing in and out for a brief look at the wonders that waited within. The scene in the neighborhood of the office "reminded one of an election day in the First Ward." Before many weeks in that new year of 1870 had passed, it was estimated that seven thousand visitors had set aside the "calls" of exchange in favor of "calls" at 44 Broad. The unprecedented had happened. Dr. Johnson's legendary dog had stood upon his hind legs. While the Bulls and the Bears were tossing prices as they would shuttlecocks, a new firm had started a brokerage business. But Woodhull, Claflin & Company was unlike any other firm ever known to the street. For the principals of Woodhull, Claflin & Company were women. Moreover, they were young and beautiful women with a somewhat dubious history. Woodhull's first name was Victoria; Claflin's was Tennessee. They were sisters, one of whom had been named after a queen, the other after a state. Now, in the street of tumult and confusion that boasted at one end a church and at the other a stream, a new landmark had appeared—the first firm of women brokers in history. Only the spire of Trinity remained unmoved as it looked down upon the incomprehensible marvel.

Had Woodhull and Claflin been men, their firm would have been accepted for precisely what it was. Since they were women, it was either scorned and belittled or ridiculed and made the butt of new Wall Street witticisms. Even those who championed their audacity did so with a cry of *"Vive la frou-frou!"* Whatever the reactions, nearly all were in accord on one point. Since Woodhull and Claflin were women, there must be one or more representatives of the stronger, sager sex behind them, not merely to give occasional tips or counsel, but to keep them from floundering in the maelstrom of financial disaster. The point of view of 1870 has persisted through the emancipated twentieth century until now. Because Woodhull and Claflin were women, fascinating and fashionably dressed, they could not possibly have been shrewd speculators on the street. Because their private lives were glamorously questionable, they could not possibly have manipulated the complex strings of finance. Such illogical non sequiturs have been harbored by the hosts who have reported their lives and recorded their careers. Yet the fact remains. The sensation that Wall Street witnessed in 1870 was no hallucination, but a *fait accompli.*

None the less, the wits continued to hint that Victoria Woodhull had started a brokerage firm to buy and sell stocks on the system of clairvoyance, and had founded a bank to fulfill a prophecy and follow a celestial mandate. Like most witticisms, this barb had some point of truth in it, for Victoria had been subject to visions from her third year and had packed enough varied adventure into the first thirty-one years of her life to merit almost any epithet, from that of unprincipled adventuress to that of hub of the world.

She had been born in September 1838, at Homer, Ohio, one of a family of ten all of whom bore fanciful names and equally fanciful histories. Her father, Reuben Buckman Claflin, was variously described as an eminent lawyer descended from the ducal family of Hamilton, a bosom friend of the Governor of Pennsylvania, and as a conniving fraud who burned down his own grist mill to pocket the insurance. The possibility that Claflin may have been all of these seems not to have occurred to those writers who prefer their subjects all of a piece. Similarly, Victoria's mother, Roxanna Hummel Claflin, has been depicted as a lady of royal German ancestry and as a shrewish termagant born out of wedlock. Again, there is no reason why she may not have been both. Even Victoria's birthplace varies with the describer, from a picturesque, white-painted, high-peaked cottage to a slovenly, squalid shack. Once again, there is no reason why it may not have been both— at different times.

Against this somewhat bewildering background, the young Victoria emerged to face a youth that reflected the humbugs and eccentricities of the times. Her wildly various life paralleled the fluid society of the country. With her family, especially her sister Tennie, the girl who was named after a queen earned money as spiritualist and clairvoyant, mesmerist and magnetic healer, dispenser of an elixir of life and a cancer cure. Through Ohio and Illinois, Kansas and Missouri, the Claflins wandered, an errant side show in the mammoth attraction that was America. Along the way, while Tennie picked up a charge of manslaughter for a cancer treatment that ended fatally, the fifteen-year-old Victoria picked up the first in that series of "husbands" for which she would be classified either as a prostitute or as one who had been "married rather more extensively than most American matrons." By Dr. Canning Woodhull, whose career was to end in alcoholism, she had two children, Byron, an idiot, and Zula Maud. While Tennie gained what she was to call a "long practice in female complaints," Victoria served a turn on the California stage before she met her second "husband," James Harvey Blood, in St. Louis. After her divorce from Woodhull, she joined forces in 1866 with the virile Colonel Blood, late of the Sixth Missouri Volunteers, spiritualist, intellectual, and reformer, who was destined for immortality as the "Company" in Woodhull, Claflin & Company. Not long after, the rather incongruous appearance of the spirit of Demosthenes in the city of Pittsburgh directed Victoria to move her ménage to New York. She obeyed the ethereal ukase and found herself in the metropolis of Bulls and Bears, of a Wall Street that was dominated by its own special spirit known as Commodore

Cornelius Vanderbilt. If Victoria had learned anything at all from her early checkered career as individualistic eccentric in a land of individualistic eccentrics, she had learned the importance and the value of money, and the frauds that were perpetrated to obtain that essential commodity. This was the double-headed coin she was to fling into the coffers of Wall Street.

Victoria was quick to learn that she had entered a New York that held vast possibilities. The Erie war was at its height. In the tens of thousands, miles of track were being laid to open up the West, and the result of the unprecedented building of railways was reflected in a stock exchange that existed principally as a market for railroad securities. The railroads had created the wealth of the country, and, to a large extent, Commodore Cornelius Vanderbilt had created the railroads, or at least the profits in railroads. Victoria Woodhull, clairvoyant and healer, bearded the lion in his den, for the lion happened to be as responsive to the soft touch of feminine magnetic fingers as he was to a good race horse or a saddle of venison.

Possibly through their father, or less possibly through the wily machinations of the mustachioed, dark-haired Colonel Blood, the sisters were introduced to the aging monarch of Wall Street and promptly served him as magnetic healers and clairvoyants. In return for their services, it was said, the Commodore either set them up in business or promised market tips. It was also said, however, that Victoria emerged from her clairvoyant trances with valuable tips for the Commodore. Whoever profited more from these exchanges, Victoria Woodhull had found an entrée into Wall Street at a time when most men agreed that the profession of stockbroker was "unsuited to woman's nature" since it would "change her tender heart into stone," doom her to failure, and cause her crinolines to be crushed.

Although Woodhull, Claflin & Company did not formally start business until February 4, 1870, they had prepared for their unprecedented undertaking much earlier. For some time they had been "bold and successful operators on the street," acting through their own brokers, Strong, Nichols, Strong. "Speculative traffic in buying, holding and selling the products of the country" had been their delight, "and to be fully acquainted with the market value of everything our pride. . . . Having gained some reputation for business ability in the management of our own affairs," they declared, "we began to be entrusted with the more intricate or delicate affairs of others. In this way we became acquainted with real estate operations; and to such we at length turned special attention. About this time we were attracted to military lands by several patents held among our acquaintances. In attending to perfecting the titles to these by clearing up tax sales, &c., we were largely drawn into dealing in them, at one time having no less than a million of dollars' worth of them wholly or partially under our control. When we were most deeply engaged 'tracing titles,' 'searching records,' 'making abstracts,' drawing powers of attorney and deeds, . . . a decision of the Supreme Court of the United States relative to the rights of widows and minors in these titles cut off most of our expected realizations and determined us to abandon the business, which we did, finding ourselves left possessed of some thousands of acres of lands. These we sold, investing the proceeds in oil stocks. Making some losses we turned our attention to railway stocks, and at times have operated quite largely, . . . Our best ventures have been in Chicago and Alton, Northwestern, Toledo, Wabash and Western, and latterly in New York Central and Hudson River." As early as January 1869, Victoria had been "conversing with engineers and others, . . . as to the . . . practicability of 'elevated railways and pneumatic despatches.'" During the September panic, she had sat in her carriage from morning till evening on Broad Street, operating heavily and coming out a winner. Before its formal opening, it was claimed, her operations, conducted through agents in the street, had netted the as yet unofficial firm some $700,000. If her claims were true, then Commodore Vanderbilt must have foreseen a sure profit from a silent partnership in Woodhull, Claflin & Company. If they were not true, the spirit of Demosthenes must have bestowed upon his protégées the gift of tongues—glib, plausible, and convincing.

Before the formal opening on Broad Street, the company operated for a short time in their parlors, Nos. 25 and 26 in the Hoffman House. Against a background of oil paintings and statuary, sofas, chairs and a piano, they continued their speculations, reassured perhaps by a framed and "gracefully finished" motto: "Simply to Thy Cross I cling."

Apparently the assurance had been forthcoming, for by January of 1870 the sisters had moved to larger and more business-like quarters at 44 Broad Street. Victoria and Tennessee, in their handsome dark blue cloth walking-suits trimmed with black silk, their close-cropped hair topped with neat jockey hats, sat for a portrait in words entitled the "Bewitching Brokers." To the merry brown eyes and chubby face that gave Tennie the appearance of one of the most charming brigands of Wall Street, Victoria presented a startling contrast. With an intellectual beauty of face, her countenance was "never twice alike" for her "soul comes into it and goes out of it." But whatever the vagaries of her soul, she radiated an intensity, a prepossessing intelligence and a magnetic beauty startling in a broker of 1870.

William Gray, lately connected with the New York Bounty Loan frauds, had vacated the offices at 44 Broad, but not before he had furnished them in an elaborate style at an expense of $7000. The furniture, sold at a sheriff's sale, had been bought by Woodhull and Claflin for $1400. It had been a wise purchase, for it included plate glass, marble counters, leather lounges and sofas, Marvin safes and walnut desks covered with green baize. A portion of the office was taken for a time by the stockbroker, John J. Ogden. When the gentlemen on exchange, in their pearl-colored pantaloons and green kid gloves, besieged the "speculative daughters of Eve," they noted the clarence waiting in front to convey the ladies on their business missions, and were admitted by a uniformed doorman to the front office. The inner room, with the private desks of the firm, was guarded by a card that cautioned gentlemen to "state their business and then retire at once." Visitors were treated not only to a vision of the bewitching brokers at work, but to the latest figures on Mariposa or a disquisition on woman's rights. In an ivory memorandum book, Woodhull and Claflin jotted down some points on Long Island stock, while they revealed to those who listened in grim silence or scepticism the reasons for their strange new venture.

It was primarily, Victoria claimed, to prove woman's ability that they had invaded Wall Street. While others were arguing the equality of woman with man she would prove it by successfully engaging in business. Their petticoats would not take up more room in the street than the other brokers' trousers. "Women have every right. All they need do is exercise them. . . . We are doing daily more for women's rights, by practically exercising the right to carry on our own business, than all the diatribes of papers and platform speeches will do in ten years." And surely it was neither Vanderbilt nor Blood nor yet the spirit of Demosthenes, but her own varied experiences which had convinced Victoria that "woman's ability to earn money . . . is a better protection against the tyranny and brutality of men than her ability to vote."

That ability the firm of Woodhull and Claflin proceeded to exercise while reporters mused about "female ursines," cartoonists sharpened their pens to depict "The Wall Street Hippodrome" in which the ladies drove a chariot drawn by "two furious animals, Fisk and Vanderbilt," editors amused themselves with witty articles on the Princesses of Erie, and Susan B. Anthony descended upon the balmoral brokers to interview them for her paper and wish them success. In the Gold Room and the Stock Exchange the new opening was announced, while songs were sung and jokes cracked at the expense of the newcomers. Unperturbed, the firm of Woodhull, Claflin & Company advertised that they

Buy and sell Gold, Government Bonds and Securities; Railway, Mining and Oil Stocks and Bonds; Bonds of any State, County or City, and will make liberal advances on same; will make collections on and issue certificates of deposit available in all parts of the Union. . . .

Interest allowed on daily balances of depositors.

The fascinating brokers had flung their banner to the breeze.

One of their first acts was to deposit a check for $7000 or $7500 and establish credit. With accounts at the Fourth National and the Bank of New York, they were ready for business. Although commissions were only one-eighth of one per cent, margin requirements at ten per cent promised possibilities. Victoria Woodhull was prepared to investigate them.

One of the firm's pet projects early in its career was the Arcade Underground Railway designed to relieve traffic on Broadway, but destined for a gubernatorial veto. To this, Woodhull and Claflin swiftly added other schemes—a Nevada silver ledge company, and, of course, investment in the country's railways. Not all their projects were profitable—$12,000 invested in railroad bonds was lost when the bonds proved worthless—but the firm was learning perhaps as much from its mistakes as from its successes. Certainly Victoria Woodhull was learning the mysteries of sharp practice and false claims, of watered stocks and bogus bonds—knowledge that she would expose in due time to the discomfort of many of the magnates of Wall Street.

Meanwhile, the investments and the commissions continued, while speculation ran rife. Was Peter Cooper a client of Woodhull and Claflin? Was Commodore Vanderbilt lending his money or merely his counsel? Was the Commodore or the Colonel or the orator Demosthenes the power behind the firm? Had the gentlemen of the street hired detectives to trace their eventful history? Represented by brokers on the Gold and Stock Boards, the queens of finance placidly continued their business. The women of the metropolis rode up in their carriages to 44 Broad Street, entered the private room in the rear, left deposits of money with the business-like brokers, gave orders for the buying and selling of stocks, and went their way. Victoria, shrewd and energetic, was ready to transact business in gold or bonds or stocks for all who wished to make ventures on the street. To expand their facilities, Woodhull and Claflin added to their brokerage activities a banking business "upon a solid and wide basis." On that extension of Nassau below Wall known as Broad Street, the lady brokers were in full swing.

The incidents, the difficulties, the speculations mounted. Women visitors queried, "How do you manage to get along with so many different men without being insulted?" Men refused to admit the bewitching brokers to their offices when their wives were present. One Achsah M. Truman alleged she had deposited $400 with Woodhull and Claflin but had received no interest on the deposit. Susan A. King was to assert that she had invested $18,000 with the firm, but that no stocks had been bought for her. Forgers who attempted to victimize the female brokers by altering Park and Tilford checks from small amounts to large were outwitted by the ladies of Broad Street, who demanded certification. Through the months, they watched the market as it reflected the life of the nation. Gold might be dull and state bonds steady, Rock Island weak and Erie strong, the ladies watched and listened and acted. They stood by, observing the results of rumors of a European war or the passage of the currency bill, of the Chicago fire and the

Boston fire on the fluctuating market, observing how certain securities had a formidable way of passing into the hands of cliques and rings. In "Puts" and "Calls," "Spreads" and "Straddles" they became adept, while rumors spread about the intrepid pair. In the midst of exciting talk about stocks, it was said, they languidly called for Vichy water. They gambled their profits in the policy shop at the rear of Clute's brokerage office. They kept dubious assignations in the restaurant on Broad Street where they had "apartments subject to call."

Despite the rumors, the profits, for a time at least, mounted. In eleven days they had made $500 by commissions on sales alone. Their banking capital was estimated at a quarter of a million. Tennie could remark, "What do present profits amount to when it costs us over $2,500 a month to live?" Certainly, Victoria could point to the palatial mansion on Murray Hill that housed her entire family and her hangers-on as proof that money was flowing in from one source or another. If Vanderbilt had helped her with tips, he had helped other women before. If she had "made and lost fortunes," so had the monarchs of Wall Street who frequently sandwiched periods of prosperity between two sizable bankruptcies. Accused of being a prostitute who specialized in brokers rather than in brokerage, she could point to the roster of visitors to her home—a list that included the Presidents of the Western Union Telegraph Company, of the Home Fire Insurance Company, of the Continental Bank and of the Stock Board, the Vice-President of Union Pacific Railroad, and Henry Clews, the celebrated banker with mutton-chop whiskers and strong views on women's inequality. Surely she could not have "specialized" in all these distinguished gentlemen?

Surely, too, despite the charges and the notoriety, Victoria Woodhull had proved what she had set out to prove. For the first time in history, a woman had entered upon Wall Street and faced it on its own terms. Now, only a few months after she had formally established her company, she set out to prove something else. If she had succeeded in astounding Wall Street, she would now attempt to astound the entire country. For the bewitching broker was about to become petticoat politician.

On March 29th, 1870, her pronunciamento was dispatched to *The New York Herald,* where it appeared a few days later:

As I happen to be the most prominent representative of the only un-
represented class in the republic, and perhaps the most practical
exponent of the principles of equality, I request the favor of being
permitted to address the public through the medium of the Herald.
While others of my sex devoted themselves to a crusade against the
laws that shackle the women of the country, I asserted my individual
independence; . . . while others sought to show that there was no
valid reason why woman should be treated . . . as a being inferior to
man, I boldly entered the arena of politics and business and exercised
the rights I already possessed. I therefore claim the right to speak for
the unenfranchised women of the country, and . . . I now announce
myself as a candidate for the Presidency.

The charming little jockey hat had been hurled into the ring.
As a Wall Street broker, however, Victoria Woodhull could not
possibly hope to ensconce herself in the White House. Only by a
radical about face could she attempt to garner the votes of the
male population. She had learned enough about the nerve center
of American finance to expose its machinations to the public. This
she proceeded to do. In the case of the "People *versus* Fraud"
she flung her gauntlet. The bewitching broker, for political expediency or for the glow of the limelight, turned iconoclast, crusader
against the very street she had invaded.

What better medium than printer's ink to endorse her campaign
and what better end for her brokerage profits than a weekly paper?
Although it was said that the journal was "edited in one world
and published in another," *Woodhull & Claflin's Weekly,* from its
first issue of May 14, 1870, was very much of this world. From
prostitution and the social evil to free love, abortion and divorce,
from suffrage to new employments for women, from spiritualism
to puffs for the self-appointed candidate, from currency reform
to industrial justice, it ran a wide and ruthless gamut. If it expressed the opinions of its managing editor, Colonel Blood, and
of its contributor, the eccentric philosopher, Stephen Pearl Andrews, whose "Cardinary News" from the "Pantarchy" made it
the organ of "Social Regeneration and Constructive Reform," it
also reflected the views and experiences of a Broad Street broker
who, to fulfill her political ambitions, had decided to elucidate the
mysteries of finance to the people and drive the money-changers
from the temple.

On September 10, 1870, *Woodhull & Claflin's Weekly*—despite the fact that its advertising columns resembled a roster of the country's financial institutions—began its muckraking campaign:

There are frauds in railroad companies to an alarming extent, the exposure of which has long been neglected by the public press—the only medium through which it could be clearly made to the people.

This exposure we deem a necessity . . . for the protection of a large class of citizens who, as shareholders, are now subjected to heartless plunderings daily, . . .

There are other frauds of bolder character practiced by the trained brains of scheming bankers . . . by which they swindle the abundance of the rich and the scanty savings of the poor. . . .

The peculiar species of *swindling* in each instance will spread astonishment, when it is set forth, as it will be in the columns of this journal. . . .

. . . we are prepared with the names of each party, the description and extent of the frauds perpetrated, the swindles intended, the quantity or amount of bonds and shares in many cases which gratuitously and dishonestly went to each director, banker, Congressman, Governor and State Legislator. Each in their turn will be brought to light.

. . . We are nearly ready to commence the work, and in advance call close attention to the forthcoming revelations. . . .

We shall not hesitate to give names, acts, transactions; and we shall stand ready with evidences, with moral and financial strength to sustain us in this bold effort to protect the interest of the people.

Victoria had begun with the railroads, but she did not end there. Under her tireless whip, the "fraudulent, the rotten, the mushroom, and the speculative" were scourged—the insurance companies with fictitious policies, the Wall Street corners, the watered stocks, the land jobbery in Congress, the swindles in Southern State bonds and in spurious Mexican bonds. "Subjected to all kinds of influence" to induce her to cease her revelations, she could blithely reply that her columns were "open to evidences of error," but that no such "evidences" were forthcoming. To charges that she was engaged in blackmailing, she pointed out the obvious fact that the companies accused of fraud would doubtless have offered her large amounts to suppress her exposures, but she had not suppressed them.

Indeed, she continued those exposures until it seemed as though Victoria Woodhull must have embarked upon a brokerage career only to destroy Wall Street. To this, too, the fascinating financier had an answer. "We entered upon the 'walks of money 'change' to do a legitimate business in American securities. . . . It opened to us unusual facilities and sources for correct information . . . . soon revealed the startling fact that frauds existed in many of the securities deemed first-class. . . . We were enabled to save many of our customers from serious losses. In doing this we discovered that larger, bolder and deeper frauds were contemplated by . . . shoddy bankers, who, like scum, had risen to the surface in boilings of the dishonest caldrons of the war."

The prepossessing Victoria Woodhull of the magnetic eyes, handsomely arrayed in her blue walking suit, stirred that caldron until it erupted. Actually, for a time during her race for the White House, she followed her theories to their logical—or illogical—end, by becoming the dominant personality in Section 12 of the International Workingmen's Association which had been organized in 1864 by Karl Marx! The section met at the brokerage office on Broad Street until it caused a split in the International and formed a Federal Council of its own. Meanwhile, the Woodhull faction had staged an international parade after the execution of the Paris Communists, and—of far greater significance—the Woodhull weekly had published the first English translation of the *Communist Manifesto* to appear in the United States.

For the enlightenment of her comrades, as well as for their votes, the would-be President varied her activities as broker and publisher with lectures and tracts on the times. She was "always glad to extend whatever favor my limited time permits, to such as have, at heart, . . . the needed reforms that must precede any decided improvement in the human race." Holding her manuscript in one hand, she mounted the platform arrayed in black with a single red rose on her dress, and "quivering under the fire of her own rhapsody," emitted the "eloquence" that "poured from her lips in reckless torrents." It was eloquence on spiritualism and its relations to political reform, on free love to which she announced her *"inalienable, constitutional* and *natural* right," on the scarecrows of sexual slavery that existed only in marriage, the "hotbed of license." And, of course, it was eloquence on finance.

On August 3, 1871, Victoria Woodhull appeared at Cooper Institute to deliver a speech on "The Principles of Finance," announcing that gold was merely an arbitrary standard of value, that the present system of banking was a swindle upon the people, and that bank notes should give way to a purely people's money, a national currency. *"No person,"* she declared, *"has any just claim to the ownership of anything which he did not produce or which he did not acquire by an equitable exchange of something which he did produce."* A singular point of view for a banker-broker, perhaps, but less singular for a banker-broker in quest of support as presidential nominee.

If, as was remarked, Victoria Woodhull's speeches were written by the men in her background, she would not have been the first public figure to employ the services of a ghostwriter. Her lectures had a habit of arousing either incredulity or "a spasmodic convulsion of virtue" on the part of the audience. None the less, she continued to deliver them, following up the Cooper Union tirade with a disquisition on "The Impending Revolution" at the Academy of Music.

"Before the largest assemblage ever seen in that Hall," Victoria Woodhull unhesitatingly, if rather ungratefully, castigated the Vanderbilt who sits in his office manipulating stocks, the Astor who watches his inherited wealth increase and is worshiped for his own business capacity, and the Stewart who entraps his customers into millions of dollars of purchases—the individuals who "represent three of the principal methods that the privileged classes have invented by which to monopolize the accumulated wealth of the country."

Whoever had written the words against the privileged few, it was Victoria Woodhull who had delivered them. If she had written the series of articles on "The Tendencies of Government" that appeared over her name in the *Herald,* she was capable of writing her speeches. If she had not written the articles, then she had probably not written the introduction to Goethe's *Elective Affinities* commissioned of her by a Boston publisher. And if she had not written that introduction, she had probably not written anything at all. Indeed, there were some who went so far as to say that Victoria Woodhull could not even write her name, basing the charge no doubt upon her checkered early history, her scanty edu-

cation, her ideological about face, her attractiveness to men, or
even possibly upon the fact that she was a woman. That she
was a woman who had founded a bank and published a journal
seemed to make no difference.

At all events, no one questioned, or could question, the fact
that she could speak. Her début as lecturer had been made in
the national capital itself before no less august an assemblage
than the House Judiciary Committee in January of 1871. Upon
that occasion it was remarked that her speech had been written
either by the greenbacker and champion of woman's rights, Ben
Butler, or by Victoria's Greek guardian, Demosthenes. In this case
the allegations were surely tributes, for with or without earthly
or astral aid, the would-be presidential candidate had prepared a
Memorial for Congress that was to raise the vexed problem of
woman suffrage into a question of constitutional law. The petticoat
politician may have been no more sincere than the bewitching
broker. But she was to prove no less effective.

As Susan B. Anthony put it, Victoria "came to Washington
from Wall street with a powerful argument and with lots of cash
behind her." She came in a blue naval cloth costume and jacket
with coat-tails behind, and having removed her Alpine hat, arose
before the tribunal to read a Memorial that was indeed powerful,
simple and comparatively novel. No new amendment was required
to enfranchise women. If women were citizens, then their right to
vote was already guaranteed by the Constitution, and all that was
needed was that Congress see that that right be exercised. The
"Youth, Beauty and Wealth of the Woodhull" on this occasion
also "carried the day." She had impressed not only the "grave
legislators" but the suffragettes—Mrs. Beecher Hooker in her curl-
ing feathers of blue, Susan B. Anthony in her black silk with
spectacles clinging to her nose and her benign finger marking off
the elocutionary pauses. For a time at least, the cause of woman
suffrage seemed to have discovered the paladin "best fitted to
rescue it from dusty oblivion."

Although the Committee's majority report recommended that
the Memorial be laid on the table and that the petitioner's prayer
be not granted, it evoked a strong minority report in its favor, and
Victoria followed up her oratorical début swiftly. Before a suffrage
convention that met in Washington on the same day that the

Memorial had been presented, she repeated her argument. Armed with the Constitution, she had become the "lively little yacht" that took the wind out of the convention's drooping sails.

At the November elections, Victoria made a bold, albeit unsuccessful attempt to apply her convictions. Leading a group of thirty-two women, who "advanced on the universal suffrage question with the solidity of a Grecian phalanx and the tread of a Roman legion," she unsheathed her parasol and sallied forth to the polls. Despite a Woodhull peroration on the science of government, the inspectors stroked their beards and regretted. Perhaps they had not heard of the Woodhull Memorial.

Meanwhile, the brokerage office on Broad Street had been converted into campaign headquarters for the political aspirant, a Victoria League was organized to support the candidacy of one whose name inspired "the cheerful prescience of victory," and in May 1872, at an Apollo Hall convention, Victoria Woodhull was at long last nominated as a candidate for the presidency of the United States. The fascinating financier heard the roaring shouts that greeted the proposal, and, her face beaming under her high-crowned Neapolitan black hat, she "shook hands with the gentlemen" and was embraced by the women in scenes of wild political osculations. A grand rally at Cooper Institute ratified the nomination of the Equal Rights Party, *Woodhull & Claflin's Weekly* blossomed forth as a campaign sheet, banners were planned, bonds announced, and, to the tune of "John Brown's Body" the constituents of the petticoat politician chanted, "Victoria's marching on!"

Through campaign lectures and printer's ink Victoria marched, announcing a platform that would completely reconstruct the most important functions of government, remove the "oppressive weight" which capital laid upon labor, and advance the freedom of woman and the freedom of the worker. There was something that appealed to the candidate in the idea of a "twin sisterhood of Victorias" presiding over two great nations, and she believed that the "fatality of triumph" adhered somehow in her name.

That there was a different kind of fatality adhering in her name shortly became apparent. By the time Grant was re-elected at the polls in November 1872, the Equal Rights Party had no electoral ticket, and its erstwhile candidate was in Ludlow Street Jail.

The name of Victoria Woodhull had had a fatality indeed, but not one connected with triumph in the White House. By November of 1872, Victoria Woodhull had lit the spark under a bonfire that was to roar across a nation, implicate one of its greatest idols, and ruin her own career as broker, publisher and would-be politician. The bonfire was known as the Beecher-Tilton Scandal. The spark that lit it was the November 2, 1872 issue of *Woodhull & Claflin's Weekly*.

In that issue there appeared two articles, one entitled "The Philosophy Of Modern Hypocrisy" which revealed the debauches of a broker named Luther C. Challis, the other entitled "The Beecher-Tilton Scandal Case" which revealed Henry Ward Beecher's liaison with the wife of his friend and parishioner, Theodore Tilton, and which was intended to "burst like a bomb-shell into the ranks of the moralistic social camp." For the first article, Victoria Woodhull was charged with sending obscenity through the mails. For the second, she was to be rewarded with such notoriety as neither the Broad Street broker nor the presidential candidate had dreamed of. In this instance at least, no one—except Stephen Pearl Andrews, who later acknowledged its authorship—expressed any doubt that Victoria had penned the eruptive revelation. It was an article that was to evoke a library of pamphlets, songs, poems and burlesques, that was to cause trials, arrests and re-arrests, that was to start a scandal that would hold its own for nearly three long years.

It was not the love of sensation for sensation's sake that led Victoria Woodhull to discharge the bombshell that wakened "echoing thunders from the country." By November of 1872, the bewitching broker had been sore tried. Harriet Beecher Stowe, sister of the distinguished pastor of Plymouth Church, had written a novel, *My Wife and I*, which portrayed in Audacia Dangyereyes a somewhat unappetizing caricature of Victoria Woodhull. Catherine Beecher, another sister of the pastor, was to declare in the *Tribune* that Victoria was "either insane or the hapless victim of malignant spirits." *The Independent*, published by Beecher's friend, Henry Bowen, had noted in an editorial that "Mrs. Woodhull, about whose private affairs all gossip is needless . . . does more harm than good."

Gossip about Victoria's affairs may have been needless, but it had been much bruited. If it was not common knowledge that her household had included not only her present "husband," James

Harvey Blood, but her former husband, Dr. Canning Woodhull, that tri-partite domestic arrangement became common knowledge when Victoria's mother lodged a court complaint against the Colonel in what was called the "Claflin Scandal Case." Victoria's free love platform, the *Harper's Weekly* cartoon that caricatured her as Mrs. Satan exhorting a wife to "Be Saved by Free Love" had not helped her anomalous position. Even her biography prepared by the enamored Theodore Tilton, and his announcement that she was the "Joan of Arc" of the woman's movement, a "gentle but fiery genius" and "one of the most remarkable women of her time" did not help. Henry Ward Beecher was, like Caesar's wife, above suspicion. Victoria Woodhull was not. She was forced to give up her mansion on Murray Hill. No hotel would admit her. She slept on the floor of her brokerage office. When the landlord raised the rent of that office by $1000 a year, she was forced to move. She was being hounded for practising more or less in public what the pastor of Plymouth Church practised more or less in private. It was a situation that called for correction.

Elizabeth Cady Stanton, who confirmed to Victoria the rumor that Beecher was enjoying an extra-curricular relationship with Elizabeth Tilton, had supplied the ammunition for her guns. Victoria fired them first in a letter to the *Times* and to *The World*:

One of the charges made against me is that I lived in the same house with my former husband, Dr. Woodhull, and my present husband, Colonel Blood.

. . . Dr. Woodhull being sick, . . . and incapable of self-support, I felt it my duty . . . that he should be cared for, . . . I esteem it one of the most virtuous acts of my life; but various editors have stigmatized me as a living example of immorality. . . .

I do not intend to be made the scapegoat of sacrifice. . . .

I know that many of my self-appointed judges . . . are . . . tainted with the vices they condemn; . . . My judges preach against "free love" openly, practice it secretly; . . . For example, I know of one man, a public teacher of eminence, who lives in concubinage with the wife of another public teacher, of almost equal eminence. All three concur in denouncing offences against morality. . . . I shall make it my business to analyze some of these lives, and will take my chances in the matter of libel suits.

Victoria's guns were as yet muffled. When she fired them a second time, in a bold revelation before a convention of spiritualists in Boston, her guns were not muffled, but they did not reverberate far. They were both unmuffled and far-reaching when, on November 2, 1872, they shot like a thunderbolt from the columns of *Woodhull & Claflin's Weekly*.

Then, not Henry Ward Beecher, but the self-appointed guardian of public morality, Anthony Comstock, hauled Victoria Woodhull to jail ostensibly because of her obscene article about the broker, Challis, but actually because of her libelous exposures about America's most distinguished preacher. Victoria's bombshell had backfired. In Cell No. 11 of Ludlow Street Jail she was held until Ben Butler came to the rescue with his interpretation of the law regarding obscene literature, and until her counsel, the glittering, bediamonded Howe of Howe & Hummel, won one of the most notable censorship trials of the country. She was arrested and re-arrested and labeled as part of a "nest of free-lovers and mountebanks" bent upon blackmailing Henry Ward Beecher. When the eccentric philosopher, George Francis Train, who had circled the world in eighty days, championed her, he, too, was incarcerated and declared a lunatic. Her paper was suspended. Her clients abandoned her. For Victoria Woodhull, the wages of Beecher's sin was ruin. Not so for Beecher. A "trial" at Plymouth Church exonerated its pastor and expelled his inamorata. The more official trial of Tilton vs. Beecher, which lasted for nearly six months and involved most of the bigwigs of the country, ended in a hung jury. The odds were with Beecher, who went forth to lecture at $1500 a night. Victoria Woodhull went forth to lecture, too, but the odds were against her. On one occasion she had been forced to don the disguise of a Quakeress in a coal-scuttle bonnet to evade the United States marshals who tried to prevent her from discussing "The Naked Truth" at Cooper Institute.

Yet nothing was able to clip irreparably the wings of the Broad Street broker. She revived her paper to resume her anti-Beecher crusade and to publicize her prison experiences. Even her brokerage activities were not entirely discontinued, despite her loss of clients, for the name of Woodhull, Claflin & Company, bankers or brokers, persisted in the *New York Directories* intermittently until 1876. In lectures especially she clung to the foreground. Taking her text now from Corinthians and appearing with a Bible in one hand, she toured the South and mounted the platform to announce that the human body was the temple of God and that the elixir of life was to be found in sexual freedom. Victoria Woodhull, it seemed, had come full circle. She had started her career by dispensing an elixir of life in bottles and now she was dispensing another elixir in words. Between two elixirs she had sandwiched a formidable if notorious career as the first woman broker, the first woman aspirant to the White House, and the first woman to point an accusing editorial finger at the country's strongest bulwark of morality. Victoria Woodhull's American career was ending on an apt note. But it was ending only to open the way for another career three thousand miles away. In America, Victoria Woodhull had invested her wherewithal in a bank. In England, she was to invest it in a banker.

Once again, rumor had it that Cornelius Vanderbilt was the power behind Victoria's decision to leave her native land, except that this time it was, even more appropriately, the ghost of Vanderbilt dead. The Commodore died in 1877, leaving the bulk of his enormous estate to his son William and comparatively minor bequests to his remaining progeny, who proceeded to contest the Will. The magnate's propensities for electrical physicians and clairvoyants naturally played no small part in determining his soundness of mind and, in order to avoid the summoning of Victoria Woodhull as a witness, it was whispered, William H. Vanderbilt had offered her a sizable amount to go abroad. Whether she had left, fortified with part of the Vanderbilt fortune, or whether she had departed, "shattered in health, reduced in pocket, almost heartbroken, . . . with the instinct of a wounded deer, to hide in solitude," Victoria arrived in England with her sister Tennie and her parents, but minus her discarded "husband," Colonel Blood. She was not to "hide in solitude" for long.

Having appeared as lecturer in the provinces, the thirty-nine-year-old ex-Princess of Erie opened her London season with an address at St. James's Hall on "The Human Body, the Temple of God." In the audience on that eventful December evening of 1877 was a thirty-six-year-old gentleman who had followed her work and career in America, clipped newspaper articles about her, and "treasured every mention of her name." Prompted perhaps by the nature of Victoria's oration, which disclosed a paradise and a Garden of Eden in the human body, or by the nature of the lecturer herself as she walked upon the platform much in the manner of Charlotte Cushman as Queen Elizabeth, the young gentleman decided to make her his wife.

After all, they had much in common. John Biddulph Martin was descended, on his mother's side, from Martha Washington. Victoria Woodhull, it was said, was descended on her father's side from the ducal house of Hamilton. After a century, "the families of Washington and of his dearest friend, Alexander Hamilton," would again be united. John Biddulph Martin was a partner in Martin's Bank, one of the oldest firms in the City, older than the Bank of England. At its ancient sign of "The Grasshopper" in Lombard Street, Nell Gwyn had kept accounts. Victoria Woodhull had been a partner in Woodhull, Claflin & Company, at whose less ancient sign on Broad Street, it was said, Cornelius Vanderbilt had kept accounts.

These familial and financial common interests were more convincing to John Biddulph Martin than to his family, who took six years to acquiesce to the proposed union. It was not until October 31, 1883, that the queen of finance received her official crown as wife of John Biddulph Martin, product of Harrow and Oxford, philanthropist, leading member of the Institute of Bankers and the Royal Statistical Society, and partner in the distinguished firm at the sign of "The Grasshopper" in Lombard Street.

Victoria Woodhull Martin at the age of forty-five took her place as mistress of 17 Hyde Park Gate, South Kensington, a residence even more palatial than her Murray Hill mansion. Against a background of rich carpets, elaborate paintings, and potted palms, the fascinating financier was ensconced. Seated in her drawing-room, where American and English flags were crossed and the emblem of "The Grasshopper" looked over at a statue representing "Liberty," Victoria could converse with her distinguished husband on the subjects that interested him most deeply—the gold coinage and the currency question, statistics and the circulation of bank notes, the development of railways and the American national debt. She could vary her background by a sojourn at the Martin manor house in Bredon's Norton near Tewkesbury, and at the base of lofty Bredon Hill overlooking the fertile valley of the Severn, could continue her marital discussions about the relative merits of the gold standard and a more fluid currency.

Only the reverberations of early scandal marred an otherwise perfect union. As Harriet Beecher Stowe's *My Wife and I* had caricatured Victoria at home, Henry James's *Siege of London* presented in the portrait of the social climber, Mrs. Headway, a woman who "must have repudiated more husbands than she had married," a disguised sketch of Mrs. Woodhull. The woman who in her own eyes had upheld liberty was still accused of defending licence, and to unearth "those vile traducers" who wantoned with her good name, she and her husband paid periodic visits to the United States and even started an action against the British Museum for allowing two pamphlets about the Beecher-Tilton Scandal to remain on the shelves!

While she was not defending her new name from libelous attacks, Mrs. Woodhull-Martin could enjoy the spoils of high life. In 1885 her sister Tennie passed her on the social ladder, marrying the merchant, Francis Cook, and shortly thereafter becoming Lady Cook with all the rights to the Chateau of Monserrate on "Cintra's Fair Rock" in Portugal and to the great Cook art collection housed in Doughty House, Richmond. Yet Victoria, lacking both title and art gallery, surely found deep satisfaction in her new life. In 1892 she began the publication of a monthly, *The Humanitarian,* with her daughter, Zula Maud, as associate editor and her husband as occasional contributor. Although Victoria's aim was "to discuss all subjects appertaining to the well-being of humanity," she had not forgotten the important role that finance played in what she called humanitarian government. Now, without a James Harvey Blood or a Stephen Pearl Andrews to guide her pen, she could still announce a humanitarian platform which held that "social evils are caused, *first*, by unequal distribution of wealth," and she could fill the columns of her monthly not only with articles on psychical research, astrology and palmistry, but with essays on the financial crisis in America, co-operative credit and the inequalities of wealth. Broad Street may have been a far cry from South Kensington, but the mistress of 17 Hyde Park Gate had not forgotten the principles of finance. If John Biddulph Martin taught her something of statistics, he doubtless learned much about market manipulations from the bewitching banker who had become the banker's bewitching wife.

Between writing on stirpiculture or the rapid multiplication of the unfit and conducting epistolary campaigns for the presidency of the United States, Victoria persisted in her attempt to elucidate the mysteries of finance to the public. Her treatise, *Humanitarian Money,* was prepared without benefit of either Blood or Andrews, although none could prove that during its composition the guardian spirit of Demosthenes may not have hovered somewhere among the draperies of 17 Hyde Park Gate.

And long after the death of her husband in 1897, the wealthy widow Martin continued to enlighten and bedazzle the public. Until after the turn of the century *The Humanitarian* plied subscribers with her views. Having sold her London residence, Victoria moved to Bredon's Norton, where the woman who had railed against the shams of the nineteenth century embraced the twentieth century in all its aspects. As the years and then the decades passed, she founded the Women's International Agricultural Club, contributed toward the purchase of Sulgrave Manor for the Anglo-American Association, and aided in fund-raising campaigns during the First World War. The enthusiast of modernity joined the Ladies' Automobile Club, organized the Women's Aerial League of England, and offered $5000 and a trophy to the first transatlantic aviator.

Actually, Charles A. Lindbergh might well have claimed the promised prize, for Victoria Woodhull-Martin did not die until June 10, 1927, three weeks after the aviator had made his flight to Paris. The world had changed unrecognizably since the bewitching broker had first descended upon Broad Street, and Victoria Woodhull had changed from a magnetic and beautiful thirty-one-year-old banker with presidential ambitions into a benevolent if eccentric widow bowed by the weight of almost ninety intense years. She had come a long way from the Homer, Ohio of 1838, to die in her sleep in an ancestral country manor at Bredon's Norton. It had been a colorful way if a notorious way. In its rich and varied course she had proved many things. Not the least of them was the now indisputable fact that a woman could be at once a woman and a financier, and a fascinating financier to boot.

An American Woman First in
Textiles & Interior Decoration
CANDACE WHEELER
1877

AMONG the crowds who wandered through Fairmount Park, that "great pleasure-ground of Philadelphia," exclaiming at the marvels of the Centennial Exposition of 1876, was a woman not quite fifty years old who had as yet made no perceptible mark in the world. With the hosts who reveled in the art gallery and the New England kitchen, the horticultural hall and the hunters' camp, the popcorn and the soda water, Candace Thurber Wheeler enjoyed the sights and the sensations of a nation *en fête*. It was only when she walked on to the pavilion of the "Royal School of Art and Needlework," that her personal reactions to the Centennial began to differ from those of the crowds about her. Mrs. Wheeler looked at the "magnificent tent, . . . constructed of purple velvet hangings, and ornamented with a superb collection of . . . embroidery and needlework," saw the "exquisitely worked scroll over the entrance," and examined the work of the "Kensington School" —a group who were reviving with the needle those medieval arts that the pre-Raphaelites were reviving with the brush. While the School's primary object, she knew, was to benefit "decayed gentlewomen," it was also giving proof, in its revival of embroidery, that needlework could become "a means of artistic expression and a thing of value." Mrs. Wheeler suddenly realized that "the common and inalienable heritage of feminine skill in the use of the needle" could be converted into "a means of art-expression and pecuniary profit." With that realization, the purpose of Mrs. Wheeler's life was crystallized, and the decorative impetus of her country was revitalized. Candace Thurber Wheeler was soon to launch upon a career that would supply the demands of a nation awakened to artistic impulses and that would open a new profession for women—a profession that was art and industry in one, a profession that combined American textile design with American interior decoration. She would, in the long years that followed, help organize a new Society of Decorative Art, join an association that would unfold for America a renaissance of art in industry, found her own firm of decorative artists, and crown her career with the decorative work for yet another great Exposition, the Columbian of 1893.

Although Mrs. Wheeler's awareness of her purpose was brought to a sudden and dramatic crux by the Centennial of 1876, that purpose had gradually been crystallizing throughout her life. In the five decades that had already passed, she had unknowingly been grounded in all the arts and skills that she would summon to her aid, from home industries and domestic manufactures to sketching from nature. The woman who would help bring to the public a fulfillment of its artistic desires and to her fellow women a new industry, a new profession, had been equipped by the varied richness of her own life for the untried work that lay ahead.

The woman who in 1899 was to write an article on "Home Industries and Domestic Manufactures" had lived those industries and manufactures decades before. She had lived them as Candace Thurber, the daughter of Abner Thurber, who bought and sold skins and ran his own dairy farm, and of Lucy Dunham Thurber, who was herself a "domestic manufacturer" although she looked like a Roman contadina. She lived them in Delhi, a small settlement in Central New York, on the uplands of the Delaware valley, where she had been born in 1827. One of a family of eight, Candace wore linen that had been flax grown on the farm, spun and woven in her own house. She helped make butter and cheese; she joined the "sugaring off" in the maple grove; she assisted in the smoking and curing of meats; she "watered down" the flax; she dipped candles. Her grandmother showed her the bits of India chintz in "housewives" long preserved that Candace would one day hope to revive. Her father plucked flowers for her to draw, whose patterns she would one day boldly embody in textiles. On their walks she had seen "the transparent crimson bell of color which the meadow lily made between her and the sky," and the fiery pink of the wild rose with the sun behind it—colors she would one day apply to canvas. While the child dreamed of scalpings and Indians, her days were colored by the guests of the house—straggling missionaries, colporteurs with their Bibles, temperance lecturers, runaway slaves. She was close enough to her pioneer forefathers to remember their ways forever. Candace varied her readings in Cobbett's *Cottage Economy* with sums done in fox, mink and muskrat skins, and the education that was begun at home was completed at the Delaware Academy. The woman who would one day invent the Wheeler tapestry had executed a sampler at the age of six. The girl whose father prayed she would become a missionary was indeed a missionary of sorts—a missionary for a new profession in "household art" that women could follow. Her grounding in that profession had come early, for what was one day to be part of an "Art Nouveau" had been her daily life.

There was another facet of the household art that would come to be called interior decoration, the facet of art proper, and to this, too, Candace brought an almost unconscious preparation in which her husband played an important if unobtrusive part. The girl from Delhi, New York, was married in 1844, when she was seventeen, to the twenty-six-year-old Thomas M. Wheeler, who had served as a surveyor and civil engineer in the mid West and who was at the moment working in a New York commission house. At first in Brooklyn, and later in New York and Jamaica, Long Island, young Mrs. Wheeler was introduced to the world of artists and through them to the world of art. At the artists' receptions of the '40's and '50's, she circulated among the Hudson River painters—George Inness with his piercing gaze, his long hair and intense expression, the landscape artists, Jervis McEntee and Sanford Gifford. Kensett and Bierstadt, John Weir and La Farge were friends whose talk itself brought paint to life. At New York's Tenth Street Studio the Wheelers picked up paintings while Mrs. Wheeler picked up hints on brush and pigment. At the Saturday receptions of William Chase, the painter with the Van Dyck beard, she was an eager listener. The art world came to her doorstep when, in 1854, the Wheelers built their own house, "Nestledown." To the low, rambling red cottage on the flats of Long

Island near the old Dutch village of Jamaica, the men of the
Tenth Street Studio and the Hudson River School drifted out on
Sundays and holidays—Eastman Johnson, the sculptor Launt
Thompson, the gentlemanly Hubbard who, like his work, had an
air of aloofness. At close hand Mrs. Wheeler could watch Sanford
Gifford sketch a sunset or could learn from George Hall how to
mix colors and glazes.

Not all her world was art, however. Candace's children had
begun to make their appearance—the first, a daughter born in
1845, who would become the mother of Henry L. Stimson; the
third, the daughter Dora, born in 1856, who would one day be a
portrait painter in close association with her mother—alternating
with two sons. In her Quaker bonnet of a morning, Mrs. Wheeler
might transplant into her garden poet's narcissus, and on the
ferry she might catch a glimpse of a more authentic poet, William
Cullen Bryant, whose daughter became her friend. When Brooklyn
was a village of green fields and Long Island spread out behind
it, a pastoral farmland, Candace Wheeler drove a pair of Morgan
mares or a tall black pair of carriage horses and lived the life of
her time and place. That life was and would be broadened by the
poets and writers whom she came to know—Bryant, to whose
Roslyn home she might carry a basket of lilies, Lowell and Holmes
and Aldrich. But that life was most immeasurably enriched by the
artists who, unknowingly, equipped her for another life that lay
ahead. She had always drawn; she had always had an instinct for
color; after her companionship with artists at work she would find
that when she came to the study of art personally, "the way had
been prepared."

Study itself was more than talk. She might read, during the
'70's, Bezold on *The Theory of Color* or Langl on *Modern Art
Education*; she might dip into a book entitled *The Home* by Frank
Stockton and his wife, who would also be numbered among her
friends, or browse in Charles Eastlake's *Hints on Household Taste*.
But the history as well as the practice of art would be dramatically
unfolded to her in journeys abroad. In her travels early or late
she could visit Watts and Burne-Jones, Alma-Tadema and Whistler. She could drive to the Du Mauriers or meet De Morgan in
his study and catch him in the midst of his ceramic experiments.
As the years passed, she would meet Browning at Lady Jeune's

and discuss textile design with Alma-Tadema, but perhaps no trip abroad was more significant to her than the journey to Dresden when she studied in the studio of a German professor of painting. For that Dresden winter brought her face to face with "the history and accomplishments of art" which were to be bound so inextricably with her own work when she abandoned the "simply personal phase of life."

That phase was not yet over. Through the Civil War in New York, and after the Civil War in Newport, where Mrs. Wheeler sat at Julia Ward Howe's "blue teas" listening to Samuel Colman dilate upon his collection of weavings or hearing John La Farge contribute his wisdom to the weekly convocations, she was still a spectator. By 1867, with the birth of Henry L. Stimson, the lady of "Nestledown" had become a grandmother. Less than a decade later, she lost her eldest daughter—a tragic personal event that happened to coincide with a jubilant public event, the United States Centennial Exhibition in Philadelphia. Now, Candace Wheeler had the spur to move on from the personal life that had engrossed her into a realm more public. "Although . . . I was apparently absorbed in family life, and country life, and social life, . . . these things had in themselves elements of wider forms of usefulness; so that now when the loss came which changed my whole attitude toward life . . . I was not unprepared." She had indeed been prepared. The household industries she had shared as a child, the world of paint and canvas that her artist companions had unfolded to her, the study of art and its history that she had begun abroad, her own color consciousness and enthusiastic talent for drawing, her interest in flowers and their characteristic patterns—needed only to be combined and given direction. Added up, they made a whole larger than themselves, a whole known as American interior decoration and textile design. Now the fifty-year-old grandmother who was Candace Wheeler gathered together the lives she had lived and focused them into yet another life that would evolve into a new and important industry for herself and the women who came after her.

The summing up of her lives, the interweaving of its threads, began tentatively in an association called The New York Society of Decorative Art. On February 24, 1877, five people met together, each of whom knew that "there were numberless educated and dependent women to whom a legitimate outlet for their labor would be the greatest boon which society could bestow." One of them knew more than that. Candace Wheeler knew that "a new commercial opportunity for women" was not only imperative, but feasible, for she believed that "the small skill and abundant taste of the average woman could easily be made available in the production of artistic manufactures" of the kind she had seen at the Centennial. The American mind, however, must follow national impulses. The new society would differ from its English prototype, the Kensington School, as much as a republic differed from a monarchy. It would be wider in scope, more general in its benefits, and not based upon "the idea of one class helping another." It would make "daily . . . breaches in the invisible wall of prejudice and custom which had separated . . . well-bred women from . . . money-gaining enterprise." Such breaches were essential. The panic, the invention of the sewing machine which had "left the seamstress idle and hungry," the decline of domestic manufactures in the East which had coincided with the opening of the great West, the establishment of wool and cotton mills—all these, Mrs. Wheeler realized, were combining forces that compelled women to become self-supporting. If indeed "the American art renaissance had begun with the Centennial Exhibition of 1876," the taste that had been stimulated by the Centennial could be fulfilled by the Society of Decorative Art.

At 4 East 20th Street, and later on 19th Street, the new Society, of which Candace Wheeler served as vice-president and corresponding secretary, upheld its purposes. It would "encourage profitable industries among women who possess artistic talent, and . . . furnish a standard of excellence and a market for their work." It would "accumulate and distribute information concerning the various art industries . . . and . . . form classes in Art Needlework." It would exhibit and sell "Sculptures, Paintings, Wood Carvings, Paintings upon Slate, Porcelain and Pottery, Lacework, Art and Ecclesiastical Needlework, Tapestries and Hangings, and, . . . decorative work of any description, done by women, and of sufficient excellence to meet the recently stimulated demand for such work." It would form auxiliary committees in other American cities, make connections with manufacturers and importers, and obtain orders from dealers in the various branches of household art. It would teach its workers "to master the details of one variety of decoration, and endeavor to make for [their] work a reputation of commercial value." The Society of Decorative Art would be a threefold association in which education, art and industry joined hands.

Through the influence of its president, Mrs. David Lane, the Society "was equipped with a board of managers which included all the great names in New York," from Mrs. Cyrus W. Field to Mrs. Abram S. Hewitt, from Miss Bryant to Mrs. August Belmont, from Mrs. William Astor and Mrs. Hamilton Fish to Mrs. Louis C. Tiffany. General Custer's widow, in New York seeking "profitable employment," was engaged as assistant secretary. With its first "mercantile transaction"—the sale of a dozen doyleys "embroidered in Japanese designs and made by a Southern lady, from a Kensington model"—the Society of Decorative Art was launched.

From Boston, Mrs. Oliver Wendell Holmes, Jr., sent a series of embroidered landscapes done in silks and weavings. Mrs. Candace Wheeler observed the diversity of articles sent in for exhibition and sale, from wood carvings to spinning wheels, from Peruvian pottery jars to canton flannel curtains, from table covers to screens. With special interest she noted the readiness of the drygoods firms to lend "useful articles of furniture"—Herter Bros. and Roux & Co., Kimbel & Cabus, Sypher & Co. Classes were formed which she hoped would raise the approach to art industries from the amateur to the professional, classes in china and tile painting, art needlework and medieval embroidery. Under the direction of Mr. Louis C. Tiffany and Mr. Lockwood de Forest a class was opened in the decoration of unbaked pottery. From her painter friends Mrs. Wheeler enlisted a committee of judges on articles submitted for sale, and at their evening sessions she watched, benefiting from criticisms which would soon stand her in good stead. With her charming manner, her hair parted in the middle and puffed on the sides, her emerald and sapphire rings glittering on her ruffled hands, Candace Wheeler was a whirl of activity. She attended meetings, served as chairman of a special committee on the work of contributors, sent in a mantel lambrequin for the Society's Loan Exhibition, and acted as a supervisor of *The Art Interchange* and as a judge in its prize design competition.

Yet she was not completely satisfied. The Society of Decorative

Art would, she knew, continue to prosper. It had found a public demand for the work of amateur producers and it had offered to those producers special training in industrial art. Despite its success and its promise, Candace Wheeler felt that philanthropy and art were not "natural sisters." Perhaps the Society was too confined in its emphasis upon art. Perhaps a more liberal plan of management would benefit more women. When Mrs. William Choate suggested that Candace join in founding another society— a society to which a woman could send a pie if not a picture, a basket of eggs if not a piece of decorated china—she agreed. For a short time Mrs. Wheeler's efforts were directed to the work of the newly organized Woman's Exchange of which she was a charter member, but for a short time only. By 1879 another opportunity had arisen which was to channel her purposes in the pioneer fields of interior decoration and textile design.

Louis Comfort Tiffany, whom Candace knew from the Society of Decorative Art, had offered the opportunity—as exhilarating as it was irresistible. The thirty-one-year-old son of the jeweler proposed an association of artists who would serve industry, apotheosize most of the handicrafts, bring the cult of art into the finest homes of the country, and raise the level of taste in the industrial arts. With her own "larger ambitions, . . . toward a truly great American effort in a lasting direction," Candace Wheeler felt that such an association of the different forms of art must result in a new era in house decoration—the first-fruits of the American renaissance that had been planted by the Centennial, watered by the Society of Decorative Art, and that would bloom forth in the Art Nouveau. This was neither philanthropy nor an amateur educational scheme; this was a business based in the newly awakened American taste for art. What William Morris and Walter Crane had projected in England, and Eugène Grasset and Emile Gallé in France, Louis C. Tiffany proposed to accomplish in America. Mrs. Wheeler, by her own association in the scheme, could demonstrate the fact that "woman's labor, *if well trained,* was needed in the world, and could not only make its demand but find its wages."

To this combination for a new interior decoration Candace Wheeler gave the name of Associated Artists. The associates were only four in number, each a specialist in his field. The flamboyant, red-bearded Mr. Tiffany, Candace knew, had studied painting with George Inness, had traveled through France and North Africa, and had ideas for new decorative expression in the medium of glass. Like herself, he believed that "our climate invites to sumptuous colors," and like herself, he had been profoundly influenced by the Centennial of 1876, at which he had exhibited oils and water colors. With him was allied the Hudson River painter, Samuel Colman, whom Candace knew from Julia Ward Howe's "blue teas" in Newport, and who was a specialist in color decoration and textiles and a collector of Oriental art. The third member of the Associated Artists was Lockwood de Forest, expert in carved and ornamental woodwork, researcher in Oriental color and design. The fourth member would be a woman—Mrs. Candace Wheeler, who would superintend the execution of embroideries, needle-woven tapestries and loom weaving.

As I was the woman member of this association of artists, it rested with me to adapt the feminine art, . . . to the requirements of the association. . . . It meant the fitting of any and every textile used in the furnishing of a house to its use and place, whether . . . curtains, portieres, or wall coverings. I drew designs which would give my draperies a framing which carried out the woodwork, and served as backgrounds for the desired wreaths and garlands of embroidered flowers.

In their atelier on Fourth Avenue, where Augustus Saint-Gaudens might lend a hand in a design for low relief, or Maitland Armstrong might arrange a mosaic in glass, or Stanford White might discuss the circumvention of conventionality in architecture, Samuel Colman traced his Oriental arabesques and Candace Wheeler surrounded herself with "rich stuffs and delicate embroideries." In the embroidery rooms in the Fourth Avenue lofts, below Louis Tiffany's glass rooms, she saw silks brought together in wonderful combination for a portièred world—a world that believed in "a room liberally hung with curtains and portières" that "shut out the disagreeable . . . and . . . enclosed within itself the peaceful serenities of home." In the atelier Candace Wheeler worked, while the arts of weaving and embroidery were carried on with the kindred arts of mural painting, stained glass and illustration—arts that were combined to serve the theme of fitness and the color consciousness of a nation mad for decoration. From her workroom flowed sumptuous hangings of opalescent plushes, "like the moonstone, full of imprisoned light," embroideries in gold and silk, "a feast of fleeting color," friezes embroidered on plush, wall hangings, panels of appliqué, mantel lambrequins—needlework that embodied daring experiments in fitness, wonderful studies in color, a "largeness of purpose" for a new era in interior decoration.

While the Board of Managers of the Society of Decorative Art entered into an arrangement with Tiffany and Mrs. Wheeler, becoming "the sole agent for the sale of the beautiful embroideries, executed from their designs and under their supervision," the Associated Artists received the first important order that would launch them as a potent force in American decorative art. The Madison Square Theatre would open in New York on February 4, 1880, with *Hazel Kirke,* a drama by Steele MacKaye. The drop-curtain that rose on the scene would be a drama in color and appliqué by Mrs. Candace Wheeler and her associates.

She found delight in marking the difference between the oak and birch trees that figured in the curtain's design, and the building of a yucca tree was as exciting to her as if it had been standing for its portrait. The curtain itself, depicting a realistic view of a woodland vista, was an unusual treatment of appliqué. Directing its execution, while Tiffany superintended the design, Colman the color and de Forest the materials, Candace Wheeler produced a landscape in textiles that used velvet and plushes for trees, shadowy silks for perspectives, and iridescent stuffs for the misty blue distance. She had produced a painting in textiles, translating the artist's methods into needlework, but she had done more, for she had "learned a lesson in the use of applied materials and large effects, which could be adapted to many beautiful uses."

Mrs. Wheeler proceeded to adapt that lesson in rich and varied ways to the work that lay ahead. The Knickerbocker Greys, who were building a new armory on Park Avenue, had commissioned Tiffany's Associated Artists, for $20,000, to decorate their Veterans' Room and Library, where the theme of fitness could be applied in a manner at once striking and unique. And in the curtained, bedraped world of 1880, Mrs. Wheeler's department must play a potent role. One of the "noble public rooms" had been taken "out of the hands of the man-milliners, who put fine furniture in them, and fine frescos on them, and finest satins about them,—all meaning nothing," and placed in the hands of a group of artists who understood "the significance of decorative *media*, . . . the power in colors and in lines, to make an atmosphere . . . redolent of the aims and purposes . . . that belong . . . to the occupants." In the hands of the Associated Artists, the Veterans' Room would embody the idea of the veteran.

While Louis Tiffany's Associated Artists integrated the dragon and Celtic motifs in the carved moldings, using iron and oak as symbols of military strength, Candace Wheeler designed "superb embroideries," portières heavy with banded plush, sparkling with steel and brass, curtains set off with rings of gold and silver "broidery." Out of dull Japanese brocade and plush representing leopard-skin, appliqués of velvet and gilded leather, she had suggested the days of knighthood and romantic warfare, the slashings of the ancient doublet and the coat of mail. She had adapted the decorative to the functional, enlarged the purposes of needlework, and created a work of Victorian art that held promise of the Art Nouveau.

Less than a year after New York's Seventh Regiment marched into its new armory, the less military membership of the Union League, of which Tiffany's father had been a founder and Mrs. Wheeler's brother and husband were members, walked into its new Club House on Fifth Avenue. A major part of the decoration had been assigned to Tiffany's Associated Artists, and once again Mrs. Wheeler's artistry in cloth of gold was put to work for a curtain framed in massive plush. While she superintended a portière that depicted a net entangling fishes with jeweled scales, she observed how Tiffany conquered the problem of economizing light and gaining the "choicest effects" at night. She had the satisfaction, too, of reading in *The Art Amateur* an article devoted to the "Draperies of the Union League Club":

The sumptuousness of the Union League Club house is a matter of common remark. This is nowhere more manifest than in its draperies. . . . there is no misapprehension in the mind of the most indifferent club man, though he be accustomed to classing all textile fabrics under the head of calico, as to the elegance of these lustrous folds which drape the windows and the doors.

To the plush, the velvet and the cloth of gold, had been added, she read, "the latest results of the progress of art embroidery in this country."

During the summer of 1881, she applied those latest results to the Hartford home of Samuel Clemens, where Tiffany contributed stenciled decorations designed after Indian motifs and Mrs. Wheeler transmuted a mid-Victorian drawing room into a more contemporary style. She would come to know Clemens well in later years, when he sat to her daughter for his portrait and visited her home in Onteora.

Meanwhile, there were other celebrities to contemplate, and there was other work to be done. Oscar Wilde, who had come to America with nothing to declare but his genius, must of course visit the Fourth Avenue atelier to observe the latest in home decoration, and Sir Henry Irving could not resist a chat on textiles with the expert Candace Wheeler. From Ellen Terry to Mrs. Potter Palmer, commissioning embroidered tapestries for her Lake Shore mansion, the visitors came, and the work mounted. For Lily Langtry, "susceptible to the fascination of our manufactures," Mrs. Wheeler must produce a set of bed-hangings to astonish the London world.

I suggested a canopy of our strong, gauze-like, creamy silk bolting-cloth, the tissue used in flour mills for sifting the superfine flour. I explained that the canopy could be crosses on the under side with loops of . . . roses, and the hanging border heaped with them.

The idea of "a coverlet of bolting-cloth lined with . . . rose-pink satin, sprinkled . . . with rose petals" appealed to the Jersey Lily, who was "triumphantly satisfied" with Mrs. Wheeler's roseate creation. Others, too, were triumphantly satisfied with the work of Tiffany's Associated Artists, from Hamilton Fish to John Taylor Johnston, from Dr. William T. Lusk to James Gordon Bennett, whose steam yacht was enlivened with the Tiffany touch. Visitors walked in, and orders flowed out—a portière for one of the Vanderbilt houses, a portière for California, embroidery designed by Mrs. Wheeler for Louis Prang as a study in color, mantel lambrequins, the panel for a firescreen. From a piano scarf of silk canvas to a purple velvet pall, Mrs. Wheeler's creations mounted along with her customers.

One of the Tiffany customers was a gentleman of particular eminence—the President of the United States. Chester Arthur, with his side whiskers and scrupulous attire, had refused to move into the White House until it had been cleaned and renovated, and

Congress had rather reluctantly appropriated the money to pay the bill. In return for $15,000, Tiffany's Associated Artists spent seven weeks decorating the Blue Room, the East Room, the Red Room and the Hall between the Red and East Rooms. Mrs. Wheeler, observing Tiffany's motifs of eagles and flags, his hand-pressed paper touched out in ivory, his elegant glass screen, added her own harmonious touch to the hangings, and doubtless agreed with the critic who concluded that "the beauty and artistic value of the Messrs. Tiffany's decorations are best appreciated by those guests who know how the White House used to look."

In between her work on decorations that applied the theme of fitness and the consciousness of color to American interiors, Mrs. Wheeler tried her hand at yet another form of industrial design—wall paper. The paper manufacturers, Warren, Fuller & Co., had offered $2,000 in prizes for the four best designs submitted, and Mrs. Wheeler decided to compete. For her this meant a "new study in adaptation, the use of different mediums, and due regard to the limitations of printing-machines." To the Warren, Fuller Competitive Designs she contributed her design of a silver honey-comb filled with honeycells of gold "and very lively and gorgeous bees . . . roaming at will." The "dado of metallic green" was broken with "a tangle of clover, gold disks, and more bees." The result, exhibited at the American Art Gallery along with some seventy other designs, many of which were sent from overseas, carried off the first prize of $1,000. The designer had the added satisfaction of learning that her daughter Dora had won fourth prize with a peony motif and that the second and third prizes had both gone to women as well. What was more, Candace Wheeler had not only secured for herself a market for "new and artistic patterns" in wall paper, but had paved the way for a new medium for American design by American women.

Another great communal effort of Tiffany's Associated Artists—and their only church venture—was applied to the interior of the Church of the Divine Paternity on Fifth Avenue, for which Mrs. Wheeler created embroideries copied from old ecclesiastical mo-tifs. On the field of the gallery hangings she worked, in wine-colored plush appliqué, texts by the late Dr. Chapin, while the choir hangings bore the score of "Old Hundred." Here surely was functional design carried to its ultimate.

Creations less functional perhaps, but no less extraordinary, were contributed by Mrs. Wheeler to the Art Loan Exhibition of December 1883, in aid of the Pedestal Fund for Bartholdi's Statue of Liberty. At the National Academy of Design her work was hung—portières, embroideries, door hangings and curtains created by Mrs. Wheeler in the workroom of Tiffany's atelier. Among the exhibits Candace had included "a series of bold and original needle-woven tapestries" that marked "the most decided advance in needlework known to the century." The tapestries, designed by Dora Wheeler and executed by Mrs. Wheeler and the Associated Artists, had been made for Cornelius Vanderbilt the Younger. "The Winged Moon" and "The Air Spirit," "The Water Spirit," "The Flower Spirit" and "The Birth of Psyche" were paintings of life in its holiday aspect sketched not with the brush, but with the needle.

In order to produce them, Candace Wheeler had filed letters patent in England on March 14, 1882, for her invention of "Improvements in Needle Woven Tapestry and in Fabric Therefor." She had followed up her English patent with two American patents, the first for "a new and useful Improvement in the Art of Embroidering, . . . by which tapestry or picture effects may be produced," and the second for an equally "new and useful Fabric for Needle-Woven Tapestries" that would "provide a material to form a ground or support" for her needlewoven designs. She had applied her invention to a tapestry entitled "Penelope" as well as to the series for Vanderbilt. She had supervised as the design was sketched upon her canvas and the strong outline in silks was applied. To her worker she had supplied a carefully colored sketch of the subject and she had watched patiently during the four long months required for the "atmosphere" alone to be filled in. With bits of silk and threads of gold and silver she had created an Undine or a nymph, *amorini* and dancing figures, "a play of changing tints," a mood. She had created indeed the Wheeler tapestry, pictorial needlework that was both a work of art and a business enterprise. She had created an American tapestry whose "production took account of the methods and materials which belonged to present periods" and was "adapted . . . to modern demands." She had fulfilled her dream of "American Tapestries made by embroidery alone, carrying personal thought into method." She had gone so far that she must go still farther.

Mrs. Wheeler herself had grown as her work had grown. From the more or less dilettante official of the Society of Decorative Art who worshiped at the shrine of aesthetic South Kensington, she had developed into a rebel against conventional High Art Needlework. Her views had been enlarged; working with Louis Tiffany she had gained practical knowledge as well as fruitful relations with manufacturers; she was evolving both a philosophy and a credo of interior decoration. The true decorator's function, she believed, was akin to that of the portrait painter—he must represent the individual or the family in his performance, with the "added gift of grace or charm of colour which he possesses." Color was all important, for it satisfied "as insistent a demand of the mind as food does to the body." In private houses, "wherever design or composition has an unimportant place, color establishes its court and beautifies the whole interior." But color and its variations must be applied as in an impressionist painting, and yet must be eminently American, for the color gift belonged to the American people. To color, the true decorator must of course add the theme of fitness, for the "perfectly furnished house" was "a crystallization of the culture, the habits, and the tastes of the family." It not only expressed, but *made* character, and the "final charm of the home" could be attained only by the "perfect adaptation of principles to conditions both of nature and humanity." The true decorator must be educated, and Candace Wheeler, through her life and her work, had been educated. Whatever she did would hold all she had learned, whether it was a patchwork quilt or a tapestry. The furnishing of a home was to her as the making of a picture, "but a picture within and against which one's life, and the life of the family, is to be lived." It was "by no means an unimportant thing to create a beautiful . . . interior. . . . truth and beauty are its essentials and these will have their utterance."

To give utterance to that truth and beauty, to create a business of her own out of the applied arts she practised, Candace Wheeler decided to break away from Tiffany and his associates. Despite the advantages she had gained from their collective efforts, there was still an impracticality in such group work. She found it no easier to work with three associates under Tiffany than with twenty in the Society of Decorative Art. Moreover, by 1883, Lockwood de Forest was spending considerable time in the Far East, and

Samuel Colman was established in Newport. Tiffany's department of design, embroidery and textiles had assumed under Candace Wheeler both a national and a commercial importance. It could and would be detached. The growth in American taste had made her work not only possible but remunerative. Amateurs no longer crept in where artists dared not tread. The field belonged to the legitimate adorners of America's homes. Taking with her not only her practical experience, but the name, Associated Artists, Candace Wheeler set up her own workrooms and launched upon her own business that would be conducted exclusively by American women for the decoration of American interiors.

Mr. Wheeler bought and converted a large, old-fashioned brownstone at 115 East 23rd Street, where a wistaria vine climbed up the four stories to the roof, and Mrs. Wheeler embarked upon her enterprise that would blend art and the manufacturing industry. Behind "the modest dark green portal" Mrs. Wheeler's Associated Artists proceeded to conjure up their marvels. Round the large table in her workroom she gathered in time her principal assistants, a "unique little band of accomplished American gentlewomen"—her daughter, Dora Wheeler, who had studied in William Chase's Tenth Street Studio, as well as in Germany and in Paris after she had won the Prang Christmas card competition, who had illustrated a book for Tiffany's Associated Artists, and whose talents would be put to use in the designing of papers and fabrics; Rosina Emmet, like Dora a student of Chase and of Julien in Paris as well as a Prang prize winner, who had begun her career by painting on china; and Ida Clark who had won second prize in the Warren, Fuller wall paper competition and who, after studying under Mrs. Wheeler, would furnish the more conventional designs for the Associated Artists, while Dora Wheeler and Rosina Emmet rendered the "figure subjects." In the studio, itself a study in color, Dora could paint while Mrs. Wheeler invited visitors to the showroom or stacked materials on the shelves in an ante-room or stored thinner stuffs in ancient dower-chests in a corner of the rooms. Her design room would before long become an important part of her establishment, for "every girl in it was there because she knew how to draw and had a special faculty for composition." Twice a week, Mrs. Wheeler discussed with them the spirit and the technique of design, before she flew off to examine mummy wrappings sent from Lima or, with her cordial manner and "winsome" smile, displayed color studies in textiles and tapestries to visitors in her showroom. In time, for the stock company or corporation of women that formed the Associated Artists, she developed a trade mark—two *A's* hooked together. But her work itself would be her trade mark, work that embodied the results of applying art education to manufactures and national industries.

The Associated Artists were queens of the reign of stuffs. While women sighed "before a yard of imperial yellow damask" or caressed "a bit of plush as a lover might the cheek of his fair one," Mrs. Wheeler's concern would be assured a market for the fabrics and textiles she produced, and when the market was not assured it could be created. With the careful study of ancient textiles and the equally careful pursuit of appropriate designs for modern fabrics, she would boldly supply American textiles for American homes. The designing, manufacture and embellishment of textile fabrics would be one of her chief activities. Through her efforts, the artistic fabrics made in America would equal those produced anywhere in the world.

With the great American silk manufacturers, the Cheney Brothers of Connecticut, as well as with fabric houses in New Jersey, Mrs. Wheeler entered into commercial relations, supplying original American designs to their mills.

We had no original American design in textiles, embroideries, or even in wall-papers; . . . I could not see why American manufactures should be without American characteristics any more than other forms of art. Art applied to manufacture should have its root in its own country.

This root the Associated Artists supplied, in the form of American design—designs of American fauna and flora—wildflowers, dandelion weeds, pond lilies—geometrical "Moorish" designs that were merely "the patchwork of our grandmothers used with a more highly developed artistic taste," designs that were studied with reference to use—the design for a palace car patterned with bells and car wheels and drifting smoke—a design for Andrew Carnegie patterned with the Scottish thistle—a design for a millionaire studded with coins—designs that embodied a new American school of workmanship while they pointed the way to a "profession for women and a profitable outlet for their . . . talents."

Out of the designing room the patterns flowed, and into the showroom came the fabrics—velvets and printed linens, cotton weaves and changeable silks, silks "soft and fine as any woven in Oriental looms," brocades and metal cloth, filmy India silks, silk canvases and damasks, moss stuff. In tints that ranged from silver white to amber, gold and orange, from bluish pink to copper and pomegranate, tints that suggested a Tiffany stained glass window in stuffs, the "beauty of light strained through color," the textiles unfolded their lustrous beauty before they were metamorphosed into portières and curtains. Experimenting in color, Mrs. Wheeler produced shadow silks whose variations, with every change of position, "brought out the design of the textile in a new aspect." She was deeply gratified by William Chase's encomium, "You can do more with silk than we can with pigments, because it reflects color as well as holds it."

It was not alone luxurious silks and brocades in a "profusion of almost Oriental splendor" that preoccupied Candace Wheeler. One of her major problems was to reduce the cost and extend the variety of stuffs, to experiment in cheap materials, chintzes and cottons, Kentucky jean and denim, whose dark blues looked rich against oil-rubbed woodwork and salmon or reddish colored walls. Through her brothers, the importers, manufacturers and grocers, H.K. & F.B. Thurber & Co., she had access to the *American Grocer and Dry Goods Chronicle,* where she could learn of the fabrics most in demand. Her range of prices was "as great as the variety of designs." Always she searched for "the missing textile," as she studied home dyeing and weaving—a fabric that would "combine inexpensiveness, durability, softness, and absolute fidelity of colour," a non-inflammable material that could be cleaned by flame.

And as she searched and studied, she superintended the work of her atelier, while ornaments were cut and designs stamped upon the ground. In her workroom she watched while the ornament was transferred to its proper place on the ground by pasting —a task assigned to one employee alone, who did nothing else but apply a paste of flour, water and a few drops of carbolic acid to the ground with a camel's hair brush. When it was dry, she waited until the piece was transferred to the embroidery frame and rolled with care.

She experimented in all aspects of her work, from embroidery silk itself that would take the place of filoselle, to the development of color schemes, from appliqué work which she found "particularly suited to our new era of building," to embroidery that would express "the national temperament." In all her experiments she did not lose sight of their ultimate purpose—the decoration of American interiors by American women. What she had done "as a widening of the field of woman's labor was really of national importance in commerce." Through her Associated Artists, "American women had won respect for American-made fabrics." The mill owners had adopted her designs, her choice of colors and the effects invented for her, and she had been "the principal agent in bringing about considerable improvements in our textile manufactures." She had gone direct to nature—to American nature—for her designs. She had had her fabrics produced in American mills. As a result, American walls, upon which the first impression of a room depended, could be hung with American textiles created by an association of women under the direction of one woman in her fifties working in a four-story brownstone on New York's East 23rd Street.

In her fascination with American textiles, Mrs. Wheeler had not forgotten her dream of American tapestries. "Threads of cotton and wool and silk, with their myriad possibilities of expression" still haunted her "like attenuated ghosts." The Wheeler tapestry, for which she had received letters patent while she was still working with Tiffany, would be produced now by her own Associated Artists and its scope extended. For years she had been experimenting with varieties of stitches in varieties of materials with the purpose of producing an embroidered surface that possessed the softness of water colors combined with "the enduring quality of ancient hand-wrought tapestries." Standing by the Jacquard loom, watching the work of silkweaving to her order, she observed "the very arrangement of threads so long desired. A discarded remnant of imperfect texture" seemed to suggest what she had been seeking. She would weave the design upon a heavy silk canvas—material specially made by the Cheney Brothers—by introducing threads of the colors needed along the woof. Nothing but moth-proof silk, and occasionally threads of gold and silver, would enter into the composition of Candace Wheeler's American tapestries. The silk threads would be drawn under the woof and so become an integral part of the silk canvas that had been created for them. Experiments with the ground were coupled with experiments with the stitches. In the Wheeler tapestry "darned threads" would be carried across woof or warp to produce the impression of a vignette in which the atmosphere faded into the ground tint. Upon a ground of silk the Associated Artists would "invest fibers, . . . with . . . color and subject them to the magic of machinery and the manipulations of living fingers."

The tapestry department of 115 East 23rd Street, where Miss Lyman was placed in charge as "chief executive artist," was a busy place. While life-size cartoons were sketched in the studio, the workroom produced tapestry after tapestry embodying those designs, until the weekly payroll of the tapestry room could contribute to the comfort and the maintenance of Mrs. Wheeler's students. For Governor Alger of Michigan, a Gleaner sketched by Rosina Emmet was woven upon a gold colored silk canvas. From the workroom emerged the tapestries that offered "a semblance of nature" and cheated "with a sense of unlimited horizon," tapestries that would disguise the "restraining bound" that was a wall and masquerade it as a luxury. The 23rd Street rooms were ablaze with the creations that came to life under Candace Wheeler's supervision. She instructed, she experimented, she waited, until a Peacock Girl in medieval costume fed her peacocks and made a glory of color. Aphrodite grew into beauty on canvas, Twilight was a woman trailing somber draperies, Love gathered daisies. In Candace Wheeler's workroom, the needle and the shuttle had been raised to the rank of brush and pigment; art had been enriched with "a means of expression."

In one tapestry in particular, she had converted the needle into the brush. Spending a summer holiday in London, Candace Wheeler had been engrossed in the study of Raphael's great cartoon, "The Miraculous Draught of Fishes," and she determined to copy it in a needlewoven tapestry. She ordered two photographs made, one of them copied exactly in water color, the other ruled, cut into squares, and again photographed. These, put together, would form the working drawing for her most ambitious tapestry. In the workroom, the perforations were gone over with pin pricks and the cartoon was fastened over a sheet of silk canvas that had been woven for the background. Under Mrs. Wheeler's guidance, a prepared powder was sifted through the lines of the perforation and fixed by the application of heat until the entire composition was exactly outlined upon the ground. Then, by needleweaving, the color and shading were superimposed, each worker laboring over one small area until the tapestry was finished. In the north light of one of the great spaces of the studio it was hung, "the most important work accomplished by needle weaving" yet made in America.

Before her tapestries were packed for shipment, Mrs. Wheeler showed them to a few visitors and friends—a set of wall panels destined for a London drawing room, the Gleaner that would go to Detroit. None of her tapestries so closely fulfilled her dream of "a distinct American embroidery type" as those that grew out of the literature and the history of her country. From Hawthorne's *Marble Faun* the Associated Artists created a tapestry of Hilda in the Tower, and from *The Scarlet Letter* a tapestry of Hester Prynne, while in needlewoven embroidery Alice Pyncheon hurried through the snow in a gossamer dress and satin slippers to Matthew Maule's bridal. From Longfellow they developed an Evangeline worked upon coarse homespun cloth made by the descendants of the Acadians, and a Minnehaha bordered with beadwork and fringed with buckskin, whose face was "listening." A Zuñi girl completed the series that translated the methods and the moods of modern art to American themes in a new medium invented by a woman.

Candace Wheeler's work in textiles and in tapestries had gone to adorn the walls of American homes, since she believed that "the colour treatment of a house interior must begin with the walls," and that rooms were bad or good "in exact accordance with the wall-quality and treatment." For the walls of Harvey Kennedy, the banker, she had made portières of imperial plush, as she had made portrait panels for Mrs. Potter Palmer. But Candace Wheeler and her Associated Artists did not end their work with the walls of American interiors; rather, they "went on in constantly enlarging lines of artistic experiment" until she could boast that

We added interior decoration to our list of accomplishments, and had much to do with making that form of art a profession for women. Women were not then and perhaps are not now sufficiently instructed in art knowledge to be equal to the interior finishing and furnishing

of . . . mansions. . . . Domestic interiors, however, fall naturally
within the grasp of women, and I look forward to the time when the
education and training of women decorators will fit them for public
as well as for private patronage.

In her own work, by her own example, Candace Wheeler was so
fitting them. Her Associated Artists supplied not only "Brocades
for Wall-Hangings and Draperies in Original Designs . . . . Velvets
Printed from Our Own Designs, Interesting and Decorative Textiles, Cotton Canvases, Chintzes, and Varona Silks," but also
"Color Schemes for Rooms or Houses" and "Special Plans for
Country Houses." In time, Candace Wheeler took a hand in "everything pertaining in any way to the ornamentation of the home."
Indeed, it seemed that for this focusing of her life work there had
been no starting point. She had always been an interior decorator.
Now, in the early '90's, her Associated Artists covered almost as
much ground as Tiffany's Associated Artists had done, and Candace Wheeler found no aspect of interior decoration alien to her.
She considered the new treatment of "pulled rugs" the beginning
of an important industry, and she developed her own theories on
floors, which should "support the room in colour as well as in
construction." From the decoration of table linen to the repro-
duction of an antique spindle chair which she had found in a
Long Island farmhouse, her interests ranged, and with her interests her theories were formulated and her scope was enlarged.
She designed a kitchen for "a one-servant house," working on
the theory that "the kitchen is the heart of the house and needs
more careful study than any other room in it." For its ceiling
she planned a warm pink tone that would reflect the washable
cardinal red used in the furnishings. The ceiling she brought down
for two feet upon the side walls and finished it with a molding,
while the wall was covered with a thin enameled table oilcloth.
Her kitchen was, as she put it, anticipating the twentieth-century
dinette, "a grill-room" where the family would take breakfast and
luncheon. For a room in the Brooklyn home of Charles Hewitt,
for luxurious interiors, for summer cottages and for servants' quarters, her Associated Artists brought to use all their methods and
all their materials, as well as all the skills of Candace Wheeler.

She had learned the trick of cheating the eye, of using somber
tints in some rooms and sunny tints in others, of making a low,
dark room seem light and airy, of bringing down too high a ceiling

or widening a narrow hall. At Sypher's she could find paneled front doors or wrought iron railings, mahogany newel posts or brass doorknobs, chimney pieces in marble and wood—the "portable art" that could be applied to interior decoration. The greenish matting and the Chinese red and gold papers from tea boxes she could convert into effective wall papers. She had learned the value of the right detail which was to a room what the *mot juste* was to a paragraph—the pottery jar placed near a drapery that repeated its color, the half accidental draping of a curtain. And the Associated Artists used her tricks as they applied her principles. If decorative art was allied to architecture, it must also be subordinate to it. It must oppose things false, "things made to *sell*," dishonest manufactures that demoralized the spirit of the home. It must be functional, appropriate, characteristic of the family and of the country it was intended for. It must be imbedded in study and in education.

While her Associated Artists became "the moving force of the growth of industrial art throughout the country," Candace Wheeler tried to make of her "stock-company of women" an American school of design where the principles of interior decoration could be taught. To her pupils she explained the mysteries of embroidery and decorative drawing, designing for wall paper, tapestries and fabrics, so that, after a three-year course their talents, too, would command a "commercial value." Day after day she scanned the letters that came from applicants—from girls who could paint on china and wished to do decorative interiors, advising them to "study the elementary principles of decorative art; copy approved forms in monochrome. . . . Confine yourself to conventional designs until you can use natural forms like an artist." When she was not supervising her Associated Artists, she was working on the advisory council of the Woman's Art School of Cooper Union or lecturing at the New York Institute for Artist-Artisans, where she was instructor in textiles, for art education must, she knew, precede the development of interior decoration as a profession for women—the "serious and comprehensive study without which no profession can be worthily followed or its practice genuinely respected." By 1895 she could predict that there would be "schools and college courses where the students can be well and authoritatively trained for this dignified profession."

While her daughter Dora held Thursday teas in a studio where her portraits of Samuel Clemens and James Russell Lowell looked down from the walls, or opened that studio to Walt Whitman when he arrived for a sitting, Candace continued her practice and her precepts. Contributing articles to "The Home Department" of *The Christian Union,* elaborating plans for a co-operative woman's hotel, receiving an invitation to attend a Silk Congress in England "as an expert in silk-weaving," the head of the Associated Artists was in her own person becoming a "moving force" in the industrial art to which the Centennial Exposition of 1876 had awakened both her country and herself.

If the Philadelphia Exposition had stirred a taste for industrial art in America, another Exposition would mark the climax that taste had reached. The Columbian Exposition of 1893 would gather together in the Windy City the industrial arts the nation had developed at the end of a century of progress. It would also bring to the sixty-six-year-old Candace Wheeler the most significant public recognition that had yet been allotted her for the work she had done in creating a new art form and in metamorphosing a union of arts into an industry and a profession for women. The Woman's Building of the Columbian Exposition, designed by a woman architect, Sophia Hayden, would be decorated in part by another woman, Candace Wheeler.

On June 7, 1892, the "Board of Women Managers for the Exhibit of the State of New York at the World's Columbian Exposition" called a meeting in Albany at which they projected a department named the Bureau of Applied Arts for the exhibition of women's work in that field. Because she "had for years been closely associated with this branch of industry," Mrs. Candace Wheeler, President of the Associated Artists, was named Director, charged with the assembling of articles for that exhibit. In addition, she was appointed Color Director of the Woman's Building, an assignment that included the interior decoration of the great room provided to New York State for its woman's library.

The twofold task consumed her. She had three months and $5,000 for completing "the miracle which had been begun in Chicago," and decorating a room "which must be not only beautiful in itself, but an integral part of a scheme." She was given "absolute freedom in its treatment," although she was provided with a staff of "all sorts of incompetent women." Candace Wheeler observed the one great window "which seemed to take in all the blue of the sky and the expanse of water which lay under it," and decided to use modulations of blue and green for her color treatment. With all her principles and practices of interior decoration in mind, she confronted the problems of fitting up a great public room functionally, appropriately, colorfully.

After my scheme for walls and furniture was completed there remained two great spaces to consider—first the ceiling, an expanse of white which was overpowering in emptiness, and then a height of wall which needed to be lessened by plaster decoration of some sort to bring it within picture reach of the range of carved bookcases which surrounded the entire room.

A painted ceiling, she decided, was essential for the overhead space, and Candace commissioned her daughter, now Dora Wheeler Keith, to undertake the work. The sketch was sent in, the great roll of canvas shipped, and the ceiling put up, "with a wide deep border and a modeled frieze that brought it to within reasonable distance of the paneled bookcases." The ceiling itself, composed of five large ovals or medallions holding symbolic figures, recalled that of "some old Venetian palace in richness of coloring and style of composition." But the subject was kept strictly in its place as part of a great library. Under Candace Wheeler's expert touch, the room gradually came to life. Loops and folds of drapery in softly blended hues represented the tints of sky and landscape. Busts of notable women by notable women were decoratively used. The great window, filled with leaded glass, "gave a softened beauty of lake and sky." The bookcases Mrs. Wheeler surmounted with dark oak paneling. "The panels were carried out by the lines of the bookcases, and the furniture was designed upon the same models." From Duveen & Co., the Color Director borrowed a mantel; from Sypher & Co., four large oak chairs and several library tables; while her own Associated Artists designed and manufactured a dozen chairs and two sofas for the room. A portrait of Pocahontas looked down from above one of the bookcases, along with a bust of Harriet Beecher Stowe; Rookwood and hammered brass vases formed the small details that made perfection. And the room, struggling for life, was brought to the fullness of life by the books themselves.

Mrs. Wheeler, hurrying from her hotel room on the border of
the Fair grounds to her office in the Woman's Building, spent her
evenings discussing the principles of applied art with the artists,
Frank Millet and Anders Zorn, and her days in a whirl of furnishings and draperies. She must placate the tall and portly Turkish
commissioner because of the inadequate space allotted to the Turkish exhibit. She must meet with red Indians in their war bonnets.
Above all, she must complete the decoration of a great room in
the Woman's Building, a building that "touched women everywhere."

The Color Director of the Woman's Building was also Director
of the Bureau of Applied Arts. When she was not placing chairs
and looping draperies in Chicago, she must hold meetings in her
New York office at 1122 Broadway, forming committees on applied and decorative painting, stained glass and glass mosaics,
modeling and plaster ornament, wood-carving, ornamental leather,
wall paper, modern embroideries, pottery, bookbinding, modern
handmade lace—on all the varied aspects of applied art that would
eventually find their way to the exhibit cases of the Woman's
Building. She herself, of course, would chair the committee on
modern textiles and tapestries. Since her first general appeal
brought merely "occasional articles of no artistic merit," Candace
Wheeler decided to hold a Preliminary Exhibition in New York
from which she could cull specimens of the diverse handicrafts of
women. On March 3, 1893, therefore, the Preliminary Exhibition
was opened at the American Art Galleries, and at its close the
Director of the Bureau of Applied Arts was able to select over 450
articles for the Chicago Exposition.

One of the most interesting and certainly the closest to Candace
Wheeler's heart was the display of her own Associated Artists.
The color studies in textiles, the weavings in gold and silk, the
great needlewoven tapestry of Raphael's "Miraculous Draught of
Fishes" which had been laboriously created in the workroom of
115 East 23rd Street, appeared now under glass in the north wing
of the Woman's Building for all the world to see. It was a display
as "extensive" as it was "remarkable"—a display that not only
marked the culmination of her own work in wall decoration, but
proved to a sceptical world that Americans were "no longer pen-
sioners of Europe in the matter of designs. To-day we have an

American School of Design, with a distinct national character of its own, and our women are to the fore in every one of its branches."

The Color Director of the Woman's Building and the head of its Bureau of Applied Arts had engaged in an exhilarating experience. She had tested her knowledge and her ability to adjust the forms of European art and industries to American taste. At the formal opening of the Woman's Building, Candace Wheeler was present, sitting behind Mrs. Potter Palmer among the group of "distinguished women, both foreign and American, whose gay toilets lent a pleasing touch of color and brightness to the assembly." And in the Library of that Woman's Building, one of her own books, *Columbia's Emblem Indian Corn,* was exhibited, along with Harriet Irwin's *Hermit of Petræa* and a great row of books by Ann Stephens. For the Distaff Series issued under the auspices of the Board of Women Managers of the State of New York for the Exposition, Mrs. Wheeler edited still another book entitled *Household Art,* and before one of the Art Congresses she presented a paper on decorative and applied art. Both by her practices and her precepts she was well represented at the World's Columbian Exposition. If what she held was true—that "we owe to the Columbian Fair that in the hitherto contracted field of art in America . . . the tendency is toward less imitative and more distinctly national art, not only in our public buildings but in our homes"—then for this coming of age of the pioneer industry of interior decoration Candace Wheeler was to a large extent responsible. Making her own summation of the "Applied Arts In The Woman's Building," she had written:

Fifteen years ago, no American manufacturer thought of buying an American design for his carpet, or wall-paper, or textile. The usual thing to do was to buy a yard of French or English material, and reproduce its color and design. To-day the manufacturers all agree that the most popular designs they can furnish are made by our native designers, who are, to a very large extent, women.

For the decoration of the Library an award was made. But no award could make adequate compensation for a life work that had widened "the scope of artistic labor among women" and that had culminated in the Woman's Building of a great Exposition.

If the Woman's Building was indeed the "centre and visible sign of a new impulse in the world," then it was Candace Wheeler, the Color Director, head of the Bureau of Applied Arts, President of the Associated Artists, who had given to that impulse a spur, a shape, a direction.

The years, so full, so rich, passed swiftly. By the turn of the century, when Candace Wheeler was in her early seventies, she handed over to her son, the architect, Dunham Wheeler, proprietorship of her Associated Artists. She herself, who had devoted two decades to the practice of home decoration, would concentrate now upon the less active but perhaps no less effective pursuit of offering precepts in home decoration. Her pen was busy toward the end of the old century and the beginning of the new, recording the knowledge she had gathered throughout her professional life. In a net of words she caught her schemes, her works, her observations. Little that touched her subject escaped her, from "Decorative Art" to "Group Exhibitions," from "The Principles of Decoration" to "Home Industries and Domestic Manufactures." For *The Outlook* she had prepared her most important article in 1895, "Interior Decoration As a Profession for Women," declaring that

. . . it is only very recently that the thorough decorative artist has made his appearance. Before that the paper-hanger and painter, the cabinet-maker, upholsterer, and the carpet salesman divided the honors between them. . . .

Here is the natural field of the woman decorator. The woman with cultivation and taste and an instinct for arrangement, even without special education, is entirely competent for this limited field [of domestic interiors]. But why should she not be educated for wider work, . . . ?

To expand that education for wider work, Candace Wheeler's pen raced on. For *Corticelli Home Needlework* she served as an editor, and for *The Ladies' Home Journal* she wrote her account of "How I Devised an Attractive Kitchen." From her busy pen the articles and the books flowed forth, *How to Make Rugs,* "The Decorative Use of Wild Flowers," "Weaving Rugs from Rags," *The Development of Embroidery in America,* and the most important of all, *Principles of Home Decoration,* the book that was a crystallization of the career she had followed and the life she had lived.

There were other books, too, for Candace Wheeler through the years had led not only a professional but a personal life. There was a book for her grandchildren, *Doubledarling and the Dream Spinner,* and there was a book for her gardens called *Content In A Garden.* By 1907, the Associated Artists made its last appearance in the *New York City Directories.* "The failure of the Associated Artists business to do what I hoped it would is in his [Dunham's] hands." Yet, perhaps the tastes to which it catered had changed even before the new century advanced. With Edith Wharton she could agree that the golden age of architecture had passed into the gilded age of decoration. Candace Wheeler had seen the Eastlake style give way to Morris and the Morris to Mission. Still handsome, still erect, still gracious in manner and striking in personality, wearing her stone cameo or diamond brooch, she would see her own seventies give way to her eighties and they in turn to her nineties before she would recall the days she had lived as *Yesterdays In a Busy Life.*

At the moment, she felt no propensity for recording a life she was so busy living. As yet there were no yesterdays. Her summers she spent, as she had spent them since 1883, in her special "Garden of Content" called "Pennyroyal" in Onteora in the Catskills. There, in Onteora—Hills of the Sky—her husband and her brother had formed the Catskill Mountain Camp and Cottage Company, for which Dunham Wheeler had built an inn, "The Bear and Fox." To the colony had come the notables and the lesser notables of the day—Samuel Clemens, who remarked that "the partitions were so thin that one could hear a lady in the next room changing her mind," John Burroughs, who enjoyed the "very pleasant life in the camp of Mrs. Wheeler" when he visited with a basket of grapes from his own vineyard, Mary Mapes Dodge and "Susan Coolidge," Mrs. Custer and Frank Stockton. With Candace Wheeler they roasted corn and sat in the moonlight, played with tamed fox cubs and climbed mountains.

There was no doubt that Candace Wheeler could still climb mountains, for in her eighties she scaled Jaynes Hill, the highest point on Long Island. She still found joy in watching spring take possession of her Long Island home, "Nestledown," upon whose walls the children still trooped up to bed in Japanese costumes and Dunham was still a boy with a toy gun in his hand. Over its mantel the motto of the house was engraved:

Who lives merrily, he lives mightily;
Without'en gladness availeth no treasure.

In 1895, Candace Wheeler had lost much of that gladness with
the death of her husband. After their life together, their far-flung
travels together, she found herself "in a lonesome land where no
one remembered that I had ever been young, or called me by my
given name."

Yet there was still enough gladness in Candace Wheeler for
her to build another home and plant another garden for her winters in Georgia. On her eightieth birthday she announced to her
family that she had bought the land and built a house called
"Wintergreen" in Thomasville, Georgia. There she, who had known
Samuel Clemens and Lowell, who had met Browning and visited
Whistler, spent her days observing the magnolia buds as they
opened or the persimmons that hung upon the trees.

She was growing old serenely, who had been active for so long.
For the engaging old lady who had written on the decorative treat-
ment of wild flowers, a conductor stopped his train to pluck violets.
In place of her own *Principles of Home Decoration* connoisseurs
were reading now Elsie de Wolfe's *House in Good Taste*. With
the World War, Dora's husband, Boudinot Keith, served as Judge
Advocate in France and her son, Elisha, lay in the American
Cemetery in Bony-Aisne. Living from the rent of her property,
Candace Wheeler still found serenity as surely as spring found the
land, "in spite of wars and world-fighting and all things dreadful."

For her illustrious grandson, former Secretary of War Henry L.
Stimson, her "dear boy," she recorded the events of her later life
as she recorded her yesterdays for a larger audience. In 1921,
when she was ninety-four, she wrote:

I am very well, wonderfully well, considering all things, and I thank
God every day with uplifted hands every day—for my . . . arts.

Her "arts" were "painting and writing for I can do nothing which
is *active* but I can think and see and am painting some good
things." She was "very busy and happy in painting little and large
flower pieces for the benefit of the Public Library" as well as in
devoting "my time and brains to a political tract for women
voters." Although, she confided to her grandson, "I no longer
know people by name, . . . I generally know where they abide &

what they have done in the world." She was living perhaps "too much in the past," and she feared "to be a burden! . . . A woman who has always paddled her own canoe as I have—and sometimes given a hand to other peoples canoes." Yet, after all, there was little time for dwelling in the past—

I have very little time . . . only about three hours a day; the rest is spent in getting dressed, and being washed and combed and covered and made presentable to an amiable world, . . . But in my good three hours I paint pictures—better and better all the time.

Despite the pictures she was painting and the recollections she had been writing, Candace Wheeler was "ready to go." She was "only waiting." On August 5, 1923, when Harding's death was troubling the nation, she died at the age of ninety-six in her daughter Dora's apartment in New York's Atelier Building. She had all but rounded her own century of progress.

She had done far more than that. Although she herself had survived much of the evanescent work she had created in textiles and in fabrics, and although much of what remained would be scattered in one museum or another, she had been a "potent influence for high taste." As each country and each period must write its history in the handwork of its time, so she had written her country's history in threads of silk and gold and silver. In the development of the Art Nouveau and its spread abroad, as in the modern applications of the credo that form follows function, she had played a small but effective part. She herself had said, "I opened up a new field, . . . Understanding of applied art spread, . . . and today American women lead the world as designers." She had indeed opened up a new field, a field that made an industry for women out of woman's taste and woman's art. In the textile branches of applied art she had achieved what Tiffany had achieved in stained glass. Once, writing on "Art Education for Women," she had pondered:

What gate has been unlocked from the straitness of woman's past which tempts a headlong and multitudinous rush into the world's field of labor?

Candace Wheeler had in her own way unlocked a gate, and in the world's field of labor had planted a burgeoning seed.

NOTES ON SOURCES

The notes that follow were designed to satisfy the scholar without intruding upon the general reader, who none the less may find something of interest in them. They incidentally reveal the problems that had to be surmounted in the production of this book, the first attempt of its kind: the problem of establishing priority; the problem of coupling with priority a· colorful life and an interesting, fruitful career; the problem of locating an abundance of source material on each subject. These three considerations were paramount in the selection of the women firsts included in this volume.

Throughout, the writer's conviction has been upheld that any woman who was first to venture upon an untried field in the nineteenth century would prove an unusual personality, stimulating and courageous, whose life was as rich as her career was productive. In some instances, the women selected were first in several fields: Isabel Barrows not only in stenographic reporting for Congressional committees, but also in ophthalmology; Sarah G. Bagley not only in telegraphy, but also in labor reform. All but one of the women whose lives are recounted were married, living full personal lives while they battered down the doors of the professions and trades of their choice.

In the case of many of the women included, this book represents the first attempt to unearth the facts of their lives and work. In the case of others, about whom something has already been written, this book presents a fresh insight by highlighting certain aspects of their careers. Whether they were famous or unknown to the public, they were selected not only because they were first in their fields, but because their lives were exciting and their struggles dramatic.

The research, the detective work, the digging in the rich mines of sources in a diversity of fields that went on behind the scenes to recreate these lives and these struggles are revealed in the "Notes on Sources."

CHAPTER 1

MARY ANN LEE

Début of Mary Ann Lee

Cyril W. Beaumont, *Complete Book Of Ballets* (New York [1938]) pp. 73-78; Charles Durang, *History of the Philadelphia Stage, between the years 1749 and 1855*, 3rd Series, p. 146 (Microfilm in 2 reels at New York Public Library); James Henry Horncastle, tr., The Bayadere. A Ballet Opera in Two Acts (MS in Theatre Collection, New York Public Library) [This was translated from *Le Dieu Et La Bayadère* of Augustin Eugène Scribe]; Frederick Allen King, The Pageant of the Dance in America p. 111 (MS in Museum of the City of New York); Lillian Moore, "Mary Ann Lee First American Giselle," reprinted from *Dance Index* II:5 (May 1943) in Paul Magriel, *Chronicles of the American Dance* (New York [1948]) [Hereinafter Moore, "Lee." To date this has been the principal attempt to survey the career of Mary Ann Lee. It is most useful as a chronology of her performances. Page numbers cited will refer to the reprint in Magriel. For the début, see pp. 103 f]; *The Philadelphia Saturday Courier* (January 6, 13, 1838) p. 3; Arthur Todd, "Three Ballerinas and a Danseuse," *Dance Magazine* XXIV:9 (September 1950) p. 28; Arthur Herman Wilson, *A History of the Philadelphia Theatre 1835 to 1855* (Philadelphia 1935) pp. 9, 12.

Early Life, Parentage & Training of Mary Ann Lee

The year of Mary Ann Lee's birth is established by the passport application 2605-2606 of October 25, 1844 (National Archives) which supplies incontrovertible evidence that she was born in 1826, and not "ca. 1823" as stated in Moore, "Lee," p. 103. Thus she was eleven and not fourteen at the time of her portentous début. Her mother's first name is revealed in the same passport application. Mrs. Lee's subsequent marriage to John Broad is disclosed by the *Philadelphia Directories* of 1839, 1840-1, 1848, 1853-4, 1861, 1870 and 1872 (some of which were supplied by courtesy of the Historical Society of Pennsylvania), as well as by the records of Laurel Hill Cemetery, where she is buried.

For further details, see George Amberg, *Ballet in America* (New York [1949]) pp. 5, 188; Ann Barzel, "European Dance Teachers in the United States," *Dance Index* III:4-6 (April-June 1944) pp. 60 f; C. Blasis, *The Code of Terpsichore* (London 1830) *passim*; Joe Cowell, *Thirty Years Passed Among The Players in England And America* (New York 1844) p. 99; Durang, *op. cit.*, 2nd Series, p. 195, 3rd Series, p. 148; Moore, "Lee," p. 104; *Philadelphia Directory* 1837 lists P.H. Hazard, teacher of dancing, at 96 S 5th; Wilson, *op. cit.*, p. 171.

As a child, Mary Ann appeared in small roles prior to her début as a danseuse. She may possibly have been instructed later on by Paul Taglioni.

Rivalry of Début & Lee's Benefit

Durang, *op. cit.*, 3rd Series, pp. 148, 169; Moore, "Lee," pp. 104 ff; *The*

Philadelphia Saturday Courier (January 13, 20, 1838) p. 3; Francis Court-
ney Wemyss, *Twenty-Six Years of The Life of An Actor And Manager*
(New York 1847) pp. 292 f, 301; "With The Ballet-Dancers of Days Gone
Bye," unidentified and undated newspaper clipping in Theatre Collection,
New York Public Library; William B. Wood, *Personal Recollections of
The Stage* (Philadelphia 1855) pp. 406 f.

*Early Roles of Mary Ann Lee; Appearances in Philadelphia, Baltimore
& Pittsburgh; New York Début*
   Amberg, *op. cit.*, p. 189; George Balanchine, *Balanchine's Complete Sto-
ries of the Great Ballets* (New York 1954) pp. 379, 387, 464, 466; Thomas
Haynes Bayly, *The Swiss Cottage* (London & New York n.d.) *passim*;
Beaumont, *op. cit.*, pp. 73, 79-84; T. Allston Brown, *A History of the New
York Stage* (New York 1903) I, 115; Anatole Chujoy, *The Dance Encyclo-
pedia* (New York [1949]) pp. 173, 234 f, 459; Durang, *op. cit.*, 3rd Series,
pp. 148, 155; *The Evening Post* [New York] (July 8, 1839) p. 3; Charles
Heath, *Beauties of the Opera And Ballet* (London n.d.) p. 95; Joseph N.
Ireland, *Records of the New York Stage* (New York 1867) II, 291 f;
John Kerr, *The Wandering Boys* (London [182-?]) *passim*; King, *op. cit.*,
pp. 64 f; James Sheridan Knowles, *William Tell* (New York & Philadelphia
n.d.) *passim*; H.M. Milner, *Masaniello; or, the Dumb Girl of Portici* (New
York 1830) p. 3; Moore, "Lee," pp. 106 ff; *Morning Herald* [New York]
(June 13, 1839) p. 5, (June 15, 24, 1839) p. 3, (June 25, 1839) pp. 2, 3,
(July 4, 1839) p. 3; George C.D. Odell, *Annals of the New York Stage*
(New York 1928) IV, 318 f; *The Philadelphia Saturday Courier* (August
25, September 8, October 13, 1838) p. 3, (April 27, May 4, June 29,
December 14, 1839) p. 3, (February 1, 15, 1840) p. 3; *The Pittsburgh
Daily Advocate and Advertiser* (December 7, 1839) p. 2 (Courtesy Car-
negie Library of Pittsburgh); J.R. Planché, *The Loan of a Lover* (New
York [1840?]) *passim*; Playbill, Bowery Theatre, June 26, [1839] (Theatre
Collection, Harvard College Library); *Public Ledger* [Philadelphia] (March
22, 1838) p. 2; *Sadak and Kalasrade* (title-page missing) *passim*; *The
Spoiled Child* (London [1826?]) *passim*; *The Sun* [Baltimore] (August 1,
1838) pp. 2 & 3, (August 2, 3, 1838) p. 3, (August 6, 1838) pp. 2 & 3,
(August 7, 8, 9, 1838) p. 3, (August 10, 1838) pp. 2 & 3, (August 11,
1838) p. 3, (September 9-14, 17-18, 21, 24, 1839) p. 3, (October 1, 1839)
pp. 2 & 3, (October 7, 12, 14, 1839) p. 3, (October 15, 1839) pp. 2 & 3;
Wemyss, *op. cit.*, p. 301; Wilson, *op. cit.*, pp. 196, 218, 567, 696.

Vauxhall Garden, New York
   Amberg, *op. cit.*, p. 190; P.T. Barnum, *The Life of Barnum . . . . Written
By Himself* (Philadelphia n.d.) p. 77; George S. Bryan, ed., *Struggles And
Triumphs: or, The Life Of P.T. Barnum, Written By Himself* (New York
& London 1927) I, 178; Moore, "Lee," pp. 108 f; *Morning Herald* [New
York] (June 29, 1840) p. 3, (July 1, 1840) p. 4, (July 2, 1840) p. 2,
(July 3, 6, 1840) p. 3, (July 10, 1840) p. 2, (July 13, 1840) pp. 2 & 3,
(July 15, 1840) p. 3, (July 16, 1840) p. 2; Odell, *op. cit.*, IV, 433 f; M.R.

Werner, *Barnum* (New York [1923]) p. 40; Bouck White, *The Book of Daniel Drew* (New York 1910) p. 71.

Elssler in America; Lee's Studies with James Sylvain
    Amberg, *op. cit.*, p. 190; Balanchine, *op. cit.*, p. 466; Barzel, *op. cit.*, p. 60; Cyril W. Beaumont, *Fanny Elssler (1810-1844)* (London 1931) *passim*; Chujoy, *op. cit.*, pp. 169 ff; Durang, *op. cit.*, 3rd Series, pp. 171 f; S.M. Fuller, *Summer On The Lakes, In 1843* (Boston & New York 1844) pp. 93 f; King, *op. cit.*, pp. 87 f, 93; *The Letters and Journal of Fanny Ellsler* (New York 1845) pp. 40 f; *Memoir of Fanny Elssler* (New York 1840) pp. 20 ff; Moore, "Lee," pp. 108 f; Allan Nevins, ed., *The Diary of Philip Hone 1828-1851* (New York 1936) pp. 480 f, 483 f; Odell, *op. cit.*, IV, 479; Wemyss, *op. cit.*, p. 332.

Lee in Pittsburgh, Boston, Baltimore, & New Orleans; Her Roles
    Amberg, *op. cit.*, p. 191; *Baltimore Directory 1842* (Courtesy Enoch Pratt Free Library); Thomas Haynes Bayly, *"My Little Adopted"* (London [1840]) *passim*; Thomas Haynes Bayly, *One Hour; or The Carnival Ball* (New York n.d.) *passim*; B[u]y it, Dear 'Tis Made of Cashmere (MS in Theatre Collection, New York Public Library) *passim*; William W. Clapp, Jr., *A Record of The Boston Stage* (Boston & Cambridge 1853) pp. 379, 474; *The Daily Bee* [Boston] (May 24, 1842) p. 3; *Daily Evening Transcript* [Boston] (May 7, 9-12, 1842) p. 3, (May 13, 1842) pp. 2 & 3, (May 14, 16-20, 1842) p. 3, (October 24, 1842) pp. 2 & 3, October 25-28, 31, 1842) p. 3, (November 1, 1842) pp. 2 & 3, (November 2-4, 1842) p. 3; *The Daily Picayune* [New Orleans] (January 21, 1843) pp. 2 & 3, (January 22, 1843) pp. 2 & 3, (January 26, 1843) pp. 2 & 3, (January 28, 1843) p. 3, (February 2, 1843) pp. 2 & 3, (February 16, 1843) p. 3, (February 19, 1843) p. 3, (February 21, 1843) p. 3, (March 4, 1843) p. 3, (March 10, 1843) pp. 2 & 3, (April 9, 1843) p. 3, (April 12, 1843) pp. 2 & 3, (April 13, 1843) pp. 2 & 3, (April 22, 1843) pp. 2 & 3, (February 20, 1844) p. 2, (February 21, 1844) p. 3, (March 13, 1844) p. 3, (March 16, 1844) p. 3, (December 6, 1846) p. 2; J. Farrell, *The Dumb Girl of Genoa* (Boston n.d.) *passim*; Lucile Gafford, *A History of the St. Charles Theatre in New Orleans 1835-43* (Chicago 1932) p. 7; J.S. Jones, *The Surgeon of Paris* (Boston 1856) *passim*; John S. Kendall, *The Golden Age of the New Orleans Theater* (Baton Rouge, La., [1952]) pp. 233, 255; Mary Ann Lee to J.S. Jones, Baltimore, September 12, 1842 (Theatre Collection, Harvard College Library); N.M. Ludlow, *Dramatic Life As I Found It* (St. Louis 1880) pp. 561, 563, 566 f, 587, 589; Moore, "Lee," pp. 109 f; *The New York Herald* (September 26, 1842) p. 2; Odell *op. cit.*, IV, 494, 546 f; Playbills, Bowery Theatre, August 20 & 24, 1841, September 4, 1843 (Theatre Collection, Harvard College Library); Augustin Eugène Scribe & G. Delavigne, *Robert-Le-Diable* (Paris n.d.) *passim*; Sol Smith, *Theatrical Management in the West and South for Thirty Years* (New York 1868) p. 172; *The Sun* [Baltimore] (September 12-17, 19-24, 26, 28-30, October 1, 3-8, 1842) p. 3, (October 11, 1842) pp. 3 & 5, (October 12-13,

1842) p. 3; George Vandenhoff, *Leaves from An Actor's Note-Book* (New York & London 1860) pp. 203, 205 f; Wemyss, *op. cit.,* p. 373.

Mary Ann Lee's Studies in Paris under Coralli; Her Characteristics as a Dancer
 Amberg, *op. cit.,* p. 192; Balanchine, *op. cit.,* pp. 184, 260; Beaumont, *Complete Book Of Ballets, op. cit.,* p. 113; Charles de Boigne, *Petits Mémoires de l'Opéra* (Paris 1857) pp. 35 f, 255; *Ces Demoiselles de L'Opéra* (Paris 1887) pp. 24, 28; *The Charleston Courier* (November 16, 1846) p. 2; Chujoy, *op. cit.,* pp. 110 f, 205; Clapp, *op. cit.,* p. 437; *The Daily Picayune* [New Orleans] (December 17, 22, 1846) p. 2; Durang, *op. cit.,* 2nd Series, p. 195; Serge Lifar, *Carlotta Grisi* (London [1947]) p. 53; Serge Lifar, *Giselle Apothéose du Ballet Romantique* (Paris [1942]) pictures opp. p. 118; Moore, "Lee," pp. 110 f, 117; *The New York Herald* (April 16, 1846) p. 2; Passport Application 2605-2606 (October 25, 1844) in National Archives; Albéric Second, *Les Petits Mystères De L'Opéra* (Paris 1844) pp. 161, 177 f; *The Spirit of the Times* XV:14 (May 31, 1845) p. 164; Walter Terry, *The Dance in America* (New York [1956]) p. 29; L. Véron, *Mémoires d'un Bourgeois De Paris* (Paris 1854) III, 295 ff, 298, 301.
 Lee's dancing style was compared by Clapp, *op. cit.,* p. 437, to that of Blangy, whose gracefulness, intelligence of action, light movements and "manifestations of mind" were commented upon by the [New Orleans] *Weekly Picayune* (January 4, 1847) p. 1.

Romantic Ballets Performed by Lee
 Amberg, *op. cit.,* pp. 5 ff, 191 f; Balanchine, *op. cit.,* pp. 168 ff, 177-185, 445, 467, 553, 555; Cyril W. Beaumont, *The Ballet Called Giselle* (London 1945) *passim;* Beaumont, *Complete Book Of Ballets, op. cit.,* pp. 99-102, 129-137, 149-159; *Les Beautés De L'Opéra ou Chefs-D'Oeuvre Lyriques* (Paris 1845) pp. 23 f; *Boston Courier* (April 22, 1846) p. 2; George Chaffee, "A Chart to the American Souvenir Lithographs of the Romantic Ballet 1825-1870," *Dance Index* I:2 (February 1942) pp. 31 f; *The Charleston Courier* (November 10-12, 14, 1846) p. 3, (November 16, 1846) pp. 2 & 3, (November 17-21, 23, 1846) p. 3; *Charleston Mercury* (November 9, 12, 14, 16-17, 1846) p. 3, (November 23, 1846) pp. 2 & 3; Chujoy, *op. cit.,* pp. 205 f, 208 f, 234 f, 459; *Daily Evening Transcript* [Boston] (December 26, 27, 29-30, 1845) p. 3, (December 31, 1845) pp. 2 & 3, (January 1, 1846) p. 3, (January 2, 1846) pp. 2 & 3, (January 5, 1846) p. 3, (January 6, 1846) pp. 2 & 3, (January 8-9, 1846) p. 3; *The Daily Picayune* [New Orleans] (December 6, 1846) pp. 2 & 3, (December 8, 1846) pp. 2 & 3, (December 9, 1846) pp. 2 & 3, (December 10, 1846) p. 2, (December 13, 1846) pp. 2 & 3, (December 15, 1846) pp. 2 & 3, (December 16, 1846) p. 3, (December 17, 1846) pp. 2 & 3, (December 22, 1846) p. 2, (January 2, 1847) pp. 2 & 3, (January 3, 1847) pp. 2 & 3, (January 5, 1847) p. 2, (January 6, 1847) pp. 2 & 3, (January 7, 1847) p. 3, (January 8, 1847) p. 2; Gladys Davidson, *Stories of the Ballets* (London [1949]) pp. 77-88,

473; Heath, *op. cit.*, p. 16; Ireland, *op. cit.*, II, 452; Kendall, *op. cit.*, p. 263; Mary Ann Lee to Ludlow & Smith, Philadelphia, August 28, 1846, September 21, 1846 (Theatre Collection, Harvard College Library); Lifar, *Carlotta Grisi, op. cit.*, p. 52; Ludlow, *op. cit.*, p. 660; Ludlow & Smith to Mary Ann Lee, St. Louis, September 6, 1846 (Theatre Collection, Harvard College Library); Lillian Moore, "George Washington Smith," *Dance Index* IV:6-8 (June-August 1945) *passim*; Moore, "Lee," pp. 105, 111-115; *The New York Herald* (April 5, 1846) p. 3, (April 6, 7, 1846) p. 2, (April 8, 1846) pp. 2 & 3, (April 9, 1846) p. 3, (April 10, 1846) p. 2, (April 13, 14, 1846) p. 3, (April 15, 16, 1846) p. 2; Odell, *op. cit.*, (New York 1931) V, 181; Harry T. Peters, *America On Stone* [New York 1931] pp. 152, 166, Plate 42; *The Philadelphia Saturday Courier* (November 15, 29, December 6, 1845) p. 3; Playbill, Howard Athenæum, Boston, January 2, 1846, in newspaper clipping entitled "With The Ballet-Dancers of Days Gone Bye" (Theatre Collection, New York Public Library); Playbills, Howard Athenæum, December 23, 24, 25, 26, 29, 1845, St. Charles Theatre, December 7, 8, 9, 10, 13, 14, 15, 17, [1846] (Theatre Collection, Harvard College Library); *Public Ledger* [Philadelphia] (November 24, 1845) pp. 2 & 3, (November 25, 1845) p. 3, (November 26, 1845) pp. 2 & 3, (November 27-29, December 3, 1845) p. 3; Joseph C. Smith, "The Story of a Harlequin," *The Saturday Evening Post* (May 30, 1914) pp. 13 f; Philippe Taglioni, *La Fille du Danube* (Paris 1836) *passim*; Vandenhoff, *op. cit.*, pp. 206 f; *The Wept of The Wish-Ton-Wish* (New York [1856?]) *passim*.

Announcement of Lee's Retirement

Public Ledger [Philadelphia] (June 18, 1847) pp. 2 & 3, and *Saturday Courier* [Philadelphia] (June 19, 1847) p. 3. These announcements have been accepted by all commentators. See Amberg, *op. cit.*, p. 193; Moore, "George Washington Smith," *op. cit.*, p. 97; Moore, "Lee," p. 115; Todd, *op. cit.*, p. 44.

For a fictitious account resembling Lee's career in a few respects, see William Knight Northall, *Before And Behind the Curtain: or Fifteen Years' Observations among The Theatres of New York* (New York 1851) pp. 205-215.

Lee's Marriage to William F. Vanhook

T. Allston Brown, *History of the American Stage* (New York [1870]) p. 366 states that Mrs. W.F. Vanhook, whose maiden name was Mary Ann Lee, made her début on May 12, 1847, as a danseuse at the Chestnut Street Theatre in Philadelphia. Although no performance was given at that theater on May 12, 1847, the players were rehearsing for *The Maid of Cashmere* which began its run with Mary Ann Lee the next evening [See *Public Ledger* (May 12, 13, 1847) p. 3]. The conclusion may therefore be drawn that, by May of 1847, Mary Ann Lee had already married William F. Vanhook.

The conclusion is bolstered by other facts. On September 6, 1846, Ludlow & Smith, who were corresponding with Mary Ann regarding her New

Orleans engagement, addressed their letter to 8 Jacoby Street, Philadelphia. Two years later, the *Philadelphia Directory* reveals that 8 Jacoby Street was the home of Wilhelmina Broad, Mary Ann's mother. By 1849, another name is listed at that address, that of William F. Vanhook.

Mary Ann's eldest known child was Marie, who died in 1935 at the age of 85, and who therefore was probably born in 1850. The marriage took place, probably in 1847—certainly not later than 1849. Other children born of the union were Charles Hunt Vanhook, buried July 27, 1853, age one year and nine months, and Mabel L. Vanhook, buried December 13, 1912, age 58 (Information from Assistant Secretary, Laurel Hill Cemetery Company).

For details regarding William F. Vanhook, see *Philadelphia Directories* 1846-1889. Records regarding his work in the Custom House, where, on June 17, 1856, he was appointed an Inspector at Philadelphia at a salary of $1095 a year, may be found in Record Group 56, General Records of the Department of the Treasury. According to his Death Certificate (No. 34902) he died in Atlantic City, N.J., on July 18, 1889, of paralysis. According to the Assistant Secretary of Laurel Hill Cemetery Company, he was buried on July 22, 1889, at the age of 63.

Later Performances
American Courier [Philadelphia] (May 29, June 5, September 4, 1852) p. 2, (May 7, 1853) p. 3, (May 14, 28, 1853) p. 2, (September 3, 1853) p. 3, (September 24, 1853) p. 2; Beaumont, *Complete Book Of Ballets, op. cit.*, pp. 86-91; *The Daily Picayune* [New Orleans] (December 6, 1849) p. 3; *The Dollar Newspaper* [Philadelphia] (May 4, June 1, 1853) p. 3; Durang, *op. cit.*, Vol. 6, pp. 341, 367, 378; Kendall, *op. cit.*, p. 333; Ludlow, *op. cit.*, p. 697; Moore, "George Washington Smith," *op. cit.*, pp. 98, 114; Moore, "Lee," p. 117; Playbill, Chesnut Street Theatre, May 27, 1852 (Theatre Collection, Harvard College Library).

Details of Later Personal Life
Death Certificate of William F. Vanhook (No. 34902); Information from Laurel Hill Cemetery Company; *Philadelphia Directories* 1861, 1870, 1872, 1890-1891, 1895-1899; *Public Ledger* (July 19, 1889) p. 2, (July 20, 1889) p. 4, (July 22, 1889) p. 2 [reporting death of William F. Vanhook].

Mary Ann's Dancing Academy
Philadelphia Directories 1860-1861.
For Carpenter's activity see *American Courier* [Philadelphia] (April 21, 1855) p. 3 & *The Philadelphia Inquirer* (April 10, 1860) p. 4.

Later Events in Ballet World
Balanchine, *op. cit.*, pp. 446, 469 f; Beaumont, *Complete Book Of Ballets, op. cit.*, pp. 113, 289; Terry, *The Dance in America, op, cit.*, pp. 31 f; Marian Hannah Winter, "Augusta Maywood," reprinted in Magriel, *Chronicles of the American Dance, op. cit.*, p. 137; "With The Ballet-Dancers of

Days Gone Bye," newspaper clipping, Theatre Collection, New York Public Library.

Death of Mary Ann Vanhook

Death Certificate of Mary Ann Vanhook (No. 34901) [This states, incorrectly, that she died age 68. The passport application of 1844 provides reliable evidence that she had been born in 1826]; Information from Laurel Hill Cemetery Company; *Public Ledger* (January 27, 1899) p. 9, (January 28, 1899) p. 8.

For George Van Hook Potter, see *The Philadelphia Inquirer* (May 29, 1934) p. 4, (May 31, 1934) p. 23.

Her poverty is revealed by Letters of Administration, in the Estate of Mary Ann Van Hook, deceased, granted unto Mabel L. Van Hook, Administratrix, on May 4, 1899 (Register of Wills, Philadelphia).

CHAPTER 2

ANN S. STEPHENS

Advertisements of The First Beadle Dime Novel
New-York Daily Tribune (June 7 & 9, 1860) p. 1.

Early Appearance of Malaeska & Price Paid by Beadles

"The Dime Novel," *Beadle's Weekly* II:77 (May 3, 1884) p. 8; "Malaeska," *The Ladies' Companion* (February, March & April 1839) X, 188-195, 239-244 & 258-269.

Ann Stephens' Early Life & Background

Her date of birth is established by her death record (City Clerk, Newport, R.I.) which states that at her death on August 20, 1886, her age was 76 years, 4 months and 21 days. See also record at The Green-Wood Cemetery (Lot 4919 Sec. 48), courtesy Neil B. Watson, Superintendent. Most of the published sources give her birth year as 1813—an error.

For details of her early life see the following, many of which have been used throughout and will not be cited again: Rev. Hollis A. Campbell, William C. Sharpe & Frank G. Bassett, *Seymour, Past and Present* (Seymour, Conn., 1902) pp. 62 ff, 75, 78f, 198; Arthur Prudden Coleman & Marion Moore Coleman, "Polonica and Connecticut," *Polish American Studies* IV:12 (January-June 1947) p. 6; James A. Eastman, *Ann Sophia Stephens* (Masters Essay, Columbia University 1952) pp. 2-7 & *passim*; Samuel Orcutt & Ambrose Beardsley, *The History of the Old Town of Derby, Connecticut, 1642-1880* (Springfield, Mass., 1880) pp. 451-461, 648f [For this work Mrs. Stephens wrote recollections of her early life in Connecticut]; W.C. Sharpe, *History of Seymour, Connecticut* (Seymour, Conn., ? 9) pp. 126f; Mrs. Ann S. Stephens to Mrs. Lydia H. Sigourney, New rk, April 27, 1843 (Connecticut Historical Society) [The letter recalls

her early Connecticut days]; Mrs. Ann S. Stephens, *The Heiress. An Auto-
biography* (Philadelphia [1859]), Dedication; Mrs. Ann S. Stephens, "My
First Lesson," *Mrs. Stephens' New Monthly* (January 1858) IV, 21f; "Mrs.
Ann S. Stephens," *The American Literary Magazine* II:6 (June 1848)
pp. 335-343; "Ann Sophia Stephens," *DAB*; "Mrs. Ann S. Stephens," *Frank
Leslie's Illustrated Newspaper* II:36 (August 16, 1856) p. 158; "Ann Sophia
(Winterbotham) Stephens," *The National Cyclopædia of American Biog-
raphy* (New York 1909) X, 20; "Mrs. Ann Sophia Stephens," *Publishers'
Weekly* XXX:9 (August 28, 1886) p. 242; C. L. Weaver, "Connecticut's
Forgotten Novelist," *Connecticut Circle* XVI:7 (July 1953) p. 17; "William
Winterbotham," *DNB*; William Wrigley Winterbotham, *Recollections* (Pitts-
burgh 1950) *passim*.

For additional details concerning Col. Humphreys, see Rufus Wilmot
Griswold, *The Poets and Poetry of America* (Philadelphia 1852) p. 50;
Leon Howard, *The Connecticut Wits* (Chicago [1943]) p. 263; General
Humphreys, *The Yankey in England, A Drama, in Five Acts* [Humphreys-
ville 1815] *passim*; "David Humphreys," *DAB*; Frank Landon Humphreys,
Life and Times of David Humphreys (New York & London 1917) II, 360,
385ff, 428f.

Marriage; Life & Work in Portland

"The Female Writers of America," *The Ladies' Wreath* (New York
1848-49) II, 321; *The Maine Monthly Magazine* I:12 (June 1837) p. 568;
John Neal, *Portland Illustrated* (Portland 1874) pp. 69f; John Neal, *Wandering Recollections of A Somewhat Busy Life* (Boston 1869) p. 351;
The Portland Directory 1834; *The Portland Magazine* I & II (October 1,
1834–June 1, 1836) *passim*. For the "Address," see I:1 (October 1, 1834)
p. 1; *The Portland Sketch Book. Edited by Mrs. Ann S. Stephens* (Portland 1836) *passim* & "Preface," pp. iii ff; *The* [Portland] *Transcript* (September 15, 1886), clipping in *Scrap-book containing obituary notices, etc.,
of Mrs. Ann S. Stephens* (New York Public Library); Bertha Monica
Stearns, "New England Magazines for Ladies 1830-1860," *The New England Quarterly* III:4 (October 1930) pp. 636f; Mrs. Ann S. Stephens to
Mrs. Lydia H. Sigourney, New York, November 10, 1841 & April 27,
1843 (Connecticut Historical Society); Mrs. Ann S. Stephens, "The Diamond Necklace," *The Boston Pearl* V:10 (November 21, 1835) pp. 84-87;
Ann S. Stephens, "Mrs. Lydia Huntley Sigourney," *The Ladies' Wreath*
(New York 1850) pp. 259f; Ralph Thompson, *American Literary Annuals
& Gift Books 1825. 1865* (New York 1936) p. 148.

The Stephenses in New York City; Mrs. Stephens & The Ladies' Companion

Caroline J. Garnsey, "Ladies' Magazines to 1850," *Bulletin of The New
York Public Library* 58:2 (February 1954) pp. 78, 84; *The Ladies' Com-
panion* VIII-XI (November 1837–May 1839) *passim*. For the "$200 Prize
Article" see the issue of May 1838, p. 39; Mary Noel, *Villains Galore*
(New York 1954) pp. 37 ff; Mrs. Ann S. Stephens, MS Scrapbook (Manu-

script Division, New York Public Library); Mrs. Ann S. Stephens to James Buchanan, New York, August 17, 1858 (Historical Society of Pennsylvania) [The letter reveals her husband's salary]; Mary Alice Wyman, *Two American Pioneers Seba Smith and Elizabeth Oakes Smith* (New York 1927) pp. 110f.

Mrs. Stephens' Appearance, Character & Reputation

Charles J. Peterson, "Our Contributors.—No. XV. Mrs. Ann S. Stephens," *Graham's Magazine* XXV:5 (November 1844) pp. 234ff; Edgar Allan Poe, "The Literati of New York," *Godey's Lady's Book* (July 1846) XXXIII, 15; Mrs. Ann Stephens to Mrs. Sigourney, New York, May 16, 1839 (New-York Historical Society).

For the dates of birth of her children, Ann and Edward, see Edward Stephens to Mrs. Sigourney, New York, September 13, [1845] (Boston Public Library); Ann Stephens to Mrs. Sigourney, New York, July 31, 1845 (Boston Public Library) & New York, April 27, 1843 (Connecticut Historical Society).

Mrs. Stephens & Graham's Magazine

For George Rex Graham, who was to lose his fortune later on, see Hervey Allen, *Israfel* (New York 1927) p. 485; "Death of George R. Graham," *Orange Chronicle* (July 14, 1894), Courtesy Orange Public Library; "George Rex Graham," *DAB*; Charles J. Peterson, "George R. Graham," *Graham's Magazine* XXXVII:1 (July 1850) pp. 43f; J. Albert Robbins, "George R. Graham Philadelphia Publisher," *The Pennsylvania Magazine of History and Biography* LXXV:3 (July 1951) *passim.*

For details of the *Magazine,* see also "Graham's Magazine," *Pennsylvania Arts and Sciences* I:1 (Christmas 1935) *passim*; Frank Luther Mott, *American Journalism* (New York 1950) pp. 319f; Frank Luther Mott, *A History of American Magazines 1741-1850* (New York & London 1930) pp. 544n, 547-550, 555; J. Albert Robbins, "Fees Paid to Authors by Certain American Periodicals, 1840-1850," *Studies in Bibliography* II (Charlottesville, Va., 1949-1950), Courtesy John Cook Wyllie; John Sartain, *The Reminiscences of a Very Old Man 1808-1897* (New York 1899) pp. 196ff; Albert H. Smyth, *The Philadelphia Magazines and their Contributors 1741-1850* (Philadelphia 1892) pp. 216, 218, 223.

For Mrs. Stephens' relations with Poe and Griswold, see Joy Bayless, *Rufus Wilmot Griswold Poe's Literary Executor* (Nashville, Tenn., 1943) *passim*; *Graham's Magazine* XIX:6 (December 1841) p. 308, XXI:1 (July 1842) p. 60, & XX:1–XXII:3 (January 1842–March 1843) *passim*; Horace Greeley to Rufus W. Griswold, New York, November 13, 1843 (Griswold MSS, Boston Public Library); Rufus W. Griswold to James T. Fields, Philadelphia, March 7, 1847 (Huntington Library FI 1476); Rufus W. Griswold, *Passages From The Correspondence of Rufus W. Griswold* (Cambridge, Mass., 1898) p. 133; Rufus W. Griswold, *Statement of the Relations of Rufus W. Griswold with Charlotte Myers (called Charlotte Griswold), Elizabeth F. Ellet, Ann S. Stephens* (Philadelphia 1856) *passim*; "The

Griswold Divorce Case," *New-York Daily Tribune* (February 27, February 29 & March 1, 1856); Gordon S. Haight, *Mrs. Sigourney The Sweet Singer of Hartford* (New Haven 1930) pp. 119, 122f; John H. Ingram, *Edgar Allan Poe His Life, Letters, and Opinions* (London 1880) I, xii; Jacob L. Neu, "Rufus Wilmot Griswold," *Studies in English Number 5. University of Texas Bulletin No. 2538* (October 8, 1925) *passim*; Mary E. Phillips, *Edgar Allan Poe The Man* (Chicago, Philadelphia, Toronto 1926) I, 685, II, 953 & 1203; Edgar Allan Poe, "A Chapter on Autobiography," *Graham's Magazine* XIX:6 (December 1841) p. 286; Edgar Allan Poe, *The Letters of Edgar Allan Poe Edited by John Ward Ostrom* (Cambridge, Mass., 1948) I, 187, 197, 246; Poe, "The Literati of New York," *op. cit.*; Arthur Hobson Quinn, *Edgar Allan Poe* (New York & London 1941) p. 330; Elisabeth Oakes Smith to John H. Ingram, June 8, 1875 (Alderman Library, University of Virginia); Mrs. Stephens to Mrs. Sigourney, New York, April 27, 1843 (Connecticut Historical Society); George E. Woodberry, *The Life of Edgar Allan Poe* (Boston & New York 1909) I, 317.

Mrs. Stephens' Social Activities

Brother Jonathan VI:17 (December 23, 1843) p. 469; Mrs. Stephens to Mr. Burton, [New York], April 2, n.y. (Historical Society of Pennsylvania); Madeleine B. Stern, "The House of the Expanding Doors: Anne Lynch's Soirées, 1846," *New York History* XXIII:1 (January 1942) pp. 46f; Bayard Taylor, *Life And Letters* (Boston & New York 1885) I, 110. For her illness see Ann to My dear friend, New York, December 7, 1844 (Connecticut Historical Society).

Mrs. Stephens' Magazine Connections & Contributions

According to Joseph N. Kane, *Famous First Facts* (New York 1950) p. 40, Mrs. Stephens was the first successful woman serial writer. See also *Brother Jonathan* V:13 (July 29, 1843), advertisement at end, & VI (1843) *passim*; *Frank Leslie's Ladies Gazette of Fashion* I:1-IV:3 (January 1854–September 1855) *passim*; *The Ladies' Wreath* I (1846/1847); Frank Luther Mott, *A History of American Magazines 1850-1865* (Cambridge, Mass., 1938) pp. 32, 437f; *The New York Times* (August 21, 1886) clipping in Stephens Scrap-book of clippings, *op. cit.*; *Peterson's Magazine* XXXIV:5 (November 1858) p. 370; Stearns, *op. cit.*, p. 637; Mrs. Stephens to Wilton [Brooks] [New York], Monday (Huntington Library HM 2970); Mrs. Stephens to James Buchanan, New York, March 4, 1860 (Historical Society of Pennsylvania) [The letter introduces James Brooks to the President]; Mrs. Stephens to Carey & Hart, New York, January 23, 1839 (Historical Society of Pennsylvania); Mrs. Stephens to Mrs. Sigourney, New York, April 27, 1843 (Connecticut Historical Society); Mrs. Ann S. Stephens, "Romance of the Real; or Phases in the Life of Myra Clark Gaines," *The Columbian Lady's and Gentleman's Magazine* IX:5-8 (May, June, July & August 1848) pp. 193-200, 273-279, 321-327, 361-367; *Mrs. Stephens' [Illustrated] New Monthly* I–IV (July 1856–June 1858) *passim*; Madeleine B. Stern, *Purple Passage The Life of Mrs. Frank Leslie* (Norman, Okla.,

1953) p. 34; *Sunday Morning News* (May 22, 1842), Courtesy the late Dorothea E. Spear, American Antiquarian Society; James Grant Wilson, *The Memorial History of the City of New-York* (New York 1893) IV, 156f.

Mrs. Stephens & Peterson's Magazine

For Charles J. Peterson and his *Magazine,* see Garnsey, *op. cit.,* p. 86; Rufus W. Griswold, *Passages From The Correspondence, op. cit.,* p. 152; *The Lady's World* [early name of *Peterson's Magazine*] III:4 (April 1843) p. 102, III:6 (June 1843) p. 191; Mott, *American Journalism, op. cit.,* p. 320; Mott, *A History of American Magazines, op.cit.,* II, 306ff, 311; Charles J. Peterson, *Monody on Certain Members of the "Press Club."* (N.p. n.d.) unpaged; Charles J. Peterson, "Our Contributors," *Graham's Magazine* XXV:5 (November 1844) p. 235; "Charles Jacobs Peterson," *DAB*; *Peterson's Magazine* XVII:1 (January 1850) "Editors' Table," pp. 70f, XXVI:6 (December 1854) p. 384, III–XCI (1843-1887) *passim*; J.A. Robbins, "Fees Paid to Authors by Certain American Periodicals," *op. cit.,* p. 102; "Mrs. Ann S. Stephens. With A Portrait," *Ladies' National Magazine* X:6 (December 1846) p. 197.

The European Tour

The best reports of the journey are those published from time to time in *Peterson's Magazine.* See especially XVII:6 (June 1850) p. 270, XVIII:1 (July 1850) p. 54, XVIII:2 (August 1850) p. 94, XVIII:6 (November 1850) p. 214, XIX:3 (March 1851) p. 166, XIX:5 (May 1851) p. 246, XX:4 (October 1851) pp. 172f, XX:5 (November 1851) p. 208.

For Mrs. Stephens' own articles based upon her travels, see "The Andalusian Letter-Writer," *Mrs. Stephens' New Monthly* (February 1858) IV, 102f; "A Breakfast with Samuel Rogers," *Peterson's Magazine* XXXVII:1 (January 1860) pp. 19-24; "First View of the Alhamra," *Ibid.* XXI:3 (March 1852) p. 176; "A London Dinner-Party," *Ibid.* LXXXII:1 (July 1882) pp. 29-35; "To The Reader," *Ibid.* XX:6 (December 1851) p. 251; "A Visit to Edgeworthstown. Memories of Maria Edgeworth," *Mrs. Stephens' New Monthly* (January 1858) IV, 39ff.

See also Stephens Scrap-book of clippings, *op. cit., passim*; Passport Application 4191, March 20, 1850, Received March 25, 1850, National Archives. [Details of Mrs. Stephens' appearance are listed including blue eyes, stout nose, large mouth, round chin, reddish hair, florid complexion and full face].

For details about George W. Pratt, who died in the Civil War, and of Julia Pratt, who married the Hon. Colin M. Ingersoll, see *Biography of Zadock Pratt, of Prattsville, N.Y.* (N.p. n.d.) *passim*; F.W. Chapman, *The Pratt Family* (Hartford 1864) pp. 225f; *Collection of Miss D . . . formed mainly from the Collections of Zadock Pratt and George W. Pratt which will be sold by auction in Paris the 14th, 15th, 16, 17th of June 1927 passim; Collections on the History of Albany* (Albany 1867) II, 122; Roswell R. Hoes, "Another Biographical Sketch of Colonel George W.

Pratt," *Olde Ulster* X:12 (December 1914) *passim*; "Colonel George W. Pratt," *Ibid.* VI:4 (April 1910) *passim*.

For Mrs. Stephens' dedication of "Palaces and Prisons," see *Peterson's Magazine* XV:2 (February 1849) p. 47.

Mrs. Stephens' Political Interests & Influence

The Diary of James K. Polk during his Presidency, 1845 to 1849 (Chicago 1910) II, 391; Philip Graham, *The Life and Poems of Mirabeau B. Lamar* (Chapel Hill 1938) pp. 70, 84, 293, 313; Mirabeau B. Lamar, *Verse Memorials* (New York 1857) pp. 9f & 125ff; Neal, *Portland Illustrated, op.cit.*, p. 70; *The Papers of Mirabeau Buonaparte Lamar* (Austin, Texas, 1924, 1925, n.d.) IV, Part I, 101f, 109f, IV, Part II, 78, VI, 163, 361f; William O. Scroggs, *Filibusters and Financiers* (New York 1916) pp. 200, 206, 354, 358; Mrs. Ann S. Stephens to James Buchanan, New York, May 26, 1854, February 10, 1857, New York, July 5, 1858, August 5, 1858, New York, August 17, 1858, New York, October 16, 1859, Willards Hotel, January 31, 1860, New York, March 4, 1860, New York, August 13, 1860 (Historical Society of Pennsylvania); Mrs. Ann S. Stephens to Samuel Sullivan Cox, New York, February 16, 1861 (Brown University Library); Mrs. Ann S. Stephens to Mrs. Day, February 4, 1860 (New-York Historical Society); Mrs. Ann S. Stephens to Mrs. Sigourney, New York, April 27, 1843 (Connecticut Historical Society) [The letter refers to her visit to Seward]; Ann S. Stephens, MS Scrapbook (Manuscript Division, New York Public Library); Mrs. Ann S. Stephens, "Lines to Gen. Mirabeau B. Lamar," *The Knickerbocker* XXV:3 (March 1845) p. 242; Mrs. Ann S. Stephens, "A London Dinner-Party," *Peterson's Magazine* LXXXII:1 (July 1882) p. 29; Stephens Scrap-book of clippings, *op. cit.*, *passim*; Jane McManus Storms to James Buchanan, New York, June 14, 1847 (Historical Society of Pennsylvania), Courtesy Mrs. Jane Durgin [The writer refers to Mrs. Stephens' "plan of going to Europe when dispatches were given"].

For another instance of her political interests, see a curious letter from Ann S. Stephens to Hon. A.R. Boteler, New York, February 5, 1860 (Special Collections, Columbia University):

> Permit me to thank you for all the attentions so kindly bestowed on me while in Washington. In the whirl of excitement there, I could not sufficiently express the pleasure your appreciation of my poor efforts to prove the existence of a general love of the South in this portion of the country, gave me. It was reward enough for any little responsibility I had taken. . . .

Mrs. Stephens & The Atlantic Cable

Atlantic Telegraph Celebration. Order of Exercises at the Crystal Palace, . . . September 1, 1858 passim; C.T. McClenachan, *Detailed Report of the Proceedings . . . In Commemoration . . . of the Atlantic Telegraph Cable* (New York 1863) *passim*; *New-York Daily Tribune* (September 2, 1858) p. 4; Mrs. Stephens to James Buchanan, New York, August 17, 1858 (Historical Society of Pennsylvania).

Mrs. Stephens' Books

Besides the books themselves, see *Brother Jonathan* V:13 (July 29, 1843) advertisement at end; Herbert Ross Brown, *The Sentimental Novel in America 1789-1860* (Durham, N.C., 1940) p. 403; Alexander Cowie, *The Rise of the American Novel* (New York et al. [1948]) pp. 425, 819; Evert A. & George L. Duyckinck, *Cyclopædia of American Literature* (New York 1855) II, 530; Rufus Wilmot Griswold, *The Female Poets of America* (Philadelphia 1854) p. 210; Sarah Josepha Hale, *Woman's Record* (New York 1855) p. 797; *Frank Leslie's Ladies Gazette of Fashion* II:1 (July 1854) p. 132; *New-York Daily Tribune* (September 11, September 14, October 7, 1854, November 3, 1856); George C.D. Odell, *Annals of the New York Stage* (New York 1931) VI, 372 & 558; Helen Waite Papashvily, *All The Happy Endings* (New York [1956]) p. 143; *Peterson's Magazine* XXVI:2 (August 1854) p. 128, XXVI:4 (October 1854) p. 253, XXVII:1 (January 1855) p. 99; *The Saturday Evening Post* (August 5, 1854); Mrs. Ann S. Stephens, *Fashion and Famine* (Philadelphia [1854]) Preface, pp. v f; Ralph Thompson, *American Literary Annuals & Gift Books, op. cit., passim*; Lyle H. Wright, *American Fiction 1774-1850* (San Marino, California, 1948) #2495-#2501.

The Old Homestead was dramatized in 1856 by the actor-playwright, George L. Aiken, who also dramatized *Uncle Tom's Cabin*. It was performed at Purdy's National Theatre.

Mrs. Stephens & Beadle; Malaeska

Besides the dime novels themselves, see Ralph Admari, "The House That Beadle Built 1859 to 1869," *The American Book Collector* IV:5 (November 1933) p. 224; *The American Annual Cyclopædia . . . of . . . 1864* (New York 1867) IV, 473; *The Banner Weekly* (September 25, 1886) p. 4; *The Beadle Collection of Dime Novels Given to The New York Public Library By Dr. Frank P. O'Brien* (New York 1922) *passim*; "Beadle's Dime Books," *North American Review* XCIX:204 (July 1864) pp. 303f; *Beadle's Illustrated Catalogue of Dime Books* (New York & London [1860]) unpaged; "The Dime Novel," *Beadle's Weekly* II:77 (May 3, 1884) p. 8; Philip Durham, "Dime Novels: An American Heritage," *The Western Humanities Review* IX:1 (Winter 1954-1955) p. 34; Nolan B. Harmon, Jr., *The Famous Case of Myra Clark Gaines* (Baton Rouge 1946) pp. 393f, 473; James D. Hart, *The Popular Book* (New York 1950) p. 154; Charles M. Harvey, "The Dime Novel in American Life," *The Atlantic Monthly* (July 1907) C, 37-45; Albert Johannsen, *The House of Beadle and Adams* (Norman, Okla., [1950]) I, *passim* & II, 262; Della T. Lutes, "Erastus F. Beadle Dime Novel King," *New York History* XXII:2 (April 1941) pp. 147-157; Frank Luther Mott, *Golden Multitudes* (New York 1947) pp. 149f, 308; *New-York Daily Tribune* (June 7 and June 9, 1860) p. 1; Mary Noel, *Villains Galore, op. cit.*, p. 121; Papashvily, *op. cit.*, pp. 142ff; Edmund Pearson, *Dime Novels* (Boston 1929) pp. 8, 46; Quentin Reynolds, *The Fiction Factory* (New York [1955]) pp. 71f, 74f; Henry Morton Robinson, "Mr. Beadle's Books," *The Bookman* LXIX:1 (March 1929) p. 20;

The Saturday Journal (May 5, 1877), Courtesy Serial Division, Library of Congress; Frank L. Schick, *The Paperbound Book in America* (New York 1958) pp. 50 ff; Mrs. Ann S. Stephens to James Buchanan, Willards Hotel, January 31, 1860 (Historical Society of Pennsylvania); Mrs. Ann S. Stephens, *Malaeska* (New York [1929]) p. v; Mrs. Ann S. Stephens, *Sybil Chase* (New York & London [1861]) inserted slip.

For the quotations from *Malaeska*, see Mrs. Ann S. Stephens, *Malaeska: the Indian Wife of The White Hunter* (New York [1862]) pp. 7, 9, 18, 40, 57, 81, 122f, 126f.

Death of Edward Stephens

New-York Daily Tribune (August 22, 1862) p. 5; *The New York Herald* (August 21, 1862) p. 5; Record of Green-Wood Cemetery.

Mrs. Stephens in Washington; Civil War Activities

Victor Hugo's Letter on John Brown, with Mrs. Ann S. Stephens' Reply (New York 1860) *passim*; Ann Stephens to her brother John Winterbotham, Newport, August 5, 1874 (Courtesy Mrs. M.H. Sibley, Chicago); Mrs. Ann S. Stephens, *Address To the Women of the United States . . . for the Executive Committee of the "Ladies National Covenant" at Washington* (Washington 1864) *passim*; Mrs. Ann S. Stephens, *Pictorial History of the War For The Union* (New York 1866) I, Introduction; Ann Stephens (daughter of Mrs. Ann S. Stephens) Will of May 1, 1916 (Courtesy Mrs. M.H. Sibley); *Washington Critic* (August 21, 1886) in Stephens Scrapbook of clippings.

For the reporting of the Lincoln assassination plot in 1861, see William Roscoe Thayer, *The Life and Letters of John Hay* (Boston & New York [1916]) I, 93 f.

Vanderbilt Golden Wedding

Memorial of the Golden Wedding of Cornelius And Sophia Vanderbilt, December 19, 1863 (New York 1864) *passim*; *New-York Daily Tribune* (December 21, 1863); Mrs. Ann S. Stephens, *The Rejected Wife* (Philadelphia [1876]) Dedication.

Mrs. Stephens' Reputation & Literary Activities

Besides her books, see *Appletons' Journal* IV:66 (July 2, 1870) p. 22; *Frank Leslie's Chimney Corner* XXII:569 (April 22, 1876), XXIII:586-587 (August 19-26, 1876); Information from Mrs. Frank Burroughs Mulford, Stonington, Connecticut; *The New York Weekly* XVI:5 (December 27, 1860) p. 3; *Peterson's Magazine* XLII:6 (December 1862) p. 479 & LXII:6 (December 1872) p. 446; Mrs. Ann S. Stephens to My dear friend, Huntington, Long Island, June 24, 1869 (Historical Society of Pennsylvania); Mrs. Ann S. Stephens, *The Curse of Gold* (Philadelphia [1869]) advertisement at end; Mrs. Ann S. Stephens, *A Noble Woman* (Philadelphia [1871]), Title-page; "The Working Women of New York," *Street and Smith's New York Weekly* XIX:21 (April 14, 1864) p. 4.

Mrs. Stephens' Appearance & Social Life in Later Years
Olive Harper, "Mrs. Ann S. Stephens," clipping in Stephens Scrap-book of clippings; *Opinions of the Press Malaeska* [1929] unpaged excerpt from *The Hartford Courant*; Ann S. Stephens to her brother John Winterbotham, Newport, August 5, 1874 & St. Cloud [Hotel], February 15, 1876 (Courtesy Mrs. M.H. Sibley); Ann Stephens Will (Courtesy Mrs. M.H. Sibley) mentions many of her mother's jewels and the appurtenances of her home; John E. Stillwell, *The History of The Burr Portraits* (N.p. 1928) pp. 86f; *The Sun* (August 21, 1886), clipping in Stephens Scrap-book of clippings; *Times-Democrat* (September 26, 1886) in *Ibid*.; *Town Topics* (August 28, 1886) in *Ibid*.; *The Tribune* (September 4, 1886) in *Ibid*.

Decline of The Dime Novel
"Dime Novel Work," *New-York Daily Tribune* (March 10, 1884) p. 4; Harvey, *op. cit.*, p. 41; William McCormick, "The Dime Novel Nuisance," *Lend A Hand* V:4 (April 1890) p. 257; "Prohibition of Dime Literature," *Publishers' Weekly* XXIII:17 (April 28, 1883) p. 500; Robinson, *op. cit.*, p. 23.

Death of Mrs. Ann S. Stephens
The Banner Weekly (September 25, 1886) p. 4; Death Record of Mrs. Ann S. Stephens (Courtesy City Clerk, Newport, R.I.); *Peterson's Magazine* XC:4 (October 1886) p. 360; Record from The Green-Wood Cemetery, Brooklyn; Resolution of The Nineteenth Century Club on Mrs. Stephens' death in Miscellaneous Folder, Manuscript Division, New York Public Library; Stephens Scrap-book of clippings, *passim* [See especially clippings from *Baltimore American and Commercial Advertiser* (August 24, 1886), *The Daily News* (August 21, 1886), *Every Saturday* (September 4, 1886)].

Reprint of Malaeska
Merle Curti, "Dime Novels and The American Tradition," *The Yale Review* XXVI:4 (June 1937) p. 761; *Opinions of the Press Malaeska* [1929] unpaged; Reynolds, *The Fiction Factory*, *op. cit.*, p. 72; Ann S. Stephens, *Malaeska* (New York [1929]) *passim*.
American Book-Prices Current, 1944-1945 records the sale of a defective copy of the first edition with two variant copies from the Frank J. Hogan Library for $110.
It is interesting to note that Mrs. Stephens' granddaughter, who was known both to the social and theatrical worlds as Clara Bloodgood, lived a more violent dime novel than her grandmother had ever written. For her acting career, three husbands, and suicide, see *Baltimore Sun* (December 6, 1907) p. 14 (Courtesy Anna Mary Urban, Reference Librarian, University of Maryland Library).

CHAPTER 3

IRWIN, BETHUNE, HAYDEN

General Ignorance regarding Women Architects
Building. *An Architectural Weekly* IX:17 (October 27, 1888) p. 135;
[Ethel M. Charles], "A Plea For Women Practising Architecture," *The American Architect and Building News* LXXVI:1373 (April 19, 1902) p. 20; H.W. Domett, "Women in Art and Architecture," *Building. An Architectural Monthly* I:9 (June 1883) p. 118; *The Woman's Journal* XII:44 (October 29, 1881) pp. 348 f. Martha N. McKay in an article entitled "Women As Architects," *The Western* N.S. VI:1 (January 1880) declared that "in domestic architecture, men have *failed*, and women *have not tried*." (p. 31). The author mentions Mrs. Trollope as the architect of Cincinnati's Bazaar Building. At least one man concurred that architecture might be a possible pursuit for women—E.C. Gardner, who wrote *The House that Jill Built, after Jack's had Proved a Failure* (Springfield, Mass., 1896). The work bears copyright date of 1882, when it ran in *Our Continent*.

Personal Life of Harriet Morrison Irwin
I am indebted to many Southerners for details regarding Mrs. Irwin's life, but most especially to Charles R. Brockmann, Archivist of the Public Library of Charlotte, for his wealth of information so generously given. Others who aided with details were Dr. Frances Campbell Brown, Duke University; Mrs. Penelope Jarrell Fitch, North Carolina State Library; F.W. Haas, Superintendent, Elmwood Cemetery Office, Charlotte; Louise Hall, Durham, North Carolina; Mrs. Emma C. Harris, Mobile Public Library; Lelia Graham Marsh, Alumnae Secretary, Salem College, Winston-Salem, North Carolina; Robert Hall Morrison, II, Charlotte, North Carolina; Mae S. Tucker, Public Library of Charlotte.
For printed sources, see Paul B. Barringer, *The Natural Bent* (Chapel Hill, N.C., [1949]) p. 74; Mrs. Laura M. Brown, *Historical Sketch of the Morrison Family* (Charlotte, N.C., 1919) pp. 17-21; *In Memoriam. Mrs. Harriet Morrison Irwin. Born, . . . 1828. Died, . . . 1897* (Courtesy William S. Powell, Librarian, University of North Carolina Library); "Mrs. Irwin Dead," *Charlotte Democrat* (January 28, 1897) p. 4; Mary Anna Jackson, *Life and Letters of General Thomas J. Jackson (Stonewall Jackson)* (New York 1892) pp. 89 ff; Adelaide and Eugenia Lore and Robert Hall Morrison, *The Morrison Family of the Rocky River Settlement of North Carolina* [Charlotte, N.C., 1950] pp. 282 f, 305 f; "Morrison Sisters Make History," *The Charlotte Observer*, Junior League Edition (November 7, 1934) unpaged; *Salem College 175th Anniversary* (N.p. [1947]) p. 7.

Civil War & Reconstruction in Charlotte
Charlotte *A Guide to the Queen City of North Carolina* ([Charlotte, N.C.,] 1939) pp. 28 f, 51.

Stonewall Jackson's daughter, Julia, was born in the Irwin house in Charlotte in 1862, at which time Mrs. Irwin wrote to the celebrated father a letter announcing the birth in the "person of the little daughter." [See Mary Anna Jackson, *op cit.*, p. 374].

Mrs. Irwin's husband, James P. Irwin, published with General D.H. Hill *The Land We Love. A Monthly Magazine Devoted to Literature, Military History, and Agriculture,* starting with the first issue of May 1866.

Mrs. Irwin's Architectural Work

Annual Report of the Commissioner of Patents for The Year 1869 (Washington 1871) I, 165, II, 474, IV, (Washington 1876) 94, 116; Information from Charles R. Brockmann, Public Library of Charlotte; Information from Professor Chalmers G. Davidson, Davidson, N.C.; O. S. Fowler, *A Home For All or The Gravel Wall and Octagon Mode of Building* (New York [1853]) *passim*; Information from Mrs. Irwin P. Graham, Greenville, S.C.; Information from Peter W. Hairston, Mocksville, N.C.; Information from Arthur C. Holden, New York City; Information from H.M. Irwin, Jr., Charlotte, N.C.; Mrs. James P. Irwin, *The Hermit of Petræa* (Charlotte, N.C., 1871) pp. [3], 10 ff, 30, 51; Information from Robert Hall Morrison, II, Charlotte, N.C.; "Morrison Sisters Make History," *The Charlotte Observer,* Junior League Edition (November 7, 1934) unpaged; Bindon B. Stoney, *The Theory of Strains in Girders and Similar Structures* (New York 1873) *passim*; Information from Mae S. Tucker, Public Library of Charlotte; Mrs. L.C. Tuthill, *History of Architecture from The Earliest Times* (Philadelphia 1848) dedication & *passim*; United States Patent Office. H.M. Irwin, Of Charlotte, North Carolina. Letters Patent No. 94, 116, dated August 24, 1869. Improvement In The Construction Of Houses; "Woman as Architect," *The Revolution* V:5 (February 3, 1870) p. 74; "Women Architects," *The Revolution* V:14 (April 7, 1870) pp. 220 f.

According to *Southern Home* (February 17, 1870) p. [2] (Courtesy Charles R. Brockmann, Public Library of Charlotte), "A wall eighty feet built in the hexagonal form encloses a third more space than the same length of wall built in square form, and as these hexagonal rooms fit into each other without loss of space the gain in the whole building is very great."

According to Mr. Clay Lancaster, there were "many other hexagonal buildings in America predating 1869." See also his *Architectural Follies in America* (Rutland, Vt., [1960]) pp. 130, 141.

Louise Bethune's Personal Life, Architectural Training & Marriage

John E. Becker, *A History of the Village of Waterloo New York* (Waterloo, N.Y., 1949) p. 200; *Buffalo Courier* (July 20, 1915) p. 7; *Journal of the American Institute of Architects* III:9 (September 1915) p. 401; Mrs. John A. Logan, *The Part Taken By Women In American History* (Wilmington, Del., 1912) p. 787; *The National Cyclopædia of American Biography* (New York 1904) XII, 8 f; *Who's Who in America 1914-1915* p. 184;

Who Was Who In America 1897-1942 I, 90; Frances E. Willard & Mary A. Livermore, *American Women* (New York, Chicago, Springfield, Ohio, [1897]) I, 80 f; Henry F. Withey & Elsie Rathburn Withey, *Biographical Dictionary of American Architects (Deceased)* (Los Angeles [1956]) pp. 55 f, 377; "A Woman Architect," *Buffalo Express* (Clipping, courtesy Paul M. Rooney, Grosvenor Reference Division, Buffalo and Erie County Public Library); *Woman's Who's Who of America 1914-1915* p. 98.

Architectural Work of Louise Bethune & Her Firm; Her Architectural Principles

I am especially indebted to George E. Pettengill, Librarian of the American Institute of Architects, for information regarding the work of Mrs. Bethune. See also *The Architectural Era* II:5 (May 1888) p. 84, II:8 (August 1888) p. 149, II:11 (November 1888) p. 214, III:8 (August 1889) p. 179, III:12 (December 1889) p. xiv, IV:2 (February 1890) p. 47, IV:3 (March 1890) p. 64, IV:6 (June 1890) p. 138; Louise Bethune, "Women and Architecture," *The Inland Architect and News Record* XVII:2 (March 1891) pp. 20 f; *Buffalo City Directories* 1881-1913 (Courtesy Paul M. Rooney); *Buffalo Courier* (December 19, 1913) p. 7, (July 20, 1915) p. 7; *Buffalo Evening News* (May 26, 1954) Section III p. 65; *The Buffalo Express* (August 28, 1891) p. 2, (May 29, 1904) p. 11, (June 2, 1904) p. 7; [Ethel M. Charles], "A Plea For Women Practising Architecture," *The American Architect and Building News* LXXVI:1373 (April 19, 1902) p. 21; Information from F.N. Farrar, Denton, Cottier & Daniels, Buffalo; Henry-Russell Hitchcock, Jr., "Buffalo Architecture in Review," *The Art News* XXXVIII:16 (January 20, 1940) pp. 8 f; A. Parlett Lloyd, *A Treatise on the Law of Building and Buildings* (Boston & New York 1888) p. 9; Information from Alexis V. Muller, Jr., Lockport, N.Y.; Information from S.W. Murray, Iroquois Door Company, Buffalo; *The National Cyclopædia of American Biography* XII, 9; *100 Years of Education* (Lockport, N.Y., [1947]) pp. 42 f (Courtesy Alexis V. Muller, Jr.); Ulrich Thieme & Felix Becker, *Allgemeines Lexikon der Bildenden Künstler* (Leipzig 1909) III, 540; Willard & Livermore, *op. cit.*, p. 81; Withey, *op. cit.*, pp. 55 f; "A Woman Architect," *Buffalo Express* (Clipping, courtesy Paul M. Rooney); Information from Walter A. Yates, Hotel Lafayette, Buffalo.

Association Activities of Mrs. Bethune; Later Interests; Firm Changes; Death

American Institute of Architects, *Proceedings of the Twenty-Second Annual Convention . . . in Buffalo, October 17-18-19, 1888* (N.p. n.d.) p. 120; *Annuary of The American Institute Of Architects for 1913* (N.p. n.d.) p. 35; *The Architects' Directory and Specification Index For 1904-05* (New York 1904) p. 64; *The Architectural Era* I:12 (December 1887) p. 183, II:11 (November 1888) p. 210, III:12 (December 1889) p. 268, IV:12 (December 1890) pp. 254, 258; Information from G.N. Bethune, Toronto; Jennie Louise (Blanchard) Bethune, Application for Membership to The National Society of the Daughters of the American Revolution.

·No. 49584; Mrs. Louise Bethune, Deacon John Blanchard of Dunstable His Family And Descendants (Clippings, New York Public Library); Louise Bethune, "Women and Architecture," *op. cit.*, pp. 20 f; Jennie Louise Bethune, Last Will and Testament, November 28, 1906; Robert A. Bethune, Last Will and Testament, December 31, 1913; Information from Nancy W. Boone, Burnham Library of Architecture, The Art Institute of Chicago; *Buffalo Courier* (December 19, 1913) p. 7; *Buffalo Express* (Clipping, courtesy Paul M. Rooney); *Building. An Architectural Weekly* IX:17 (October 27, 1888) p. 138, IX:22 (December 1, 1888) pp. 201, 203; Louis Greenstein, "History of Buffalo-Western New York Chapter The American Institute of Architects, Inc.," *Empire State Architect* IV:5 (September-October 1944) pp. 19 ff (Courtesy Arthur C. Holden, New York City); *Journal of the American Institute of Architects* III:9 (September 1915) p. 401; Information from Mrs. J. Randolph Kennedy, Registrar General, National Society of the D.A.R.; Information from Harley J. McKee, School of Architecture, Syracuse University; *The National Cyclopædia of American Biography* XII, 9; Information from George E. Pettengill, American Institute of Architects; Information from Henry H. Saylor, Historian, American Institute of Architects; Willard & Livermore, *op. cit.*, p. 81; Withey, *op. cit.*, pp. 55, 225.

The Bethune office furniture, books, etc., were bequeathed by Robert A. Bethune, who died in 1915, to William L. Fuchs, who died in 1930. According to Margaret D. Fuchs, daughter of William L. Fuchs, the office records "have long since been disposed of."

Mrs. Bethune, Mrs. Irwin, & The Columbian Exposition
For Mrs. Bethune's opinions on the competition for the Woman's Building, see Louise Bethune, "Women and Architecture," *The Inland Architect and News Record* XVII:2 (March 1891) p. 21 and Willard & Livermore, *op. cit.*, p. 81.

The copy of Mrs. James P. Irwin's *The Hermit of Petræa* (Charlotte, N.C., 1871) at Northwestern University Library is inscribed, on the verso of the flyleaf: "Presented to the Woman's Library by the Author . . . . Chicago, May-1893." See *List Of Books Sent . . . to the Library of the Woman's Building, World's Columbian Exposition, Chicago, 1893* (N.p. n.d.) p. 45.

Early Life & Background of Sophia G. Hayden
Information from John B. Casey, Head Master, Jamaica Plain High School; Death Record, Sophia Georgianna [sic] (Hayden) Bennett, Commonwealth of Massachusetts, Division of Vital Statistics; "Girls As Architects," *The Woman's Journal* XXII:16 (April 18, 1891) p. 122; Graduating Exercises of the West Roxbury High School, . . . June 29, 1886 (Courtesy John B. Casey); Information from Caroline Shillaber, Librarian, School of Architecture & Planning, Massachusetts Institute of Technology; Enid Yandell & Laura Hayes, *Three Girls in a Flat* [Chicago 1892] p. 64 [This is a discursive novel more or less narrating the story of the Woman's

Building of the Columbian Exposition. Enid Yandell of Louisville, Kentucky, was a sculptress who modeled caryatids for the Woman's Building, and Laura Hayes of Chicago won third prize for the design of the Woman's Building].

Miss Hayden's Studies at M.I.T.

"Abstract of Thesis. Sophia G. Hayden, 1890," *Technology Architectural Review* III:5 (September 31, [sic] 1890) pp. 28, 30; *Annual Exhibition of the Dept. of Architecture. Mass. Inst. of Tech. Boston* [N.p. 1891] *passim*; "Girls As Architects," *op. cit.*, p. 122; Massachusetts Institute of Technology, *Twenty-Third - Twenty-Seventh Annual Catalogue[s]* (Boston & Cambridge 1887-1892) *passim*; *Massachusetts Institute of Technology, Boston. Department of Architecture* (Boston 1901) pp. 17 ff & *passim*; Arthur Rotch, "Eugène Létang," *Technology Quarterly* V:4 (December 1892) pp. 295 f; Information from Caroline Shillaber, M.I.T.; Thomas E. Tallmadge, *The Story of Architecture in America* (New York [1936]) pp. 196, 212 f; Arthur Clason Weatherhead, *The History of Collegiate Education in Architecture in the United States* (Los Angeles 1941) pp. 26, 32; "Women as Architects," *Architects' and Builders' Journal* II:2 (September 1900) p. 24; Yandell & Hayes, *op. cit.*, p. 64.

There had, of course, been women architectural students and graduates at various other colleges before Sophia Hayden. According to Harley J. McKee of Syracuse, for example, there were women students of architecture at Syracuse University and Cornell University in the 1870's. See also Weatherhead, *op. cit.*, pp. 33 & 37.

Sophia Hayden & The Woman's Building

The advocates of the Isabella Society had proposed to erect a statue of Isabella and build a pavilion, but were ousted by the Board of Lady Managers, who reopened the competition for women architects. See Adelaide Nichols Baker, "The Isabella Idea" (Courtesy Mrs. Richard Borden, Women's Archives, Radcliffe College).

There is a voluminous collection on the World's Columbian Exposition at the Chicago Historical Society, including manuscript material, reports and plans.

There was a spate of books on the Columbian Exposition, of which a great many referred in some detail to the Woman's Building. The following are among the most relevant references: *The American Architect and Building News* XXXII:799 (April 18, 1891) p. 45, XXXVIII:880 (November 5, 1892) p. 86, XXXVIII:883 (November 26, 1892) p. 134, XXXVIII:885 (December 10, 1892) pp. 158, 170; *The Artistic Guide to Chicago and the World's Columbian Exposition* (N.p. 1892) p. 264; Hubert Howe Bancroft, *The Book of The Fair* (Chicago & San Francisco 1893) pp. 257, 259 f, 265 f; Louise Bethune, "Women and Architecture," *The Inland Architect and News Record* XVII:2 (March 1891) p. 21; Information from Mrs. Richard Borden, Women's Archives, Radcliffe College; D.H. Burnham to Sophia G. Hayden, Chicago, December 23, 1891 (Courtesy Mrs. Jennie M. Manning, Sarasota, Fla.); *The Dream City A Portfolio of Photographic Views of the World's Columbian Exposition* (St. Louis 1893) p. 2; Mary K.O. Eagle, ed., *The Congress Of Women Held In the Woman's Building, World's Columbian Exposition* (New York 1894) p. 646; Maud Howe Elliott, ed., *Art and Handicraft in the Woman's Building of the World's Columbian Exposition* (Chicago 1894) pp. 37 f; John J. Flinn, *Official Guide to the World's Columbian Exposition* (Chicago [1893]) pp. 105 ff, 108 f, 111; "Girls As Architects," *op. cit.,* p. 122; *The Illustrated World's Fair* I:4 (October 1891) p. 6, II:7 (January 1892) p. 127, III:14 (August 1892) p. 283; Rossiter Johnson, ed., *A History of the World's Columbian Exposition* (New York 1897) I, 198, 201 ff, 204 ff, 238 f; Charles Moore, *Daniel H. Burnham* (Boston & New York 1921) I, 48; James Phinney Munroe, *A Life of Francis Amasa Walker* (New York 1923) pp. 344 f; Mrs. Potter Palmer, *Addresses And Reports of Mrs. Potter Palmer President of the Board of Lady Managers, World's Columbian Commission* (Chicago 1894) *passim;* Information from Mr. George E. Pettengill, American Institute of Architects; *Proceedings of the Twenty-Seventh Annual Convention American Institute of Architects Held at Chicago, July 31 and August 1, 1893* (Chicago 1893) pp. 141 f, 146, 157; Ishbel Ross, *Silhouette in Diamonds The Life of Mrs. Potter Palmer* (New York [1960]) pp. 74 f, 77 f; Information from Caroline Shillaber, M.I.T.; Tallmadge, *op. cit.,* pp. 198 ff, 212 f; *Technology Architectural Review* III:5 (September 31, [sic] 1890) p. 30; Information from Mrs. Dorothy Thomas, New York City; Ben. C. Truman, *History of The World's Fair* (Philadelphia & Chicago [1893]) pp. 83, 85, 87, 91, 155, 157, 164 f, 173, 175, 184; "An Unusual Opportunity for Women Architects," *The Woman's Journal* XXII:8 (February 21, 1891) p. 63; Henry Van Brunt, "Architecture at the World's Columbian Exposition.—IV," *The Century Magazine* XLIV:5 (September 1892) pp. 729 ff; Trumbull White and Wm. Igleheart, *The World's Columbian Exposition* (Philadelphia & St. Louis [1893]) pp. 444 f; "Woman In Architecture," *Congrès International Des Architectes Exposition Universelle Internationale de 1900* . . . . *Compte Rendu Et Notices* (Paris 1906) pp. 111 f; *The Woman's Book* (New York 1894) I, 15; *The Woman's Journal* XXIII:21 (May 21, 1892) p. 163, XXIII:41 (October 8, 1892) p. 330, XXIV:16 (April 22, 1893) p. 126, XXIV:18 (May 6, 1893) p. 140, XXIV:37 (September 16, 1893) p. 294, XXIV:45 (November 11, 1893) p. 359; *World's Columbian Exposition. Committee on Grounds and Buildings* [Chicago 1891] p. 3 [Here E.T. Jeffery, Chairman of the Committee on Grounds and Buildings, stated that Miss Hayden's "elevations are of the highest grade of excellence, and have met the approval of the best critics who have examined them. They show a clear scholarly quality, of which any architect might be proud."]; *World's Columbian Exposition Illustrated* I:4 (May 1891) p. 11, I:5 (June 1891) pp. 10 f, I:7 (September 1891) p. 15, I:9 (November 1891) p. 16, I:11 (January 1892) p. 5, I:12 (February 1892) p. 3, II:4 (June 1892) p. 85; Yandell & Hayes, *op. cit.,* pp. 64 ff, 67. For Sophia Hayden's own description of the building, see *Rand, McNally & Co.'s A Week At The Fair* (Chicago 1893) p. 180.

The opposing view regarding the architectural influence of the Exposition is summarized by Henry Steele Commager in *The American Mind* (New Haven 1950) p. 394: "It was the World's Columbian Exposition of 1893 that condemned American architecture to the imitative and the derivative for another generation."

Sophia Hayden's Breakdown, Later Life, Marriage & Death

The American Architect and Building News XXXVIII:883 (November 26, 1892) p. 134; *Boston Herald* (February 5, 1953) p. 31; Death Record, Sophia Georgianna [sic] (Hayden) Bennett, Commonwealth of Massachusetts, Division of Vital Statistics; Information from Mrs. Jennie M. Manning, Sarasota, Fla.; Information from Alfred B. Marsh, Alfred B. Marsh Funeral Home, Inc., Winthrop, Mass.; Palmer, *op. cit.,* pp. 199 f; Information from Caroline Shillaber, M.I.T.

Sophia Hayden is listed as an architect in the *Boston City Directory* 1894-1897 (Information courtesy Bradford M. Hill, Boston Public Library). According to Mrs. Adelaide Nichols Baker of Westport, Conn., Miss Hayden may have worked "in a decorator's office." The M.I.T. Annual Catalogs for 1895 and 1896 list her as an architect. In 1897 she is listed as designer and decorator (Information courtesy Katherine Murphy, Assistant Reference Librarian, Massachusetts Institute of Technology).

For the contemporary figures on registered women architects in the United States, see *Architectural & Engineering News* (April 1959) p. 13 (Courtesy Charles E. Peterson, Philadelphia). The Association of Women in Architecture included a membership of 1057 women in 1958.

CHAPTER 4

SARAH G. BAGLEY

Annie Ellsworth & The First Telegraphic Message

The principal source for the story is S.F.B. Morse to Bishop Stevens of Pennsylvania, Paris, November 1866, quoted in *Samuel F.B. Morse His Letters And Journals* (Boston & New York 1914) II, 198 ff and in Samuel Irenaeus Prime, *The Life of Samuel F.B. Morse* (New York 1875) pp. 465, 495 f.

The story is repeated in James D. Reid, *The Telegraph in America* (New York 1879) pp. 101 f, 105.

It is questioned in Alvin F. Harlow, *Old Wires and New Waves* (New York & London 1936) pp. 85 f, 98 f; Carleton Mabee, *The American Leonardo* (New York 1943) pp. 259 ff; John Bach McMaster, *A History of the People of the United States* (New York & London 1910) VII, 129; Robert L. Thompson, *Wiring A Continent* (Princeton, N.J., 1947) pp. 18 f.

For further details regarding the sending of the first telegraphic message, see also Charles F. Briggs & Augustus Maverick, *The Story of The Telegraph* (New York 1858) p. 26.

Morse's verses, "To Miss A.G.E. The Sun-Dial," appear in *Scribner's Monthly* XI:5 (March 1876) p. 757.

Sarah G. Bagley's Background & Work in the Lowell Mills

According to the Hamilton Manufacturing Company records in Baker Library, Graduate School of Business Administration, Harvard University (Courtesy Mr. Robert W. Lovett), Miss Bagley was a native of Meredith, N.H. Her name is mentioned in Mary E. Neal Hanaford, *Meredith, N.H. Annals and Genealogies* (Concord, N.H., 1932) p. 467.

According to her own testimony, given in February, 1845 before the Special Committee investigating petitions for the Ten-Hour Day (*Massachusetts General Court Legislative Documents 1845. House. No. 50. Commonwealth of Massachusetts* pp. 3 f) she had worked 8½ years in the Lowell Mills—6½ in the Hamilton Corporation and 2 in the Middlesex. In S.G.B., "Pleasures Of Factory Life," *The Lowell Offering* No. 2 (December 1840), Courtesy Dr. Clarence S. Brigham, American Antiquarian Society, she describes herself as "having been engaged as an operative the last four years."

Her sketch, "Tales of Factory Life, No. 1," *The Lowell Offering* I, 65-68 may be partly autobiographical. Its heroine is named "Sarah."

She describes herself as "a common schooled New England female factory operative" in *Voice of Industry* (May 15, 1846).

See also, for various phases of her career, the best source on the Lowell mills and their operatives, Hannah Josephson, *The Golden Threads* (New York [1949]) pp. 199 f, 202 f, 247 f, 250 ff, 253, 256 ff, 263 f, 271 ff.

Lowell Background: Reforms, Visitors, Mills & Their Regulations

The literature regarding this "model industrial town" is voluminous. Among the major sources may be mentioned Edith Abbott, *Women In Industry* (New York & London 1910) *passim*; Daniel D. Addison, *Lucy Larcom Life, Letters, And Diary* (Boston & New York 1895) pp. 6, 15; "Association in Lowell, Mass.," *The Harbinger* III:17 (October 3, 1846) p. 271; C.E. Beecher, *The Evils Suffered by American Women And American Children* (New York [1846]) pp. 7 ff; "The Campaign Begun," *The Harbinger* III:5 (July 11, 1846) p. 80; John Coolidge, *Mill and Mansion* (New York 1942) pp. 129-132; Lillian W. Betts, "Lowell, the City of Spindles," *The Outlook* 69:6 (October 12, 1901) p. 374; Charles Cowley, *A Hand Book of Business in Lowell* (Lowell 1856) *passim*; Charles Dickens, "American Notes for General Circulation," *Works* (Philadelphia n.d.) pp. 408 ff; *Hand-Book for the Visiter To Lowell* (Lowell 1848) pp. 9 f, 14, 16, 38 ff, 42 ff; Josephson, *op. cit., passim*; Lucy Larcom, "Among Lowell Mill-Girls: A Reminiscence," *The Atlantic Monthly* XLVIII:289 (November 1881) pp. 593-609; "Lowell Factories," *Voice of Industry* (December 26, 1845); Louis Taylor Merrill, "Mill Town on the Merrimack," *The New England Quarterly* XIX:1 (March 1946) pp. 25 ff; Henry A. Miles, *Lowell, As It Was, And As It Is* (Lowell 1845) *passim*; Margaret Terrell Parker, *Lowell A Study of Industrial Development* (New York

1940) *passim*; Harriet H. Robinson, *Early Factory Labor in New England* (Boston 1889) *passim*; Harriet H. Robinson, *Loom And Spindle* (New York [1898]) *passim*; William Scoresby, *American Factories and their Female Operatives* (London 1845) *passim*; [John Greenleaf Whittier], *The Stranger In Lowell* (Boston 1845) p. 20.

The newspapers, *Voice of Industry* May 29, 1845—April 14, 1848, *passim* and *Vox Populi* January 17, 1845—November 20, 1846, *passim* give the best insight into Lowell background, events and reformers.

A roseate picture of Lowell appears in "Visit to Lowell," *New-York Daily Tribune* (August 16, 1845).

The Lowell Offering & Sarah Bagley

The *Lowell Offering; A Repository of Original Articles On Various Subjects, Written By Factory Operatives* appeared in four preliminary numbers of 16 pages each, quarto size, in October and December 1840 and February and March 1841. These were followed by five volumes of a new series of the periodical from 1841 through December 1845, each number consisting of 32 pages, octavo. *The Lowell Offering* was superseded by the *New England Offering*. The early issues were edited by the Rev. Abel Charles Thomas, pastor of the Second Universalist Church in Lowell. After October 1842, when *The Operatives' Magazine,* which contains three contributions by "Sarah," was merged with it, the magazine passed into the hands of the reactionary printer, William Schouler, proprietor of the *Lowell Courier,* who was to report adversely on operatives' demands for a ten-hour day. Two women operatives, the Misses Farley and Curtis, became editors.

Sarah Bagley's articles, all signed "S.G.B.," consist of "Pleasures Of Factory Life," No. 2 (December 1840), and "Tales of Factory Life, No. 1," "Moving Into The New House," and "Tales Of Factory Life. No. 2. The Orphan Sisters," all in Vol. I of the new series.

From the start, the magazine was pledged to the exclusion of "politics and sectarian religion." None the less, when Orestes A. Brownson challenged "the system of labor at wages" in his article on "The Laboring Classes" in the *Boston Quarterly Review,* the *Offering,* interpreting his remarks against the factory system as a slander against the factory girls, replied to his article [See "Factory Girls" in No. 2 (December 1840) pp. 17 ff]. It was this controversial article in an otherwise uncontroversial magazine that inspired Sarah Bagley to deliver her speech at Woburn, which is reported in *Voice of Industry* (July 10, 1845). There followed in the local press a full-scale journalistic warfare between Sarah Bagley and Harriet Farley. See, e.g., *Voice of Industry* (July 17, July 24, September 25, 1845); *Lowell Daily Courier* (July 9, 1845), Courtesy Concord Free Public Library.

Despite the renown enjoyed by the *Offering*—selections from it were published in England as *Mind Amongst the Spindles* (London 1844)—the *Voice of Industry* (January 2, 1846) castigated it after its demise as having exerted an influence "detrimental to the interests of those it professed to protect.

Led on by the fatal error of *neutrality,* it has neglected the operative
as a working being, . . . to convince the world that factory girls can write
sentimental tales."

For details of the magazine, see Addison, *Lucy Larcom, op. cit.,* pp. 10 f;
Josephson, *op. cit.,* pp. 199 ff, 202; George F. Kenngott, *The Record of
a City* (New York 1912) p. 15; Lucy Larcom, *A New England Girlhood*
(Boston, New York & Chicago [1889]) pp. 209 ff; "The Lowell Offering,"
Old South Leaflets Vol. VII No. 157; Allan Macdonald, "Lowell: A Commercial Utopia," *The New England Quarterly* X:1 (March 1937) pp. 48-
56; H.C. Meserve, *Lowell—An Industrial Dream Come True* (Boston 1923)
p. 65; Robinson, *Early Factory Labor in New England, op. cit.,* pp. 17-22;
Bertha Monica Stearns, "Early Factory Magazines in New England," *Journal of Economic and Business History* II:4 (August 1930) *passim;* Rev.
Abel C. Thomas, *Autobiography* (Boston 1852) pp. 266 f; Caroline F.
Ware, *The Early New England Cotton Manufacture* (Boston & New York
1931) p. 220.

Sarah Bagley & Labor Reform; The Ten-Hour Movement

Referring to Sarah Bagley as President of the Lowell Female Labor Reform Association, and to its Secretary, Huldah J. Stone, Charles E. Persons,
et al, *Labor Laws and Their Enforcement* (New York 1911) p. 36, state:
"As the earliest labor leaders of American women, they deserve a larger
measure of fame than has so far fallen to their lot."

According to *United States Congress Senate Documents 5694 61st Congress 2d Session 1909-1910. Senate Documents.* Vol. 95 (Washington, D.C.,
1911). *Document No. 645. Report on Condition of Woman and Child
Wage-Earners in the United States.* Vol. X. *History of Women in Trade
Unions* (pp. 13, 71, 73), Miss Bagley, a "woman of unusual charm and
ability," had "witnessed the growth of the factory system" and was the
"most prominent organizer of women wage-earners" at this time. When she
testified before the Massachusetts legislative committee in 1845, she testified before the "first American governmental investigation of labor conditions."

For details regarding Sarah Bagley's labor reform activities, see also
Benjamin F. Butler, *Butler's Book* (Boston 1892) pp. 91 f; John R. Com-
mons, et al, *History of Labour in the United States* (New York 1918)
I, 539; Ruth Delzell, *Articles on The Early History of Women Trade
Unionists of America* (Chicago [1914]) p. 5; "Female Labor Reform Asso-
ciation," *The Awl* [Lynn, Mass.] (April 12, 1845), Courtesy Mrs. Charles
F. Haywood, The Lynn Public Library; Eleanor Flexner, *Century of Strug-
gle* (Cambridge, Mass., 1959) pp. 56 ff, 59 f; Alice Henry, *Women and The
Labor Movement* (New York [1923]) pp. 45 f; Josephson, *op. cit., passim;
Lowell A City of Spindles* (Lowell 1900) p. 252; *Massachusetts General Court Legislative Documents 1845, op. cit.,* pp. 3 f; Persons, *op. cit.,*
pp. 36 f, 45, 47; Stearns, *op. cit.,* pp. 698 ff, 701; J.Q.A. Thayer, *Review of the Report of the Special Committee of the Legislature of the
Commonwealth of Massachusetts, on the Petition relating to hours of La-*

bor (Boston 1845) *passim*; *Voice of Industry* (May 29, 1845—April 14, 1848) *passim*; *Vox Populi* (January 17, 1845—November 20, 1846) *passim*; Norman Ware, *The Industrial Worker 1840-1860* (Boston & New York 1924) pp. 125, 127, 139, 202; "Workingmen's Convention," *The Awl* [Lynn, Mass.] (July 19, 1845).

A petition "To the Senate and House of Representatives of the State of Massachusetts" signed by Sarah G. Bagley and others (Senate Document 11983, Archives Division, State House, Boston) states that "the present hours of labor are too long, and tend to aggrandize the capitalist and depress the laborer." The report on the petition was submitted to the Senate on March 26, 1846, and was unfavorable (Information from Mr. Edward J. Cronin, Secretary of the Commonwealth). See also *Documents printed by order of The Senate of the Commonwealth of Massachusetts, during the session of the General Court, A.D. 1846* (Boston 1846) No. 81.

The *Voice of Industry,* a weekly first published in Fitchburg, Mass., May 29, 1845, "By an Association of Workingmen," William F. Young editor, was moved to Lowell in October 1845, and the first number issued from that city was that of November 7, 1845, as an organ of the New England Workingmen's Association. The publishing committee consisted of William F. Young, Sarah G. Bagley, and Joel Hatch. Announcement of its purchase by the Female Labor Reform Association was made on March 6, 1846. On April 24, 1846, notice was given of William F. Young's withdrawal, because of ill health, and of the assumption of his duties by the publishing committee. In the May 15, 1846 issue, the new editor—though unnamed—is obviously Sarah G. Bagley. Her name continues as one of the publishing committee through the issue of September 18, 1846. On November 20, 1846, Young returned as editor, and on February 12, 1847 it was announced that publication would be an "individual affair." D.H. Jaques became editor on September 3, 1847, and the following week it was announced that publication would take place simultaneously in Boston and Lowell. Jaques and John Orvis were publishers November 5, 1847, and John Orvis & Co. April 14, 1848, when the last issue appeared. The weekly was succeeded for a short time by *The New Era of Industry,* published in Boston by John Orvis.

Quotations from Sarah Bagley's contributions appear in the issues of May 15 & September 11, 1846. Philip S. Foner, in his *History Of The Labor Movement In The United States* (New York [1947]) p. 198 calls her "one of the first woman labor editors in America."

Sarah Bagley's Appointment as Superintendent of Lowell Telegraph Depot
   Voice of Industry (February 13, 1846).

Statistics on Women Telegraphers
   Virginia Penny, *The Employments of Women* (Boston 1863) p. 102; "Women in Telegraphy," *Telegraph News* No. 10 (September 1953) p. 6.

F.O.J. Smith & The New York and Boston Magnetic Telegraph Association

Paul A. Hardaway, "Samuel Finley Breese Morse and the Electric Telegraph in Boston," *Proceedings of The Bostonian Society* (Boston 1947) pp. 33 f, 43 f; Harlow, *op. cit.*, p. 113; Alexander Jones, *Historical Sketch of the Electric Telegraph* (New York 1852) pp. 77 f; John Neal, *Wandering Recollections of A Somewhat Busy Life* (Boston 1869) p. 341, Reid, *op. cit.*, pp. 351 ff, 357; Joseph S. Rich, *Some Notes on the Telegraph Companies of the United States* (New York 1900) pp. 6 f; Francis O.J. Smith, *The Secret Corresponding Vocabulary; adapted for use to Morse's Electro-Magnetic Telegraph* (Portland, Me., 1845) *passim*.

Paul R. George

For the fascinating career of "Apostle Paul," see John Hatch George, *Sketch of Capt. Paul Rolfe George of Hopkinton, N.H.* (Concord, N.H., 1885) *passim*; *Vox Populi* (May 8, 1846).

Beginnings of Telegraph in Lowell

Hardaway, *op. cit.*, p. 44; Harlow, *op. cit.*, p. 114; *Lowell Daily Courier* (February 16, 1846), Courtesy Fred B. Bloomhardt, Librarian, Concord Free Public Library, Concord, Mass.; Reid, *op. cit.*, p. 357; *Voice of Industry* (October 2, 1845).

Telegraphic Technique & Qualifications for Telegraphers

[Daniel Davis], *Book of the Telegraph* (Boston 1851) pp. 14, 17, 20; Hardaway, *op. cit.*, pp. 36 f; Virginia Penny, *How Women can Make Money* (Springfield, Mass., [1870]) pp. 100 ff; Alfred Vail, *Description of the American Electro Magnetic Telegraph* (Washington 1845) pp. 18 f.

For Sarah Bagley's "Pleasures Of Factory Life," see *The Lowell Offering* No. 2 (December 1840) p. 25 (Courtesy Dr. Clarence S. Brigham, American Antiquarian Society).

Press Comments on The Telegraph; Difficulties with The Line

Harlow, *op. cit.*, pp. 144 f; *Lowell Daily Courier* (February 17, February 19, 1846), Courtesy Concord Free Public Library; Reid, *op. cit.*, p. 358; *Voice of Industry* (February 27, September 4, 1846); *Vox Populi* (February 27, September 18, 1846).

Sarah Bagley's Duties at Telegraph Depot, Information Received, Salary

Jones, *op. cit.*, pp. 98 f, 191; Penny, *How Women can Make Money, op. cit.*, pp. 100 ff; *Voice of Industry* (March 20, June 19, September 4, 1846, July 9, October 22, 1847, June 8, 1848); *Vox Populi* (September 4, 1846).

According to Joseph Edgar Chamberlin, *The Boston Transcript* (Boston & New York 1930) p. 81, "A noteworthy date in Boston journalism was the appearance on November 12, 1846, of the first dispatch 'By Magnetic

Telegraph.' This dispatch gave the result of an election in Delaware, a few stock prices in New York, and one or two other matters." Yet, Lowell's *Vox Populi* of September 4, 1846 printed "through the kindness of Miss Baglay, [sic]" an item "By Telegraph!" regarding the steamship *Hibernia*—more than two months before the "noteworthy date in Boston journalism."

Gardner Quincy Colton

For the career of this remarkable pioneer, whose activities were also important in the development of the electric railway, see Henry Lovejoy Ambler, *Facts Fads and Fancies about Teeth* (Cleveland 1900) p. 231; Information from Miss Gertrude L. Annan, Librarian, The New York Academy of Medicine; *Appletons' Cyclopædia of American Biography* I, 696; G.Q. Colton, *Boyhood and Manhood Recollections* (New York [1897]) pp. 8 f; G.Q. Colton, *A Few Selected Letters . . . for The Thomasville Ga., Times* (New York 1888) pp. 5 f; G.Q. Colton, *Personal and Family Reminiscences* (New York 1894) *passim*; "Gardner Quincy Colton," *DAB*; George W. Colton, *A Genealogical Record of the Descendants of Quartermaster George Colton* (Philadelphia 1912) pp. 229 f; Van Broadus Dalton, *The Genesis of Dental Education In The United States* (Cincinnati 1946) p. 44; Information from the late Dr. John F. Fulton; Information from Mrs. Elisabeth H. Gazin, Smithsonian Institution Library; T.C. Martin, "The Electric Railway Work of Dr. Colton in 1847," *The Electrical Engineer* XVI:272 (July 19, 1893) pp. 49 f; *The National Cyclopædia of American Biography* II, 198; George B. Prescott, *Dynamo-Electricity* (New York 1884) p. 717.

Telegraphic Exhibition at Lowell

Harlow, *op. cit.*, p. 145; *Lowell Daily Courier* (August 25, 26, 27, September 12, 1846), Courtesy Concord Free Public Library; *Vox Populi* (August 21, 28, 1846).

Last Recorded Activities of Sarah Bagley

The Harbinger III:12 (August 29, 1846) p. 191; Josephson, *op. cit.*, pp. 264, 273 f; *Voice of Industry* (September 18, October 2, 16, 1846, February 12, 19, 1847).

A search conducted by the Registrar of the Division of Vital Statistics, New Hampshire State Department of Health, Concord, N.H. failed to disclose a record of Sarah Bagley's birth or death. The Superintendent of the Franklin Cemetery Association found no record of Sarah Bagley in the Franklin Cemetery books.

For the other Sarah Bagleys, not to be confused with Sarah G. Bagley, see [Bela Bates Edwards], *Biography of Self-Taught Men* (Boston 1846-1847). The preface of Vol. II of this work is signed S.G.B. According to the *British Museum Catalogue,* William Cushing, *Initials and Pseudonyms* (New York 1885) I, 27, and Halkett & Laing, *Dictionary of Anonymous and Pseudonymous English Literature* I, 204, the initials are those of Sarah G. Bagley. According to the *Library of Congress Catalogue,* the initials are those of Stephen Greenleaf Bulfinch. This attribution is correct. For Sarah O. Bagley of Amesbury, see Mary Beecher Longyear, *The History of a House* (Brookline, Mass., 1925) *passim* and Sibyl Wilbur, *The Life of Mary Baker Eddy* (Boston [1929]) pp. 171 ff. For the Sarah Bagleys in Lowell, see Information from Robert W. Lovett, Baker Library, Harvard University Graduate School of Business Administration (who finds two Sarah Bagleys in the Hamilton Mills Register for 1845) and *Vital Records of Lowell Massachusetts to the End of the Year 1849* (Salem, Mass., 1930) II, 32 (where the marriage of Sarah B. Bagley to Seth Gage is recorded).

United States Congress Senate Documents 5694, op. cit., p. 77, states, "In the fall of 1846, one of the officers of the Lowell union broke down under the strain of work in the mills, and made a tour of the factory towns to arouse interest in labor reform." This may be a reference to Sarah Bagley.

CHAPTER 5

LUCY HOBBS TAYLOR

The Ohio College of Dental Surgery—Commencement of 1866
Van Broadus Dalton, *The Genesis of Dental Education In The United States* (Cincinnati 1946) pp. 173, 175; *The Dental Register* XX:3 (March 1866) p. 145, XX:4 (April 1866) p. 153; Lucy Hobbs' Diploma (Kansas State Historical Society). Shortly before her death, Lucy gave her diploma to Dr. Edward Bumgardner of Lawrence, who subsequently deposited it in the Archives of the Kansas State Historical Society.

According to Dr. Wilbur G. Adair of Vero Beach, Florida, there is some doubt regarding the exact number of graduates.

Early Women in Dentistry & Early Dental Practice
The author wishes to express her hearty gratitude to Miss Gertrude L. Annan, Librarian of The New York Academy of Medicine, for her generous help in the preparation of this chapter. Specific acknowledgments appear in the notes. In addition, the author wishes to thank the following for their co-operation and assistance: Dr. Wilbur G. Adair of Vero Beach, Florida; Rose-Grace Faucher, Librarian, University of Michigan School of Dentistry; Mr. Irvin W. Kron, Librarian, College of Medicine Library, University of Cincinnati; Clara Louise Meckel, University of Illinois Library of Medical Sciences; Judge Charles Rankin of Lawrence, Kansas.

For details, see M.D.K. Bremner, *The Story of Dentistry* (Brooklyn, N.Y., 1939) p. 195; *The Dental Cosmos* XXXV:9 (September 1893) p. 1077; Otto Juettner, *Daniel Drake And His Followers* (Cincinnati [1909]) p. 92; Elizabeth Neber King, "Women in Dentistry," *The Washington University Dental Journal* XII:1 & 2 (August-November 1945) p. 37; *Ohio State Journal of Dental Science* VI:12 (December 1, 1886) p. 588; Virginia

Penny, *How Women Can Make Money* (Springfield, Mass., [1870]) p. 14; *The Sibyl* II:17 (March 1, 1858) p. 328 (Courtesy Miss Ada M. Stoflet, Reference Librarian, State University of Iowa Libraries); Emeline A. Street, "Emeline Roberts Jones: Pioneer Woman Dentist," *The Dental Cosmos* LXV:9 (September 1923) pp. 991 f; *Transactions of the Iowa State Dental Society . . . 1893* (Chicago 1893) p. 122; George Watt, "Historical Sketch of the Ohio College of Dental Surgery," *The Dental Register* XXXIII:5 (May 1879) pp. 185 f; Amelia Rose Weidenbach, History of the University of Iowa. The College of Dentistry (MA Thesis, State University of Iowa, 1944) p. 3; Chase Going Woodhouse & Ruth Yeomans Schiffman, *Dentistry Its Professional Opportunities* (Greensboro, N.C., 1934) p. 80.

Early Life of Lucy Beaman Hobbs, 1833-1859

There is some confusion regarding the birthplace of Lucy Hobbs. Most sources, including the cemetery records supplied by the City Clerk of Lawrence, Kansas, give Ellenburg, [Clinton County] New York as her birthplace. She herself, however, stated that she was born in Franklin County, New York [See Elizabeth Cady Stanton, Susan B. Anthony, and Matilda Joslyn Gage, eds., *History of Woman Suffrage* (Rochester, N.Y., 1887) III, 401]. Lucy's Beaman grandparents in 1819 removed to Chateaugay, Franklin County, New York, and it is quite possible that Lucy herself was born in that vicinity and that the family moved to Ellenburg in Clinton County, the county next to Franklin County, when she was a young child. She may have been born in Constable, Franklin County, where her brother Thomas was born in 1831.

While the best overall source for Lucy Hobbs Taylor's professional career is Ralph W. Edwards, "The First Woman Dentist Lucy Hobbs Taylor, D.D.S. (1833-1910)," *Bulletin of the History of Medicine* XXV:3 (May-June 1951) pp. 277-283, the best source for her early life is Wilbur G. Adair, "Sketch of Lucy Hobbs Taylor, D.D.S.," *Journal of the Ohio State Dental Association* XXIII:2 (May 1949) pp. 89 ff. Of inestimable value, despite minor inaccuracies, is Lucy Hobbs Taylor, "The Early Women in Dentistry," 4-page typescript [1893] (Courtesy Alberta Pantle, Librarian, Kansas State Historical Society).

See also [Alfred T. Andreas], *History of the State of Kansas* (Chicago 1883) p. 345; Edward Bumgardner, "Doctor Lucy Hobbs Taylor America's First Woman Dentist," (Lawrence, Kansas, 1943) typescript (Courtesy Laura Neiswanger, Kansas Collection, University of Kansas Libraries); Edward Bumgardner, "The First Woman Dentist," 1-page typescript & 5-page typescript (Courtesy Alberta Pantle, Kansas State Historical Society); *The Dental Cosmos* LII:11 (November 1910) p. 1315; *Dental Radiography and Photography* XXVI:2 (1953) p. 20; Information from Rollin G. Everhart, La Cañada, California; Marian Palmer Greene, "Reflections in the River Raisin," *Michigan History* XXXIII:1 (March 1949) p. 59; *History of Jackson County, Michigan* (Chicago 1881) pp. 778, 780, 789 ff; Information from Lucy E. Hobbs, Fort Dodge, Iowa; Information from Mrs. Kate Hobbs Honsinger, Plattsburgh, N.Y.; Franklin B. Hough, *A History of St. Lawrence And Franklin Counties, New York* (Albany 1853) p. 507; Duane Hamilton Hurd, *History of Clinton and Franklin Counties, New York* (Philadelphia 1880) pp. 312 f, 317, 410; Harry F. Landon, *The North Country* (Indianapolis 1932) I, 369; *Plattsburgh Press-Republican* (May 13, 1943) p. 5; *Portrait and Biographical Record of Leavenworth Douglas and Franklin Counties . . . Kansas* (Chicago 1899) pp. 717 f; Frederick J. Seaver, *Historical Sketches of Franklin County* (Albany 1918) p. 422; Adelaide Schmidt Wayland, "Lucy Hobbs Taylor," *Daughters of America* VII:5 (May 1893) p. 8; Emily Beaman Wooden, *The Beaman and Clark Genealogy* (N.p. 1909) pp. 51 ff.

Dental Apprenticeship in Cincinnati: Drs. Cleaveland, Taft & Wardle; Mechanics' Fair of 1860; Hobbs' Cincinnati Office 1861
Adair, *op. cit.*, pp. 89 f; Bremner, *op. cit.*, p. 196; Bumgardner, "Doctor Lucy Hobbs Taylor," *op. cit.*, *passim*; Bumgardner, "The First Woman Dentist," *op. cit.*, *passim*; *The Cincinnati Dental Lamp* I:1 (November 1858) p. 16, I:2 (March 1859) p. 54; *Cincinnati Directories 1859-1861*; C.H. Cleaveland, *Galvanism; Its Application as a Remedial Agent* (New York 1853) pp. iv f; Dalton, *op. cit.*, pp. 87 ff, 174; Edwards, *op. cit.*, *passim*; Harvey Wickes Felter, *History of the Eclectic Medical Institute Cincinnati, Ohio 1845-1902* (Cincinnati 1902) pp. 37, 53, 116 f; Chapin A. Harris, *The Principles and Practice of Dental Surgery* (Philadelphia 1866) pp. 384 f; *History of Cincinnati And Hamilton County, Ohio* (Cincinnati 1894) pp. 227, 241, 724 f; Information from Ethel L. Hutchins, Head, History and Literature Department, Public Library of Cincinnati; Juettner, *op. cit.*, pp. 92, 363; Charles R.E. Koch, ed., *History of Dental Surgery* (Chicago 1909) I, 417; *Ohio State Journal of Dental Science* VI:6 (June 1, 1886) pp. 289 f; *Plattsburgh Press-Republican* (May 13, 1943) p. 5; *Portrait and Biographical Record of Leavenworth Douglas and Franklin Counties, op. cit.*, pp. 717 f; *Report of the Eighteenth Exhibition of the Ohio Mechanics' Institute, Held In Cincinnati, From September 13, To October 10, 1860* (Cincinnati 1860) pp. 5, 22, 78 & *passim*; George Mortimer Roe, ed., *Cincinnati: The Queen City Of The West* (Cincinnati 1895) pp. 378 f; Stanton, Anthony & Gage, *op. cit.*, III, 401 f; Taylor, "The Early Women in Dentistry," *op. cit.*, *passim*; George Watt, *An Essay on Dental Surgery for Popular Reading* (Cincinnati 1858) p. 66; Wayland, *op. cit.*, p. 8; Weidenbach, *op. cit.*, pp. 6 ff; Wooden, *op. cit.*, p. 53.
There may be some doubt regarding the date of Lucy's first application to the Ohio College of Dental Surgery and regarding the number of times she sought admission there. According to *The Ohio Journal of Dental Science* VII: 2 (February 1, 1887) p. 89, the time of the application of Lucy Hobbs and the Liberian was "perhaps, in the autumn of 1857." The anonymous writer was George Watt, then serving as Dean. In his article in the *Ohio State Journal of Dental Science* VI:6 (June 1, 1886) pp. 289 f, Watt also states he was Dean when the applications were made. If Lucy applied in 1857, she may have done so by correspondence from Michigan, and then she would have applied three times to the Ohio College of Dental Surgery—in 1857, 1861, and, successfully, in 1865.

Lucy Hobbs' Iowa Practice; The Iowa State Dental Society; American Dental Association in Chicago 1865

Adair, *op. cit.*, p. 90; [Andreas], *op. cit.*, p. 345; Bremner, *op. cit.*, p. 196; Bumgardner, "Doctor Lucy Hobbs Taylor," *op. cit., passim*; Bumgardner, "The First Woman Dentist," *op. cit., passim*; J.V. Conzett, "A Brief History of the Iowa State Dental Society," *Official Program Iowa State Dental Society Diamond Anniversary 1863-1937* (Des Moines [1937]) pp. 16-20, 22; J.V. Conzett, "Dr. L.C. Ingersoll—an Appreciation," *Iowa Dental Bulletin* XIX:1 (February 1933) p. 9; *The Dental Register* XIX:8 (August 1865) pp. 346 f, XIX:9 (September 1865) pp. 358 f, 365, 373, 380 f, 384, XIX:10 (October 1865) pp. 429 ff, 432; Edwards, *op. cit.*, pp. 279 ff; *A Guide To McGregor . . . . Work Projects Administration* (McGregor, Iowa, 1940) pp. 13 f; Flora N. Haag, "Women In Dentistry," *The Dental Cosmos* LIII:10 (October 1911) p. 1143; Information from Dr. Homer N. Hake, Secretary, Iowa Dental Association [from the Minutes of the Iowa Dental Association]; *History of Clayton County, Iowa* (Chicago 1882) I, 180, 187; *A History of Jackson County, Iowa* (Chicago 1879) p. 542; Information from Mrs. Kate Hobbs Honsinger; *The Iowa Dental Bulletin* XXXIX:1 (January-February 1953) p. 27; *Jackson County History Iowa . . . . Work Projects Administration* (N.p. 1942) p. 68; Koch, *op. cit.*, II, 905; Dr. J.B. Monfort, "The History of the Iowa State Dental Society," *Iowa Dental Bulletin* VIII:3 (June 1922) pp. 7 f, 12, 14; *Ohio State Journal of Dental Science* VI:6 (June 1, 1886) pp. 289 f; *Plattsburgh Press-Republican* (May 13, 1943) p. 5; *Portrait and Biographical Record of Leavenworth Douglas and Franklin Counties, op. cit.*, pp. 717 f; Iola B. Quigley, "A Metropolis of the Fifties," *The Palimpsest* XII:1 (January 1931) pp. 21 f, 27; Stanton, Anthony & Gage, *op. cit.*, III, 402; Information from Miss Ada M. Stoflet, Reference Librarian, State University of Iowa Libraries; Taylor, "The Early Women in Dentistry," *op. cit., passim*; Weidenbach, *op. cit.*, pp. 12 f, 103 f, 135; "Women In Dentistry—1855-1880," *The Journal of the American Dental Association* XV:9 (September 1928) p. 1739; Woodhouse & Schiffman, *op. cit.*, p. 80.

Studies at the Ohio College of Dental Surgery

Adair, *op. cit.*, p. 90; Bremner, *op. cit.*, pp. 195 f; Bumgardner, "The First Woman Dentist," *op. cit., passim*; Dalton, *op. cit.*, pp. 173, 175, 204; *The Dental Register* XX:1 (January 1866) *passim*, XX:3 (March 1866) p. 145, XX:4 (April 1866) p. 153, XX:9 (September 1866) pp. 403 f; Edwards, *op. cit.*, p. 281; *Fourteenth Annual Announcement of the Ohio College of Dental Surgery, Cincinnati* (Cincinnati 1858) *passim*; William J. Gies, *Dental Education In The United States And Canada* (New York 1926) pp. 42, 486, 490; Harris, *op. cit.*, pp. 276 f, 285, 378 f, 381 f, 386, 596 & *passim*; *History of Cincinnati And Hamilton County, Ohio, op. cit.*, p. 241; *A History of Dental And Oral Science In America* (Philadelphia 1876) pp. 182 f; Juettner, *op. cit.*, p. 92; Koch, *op. cit.*, I, 417; Edward C. Mills, "Dental Education in Ohio," *The Ohio State Archæological and Historical Quarterly* LII:4 (October-December 1943) pp. 356 f, 366 f, 369 f; *Ohio State Journal of Dental Science* VI:6 (June 1, 1886) p. 290; *Portrait* and *Biographical Record of Leavenworth Douglas and Franklin Counties,* *op. cit.,* p. 718; Stanton, Anthony & Gage, *op. cit.,* III, 401 f, 455; Taylor, "The Early Women in Dentistry," *op. cit., passim;* George Watt, *Register Papers* (Philadelphia 1868) pp. 253 f & *passim;* Weidenbach, *op. cit.,* p. 12; "Women in the Dental Profession," *The Woman's Journal* I:33 (August 20, 1870) p. 264; "Women In Dentistry," *The Dental Register* XXXI:3 (March 1877) p. 101.

Reaction of Critics to Women Dentists

Henry Lovejoy Ambler, *Facts Fads and Fancies about Teeth* (Cleveland 1900) p. 71; George T. Barker, "Dental Surgery—Should Females Practice It," *The Dental Times* III:4 (April 1866) pp. 152, 154 f; Bremner, *op. cit.,* pp. 195 f; *The Dental Times* III:4 (April 1866) p. 162; "Ho! Every One To The Breeches!!," *The Dental Register* XX:8 (August 1866) pp. 374 f; *Items of Interest* XI:11 (November 1889) pp. 530 f; "Women In Dentistry—1855-1880," *The Journal of the American Dental Association* XV:9 (September 1928) p. 1747.

Lucy Hobbs in Chicago; Her Address on the Mallet; Her Marriage; Sale of Her Office

Adair, *op. cit.,* p. 90; [Andreas], *op. cit.,* p. 345; Edward Bumgardner, "America's First Woman Dentist," *Oral Hygiene* XXXIII:5 (May 1943) p. 641; Bumgardner, "The First Woman Dentist," *op. cit., passim; Chicago Directory* 1866-1867; Conzett, "A Brief History of the Iowa State Dental Society," *op. cit.,* p. 19; *The Dental Cosmos* LII:11 (November 1910) p. 1315; *Dental Radiography and Photography* XXVI:2 (1953) p. 40; *The Dental Register* XX:6 (June 1866) p. 281, XX:7 (July 1866) p. 327; Edwards, *op. cit.,* p. 281; *Historical Booklet of the Illinois State Dental Society . . . 1865-1914* (N.p. n.d.) p. 57; Lucy B. Hobbs, "The Use Of The Mallet," *The Dental Register* XX:11 (November 1866) pp. 483-486; Information from Mrs. Kate Hobbs Honsinger; *Items of Interest* XII:2 (February 1890) p. 78; [Lawrence] *Daily Journal* (December 15, 1886) p. 3; Edmund Noyes, "Pioneer Women Dentists," *The Dental Summary* XLV:11 (November 1925) pp. 943 f; *Portrait and Biographical Record of Leavenworth Douglas and Franklin Counties, op. cit.,* p. 718; Information from Mrs. Roberta B. Sutton, Chief of Reference Department, Chicago Public Library.

The Taylors in Lawrence: Dental Practice; Later Personal Life; Death

Adair, *op. cit.,* p. 91; [Andreas], *op. cit.,* p. 345; Information from Mr. Frank E. Banks, Lawrence, Kansas; Bumgardner, "Doctor Lucy Hobbs Taylor," *op. cit., passim;* Bumgardner, "The First Woman Dentist," *op cit., passim;* Information from Mrs. A.M. Burbank, Concordia, Kansas; Samuel J. Crawford, *Kansas In The Sixties* (Chicago 1911) pp. 281 f, 284; *Daily Kansas Tribune* (November 26, 1871) p. 1 (Courtesy Alberta Pantle, Kansas State Historical Society); *The Dental Cosmos* LII:11 (November 1910) p. 1315; *Dental Radiography and Photography* XXVI:2 (1953) p. 40; Edwards, *op. cit.*, pp. 281 ff; *A History of Dental And Oral Science In America*, *op. cit.*, pp. v ff; Information from Lucy E. Hobbs, Fort Dodge, Iowa; Information from Dr. Albert R. Kennedy, Lawrence, Kansas; *Lawrence Directories* 1868-1911 (Courtesy Laura Neiswanger, Kansas Collection, University of Kansas Library, & Alberta Pantle, Kansas State Historical Society); [Lawrence] *Daily Journal* (December 15, 1886) p. 3, (October 3, 1910) p. 6; *The Lawrence Memorial Album* (N.p. [1895]) *passim*; *The Leading Industries of Lawrence, Kansas* (Lawrence 1883) *passim*; Information from Mrs. Betty Mole, Secretary, Adah Chapter No. 7, Lawrence, Kansas; *Portrait and Biographical Record of Leavenworth Douglas and Franklin Counties*, *op. cit.*, p. 718; *Proceedings of the Thirty-Fifth Annual Session of the Grand Chapter Order of the Eastern Star of . . . Kansas . . . May 10 and 11, 1911* (Leavenworth 1911) p. 121 (Courtesy Kansas State Historical Society); Information from Mrs. Beulah Rogers, Secretary, Rebekah Assembly, Lawrence, Kansas; Information from Ed Smith, Sexton, Oak Hill Cemetery, Lawrence, Kansas; *A Souvenir History of Lawrence, Kansas, 1898* (Lawrence [1898]) *passim*; Lucy Hobbs Taylor to Elizabeth Cady Stanton [Lawrence ca. Spring 1880?] (Chicago Historical Society); Lucy Hobbs Taylor, Last Will and Testament (Probate Court, Douglas County, Kansas); Topeka *Capital* (August 9, 1908) p. 6; Wayland, *op. cit.*, p. 8; *The Woman's Journal* XLI:49 (December 3, 1910) p. 228; "Women In Dentistry," *The Dental Register* XXXI:3 (March 1877) p. 101.

Later Women in Dentistry; Dental Progress; Interest in the History of Dentistry

Ambler, *op. cit.*, p. 68; American Dental Association, Chicago, Package Library on Women Dentists, *passim*; Bremner, *op. cit.*, pp. 196 f; Bumgardner, "The First Woman Dentist," *op. cit.*, *passim*; Henry S. Chase, *Causes of the Degeneracy of the Teeth* (N.p. n.d.) p. 127; Conzett, "A Brief History of the Iowa State Dental Society," *op. cit.*, p. 19; *Cook Book of The Northwest* (Keokuk, Iowa, 1875) dental advertisement at end; *The Dental Brief* XIII:10 (October 1908) p. 650; *The Dental Cosmos* XXXV:9 (September 1893) pp. 1076 f, LII:11 (November 1910) p. 1315; Luman C. Ingersoll, *Dental Science* (Keokuk, Iowa, 1886) *passim*; *Items of Interest* XI:10 (October 1889) p. 470, XI:11 (November 1889) pp. 531 f, XI:12 (December 1889) p. 541, XII:2 (February 1890) p. 78; Monfort, "The History of the Iowa State Dental Society," *op. cit.*, p. 14; Noyes, "Pioneer Women Dentists," *op. cit.*, pp. 943 f; *Pacific Medico-Dental Gazette* VI:1 (January 1898) pp. 57 f; Stanton, Anthony & Gage, *op. cit.*, III, 401 f, 455; *Statistical Report of the Women of The State Of New York* (Chicago 1893) pp. 39 f; Nell Snow Talbot, "Why not more women dentists?," *The Journal of the American Dental Association* LX:1 (January 1960) *passim*; *Transactions of the American Dental Association, at its Ninth Annual Meeting, . . . Saratoga, August 3 to 6, . . . 1869* (Chicago 1870) p. 23; *Transactions of the World's Columbian Dental Congress Chicago, . . . 1893* (Chicago 1894) I, 216, II, 1036; James Truman, "The

Entrance Of Women Into Dentistry," *Second Annual Report of the Woman's Dental Association* . . . Chicago . . . *1893* (N.p. n.d.) p. 45; James Truman, "Henriette Hirschfeld . . . And The Woman Dentists Of 1866-73," *The Dental Cosmos* LIII:12 (December 1911) pp. 1383, 1385; *United States Department of Labor. Women's Bureau. Bulletin 203, Number 9. Women Dentists* [1945] *passim*; Watt, "Historical Sketch of the Ohio College of Dental Surgery," *op. cit.*, p. 186; Weidenbach, *op. cit.*, pp. 6 f; "Woman and Dentistry," *The Revolution* IV:6 (August 12, 1869) p. 92; "Women in the Dental Profession," *The Woman's Journal* I:33 (August 20, 1870) p. 264; "Women In Dentistry," *The Dental Register* XXXI:3 (March 1877) p. 101; "Women In Dentistry—1855-1880," *The Journal of the American Dental Association* XV:9 (September 1928) pp. 1735, 1755; Woodhouse & Schiffman, *op. cit.*, pp. 7, 10, 80, 82, 84 f.

Lucy Hobbs Taylor's letter to Matilda Joslyn Gage, written for the *History of Woman Suffrage, op. cit.*, III, 401 f, also appeared in *The Odontographic Journal* VII:1 (April 1886) p. 39 and *Ohio State Journal of Dental Science* V:6 (June 1, 1886) p. 267.

Her article, "The Early Women in Dentistry," contributed at the request of Mary Gage Day, M.D., Chairman of the Kansas Branch of the Medical Department of the Queen Isabella Association, was published in *The Dental Register* XLVIII:1 (January 1894) pp. 31-35, *The Odontographic Journal* XV:1 (April 1894) pp. 31-34, and *The Southern Dental Journal and Luminary* XIII:6 (June 1, 1894) pp. 242-244.

CHAPTER 6

ELLEN H. RICHARDS

Vassar College & Professor Farrar
Anna C. Brackett, "Vassar College," *Harper's New Monthly Magazine* LII:309 (February 1876) pp. 356 ff; *Godey's Lady's Book* (January 1864) LXVIII, 94; Caroline L. Hunt, *The Life of Ellen H. Richards* (Boston 1912) [Hereinafter Hunt] pp. 35, 38 f, 52; [John H. Raymond], *Vassar College. A College for Women* (New York 1873) pp. 53 f; Ellen H. Richards & Alpheus G. Woodman, *Air, Water, And Food* (New York & London 1906) p. 139; James Monroe Taylor & Elizabeth Hazelton Haight, *Vassar* (New York 1915) p. 55; Frances A. Wood, *Earliest Years at Vassar* (Poughkeepsie, N.Y., 1909) pp. 18 f & *passim*.

Ellen Swallow's Early Life & Background; Studies at Vassar
Anna Barrows, "Recollections of Ellen H. Richards," *Journal of Home Economics* XXIII:12 (December 1931) p. 1125; Brackett, *op. cit.*, pp. 356 ff; Helen Dodd, *The Healthful Farmhouse* (Boston 1911) p. vi; "The Early Days of Vassar. Series I," *The Vassar Miscellany* XXVIII:4 (January 1899) pp. 145-149, Series II, *Ibid.*, XXVIII:5 (February 1899) pp. 196-204 (Courtesy Miss Dorothy A. Plum, Vassar College); Extracts from

letters written by Ellen Henrietta Swallow to her mother, from Vassar College, from September, 1868 to June, 1870 (Courtesy Miss Dorothy A. Plum); Hunt, *op. cit., passim*; *Life at Vassar Seventy-Five Years in Pictures* (Poughkeepsie [1940]) p. 17; *Prospectus of the Vassar Female College, Poughkeepsie, N.Y. May, 1865* (New York 1865) *passim*; Ellen H. Richards Papers, Education of Women Folder, Sophia Smith Collection, Smith College Library (Courtesy Mrs. Margaret S. Grierson & Miss Elizabeth S. Duvall); Ellen H. Richards, *The Cost of Living as modified by Sanitary Science* (New York 1915) p. 94; Ellen H. Richards, "Housekeeping from the College Woman's Standpoint," *The Vassar Miscellany* XXV:3 (December 1895) p. 123; "Ellen Henrietta Swallow Richards," *DAB*; Robert Hallowell Richards, *Robert Hallowell Richards His Mark* (Boston 1936) p. 154; *The Vassar Miscellany* XL:8 (May 1911) pp. 575 f; *Who's Who in America 1910-1911* p. 1599; Frances E. Willard & Mary A. Livermore, *American Women* (New York, Chicago & Springfield, Ohio, [1897]) II, 606; Wood, *op. cit., passim*; Helen Wright, *Sweeper in the Sky The Life of Maria Mitchell* (New York 1949) p. 164; Edna Yost, *American Women of Science* (Philadelphia & New York [1955]) pp. 1-9.

At Massachusetts Institute of Technology: Student, Resident Graduate, Instructor; Marriage

Information from H.N. Appleton, Assistant Secretary, American Institute of Mining, Metallurgical, and Petroleum Engineers, Inc.; Lita Bane, *The Story of Isabel Bevier* (Peoria, Ill., [1955]) p. 58; Anna Barrows, *op. cit.*, pp. 1125 f; Alice G. Bryant, *Mrs. Ellen Richards and her place in the world of science* (1936) pp. 5 ff; Alice G. Bryant, *Values for Which Mrs. Ellen H. Richards Stood* (Reprinted from *The Medical and Professional Woman's Journal*, August 1933) p. 7; Margaret S. Cheney & Ellen Swallow Richards, "A new and ready method for the Estimation of Nickel in Pyrrhotites and Mattes," *The American Journal of Science and Arts* XIV:81 (September 1877), Third Series, pp. 178-181; Hunt, *op. cit., passim*; "The Institute of Technology—A Correction," *The Woman's Journal* XII:41 (October 8, 1881) p. 324; *Journal of Home Economics* XXI:6 (June 1929) pp. 405, 408 f; *Life and Letters of William Barton Rogers* (Boston & New York 1896) II, 339; Grace MacLeod, "Reminiscences of Ellen H. Richards," *Journal of Home Economics* XXXIV:10 (December 1942) pp. 705 ff; *Massachusetts Institute of Technology, Boston, Mass. Department of Chemistry* (Boston 1893) *passim*; Massachusetts Institute of Technology, Minutes of Faculty Meetings, December 3 & 10, 1870 (Courtesy Registrar's Office, M.I.T., & Mrs. Astrid Steele, Assistant Reference Librarian); Massachusetts Institute of Technology, *Reports of the President, Secretary, and Departments. 1871-1872* (Boston 1872), *President's Reports 1874, 1883, 1884, 1886* (Boston 1875, 1884, 1886) *passim*; Annie Nathan Meyer, ed., *Woman's Work In America* (New York 1891) p. 52; James Phinney Munroe, *A Life of Francis Amasa Walker* (New York 1923) p. 221; William Ripley Nichols, *Publications of the Mass. Institute of Technology* (Boston 1882) p. 39; Samuel C. Prescott, *When M.I.T. was "Boston Tech"* 1861-

1916 (Cambridge, Mass., 1954) pp. 53 ff, 99, 123, 274 & *passim*; *Proceedings of The American Association for the Advancement of Science . . . December, 1902—January, 1903* (N.p. 1903) p. 153; *Public Health Papers and Reports . . . Presented at the Thirty-Seventh Annual Meeting of the American Public Health Association . . . 1909* (Columbus, Ohio, 1910) XXXV, 324; Ellen Richards to Miss Anna Mineah, [1876], May 11, 1876, June 1, 1876, [1877], December 21, 1877, March 11, 1878, [1879], March 1, 1881?, January 7, 1882, October 20, 1884, July 30, 1904 (Vassar College, Courtesy Miss Dorothy A. Plum); Ellen H. Richards Papers, Education of Women Folder, Sophia Smith Collection; Ellen H. Richards, *Conservation By Sanitation* (New York & London 1911) pp. 79 f, 225, 230, 249, 252, 257 & *passim*; Ellen H. Richards, *Domestic Economy as a Factor in Public Education* (New York & London 1889) p. [22]; Ellen H. Richards, *Euthenics The Science of Controllable Environment* (Boston 1912) p. 5; [Ellen H. Richards], *First Lessons in Minerals* (Boston 1882) p. 32; [Ellen H. Richards], *Laboratory Notes. Sanitary Chemistry and Water Analysis* [1896] *passim*; Ellen H. Richards, *Sanitation In Daily Life* (Boston 1907) pp. 37 f, 42; Ellen H. Richards, "University Laboratories in Relation to the Investigation of Public Health Problems and to Commercial Work," *Public Health Papers and Reports* XXV (1899) pp. 73-80; Ellen Swallow Richards & Alice W. Palmer, "Notes on Antimony Tannate," *The American Journal of Science and Arts* XVI:93 (September 1878), Third Series, pp. 196-198; Richards & Woodman, *Air, Water, And Food, op. cit.*, pp. 1, 8, 27, 94 f, 97 ff; "Ellen Henrietta Swallow Richards," *DAB*; "Mrs. Richards On Applied Science," *The Sunday Herald* [Boston] (April 2, 1911) p. 28; R.H. Richards, *op. cit.*, pp. 152 f & *passim*; Ellen H. Swallow, "Analysis of Samarskite from a New Locality," *Proceedings of the Boston Society of Natural History* (1874-1875) XVII, 424-428; Ellen H. Swallow, Notes on the estimation of vanadium in an iron ore from Cold Spring N.Y., Dissertation presented for Master's Degree, June, 1873, Vassar College (Courtesy Miss Dorothy A. Plum); Ellen H. Swallow, "On the Occurrence of Boracic Acid in Mineral Waters," *Proceedings of the Boston Society of Natural History* (1874-1875) XVII, 428-430; H.P. Talbot, "Ellen Henrietta Richards, A.M., Sc.D.," *The Technology Review* XIII:6 (June 1911) pp. 365 ff; *The Vassar Miscellany* XL:8 (May 1911) pp. 576 ff; *Who's Who in America 1910-1911* p. 1601; C.-E.A. Winslow, "The Teaching of Biology and Sanitary Science in The Massachusetts Institute of Technology," *Technology Quarterly* XIX:4 (December 1906) p. 418; C.-E.A. Winslow, *William Thompson Sedgwick 1855-1921* [Reprinted from *The Journal of Bacteriology* VI:3 (May 1921)] pp. 255 ff; Yost, *op. cit.*, pp. 15-19.

Ellen Richards: Chemistry Applied to Public Health—Water & Food Analysis

W.O. Atwater, *Methods and Results of Investigations on the Chemistry and Economy of Food.* U.S. Department of Agriculture. Office of Experiment Stations. Bulletin No. 21 (Washington, D.C., 1895) *passim*; Hunt, *op. cit., passim*; Isabel F. Hyams & Ellen H. Richards, "Notes on Oscillaria Prolifica (*Greville*)," *The Technology Quarterly* XIV:4 (December 1901) pp. 302-310, XV:3 (September 1902) pp. 308-315, XVII:3 (September 1904) pp. 270-276; E.O. Jordan, *et al, A Pioneer of Public Health William Thompson Sedgwick* (New Haven 1924) pp. 37, 57, 61, 66; *Journal of Home Economics* XXI:6 (June 1929) p. 411; Lily Miller Kendall & Ellen H. Richards, "Permanent Standards in Water Analysis," *The Technology Quarterly* XVII:2 (June 1904) pp. 277-280; Massachusetts Institute of Technology, *President's Reports* 1887 (Boston 1888) pp. 28 f, 1888 (Boston 1888) pp. 37 f; *Public Health Papers and Reports* (Chicago 1906) XXXI, Part II, pp. 241-243; Ellen Richards to Anna Mineah, [1879], March 1, 1888, October 20, 1888 (Vassar College, Courtesy Miss Dorothy A. Plum); Ellen Richards Papers, Metropolitan Park Commission Folder, Water Pollution Folder & Oscillaria Folder, Sophia Smith Collection; Richards, *Conservation By Sanitation, op. cit., passim*; Ellen H. Richards, *The Cost of Cleanness* (New York & London 1908) p. 76; Ellen H. Richards, *The Cost of Food* (New York 1901) p. 53; Richards, *The Cost of Living, op. cit.,* p. 29; Ellen H. Richards, *Food Materials and Their Adulterations* (Boston 1886) *passim*; Ellen H. Richards, *Laboratory Notes on Industrial Water Analysis A Survey Course for Engineers* (New York & London 1908) *passim*; [Richards], *Laboratory Notes. Sanitary Chemistry and Water Analysis, op. cit., passim*; Ellen H. Richards, *Meat and Drink*. Health-Education Series. No. 4 (Boston [1908]) *passim*; Ellen H. Richards, "Notes on the Potable Waters of Mexico," *Transactions of the American Institute of Mining Engineers* (New York 1902) XXXII, 335-343; Ellen H. Richards, "Notes on the Water Supplies in the Black Hills of South Dakota and Vicinity," *Technology Quarterly* XVI:4 (December 1903) pp. 309-312; Ellen H. Richards, *The Plague of Mosquitoes and Flies*. Health-Education Series. No. 9 [1908] *passim*; Ellen H. Richards, "Poisonous Food," *The American Kitchen Magazine* IX:4 (July 1898) pp. 129 f; Richards, "University Laboratories," *op. cit., passim*; Ellen H. Richards, "The Water Supplies of Southeastern Alaska," *Technology Quarterly* XVI:4 (December 1903) pp. 304-308; Ellen H. Richards & J.W. Ellms, "The Coloring Matter of Natural Waters," *The Journal of the American Chemical Society* XVIII:1 (January 1896) pp. 68-81; Ellen H. Richards & Arthur T. Hopkins, "The Normal Chlorine of the Water Supplies of Jamaica," *The Technology Quarterly* XI:4 (December 1898) pp. 227-240; Richards & Woodman, *Air, Water, And Food, op. cit., passim*; "Ellen Henrietta Swallow Richards," *DAB*; R.H. Richards, *Robert Hallowell Richards His Mark, op. cit.,* pp. 167 ff; Robert H. Richards, "Trip of the American Institute of Mining Engineers to Mexico," *The Technology Quarterly* XX:2 (June 1907) pp. 215 ff; State Board of Health of Massachusetts, *Fourth Annual Report* (Boston 1873) p. 108, *Fifth Annual Report* (Boston 1874) p. 64, *Twenty-Seventh Annual Report* (Boston 1896) pp. 433-442, *Thirtieth Annual Report* (Boston 1899) pp. 131 f; Talbot, "Ellen Henrietta Richards," *op. cit., passim*; Henry P. Talbot, *Thomas Messinger Drown, LL.D.* (Boston 1905) *passim*; *The Vassar Miscellany* XL:8 (May 1911) pp. 577 f; George

Chandler Whipple, *State Sanitation* (Cambridge, Mass., 1917) I, 50, 74, 79 f, II, 396; A.G. Woodman, "A Portable Outfit for Water Analysis," *The Technology Quarterly* XIV:4 (December 1901) pp. 295-301; Yost, *op. cit.*, pp. 13, 19 ff, 23 f, 26.

Ellen Richards: Chemistry Applied to Industry; Atkinson; New England Kitchen

Mary H. Abel, "Practical Experiments for the Promotion of Home Economics. The New England Kitchen," *Journal of Home Economics* III:4 (October 1911) pp. 362 ff; Mary H. Abel, *Practical Sanitary and Economic Cooking. . . . The Lomb Prize Essay* (N.p. 1890) *passim*; Edward Atkinson, *Plan for a Textile Laboratory and Museum* (Boston 1883) pp. 3 f; Edward Atkinson, *The Prevention of Loss by Fire* (Boston 1900) pp. 28, 35; [Edward Atkinson], *The Right Application of Heat to the Conversion of Food Material* (Salem, Mass., 1890) *passim*; Edward Atkinson, *The Science of Nutrition* (Springfield, Mass., 1892) *passim*; Edward Atkinson, *Suggestions regarding The Cooking of Food* (Washington, D.C., 1894) *passim*; "Edward Atkinson," *DAB*; Bryant, *Mrs. Ellen Richards and her place in the world of science, op. cit.*, p. 11; Bryant, *Values for Which Mrs. Ellen H. Richards Stood, op. cit.*, p. 13; Marshall B. Dalton, *Edward Atkinson (1827-1905)* (New York, San Francisco, Montreal 1950) *passim*; *The Factory Mutuals 1835-1935* (Providence, R.I., 1935) p. 128; Hunt, *op, cit., passim*; *Journal of Home Economics* III:4 (October 1911) pp. 367, 401; Pauline Beery Mack, "The Ellen H. Richards Institute," *Journal of Home Economics* XXXIII:4 (April 1941) p. 231; Rebecca Deming Moore, *When They Were Girls* (Dansville, N.Y., [1923]) pp. 153 f; N.E. Cotton Manufacturers' Association, *Proceedings of the Semi-Annual Meeting, . . . 1878* (Boston 1879) No. 25, *passim*; *Proceedings of The American Association for the Advancement of Science . . . August 1890* (Salem 1891) pp. 413, 415 ff, 418 f, & *August 1897* (Salem 1898) p. 148; Ellen H. Richards to Edward Atkinson, Collection of letters between November 23, 1889 & August 11, [1901] in Atkinson Papers, Massachusetts Historical Society; Ellen H. Richards to Anna Mineah [1879], Vassar College; Ellen H. Richards, "An Apparatus for Determining the Liability of Oils to Spontaneous Combustion," *Technology Quarterly* IV:4 (December 1891) pp. 346 ff; Richards, *The Cost of Cleanness*, op. cit., p. 24; Ellen H.S. Richards, "Notes on a Naphtha Process for Cleaning Wool," *Bulletin of the National Association of Wool Manufacturers* IX:2 (April—June 1879) pp. 96-101; [Ellen H. Richards], *Plain Words About Food* (Boston 1899) pp. 135-154; Ellen H. Richards, "The Social Significance of the Home Economics Movement," *Journal of Home Economics* III:2 (April 1911) p. 120; Richards, "University Laboratories," *op. cit.*, p. 75; Ellen H. Richards & Lottie A. Bragg, "The Distribution of Phosphorus and Nitrogen in the Products of Modern Milling," *Technology Quarterly* III:3 (August 1890) pp. 246-252; "Mrs. Richards On Applied Science," *The Sunday Herald* [Boston] (April 2, 1911) p. 28; "Mrs. Ellen H. Richards Dead," *Boston Evening Transcript* (March 31, 1911) p. 16; Ellen H. Richards & Elizabeth Mason, "The Effect of Heat upon the Digestibility of Gluten," *Technology Quarterly* VII:1 (April 1894) pp. 63 f; R.H. Richards, *Robert Hallowell Richards His Mark, op. cit.,* p. 160; Information from Ralph H. Robins, Personnel Manager, Boston Manufacturers Mutual Insurance Co.; "Count Rumford and the New England Kitchen," *The New England Kitchen* I:1 (April 1894) p. 8; H.P. Talbot, "Ellen Henrietta Richards," *op. cit,* pp. 365 ff; H.P. Talbot, "Mrs. Ellen H. Richards," *The Journal of Industrial and Engineering Chemistry* III:5 (May 1911) p. 353; *Who's Who in America 1910-1911* p. 1599; Harold Francis Williamson, *Edward Atkinson* (Boston 1934) *passim; The Woman's Book* (New York 1894) I, 123 ff; Dane Yorke, *Able Men of Boston* (Boston [1950]) pp. 143, 146, 148 ff, 152; Yost, *op. cit.,* pp. 14, 24.

Ellen Richards: Chemistry Applied to the Home; Domestic Economy; Euthenics
    Atkinson, *The Science of Nutrition, op. cit., passim;* Bane, *The Story of Isabel Bevier, op. cit.,* p. 72; Barrows, "Recollections of Ellen H. Richards," *op. cit.,* p. 1125; Isabel Bevier, "Mrs. Richards' Relation to the Home Economics Movement," *Journal of Home Economics* III:3 (June 1911) pp. 214 f; J. Stanley Brown, Gilbert B. Morrison, Ellen H. Richards, *The Fourth Yearbook of the National Society for the Scientific Study of Education.* Part II (Bloomington, Ill., 1905) pp. 43, 48 f; Charles Albert Browne & Mary Elvira Weeks, *A History of the American Chemical Society* (Washington, D.C., 1952) p. 50; Bryant, *Mrs. Ellen Richards and her place in the world of science, op. cit.,* p. 9; Bryant, *Values for Which Mrs. Ellen H. Richards Stood, op. cit.,* pp. 5, 7, 12 ff; Mary Kavanaugh Oldham Eagle, ed., *The Congress of Women Held in the Woman's Building, World's Columbian Exposition* (Chicago & Philadelphia 1894) p. 713; Hunt, *op. cit., passim; Journal of Home Economics* III:4 (October 1911) Memorial Number, *passim; La Follette's Weekly Magazine* II: 52 (December 31, 1910) p. 10; *Lake Placid Conference on Home Economics Proceedings* [1900, 1904] (Lake Placid, N.Y., 1901, 1904) *passim;* MacLeod, "Reminiscences of Ellen H. Richards," *op. cit.,* p. 709; H.J. Mozans, *Woman In Science* (New York & London 1913) pp. 217 f; *Public Health Papers and Reports . . . Buffalo 1896* (Concord, N.H., 1897) XXII, 87-91; Ellen H. Richards to Edward Atkinson, January 8, 1892, May 11 & 25, 1893, November 15, 1899, Atkinson Papers, Massachusetts Historical Society; Ellen H. Richards to Anna Mineah [1879], 1892, Vassar College; Ellen H. Richards to Marion Talbot, February 8, 1893, August 23, 1893, University of Chicago Library; Ellen H. Richards Papers, Education of Women Folder, Sophia Smith Collection; "Ellen Henrietta Swallow Richards," *DAB;* R.H. Richards, *Robert Hallowell Richards His Mark, op. cit.,* p. 176; "The Rumford Kitchen at the World's Fair," *The New England Kitchen* I:1 (April 1894) pp. 11 f; *Society To Encourage Studies At Home founded in 1873 by Anna Eliot Ticknor* (Cambridge, Mass., 1897) pp. 31 f, 34; Marion Talbot, *More Than Lore Reminiscences* (Chicago [1936]) pp. 118 f, 145; "Tendencies in Women's Professional Education," *The Woman's Journal* XXXVIII: 46 (November 16, 1907) pp. 181, 184; U.S. Department of Agriculture.

Office of Experiment Stations—*Bulletin No. 129* (Washington, D.C., 1903) *passim*; Frederic A. Washburn, *The Massachusetts General Hospital* (Boston 1939) p. 485; *The Woman's Book, op. cit.,* I, 124 f; Yost, *op. cit.,* pp. 24 ff, 26.

For some of Mrs. Richards' more significant writings on the subject, see *The Art of Right Living* (Boston [1904]) *passim*; "Carbon Dioxide as a Measure of the Efficiency of Ventilation," *The Journal of the American Chemical Society* XV:10 (October 1893) pp. 572 ff; *The Chemistry of Cooking and Cleaning A Manual for Housekeepers* (Boston 1882) *passim*; *Conservation By Sanitation, op. cit.,* p. v; *The Cost of Cleanness, op. cit., passim*; *The Cost of Food, op. cit., passim*; *The Cost of Living, op cit., passim*; *The Cost of Shelter* (New York & London 1905) *passim*; "Count Rumford, And His Work for Humanity," *The American Kitchen Magazine* VIII:6 (March 1898) pp. 203-208; *Domestic Economy as a Factor in Public Education, op. cit.,* pp. 115 ff, 128; *Euthenics, op. cit., passim*; *First Lessons in Food And Diet* (Boston 1915) *passim*; *Food Materials and Their Adulterations, op. cit.,* pp. 7 ff, 13 ff, *passim*; "Home Economics in Elementary and Secondary Education," *National Education Association Journal of Proceedings and Addresses* (Winona, Minn., 1908) p. 489; "The Ideal Housekeeping in the Twentieth Century," *Journal of Home Economics* III:2 (April 1911) pp. 174 f; "Instructive Inspection," *Public Health Papers and Reports* . . . *1909* (Columbus, Ohio, 1910) XXXV, 154-158; *Meat and Drink, op. cit.,* p. 15; "The Need of Sanitary Schools," *The Outlook* LXXIV:14 (August 1, 1903) p. 808; "Notes on Hospital Dietaries," *American Journal of Insanity* LII:2 (October 1895) pp. 214-217; "The Place of Science in Woman's Education," *The American Kitchen Magazine* VII:6 (September 1897) pp. 224 ff; *Plain Words About Food, op. cit., passim*; "Report of the Penny Lunch Experiment in Boston, January 1 to June 30, 1910," *Journal of Home Economics* II:6 (December 1910) pp. 648-653; "Sanitary Science in the Home," *Journal of the Franklin Institute* CXXVI:2 (August 1888) pp. 95-114; *Sanitation In Daily Life, op. cit., passim*; "Value of Science to Women," *The Woman's Journal* XXXI:27 (July 7, 1900) pp. 212 f; *Wanted, A Test for "Man Power"* [Reprinted from *Clarkson Bulletin* III:3 (1906)] pp. 5 f, 10; "Who is to Blame for the High Prices?," *The Ladies' Home Journal* (December 1, 1910) XXVII, 23 & 42; Richards & Bragg, "The Distribution of Phosphorus and Nitrogen in the Products of Modern Milling," *op. cit.,* p. 246; [Ellen H. Richards & Marion Talbot, eds.], *Home Sanitation A Manual for Housekeepers* (Boston 1887) *passim*; Ellen H. Richards, assisted by Louise Harding Williams, *The Dietary Computer* (New York 1902) *passim*; Richards & Woodman, *Air, Water, And Food, op. cit., passim*.

Honors for Ellen Richards; Her Achievements & Death

Bryant, *Mrs. Ellen Richards and her place in the world of science, op. cit., passim*; Bryant, *Values for Which Mrs. Ellen H. Richards Stood, op. cit., passim*; "The Death of Mrs. Ellen H. Richards," *Journal of Home Economics* III:3 (June 1911) p. 213; Information from Mrs. Elsa Butler

Grove, New York City; Hunt, *op. cit., passim,* & Anniversary Edition
(Washington, D.C., 1958) Forewords; *Journal of Home Economics* III:4
(October 1911) Memorial Number, *passim,* XXI:6 (June 1929) pp. 403-
411; *La Follette's Weekly Magazine* II:52 (December 31, 1910) p. 10;
Information from Mrs. Mary L. Mairs, Curator, Pennsylvania State Col-
lection, The Pennsylvania State University; Prescott, *op. cit.,* p. 123; Ellen
H. Richards to Anna Mineah, February 25, 1893, Vassar College; Ellen H.
Richards Papers, Education of Women Folder, Sophia Smith Collection;
Ellen H. Richards, "The Place of Science in Woman's Education," *The
American Kitchen Magazine* VII:6 (September 1897) p. 226; *Ellen S.
Richards Monographs* No. 2 Published by Vassar College [1921]; "Mrs.
Richards On Applied Science," *The Sunday Herald* [Boston] (April 2,
1911) p. 28; "Mrs. Ellen H. Richards Dead," *The New York Times*
(March 31, 1911) p. 11; R.H. Richards, *Robert Hallowell Richards His
Mark, op. cit.,* p. 170; Smith College, Citation to Ellen Henrietta Richards,
Sc.D., 1910; H.P. Talbot, "Ellen Henrietta Richards, A.M., Sc.D.," *The
Technology Review* XIII:6 (June 1911) pp. 367 f; *The Technology Review*
XIII:2 (February 1911) p. 121, XIII:3 (March 1911) p. 230; "Tendencies
in Women's Professional Education," *The Woman's Journal* XXXVIII:46
(November 16, 1907) p. 181; *Vassar College Bulletin* II:1 (March 1912)
inset sheet; Yost, *op. cit.,* pp. 1—26.

CHAPTER 7

REBECCA PENNELL DEAN

The First Antioch Faculty Meeting
Ira W. Allen, *A Collection of Facts. History of the Rise, Difficulties &
Suspension of Antioch College* (Columbus, Ohio, 1858) p. 7; *Historical
Sketch of Antioch College, Yellow Springs, Greene County, O.* (N.p. n.d.)
passim; George Allen Hubbell, *Horace Mann Educator, Patriot and Re-
former* (Philadelphia 1910) p. 233; William G. Land, *Thomas Hill Twentieth President of Harvard* (Cambridge, Mass., 1933) pp. 115 f; Horace
Mann to Austin Craig, November 8, 1852 (Massachusetts Historical Society); Horace Mann, *Demands of the Age on Colleges* (New York 1857)
p. 37; [Mary Mann], *Life of Horace Mann* (Boston 1891) I, 365 f, 386 f;
Louise Hall Tharp, *The Peabody Sisters of Salem* (Boston 1950) pp. 229 f;
Louise Hall Tharp, *Until Victory Horace Mann and Mary Peabody* (Boston [1953]) pp. 264 f; E.I.F. Williams, *Horace Mann Educational Statesman* (New York 1937) pp. 278, 311, 329 f.

Rebecca Pennell's Background & Early Life; Influence of Horace Mann
Catherine E. Beecher, *An Essay on the Education of Female Teachers*
(New York 1835) pp. 3 ff, 16; Mortimer Blake, *A History of the Town of
Franklin, Mass.* (Franklin, Mass., 1879) pp. 175 f, 259; George W. Bungay,
Crayon Sketches (Boston 1852) p. 22; Rebecca Pennell Dean, Death Cer-

tificate, City of New York, Department of Health, Bureau of Records and Statistics [Here her birthplace is given as Deerfield, N.Y. According to her Passport Application 2068 of June 18, 1877, she was born in Utica, New York.]; Orestes T. Doe, ed., *The Record of Births, Marriages and Deaths in the Town of Franklin, from 1778 to 1872* (Franklin, Mass., 1898) p. 98; Julian Hawthorne, *Hawthorne And His Circle* (New York & London 1903) p. 43; Julian Hawthorne, *Nathaniel Hawthorne and His Wife* (Boston 1885) I, 493; Nathaniel Hawthorne, *The American Notebooks . . . edited by Randall Stewart* (New Haven [1933]) p. 141; Hubbell, *Horace Mann Educator, op. cit.,* pp. 229 ff [Rebecca's letter about Mann appears here.]; George S. Mann, *Mann Memorial A Record of the Mann Family in America* (Boston 1884) pp. 26 f; "Horace Mann," *DAB*; [Mary Mann], *Life of Horace Mann, op. cit.,* I, 15 & *passim*; Joy Elmer Morgan, *Horace Mann His Ideas And Ideals* (Washington, D.C., 1936) p. 135; *The State Teachers College at Westfield Compiled by . . . Work Projects Administration in . . . Massachusetts* (Westfield, Mass., 1941) pp. 30 f (Courtesy State College, Westfield, Mass.); Tharp, *The Peabody Sisters, op. cit.,* p. 350; Tharp, *Until Victory, op. cit., passim*; Information from Bessie L. Totten, Curator of Antiochiana, Antioch College [The writer is indebted to Miss Totten, who supplied material from Robert L. Straker's "Mann Notes," for considerable help in the preparation of this chapter.]; John Weiss, *Life and Correspondence of Theodore Parker* (New York 1864) II, 343.

For Rebecca's appearance, see her Passport Application 2068 of June 18, 1877.

The Lexington State Normal School

Jacob Abbott, *The Teacher* (Boston 1836) *passim*; Henry Barnard, *Normal Schools* (Hartford 1851) *passim*; Raymond B. Culver, *Horace Mann and Religion in the Massachusetts Public Schools* (New Haven 1929) pp. 119 ff; *The First State Normal School In America The Journals Of Cyrus Peirce And Mary Swift with an introduction By Arthur O. Norton* (Cambridge, Mass., 1926) *passim*; B.A. Hinsdale, *Horace Mann and the Common School Revival in the United States* (New York 1898) p. 153; [Mary Mann], *Life of Horace Mann, op. cit.,* I, 116, 119, 153; *The Massachusetts Teacher* XIII:5 (May 1860) pp. 179, 182 ff; Samuel J. May, *Memoir of Cyrus Peirce* (Hartford 1857) *passim*; A.D. Mayo, "Horace Mann and the Great Revival of the American Common School, 1830-1850," *Report of the Commissioner of Education for . . . 1896-97* (Washington, D.C., 1898) I, 733; Information from Martin F. O'Connor, State College at Framingham, Framingham, Mass.; Cyrus Peirce to Horace Mann, West Newton, n.d. (Typescript, Antioch College); "Cyrus Peirce," *DAB*; *Records of the First Class of the First State Normal School in America* (Boston 1903) *passim*; Tharp, *Until Victory, op. cit.,* pp. 153, 155, 157; Rebecca Viles, "Lexington Normal School," *Proceedings of Lexington Historical Society* (Lexington, Mass., 1890) I, 95-100; Albert E. Winship, *Horace Mann, the Educator* (Boston 1896) p. 35.

Rebecca Pennell's Teaching Posts in Massachusetts; Horace Mann's Influence

Lucy Ellis Allen, *West Newton Half A Century Ago* [Newton, Mass., 1917] *passim*; Barnard, *op. cit., passim*; M. Blake, *op. cit.*, p. 176; *The Common School Journal* VII:5 (March 1, 1845) pp. 66, 70 f; Doe, ed., *op. cit.*, p. 167; *Eighth Annual Report of the Board of Education* (Boston 1845) pp. 32 ff (Courtesy I. Albert Matkov, State Librarian, Massachusetts State Library); *General Catalogue of the State Normal School, at West Newton, Mass. July, 1850* (Boston 1850) p. 4; Information from John F. Gracia, Principal, New Bedford High School; J. Hawthorne, *Nathaniel Hawthorne and His Wife, op. cit.*, I, 275; J. Hawthorne, *Hawthorne And His Circle, op. cit.*, pp. 42 f; Hubbell, *Horace Mann Educator, op. cit.*, p. 235; John H. Lockwood, *Westfield and Its Historic Influences* (N.p. [1922]) II, 369 ff, 371; G.S. Mann, *Mann Memorial, op. cit.*, pp. 27 f; Horace Mann to Eli Fay, May 31, 1852 (Courtesy Bessie L. Totten, Antioch College, from Robert L. Straker's "Mann Notes"); Horace Mann to Mary Mann, March 6, 1852 (Information from Mrs. Adeline Badger Edwards, Wellesley, Mass.), January 15, 1849 (Massachusetts Historical Society); Horace Mann to Rebecca M. Pennell, October 3, 1848, April 7, 1849 (Massachusetts Historical Society); Horace Mann, *A Few Thoughts on the Powers and Duties of Woman* (Syracuse, N.Y., 1853) p. 85; Mary Mann to Horace Mann, March 7, 1852 (Information from Mrs. Adeline Badger Edwards), July 29, 1850, December 6 [or 9?] 1852 (Massachusetts Historical Society); [Mary Mann], *Life of Horace Mann, op. cit.*, I, 195; "Mary Tyler Peabody Mann," *DAB*; Mayo, *op. cit.*, p. 733; Rebecca Pennell to Horace Mann, February 12, 1849 (Massachusetts Historical Society); *Records of the First Class of the First State Normal School, op. cit.*, pp. 1, 18, 24; William C. Richards, *Great In Goodness; A Memoir of George N. Briggs* (Boston 1866) p. 221; *The State Teachers College at Westfield, op. cit., passim*; Tharp, *Until Victory, op. cit.*, pp. 99, 189, 241 f, 262; Williams, *Horace Mann, op. cit.*, pp. 277 f.

Antioch College 1852-1859

Rebecca Pennell, Mary Mann and Horace Mann joined the Christian Church on November 6, 1853. This gesture did not, however, arrest the religious differences that, along with financial and legal complications, beset Antioch College. These involvements, as well as the great educational experiments of the institution, are revealed in a wealth of sources published and unpublished. Many of the latter were supplied through the courtesy of Louise Hall Tharp of Darien, Connecticut, and Bessie L. Totten of Antioch College.

Among the most interesting unpublished sources, see Ada S. Badger to Mary Mann, Yellow Springs, Ohio, November 25, 1859 (Courtesy Mrs. Adeline Badger Edwards); [Henry] Clay Badger to Mary Mann, November 25, 1859 (Copy, Courtesy Mrs. Adeline Badger Edwards); J.E. Brush to Horace Mann, New York, September 5, 1855 (Antioch College); Austin S. Dean & Rebecca M. Pennell, Marriage Record, June 16, 1855 (Probate

Court, Greene County, Xenia, Ohio); A.S. Dean to Horace Mann, Yellow Springs, December 10, 1858 (Antioch College); Rebecca Dean, Account of Mann's Illness and Death, August 2, 1859 (Typescript, Antioch College); R.M. Dean to Committee of Senior Class, Yellow Springs, August 8, 1859 (Antioch College); Rebecca M. Dean to Austin S. Dean, New York, November 19, [1858] & [November 21, 1858] (Antioch College); Rebecca Dean to Horace, Georgie & Benjy [Mann], Ship Constitution, n.d. (Massachusetts Historical Society); Sophia Hawthorne[?], Unsigned, undated fragments, and Sophia Hawthorne to Mary Mann, Unsigned fragment, April 4, [1859] (Copies, Courtesy Louise Hall Tharp); Sophia Hawthorne to Mary Mann, England, April 20, 22, 1855 (Courtesy Henry W. and Albert A. Berg Collection of The New York Public Library); Sophia Hawthorne to Mary Mann, Pateo de Geraldes, Lisboa, November 13, 1855 (Courtesy Henry W. and Albert A. Berg Collection of The New York Public Library); Horace Mann to N.T. Allen, November 6, 1853 (Information from Adeline Badger Edwards); Horace Mann to George Combe, June 15, 1855 (Massachusetts Historical Society); Horace Mann to S.G. Howe, November 2, 1854 (Massachusetts Historical Society); Horace Mann to Mary Mann, January 24, 1853, February 24, 1853 (Massachusetts Historical Society); Horace Mann to Mary Mann, July 3, 1856 and July 12 and 14, 1856 (Massachusetts Historical Society); Mary Mann to Ada Shepard Badger, Concord, December 1, 1859 (Massachusetts Historical Society); Mary Mann to Sophia Hawthorne, Concord, March 3, 1860 (Courtesy Henry W. and Albert A. Berg Collection of The New York Public Library); Mary Mann to Horace Mann, December 10, 1852, undated, January 21, 1853, February 27, 1853, December 4, 1855 (Massachusetts Historical Society); Mary Mann to Horace Mann, Yellow Springs, November 24 [?], 1855 and November 27, 1855 (Massachusetts Historical Society); Mary Mann to Lydia Mann, [1859] (Massachusetts Historical Society); Mary Mann to Nathaniel Peabody, October 8, [1853] (Typescript copy, Antioch College); Mary Mann to Nathaniel Peabody, February 19, [1854] (Typescript, Antioch College); Mary Mann to Nathaniel Peabody, Yellow Springs, September 17, 1854 (Courtesy Henry W. and Albert A. Berg Collection of The New York Public Library); Mary Mann to Cyrus Peirce, October 28, 1853 (Massachusetts Historical Society); Mary Mann to Rebecca Pennell, May 1852 (Copy, Antioch College); Rebecca Pennell to the Trustees of Antioch College, January 13, 1854 (Antioch College); Harvard Forrest Vallance, *A History of Antioch College*. Ph.D. Dissertation, Ohio State University 1936, *passim*.

Among the published sources, see Ira W. Allen, *A Collection of Facts, op. cit., passim* [To this vituperative attack against Antioch College, Horace Mann, Mr. and Mrs. Dean, and others, a reply was published: [Eli Fay], *Rejoinder to I.W. Allen's Pseudo "History" of Antioch College* (Yellow Springs, Ohio, 1859). The *Rejoinder* contains the statements of Eli Fay, Horace Mann, Austin Craig, and others, but no statement by Austin S. Dean. It was the refusal to include his statement in this *Rejoinder* that led to Rebecca's "paralytic shock." The *Rejoinder* does, however, devote a few pages to "The Falsehood respecting Mr. Dean's College Agency, and Mr. Fay's Interest in it."]; *Antioch College Catalogues 1853/4–1858/9 passim*; "Antioch's First President," *Antioch Notes* XIII:12 (April 1, 1936) *passim* (Courtesy Bessie L. Totten); Henry Barnard, ed., *Educational Biography. Memoirs of Teachers* (New York 1859) I, 396; Mary E. Beedy, *The Joint Education of Young Men and Women in the American Schools and Colleges* (London 1873) pp. 10, 13 f; Henry W. Bellows, *The Claims of Antioch College on the Unitarian Denomination* (Boston 1865) *passim*; Paul Bixler, "Horace Mann—Mustard Seed," *The American Scholar* VII:1 (Winter 1938) p. 37; George D. Black, "Memoir of John Burns Weston," *Antioch College Bulletin* IX:1 (December 1912) p. 6; Olympia Brown, *Acquaintances, Old and New, Among Reformers* (N.p. 1911) pp. 15 f; Josephine E. Butler, ed., *Woman's Work and Woman's Culture* (London 1869) p. 71; Henry Steele Commager, *Theodore Parker* (Boston 1936) p. 146; Gabriel Compayré, *Horace Mann and the Public School in the United States* (New York [1907]) pp. 99 ff, 102 f; Moncure Daniel Conway, *Autobiography Memories and Experiences* (Boston & New York 1904) I, 261 ff, 264; "Austin Craig," *DAB*; *Dedication of Antioch College, and Inaugural Address of its President, Hon. Horace Mann; with other proceedings* (Yellow Springs, Ohio, & Boston 1854) *passim*; Rev. W.H. Doherty, *A Christian Minister's Appeal* (Rochester, N.Y., 1852) *passim*; *Educating for Democracy A Symposium* (Yellow Springs, Ohio, 1937) *passim*; Information from Mrs. Adeline B. Edwards, Wellesley, Mass.; William Albert Galloway, *The History of Glen Helen* (N.p. [1932]) pp. 59, 62 ff, 65, 77; Ezra S. Gannett, "Antioch College," *The Quarterly Journal of the American Unitarian Association* V:1 (November 1857) pp. 93 ff, 96 f, 100 f, 105; William C. Gannett, *Ezra Stiles Gannett* (Boston 1875) p. 277; Matthew Gardner, *The Autobiography* (Dayton, Ohio, 1874) pp. 126 ff; *The Gospel Herald*, December 1, 1852 (Courtesy Bessie L. Totten); Arnold Guyot, *Physical Geography* (New York & Chicago [1885]) Preface; Marie Hansen-Taylor & Horace E. Scudder, eds., *Life and Letters of Bayard Taylor* (Boston 1885) I, 297 f; W.S. Harwood, *Life and Letters Of Austin Craig* (New York, Chicago, Toronto [1908]) *passim* (Courtesy Mrs. Harry Snyder, Minneapolis, Minnesota); Algo D. Henderson & Dorothy Hall, *Antioch College* (New York & London [1946]) p. 186; Hinsdale, *op. cit.*, pp. 247, 251 ff, 259 f, 263, 265; *Historical Sketch of Antioch College, op. cit., passim*; *History of The Christian Church of Yellow Springs, Ohio* (Yellow Springs & Columbus, Ohio, 1858) *passim*; Julia Ward Howe, ed., *Sex and Education* (Boston 1874) pp. 55, 65, 68, 197; George Allen Hubbell, "Horace Mann and Antioch College," *Ohio Archæological and Historical Quarterly* XIV:1 (January 1905) pp. 12-27; Hubbell, *Horace Mann Educator, op. cit., passim* [Mann's long letter to Rebecca about her health is quoted on pp. 232 f. The original, Horace Mann to Rebecca Pennell, January 2, 1853, is in the Massachusetts Historical Society]; George Allen Hubbell, *Horace Mann in Ohio* (New York 1900) *passim;* Mary R. Keith, "Horace Mann," *The New England Magazine* N.S. II:6 (August 1890) pp. 655, 657 ff; Land, *Thomas Hill, op. cit.*, pp. 84 f, 90, 92, 94 f,

97, 115 f, 118, 120; *Life and Works of Horace Mann* (Boston 1891) V, 524; Daniel Albright Long, *Sketch of the Legal History of Antioch College* (Dayton, Ohio, 1890) *passim* (Courtesy Bessie L. Totten); Mann, *Demands of the Age, op. cit., passim*; "Horace Mann," *DAB*; [Mary Mann], *Life of Horace Mann, op. cit.,* I, 395 & *passim*; Mayo, *op. cit.,* p. 766; Annie Nathan Meyer, ed., *Woman's Work In America* (New York 1891) pp. 70 f; J.E. Morgan, *op. cit.,* p. 31; Lucy Griscom Morgan, *Pioneering Days at Antioch* (Yellow Springs, Ohio, [1947]) *passim*; Milo True Morrill, *A History of the Christian Denomination in America* (Dayton, Ohio, 1912) pp. 192 f, 195; David P. Page, *Theory and Practice of Teaching* (Syracuse, N.Y., 1847) p. 12 & *passim*; Alonzo Potter & George B. Emerson, *The School and The Schoolmaster* (New York 1842) pp. 149, 311 & *passim*; Laura E. Richards, ed., *Letters and Journals of Samuel Gridley Howe* (Boston & London [1909]) p. 473; "The Seals of Antioch College," *Antioch Alumni Bulletin* VI:1 (November 1934); Mary Somerville, *Physical Geography* (Philadelphia 1853) p. 508 & *passim;* Bertha-Monica Stearns, "Memnonia: The Launching of a Utopia," *The New England Quarterly* XV:2 (June 1942) *passim*; Robert L. Straker, *The Unseen Harvest Horace Mann and Antioch College* (Yellow Springs, Ohio, 1955) *passim*; Martyn Summerbell, ed., *Writings and Addresses of Austin Craig* (Dayton, Ohio, 1911-1913) I, 409 & *passim* (Courtesy Mrs. Harry Snyder, Minneapolis, Minn.); Tharp, *The Peabody Sisters, op. cit., passim*; Tharp, *Until Victory, op. cit., passim*; Information from Bessie L. Totten, Antioch College; Williams, *op. cit., passim*; Helen Beal Woodward, *The Bold Women* (New York [1953]) pp. 175 f, 178; Rev. J.C. Zachos, *The Phonic Text* (Boston 1865) *passim*.

For Rebecca's "adoption" of her nephew, Henry G. Blake, see *Records of the First Class of the First State Normal School, op. cit.,* p. 175.

For further information regarding Austin S. Dean, see *Annual Catalogue of the Meadville Theological School, for . . . 1850-51* (Meadville, Pa., 1850) p. 5; Information from Margaret Boell, Librarian, Meadville Theological School, Chicago; Austin S. Dean, Passport Application 7943, Received June 23, 1855; Austin S. Dean, Will, No. 6486, St. Louis Probate Court; Information from Mrs. Adeline Badger Edwards, Wellesley, Mass.; Walter Cox Green, *General Catalogue of the Meadville Theological School . . . 1844-1910* (Meadville, Pa., 1910) p. 9.

Horace Mann's remains were removed the next year to Providence, R.I.

Rebecca Dean in St. Louis; Mary Institute
Advertisement of the Academic, Collegiate and Scientific Departments of Washington University, and of Mary Institute, for . . . 1862-63 (St. Louis 1862); Galusha Anderson, *The Story of a Border City during the Civil War* (Boston 1908) pp. 9, 16; John Wright Buckham & George Malcolm Stratton, *George Holmes Howison Philosopher And Teacher* (Berkeley, Cal., 1934) pp. 45, 49; Information from Ethel Hope, Registrar, Mary Institute; Joseph G. Hoyt, *An Address at The Inauguration of Joseph G. Hoyt, . . . as Chancellor of Washington University* (St. Louis 1859) p.

73 & *passim*; Sophia Jex-Blake, *A Visit To Some American Schools And Colleges* (London 1867) pp. 110 f, 113 f, 118 f; Information from Marjorie Karlson, Washington University Libraries; Phebe Mitchell Kendall, ed., *Maria Mitchell Life, Letters, And Journals* (Boston 1896) p. 59; Mary Institute, [*Announcement*] (N.p., n.d.); Mary Institute, *Exercises of the Graduating Class . . . 1864-1869* (N.p., n.d.); [Mary Institute], *From Mary to You Centennial 1859-1959* [St. Louis 1959] *passim* (Courtesy Ethel Hope, Registrar, Mary Institute); Mary Institute, *Rehearsal . . . 1866, 1868* (N.p., n.d.); Robert J. Rombauer, *The Union Cause in St. Louis in 1861* (St. Louis 1909) *passim*; *St. Louis Directories* 1864, 1866, 1868; J. Thomas Scharf, *History of Saint Louis* (Philadelphia 1883) I, 554 & *passim*; Edmund H. Sears, *Mary Institute The Story Of Fifty Years* (N.p., 1910) *passim*; Edmund H. Sears, *Mary Institute The Story of Seventy-five Years* (St. Louis 1934) *passim* (Courtesy Ethel Hope, Registrar, Mary Institute); Denton J. Snider, *The St. Louis Movement* (St. Louis 1920) pp. 23, 54 f; Washington University, *A Catalogue of the Officers and Students . . . 1860, 1862-63, 1863-64, 1864-65, 1865-66, 1867-68* (St. Louis 1859, 1862, 1863, 1864, 1866, 1868).

Mrs. Dean's salary is revealed in the MS Journal of W.G. Eliot, May 1860-April 1861, p. 102 (Courtesy Marjorie Karlson, Reference Department, Washington University Libraries).

For Capt. A.S. Dean, see *Missouri Democrat* (July 20, 1863) p. [1] (Courtesy Georgia Gambrill, St. Louis Public Library); *The War of the Rebellion . . . Official Records* (Washington, D.C., 1902) Series II, Vol. V, 317 & Series III, Vol. II, 595.

Mrs. Dean is listed as Instructor in History, Physical Geography and other English Branches in the Washington University *Catalogue . . . for . . . 1872-73* p. 8, and her name appears in the *St. Louis Directory* for 1873—an indication that, after her resignation from Mary Institute, she may have returned for a brief period as teacher.

Rebecca Dean in St. Paul; Her Later Life, & Death

M. Blake, *A History of . . . Franklin, Mass., op. cit.*, p. 176; Henry A. Castle, *History of St. Paul and Vicinity* (Chicago & New York 1912) I, *passim*; Rebecca Mann Dean, Death Certificate; Rebecca M. Dean, Passport Application 2068, June 18, 1877; Rebecca M. Dean, Will, File 5319 in Book 8 of Wills, pp. 236-242 (Probate Court, St. Paul, Minn.); Information from James Taylor Dunn, Librarian, Minnesota Historical Society [Excerpts from the autobiographical MS of his mother, Alice Monfort Dunn]; *The New-York Times* (March 6, 1890) p. 5; *Records of the First Class of the First State Normal School, op. cit.*, pp. 114, 118, 122, 146, 169, 174 f, 195 f, 199; Information from Bessie L. Totten [From Robert L. Straker's "Mann Notes" and other sources]; Information from Neil B. Watson, Superintendent, The Green-Wood Cemetery; J. Fletcher Williams, *A History of the City of Saint Paul* (St. Paul 1876) *passim*.

CHAPTER 8

ISABEL C. BARROWS

Isabel Barrows & the "Iron Clad Oath"
    Isabel C. Barrows, Chopped Straw or The memories of Threescore Years.
Typescript autobiography dated Washington, D.C., February 23, 1908, p.
223 (Courtesy William Burnet Barrows, Burnet M. Davis and June Barrows Mussey) [hereinafter Barrows, Chopped Straw]; [J.D. Strachan],
Samuel J. Barrows. Errand-boy, telegrapher, stenographer, newspaper reporter and correspondent, private secretary, minister, editor, congressman,
linguist, author, prison reformer. Typescript at New York Public Library,
p. 12 [hereinafter [Strachan], Barrows. Errand-boy]; *The Student's Journal.*
Devoted to Graham's Standard Phonography XX:7 (July 1891) p. 16.

Early Life of Isabel Barrows
    Barrows, Chopped Straw, *passim;* "A Lady Oculist—Mrs. Bella C. Bar-
rows," *The Revolution* VII:1 (January 5, 1871) p. [3]; Information from
Harriett C. Newell, Derry Village, N.H.; [Strachan], Barrows. Errand-boy,
p. 11; *The Student's Journal* (July 1891) p. 15; George F. Willey, *Willey's*
Book of Nutfield (Derry Depot, N.H., 1895) pp. 341 f; *Woman's Who's*
Who of America 1914-1915 p. 79 [Here her maiden name is given as Hay].

Isabel's First Marriage; William Wilberforce Chapin; Life in India
    Barrows, Chopped Straw, *passim*; Samuel J. Barrows and Isabel C. Bar-
rows, *The Shaybacks In Camp Ten Summers Under Canvas* (Boston &
New York 1887) pp. 281-298; Gilbert Warren Chapin, *The Chapin Book*
of Genealogical Data (Hartford, Conn., 1924) I, 857 f; Calvin Durfee,
Williams Biographical Annals (Boston 1871) p. 643; Calvin Durfee, *Wil-*
liams Obituary Report, 1865-1875 (North Adams, Mass., 1875) pp. 20 f;
John H. Hewitt, *Williams College and Foreign Missions* (Boston, New York
& Chicago [1914]) pp. 433 ff; "A Lady Oculist," *The Revolution* (January
5, 1871) p. [3]; Daniel Smith Lamb, ed., *Howard University Medical De-*
partment Washington, D.C. (Washington, D.C., 1900) p. 117; [Strachan],
Barrows. Errand-boy, p. 11; *The Survey* XXXI:5 (November 1, 1913) p.
139.

Dansville, New York; Samuel J. Barrows & His Early Life
    Barrows, Chopped Straw, *passim*; Isabel C. Barrows, *A Sunny Life The*
Biography of Samuel June Barrows (Boston 1913) pp. 55 ff, 59-63 &
passim; Samuel J. Barrows, *A Baptist Meeting-House* (Boston 1885) *pas-*
sim; "Samuel June Barrows," *DAB*; A.O. Bunnell, ed., *Dansville 1789-1902*
Historical Biographical Descriptive (Dansville, N.Y., n.d.) pp. 97, 176 ff,
180 f; Gerald Carson, *Cornflake Crusade* (New York & Toronto [1957])
pp. 19, 22, 59, 61 ff, 65 ff, 257 f; Louis Guillaume, *Dr. Samuel J. Barrows*
. . . *Notice Biographique* (Berne 1909) pp. 12 ff; James C. Jackson, *How*
To Beget and Rear Beautiful Children (Dansville, N.Y., 1884) *passim*;

The Jackson Health Resort, *Fiftieth Anniversary Tidings* (Dansville, N.Y., [1908]) *passim*; Paul U. Kellogg, "Samuel June Barrows A Circuit Rider In The Humanities," *The Survey* (May 29, 1909) XXII, 308; "A Lady Oculist," *The Revolution* (January 5, 1871) p. [3]; Prison Association of New York, *Sixty-Fourth Annual Report* .... *1909* (Albany 1909) pp. 51 f; Nelson Sizer, *Forty Years in Phrenology* (New York 1888) p. 3; Nelson Sizer, *The Royal Road to Wealth* (New York 1883) p. 158; J.D. Strachan, "Samuel June Barrows," *Proceedings of the New York State Stenographers' Association,* . . . *December 29 and 30, 1913* (Albany 1914) p. 137; [Strachan], Barrows. Errand-boy, pp. 2 ff, 10 f; *The Student's Journal* XX:6 (June 1891) pp. 15 f, XX:7 (July 1891) p. 15.

Life in New York; Isabel's Marriage to Barrows; Her Shorthand Studies
   American Phrenological Journal XLIII:3 (March 1866) p. 83, XLIV:2 (August 1866) pp. 45 f; Barrows, Chopped Straw, *passim* [For the quotation about Bellevue, see p. 184]; Barrows, *A Sunny Life* pp. 64 ff; Barrows, *A Baptist Meeting-House* pp. 103 f; *A Complete Catalogue of Works for Shorthand Writers and Typewriters. Fowler & Wells Co.* (New York, n.d.) unpaged; Charles Dickens, *David Copperfield* (New York [1950]) pp. 554, 573; Andrew J. Graham, *The Hand-Book of Standard or American Phonography* (New York [1858]) p. ix; Kellogg, "Samuel June Barrows," *The Survey* (May 29, 1909) p. 308; "A Lady Oculist," *The Revolution* (January 5, 1871) p. [3]; Sizer, *The Royal Road to Wealth* p. 161; *Standard Phonographic Visitor* IV:25 (December 20, 1869) p. 300, IV:31 (January 31, 1870) p. 372; *The Student's Journal* (June 1891) p. 16, (July 1891) p. 15; E. Webster, *The Phonographic Teacher:* . . . *Revised by Andrew J. Graham* (New York 1856) p. xii.

Life in Washington, D.C.; Stenographic Work for Seward
   Frederic Bancroft, *The Life of William H. Seward* (New York & London 1900) II, 501 f; Bella C. Barrows to William H. Seward, New York City, January 12, 1869, Washington, D.C., January 29, 1872 (William Henry Seward Collection, University of Rochester); Barrows, Chopped Straw, *passim*; Barrows, *A Sunny Life* pp. 66 f, 73; Samuel J. Barrows to William Henry Seward, Delaware City, Del., September 30, 1868, Washington, D.C., March 9, 1869, Springfield, Mass., August 3, 1872 (William Henry Seward Collection, University of Rochester); Barrows, *A Baptist Meeting-House* p. 135; S.J. Barrows, "A Diplomatic Episode," *The Atlantic Monthly* LVI:335 (September 1885) pp. 339-353; Samuel J. Barrows & Isabel C. Barrows, "Personal Reminiscences of William H. Seward," *The Atlantic Monthly* LXIII: 377 (March 1889) pp. 379-397; "Samuel June Barrows," *DAB*; "Samuel J. Barrows Dead," *The* [New York] *Evening Post* (April 22, 1909) p. 7; Information from Arthur B. Berthold, Acting Chief, Library Division, Department of State; Kellogg, "Samuel June Barrows," *The Survey* (May 29, 1909) p. 308; "A Lady Oculist," *The Revolution* (January 5, 1871) p. [3]; Lamb, *op. cit.,* p. 117; Information from Carl L. Lokke, Archivist in Charge, Foreign Affairs Branch, General

Records Division, The National Archives; Prison Association of New York, *Sixty-Fourth Annual Report* . . . . *1909* p. 52; Frederick W. Seward, *Seward at Washington* (New York 1891) *passim*; [Strachan], Barrows. Errand-boy, pp. 5, 12; *The Student's Journal* (June 1891) p. 16, (July 1891) p. 15.

Barrows served part of the time in the Consular Bureau and as Assistant Keeper of Rolls, Chief Clerk's Bureau.

Continuation of Isabel's Medical Studies in New York; The University of Vienna

Although Isabel states, "We took our degrees in the spring [of 1869]" [Barrows, Chopped Straw, p. 194], and although she has been described as "a graduate of the Woman's Medical College of New York City" [Walter Dyson, *Howard University* (Washington, D.C., 1941) p. 241], the first class was not graduated from Woman's Medical College of the New York Infirmary until 1870. While Isabel doubtless studied there, she is not recorded as an official graduate.

See also Barrows, Chopped Straw, pp. 193-218; Barrows, *A Sunny Life* pp. 67 f; "Isabel Chapin Barrows," *The Christian Register* XCII:46 (November 13, 1913) p. 1098; "A Lady Oculist," *The Revolution* (January 5, 1871) p. [3]; Lamb, *op. cit.*, p. 117; *The Revolution* VI:2 (July 14, 1870) p. 26; Mary Safford, "Sights In Vienna," *The Revolution* VI:8 (August 25, 1870) pp. 115 f; Strachan, "Samuel J. Barrows," *Proceedings of the New York State Stenographers' Association,* . . . *1913* p. 143; [Strachan], Barrows. Errand-boy, p. 12; *The Student's Journal* (July 1891) p. 15; *The Survey* XXXI:5 (November 1, 1913) p. 107.

Medical & Stenographic Work in Washington; Congressional Committee Reporting

Barrows, Chopped Straw, pp. 219-229; Barrows, *A Sunny Life* pp. 68 f, 159; *Daily Morning Chronicle* [Washington, D.C.] (May 29, 1871) p. 1; Dyson, *op. cit.*, pp. 241 f; Walter Dyson, "Founding The School Of Medicine of Howard University 1868-1873," *Howard University Studies in History* No. 10 (November 1929) (Washington, D.C., 1929) p. 23; Guillaume, *op. cit.*, p. 15; Frank R. Hanna, "Committee Reporting in Congress," *The Shorthand Writer* II:8 (May 1907) pp. 555-558; "History Of Reporting Committees In Congress," *Browne's Phonographic Monthly* X:5 (May 1885) pp. 114 f; Kellogg, "Samuel June Barrows," *The Survey* (May 29, 1909) pp. 308 f; "A Lady Oculist," *The Revolution* (January 5, 1871) p. [3]; Lamb, *op. cit.*, pp. 23, 25 ff, 28, 77, 101, 117; Information from David C. Mearns, Chief, Manuscript Division, Library of Congress; Information from J.W. Morton, Director of Recording, Howard University; Prison Association of New York, *Sixty-Fourth Annual Report* . . . . *1909* p. 58; Robert Reyburn, *Fifty Years in the Practice Of Medicine And Surgery* (N.p. [1907]) *passim*; [Strachan], Barrows. Errand-boy, p. 12; Strachan, "Samuel June Barrows," *Proceedings of the New York State Stenographers' Association,* . . . *1913* p. 143; *The Student's Journal* (July 1891) pp. 15 f; *Washington, D.C. Directory* 1872; *Woodhull & Claflin's Weekly* II:52 (May 13, 1871) p. 13.

While the medical directories of the time fail to include Isabel Barrows, there is little doubt that she was the first regularly trained American woman to practise the specialty of ophthalmology. Credit for this pioneer work has too long been denied her.

For Barrows' colorful summers of 1873 and 1874 in the West, his work at Harvard Divinity School, and the trip to Leipzig, see Barrows, *A Sunny Life* pp. 88 ff; Barrows, *A Baptist Meeting-House* p. 193; S.J. Barrows, "The Northwestern Mule and his Driver," *The Atlantic Monthly* XXXV: 211 (May 1875) pp. 550-560; "Samuel June Barrows," *DAB*; *Biographical Directory of the American Congress* (Washington, D.C., 1950) p. 819; Guillaume, *op. cit.*, pp. 15 f; Kellogg, *op. cit.*, p. 309; *New-York Tribune* (September 6, 8, 9, 1873, August 24, 28, 1874) p. 1 of each issue; Prison Association of New York, *Sixty-Fourth Annual Report* . . . . 1909 pp. 58 f; [Strachan], Barrows. Errand-boy, pp. 5 f, 10; Strachan, "Samuel June Barrows," *Proceedings of the New York State Stenographers' Association,* . . . *1913* p. 139; *The Student's Journal* (June 1891) p. 16.

Barrows' reports of the Agassiz lectures appeared in the semi-weekly and weekly editions of the *New-York Tribune* in 1873. They were reprinted as No. 8 in the series, *The Tribune Lecture and Letter Extras* (Information courtesy Henry J. Dubester, Chief, General Reference and Bibliography Division, Library of Congress).

Barrows' Work as Minister, Editor of Christian Register, Congressman, Penologist; His Views & Interests & Isabel's Collaborations with Him

Isabel C. Barrows to Isabel Howland, Dorchester, [Mass.], February 26, 1892, Boston, March 21, 1892, Dorchester, June 20, 1892, S.S. Werkendam, September 11, 1892, Dorchester, March 28, 1897 (Sophia Smith Collection, Smith College Library, Courtesy Elizabeth S. Duvall, Bibliographer).

Isabel C. Barrows, "The Pacific Coast," *Charities and The Commons* (November 21, 1908) XXI, 305-307; Isabel C. Barrows, "Social Agencies The Home Idea in Hungary's Reformatories," *The Survey* (August 24, 1912) XXVIII, 672 ff; Barrows, *A Sunny Life, passim*; Samuel J. Barrows, "America Sober," *The Outlook* (February 20, 1909) XCI, 397-402; Samuel J. Barrows, *The Doom of the Majority Of Mankind* (Boston 1883) *passim;* Samuel J. Barrows, *The Isles And Shrines of Greece* (Boston 1898) pp. vii, ix, & *passim*; Samuel J. Barrows, *Report of Proceedings of the Seventh International Prison Congress Budapest, . . . September, 1905* (Washington, D.C., 1907) *passim;* Samuel J. Barrows, ed., *Science and Immortality. The Christian Register Symposium* (Boston 1887) *passim*; Samuel J. Barrows, *The Sixth International Prison Congress held at Brussels, . . . August 1900* (Washington, D.C., 1903) *passim*; Samuel J. Barrows, *Tour of the Interparliamentary Union* (Washington, D.C., 1905) *passim*; S.J. & I.C. Barrows, *The Shaybacks In Camp, passim*; "Samuel June

Barrows," *DAB*; "Samuel J. Barrows Dead," *The* [New York] *Evening Post* (April 22, 1909) p. 7; *Biographical Directory of the American Congress* (Washington, D.C., 1950) p. 819; Alice Stone Blackwell, "Armenians as I Have Known Them," *Armenian Affairs* I:2 (Spring 1950) pp. 149 f; Alice Stone Blackwell, ed., *The Little Grandmother of the Russian Revolution Reminiscences and Letters of Catherine Breshkovsky* (Boston 1917) p. 127; Alice Stone Blackwell, *Lucy Stone* (Boston 1930) p. 272; "Alice Stone Blackwell (1857-1950) A Symposium," *Armenian Affairs* I:2 (Spring 1950) pp. 136-144; *Boston Directories* 1877-1897 [Bella C. Barrows, physician, appears in the 1882-83 and 1884 *Directories*]; *The Christian Register* LX:4 (January 22, 1881)—LXXVI:52 (December 30, 1897) *passim*, LXXXVIII:17 (April 29, 1909) pp. 454 f, LXXXVIII:19 (May 13, 1909) p. 515, XCII:44 (October 30, 1913) p. 1054, XCII:46 (November 13, 1913) p. 1098 [For the article on "Short-Hand For Women," see LXII:43 (October 25, 1883) p. 674]; "A Good Man," *The Independent* LXVI:3153 (May 6, 1909) pp. 989-991; Guillaume, *op. cit., passim*; *Harvard Vespers* (Boston 1888) p. 3; *Index to the Congressional Record*. Fifty-fifth Congress, First Session, p. 24, Third Session, p. 22; Kellogg, *op. cit.*, pp. 307-313; *King's Hand Book of Boston* (Cambridge, Mass., [1883]) p. 168; Lamb, *op. cit.*, p. 117; Information from Carl L. Lokke, Archivist in Charge, Foreign Affairs Branch, General Records Division, The National Archives; Frank Luther Mott, *A History of American Magazines 1885-1905* (Cambridge, Mass., 1957) pp. 294, 744 f; *The Outlook* (June 21, 1913) CIV, 390 f, (November 8, 1913) CV, 513; *The Paris Prison Congress, 1895. Summary Report* (London, n.d.) p. 5; Theodore Parker, *West Roxbury Sermons* (Boston 1902) p. xv; Prison Association of New York, *Fifty-Sixth Annual Report . . . For . . . 1900* (Albany 1901) p. 133, *Fifty-Eighth Annual Report . . . For . . . 1902* (Albany 1903) pp. 30 f, 70 f, 74 ff, *Sixty-First Annual Report . . . 1905-6* (Albany 1906) pp. 33, 39, 84, *Sixty-Fourth Annual Report . . . . 1909* pp. 52, 57, 59; Information from Miss Sophie A. Siebker, Bremen, Germany; Strachan, "Samuel June Barrows," *Proceedings of the New York State Stenographers' Association, . . . 1913* pp. 139-142, 144 f; [Strachan], Barrows. Errand-boy, pp. 6-9; *The Student's Journal* (June 1891) p. 16; *The Survey* (November 1, 1913) p. 140; *Unitarian Year Book* (Boston [1909]) pp. 155 ff.

Isabel's Stenographic Work

Mrs. Dr. Barrows to Pres. & Mrs. Garfield, Buffalo, July 5, [1881] (James A. Garfield Papers, Library of Congress) [The identity of the writer is not absolutely certain]; Barrows, Chopped Straw, p. 222; Isabel C. Barrows, ed., *A Conference on Manual Training* (Boston [1891]) *passim*; Isabel C. Barrows, ed., *First Mohonk Conference on the Negro Question* (Boston 1890), *Second Mohonk Conference on the Negro Question* (Boston 1891) *passim*; Isabel C. Barrows, "The International Council of Women," *The Independent* LI:2643 (July 27, 1899) pp. 2009-2011; Isabel C. Barrows, "Ellen Johnson and the Sherborn Prison," *The New England Magazine* XXI:5 (January 1900) pp. 614-633; Isabel C. Barrows, "A Moral Citadel,"

The Outlook (March 25, 1911) XCVII, 667-679; Isabel C. Barrows, ed., *Physical Training A Full Report of the . . . Conference Held In Boston . . . 1889* (Boston 1890) *passim*; S.J. Barrows, *The Reformatory System In The United States* (Washington, D.C., 1900) p. 12; Samuel J. Barrows and Isabel C. Barrows, "Personal Reminiscences of William H. Seward," *The Atlantic Monthly* (March 1889) p. 392; "William Worth Belknap," *DAB*; *The Christian Register* XCII:46 (November 13, 1913) p. 1098; *A Complete Catalogue of Works for Shorthand Writers . . . . Fowler & Wells Co.* (New York n.d.) unpaged; *A Decade's Review of the Lake Mohonk Conference on International Arbitration 1895-1905* (Mohonk Lake, N.Y., 1904) unpaged; Kellogg, *op. cit.*, p. 308 n. 1; *Lake Mohonk Conference of Friends Of The Indian, Proceedings* [Sixth Annual Meeting 1888—Twentieth Annual Meeting 1902] (Lake Mohonk 1888-1903) *passim*; Lamb, *op. cit.*, p. 117; *List of Members of the National Prison Assoc'n.* (Nashville, Tenn., 1889) p. 4; *The Outlook* (November 8, 1913) p. 513; Prison Association of New York, *Sixty-Fourth Annual Report . . . . 1909* p. 57 n; *Proceedings of the Annual Congress of the National Prison Association of the United States, . . . 1897* (Pittsburgh 1898) p. 213, . . . *1898* (Pittsburgh 1899) p. 299; *Proceedings of the National Conference of Charities and Correction 1884-1906* (Boston 1885—N.p. n.d.) *passim*; Information from Miss Sophie A. Siebker; Strachan, "Samuel June Barrows," *Proceedings of the New York State Stenographers' Association, . . . 1913* p. 143; [Strachan], Barrows. Errand-boy, pp. 12 f; *The Student's Journal* (June 1891) p. 16, (July 1891) p. 16; *The Survey* (November 1, 1913) p. 107.

Isabel Barrows & Mme. Breshkovsky; Barrows' Death

Isabel Barrows, "After The Verdict," *The Outlook* (April 16, 1910) XCIV, 844-846; Isabel C. Barrows, "The Island Palace," *The Outlook* (August 14, 1909) XCII, 887-889; Isabel C. Barrows, "Madam Breshkovsky In Prison," *The Outlook* (March 5, 1910) XCIV, 538-542; Barrows, *A Sunny Life* pp. 238-243; "Isabel Chapin Barrows," *The Christian Register* XCII: 46 (November 13, 1913) p. 1098; "Isabel C. Barrows," *The Outlook* (November 8, 1913) CV, 513; "Samuel June Barrows," *The Christian Register* LXXXVIII:20 (May 20, 1909) pp. 557 f; Blackwell, ed., *The Little Grandmother of the Russian Revolution*, *op. cit.*, *passim*; "Madame Breshkovsky," *The Outlook* (October 29, 1910) XCVI, 477; *The Christian Register* LXXXVIII:16 (April 22, 1909) p. 425; Guillaume, *op. cit.*, p. 3; Kellogg, *op. cit.*, pp. 307 f; Alexander Kerensky, "Catherine Breshkovsky (1844-1934)," *The Slavonic and East European Review* XIII:38 (January 1935) pp. 428 f; Eloise Lownsbery, *Saints & Rebels* (New York & Toronto 1937) pp. 46, 66 ff, 69, 71; *The Survey* XXXI:5 (November 1, 1913) p. 107; Nicholas Tchaykovsky, "My Prison Story," *The Outlook* (October 22 & 29, 1910) XCVI, 429-441 & 493-500.

Isabel had journeyed to Russia with her husband before, in the summer of 1907, when, as secretary of the American Famine Relief Committee, Barrows had investigated conditions there. At that time she met Tolstoy.

See Barrows, Chopped Straw, p. 40; Barrows, *A Sunny Life* pp. 192-195; Samuel J. Barrows, "Famine Relief Work in Russia," *Charities* (June 6, 1908) XX, 353-357.

For Isabel's Armenian interests, see, e.g., "Alice Stone Blackwell . . . A Symposium," *Armenian Affairs* I:2 (Spring 1950) p. 142.

Isabel's Last Years & Death

Isabel C. Barrows, "The Personal Side of the Congress," *The Survey* (November 5, 1910) XXV, 225-236; Barrows, *A Sunny Life* p. 216; "Isabel Chapin Barrows," *The Christian Register* XCII:46 (November 13, 1913) p. 1098; Blackwell, ed., *The Little Grandmother of the Russian Revolution, op. cit.,* pp. 188, 223 f; Guillaume, *op. cit.,* pp. 4 ff; Strachan, "Samuel June Barrows," *Proceedings of the New York State Stenographers' Association, . . . 1913* pp. 136 f, 140, 144 f; *The Survey* (August 7, 1909) XXII, 613 f, (February 18, 1911) XXV, 851-858, (May 27, 1911) XXVI, 337 f, (September 9, 1911) XXVI, 831, (September 23, 1911) XXVI, 886-892, (February 10, 1912) XXVII, 1734, (July 20, 1912) XXVIII, 575 ff, (November 1, 1913) XXXI, 107, 139 f.

CHAPTER 9

BELVA ANN LOCKWOOD

Belva Lockwood's Motion to Admit Samuel R. Lowery to the United States Supreme Court

History of Woman Suffrage edited by Elizabeth Cady Stanton, Susan B. Anthony, and Matilda Joslyn Gage (Rochester 1887) III, 174; *Lockport Daily Journal* (February 11, 1880) p. [2] (Courtesy Julia H. Winner, Deputy Historian, Niagara County, N.Y.); *The National Republican* [Washington, D.C.] (February 4, 1880) p. 1.

Belva Lockwood's Early Life, Studies, First Marriage, & Teaching Activities

Alumni Record and General Catalogue of Syracuse University (Syracuse 1899) p. 220; C.W. Boyce, *A Brief History of the Twenty-eighth Regiment New York State Volunteers* (Buffalo n.d.) p. 97; *A Catalogue of the Officers And Students of Genesee College, Lima, Livingston County, N.Y., For the Academic Year 1855-6* (Lima, N.Y., 1855) pp. 13 & *passim; A Catalogue of the Officers and Students of the Genesee Wesleyan Seminary, . . . for the Academic Year ending November 21, 1855* (N.p. n.d.) pp. 29, 43, 47; Mrs. Richard Crowley, *Echoes from Niagara* (Buffalo 1890) p. 124; Harry S. Douglass, "Glimpses of Gainesville 1805-1955," *Historical Wyoming* IX:1 (October 1955) pp. 13 f; W. Freeman Galpin, *Syracuse University: The Pioneer Days* (Syracuse 1952) I, 6 f; Phebe A. Hanaford, *Daughters of America; or, Women of the Century* (Boston 1883) pp. 650 ff; Frances Hays, *Women of the Day* (Philadelphia 1885) p. 120;

Laura Kerr, *The Girl Who Ran for President* (New York, Edinburgh & Toronto [1948]) *passim*; William C. King, *Woman. Her Position, Influence, And Achievement Throughout the Civilized World* (Springfield, Mass., 1902) p. 423; Belva Lockwood to Lella, April 7, 1912 (Swarthmore College Peace Collection); Belva A. Lockwood, "My Efforts to Become A Lawyer," *Lippincott's Monthly Magazine* (February 1888) XLI, 215-220; Belva A. Lockwood, *Peace and the Outlook* (Washington, D.C., 1899) pp. 14 f; "Belva A. Lockwood," *Case and Comment* XXIV:3 (August 1917) pp. 252 f; "Belva Ann Bennett Lockwood," *DAB*; Belva Lockwood Chronology (Courtesy Reina Gardner Hamilton, State College, Pennsylvania); "Belva Lockwood, Lawyer, Dies at 85," *The New York Times* (May 20, 1917) p. 23; Mrs. John A. Logan, *The Part Taken By Women In American History* (Wilmington, Del., 1912) pp. 583, 585; J. Miller, "She Chose to Run," unidentified newspaper clipping (Courtesy Mrs. Arthur C. Holden, New York City); *National Equal Rights* III:11 (November 1884) p. 4; Irvin W. Near, *The Early History of Hornellsville, Steuben County, New York* (Hornellsville, N.Y., 1890) p. 23; *The* [Lockport] *Niagara Democrat* (August 7, 1844) *passim*; "Obituary Mrs. Belva Lockwood," *Chicago Legal News* (May 24, 1917) Vol. 49, p. 341; *Official Report of the Fifth Universal Peace Congress held at Chicago, . . . August 14 to 20, 1893* (Boston [1893]) p. 138; Information from Mrs. Evelyn Perry, Office of the Registrar, Syracuse University; John Clagett Proctor, "Belva Ann Lockwood Only Woman Candidate for President of the United States," *Records of The Columbia Historical Society* (Washington, D.C., 1935) Vol. 35-36, pp. 193 ff; Information from Dorothy Thomas; *Who's Who in America 1916-1917* IX, 1500 f; Frances E. Willard & Mary A. Livermore, *A Woman of the Century* (Buffalo, Chicago & New York [1893]) pp. 468 ff; Julia Hull Winner, "Belva A. Lockwood—That Extraordinary Woman," *New York History* XXXIX:4 (October 1958) pp. 321-340; *Woman's Who's Who of America 1914-1915* p. 496.

Belva's credo regarding woman's education appears in *The Peacemaker* X:2 (August 1891) p. 36.

Early Years in Washington, 1866-1873; Second Marriage; Struggles for Law Degree

Alumni Record . . . of Syracuse University, op. cit., p. 220; David K. Boynick, *Pioneers in Petticoats* (New York [1959]) pp. 59-89; Certificate of Issuance of Marriage License Dr. E. Lockwood and Mrs. Belva A. McNall (United States District Court for the District of Columbia); Allen C. Clark, "Belva Ann Lockwood," *Records of The Columbia Historical Society* (Washington, D.C., 1935) Vol. 35-36, pp. 206 ff, 209 f, 212; Grace Julian Clarke, *George W. Julian* (Indianapolis 1923) p. 315; *Daily Morning* [Washington, D.C.] *Chronicle* (May 20, 1867) p. 2 & (September 24, 1870) p. 2; *The Golden Age* II:32—II:51 (August 10, 1872—December 21, 1872) *passim*; Hanaford, *op. cit.*, pp. 652 f; Hays, *op. cit.*, p. 120; *History of Woman Suffrage, op. cit.*, III, 809 ff, 812; Kerr, *op. cit.*, *passim*; King, *op. cit.,* p. 423; Belva Lockwood, "Diploma" (MS, Swarthmore College Peace Collection); Belva A. Lockwood, *Arbitration and the Treaties* (N.p. n.d.) pp. 3 f; Belva A. Lockwood, "My Efforts to Become A Lawyer," *op. cit.,* pp. 221-224; Belva Lockwood and Others, Petition . . . to confer the right of suffrage without regard to sex (National Archives); Ezekiel Lockwood, Certificate of Death (Vital Statistics Section of the District of Columbia Department of Public Health); *National Equal Rights* III:11 (November 1884) p. 4, I:4 [sic] (February 1885) p. 4, I:5 (March 1885) p. 7; *The Peacemaker* XXI:8 (August 1902) p. 183; Proctor, *op. cit.,* pp. 195 f; John C. Proctor, ed., *Washington Past and Present A History* (New York 1930) I, 267; Helena Ducie Reed, "Belva Ann Lockwood First of Our Great Women Lawyers," *The Kappa Beta Pi Quarterly* 38:2 (June 1954) *passim*; Agnes Wright Spring, ed., *A Bloomer Girl on Pike's Peak 1858* (Denver [1949]) *passim*; *The Sunday Star* [Washington, D.C.] (February 7, 1854) p. D9; *Washington Directories* 1867—1873 (Courtesy Mrs. Margaret Billings, Columbia Historical Society); *Who's Who in America 1916-1917* IX, 1500 f; Willard & Livermore, *op. cit.,* p. 469; *Woman's Herald of Industry* III:10 (October 1884).

As early as May 18, 1872, *Woodhull & Claflin's Weekly* (IV:27) p. 12 carried the following statements regarding Belva Lockwood's studies and struggle for admission to the bar:

> Mrs. Lockwood and Mrs. L. S. Hall Graffan, applicants for admission to the bar, have passed their examinations credibly.
>
> *—Chronicle.*
>
> And now a woman takes her place as attorney at our District Bar. A petticoated lawyer! What would the *ante-bellum* city of Washington have said could it have known?
>
> *—Chronicle.*
>
> Female Attorneys.—In the District Supreme Court, yesterday, applications for admission to the bar of the District were presented by Mrs. Belva A. Lockwood and "Miss Lydia A. Hall," and were referred to a committee recently appointed for the examination of applicants. . . .
>
> Progress of Woman's Rights.—The judges of the Supreme Court of the District of Columbia, in revising the new code prepared by the commission to codify the laws of the District, have ordered the word "male," in connection with admission to the bar, to be stricken out, thus opening the way to women to practice in the courts here. Mrs. Lockwood, and other advocates of woman's rights, to whom the fact became known yesterday, were greatly rejoiced, regarding this action of the court as a prodigious stride towards the attainment of the object they have in view.
>
> *—Washington Star.*

Admission to Supreme Court of District of Columbia; Early Legal Career

Job Barnard, "Early Days of the Supreme Court of the District of Columbia," *Records of The Columbia Historical Society* (Washington, D.C., 1919) Vol. 22, pp. 19 ff; Clark, "Belva Ann Lockwood," *op. cit.,* p. 216; Folker vs. Folker. Equity 3426 Doc. 13 (National Archives); Information from Miss Bess Glenn, Archivist in Charge, Justice and Executive Branch, General Records Division, The National Archives [The author is deeply indebted to Miss Glenn for her aid in the legal aspects of Belva Lockwood's career]; Hays, *op. cit.*, p. 120; *History of Woman Suffrage, op. cit.*, III, 35; List of Documents Filed in Cases in Law and Equity, 1873 and 1874, of the Former Supreme Court of the District of Columbia in Which Belva Lockwood Served as Attorney (Courtesy Miss Bess Glenn, National Archives); Belva Lockwood, "Diploma" (MS, Swarthmore College Peace Collection); Belva A. Lockwood, "My Efforts to Become A Lawyer," *op. cit.*, p. 224; Belva A. Lockwood, Petition To the Honorable the Senate and House of Representatives . . . [that no woman . . . be debarred from practice before any United States Court on account of sex or coverture] (National Archives); Belva A. Lockwood, "The Present Phase of the Woman Question," *The Cosmopolitan* V:6 (October 1888) p. 469; Ellen A. Martin, "Admission of Women to the Bar," *The Chicago Law Times* I:1 (November 1886) p. 80; Annie Nathan Meyer, ed., *Woman's Work In America* (New York 1891) pp. 239 f; J. Miller, "She Chose to Run," *op. cit.*; *The Nation* XXVIII:711 (February 13, 1879) p. 110; F. Regis Noel & Margaret Brent Downing, *The Court-House of the District of Columbia* [Washington, D.C., 1919] p. 58; Proctor, "Belva Ann Lockwood," *op. cit.*, p. 195; Proctor, ed., *Washington Past and Present, op. cit.*, I, 267; *Woman's National Liberal Union. Report of the Convention for Organization* (Syracuse 1890) p. 78.

The name of the Supreme Court of the District of Columbia was changed in 1936 to the District Court for the United States for the District of Columbia, and in 1948 to the United States District Court for the District of Columbia. Although most sources give the date of Mrs. Lockwood's admission to the Court as September 23, 1873, the Index of Admission of Attorneys gives the date as September 24, 1873 (Information from Harry M. Hull, Clerk, United States District Court for the District of Columbia).

Von Cort Case & Struggle for Admission to Federal Courts

According to Belva Lockwood's own account [Belva Lockwood, "Mrs. Lockwood, and the Late Associate Justice Knott [sic]" (MS, Swarthmore College Peace Collection)] "She took her testimony in the [Von Cort] case . . . prepared with great care an elaborate brief, and asked leave for her client to read it to the court. This, they had no power to deny, as it is the privilege of every applicant to plead his own case, and sat by Mrs. Von Cort until the hearing was completed."

The case file of the Von Cort case (Court of Claims General Jurisdiction Case No. 9194) is at the National Archives. According to Miss Bess Glenn, "The first paper in the case was filed in April 1874. Between November of that year and May 8, 1876, when it was dismissed, the case seems to have been inactive. . . . The papers filed in the case contain nothing relating to Mrs. Lockwood's status as an attorney in the Court of Claims. Among the papers in the case file, however, but apparently not filed in this case, is a printed copy of Judge Nott's opinion, issued in 1874, ruling against the admission of Mrs. Lockwood to practice before the Court of Claims."

For details, see *The American Law Review* XI:2 (January 1877) p. 367 & XIII:3 (April 1879) p. 589; *The Ballot Box* I:11 (February 1877) p. 2 (Courtesy Ruth Whittier, Secretary, New Hampshire State Library); Clark, *op. cit.*, pp. 214 f; Allen C. Clark, "More About The Fourth Ward," *Records of The Columbia Historical Society* (Washington, D.C., 1932) Vol. 33-34, pp. 72 f; *Congressional Record*, 45th Congress, 1st Session VI, 240; 45th Congress, 2nd Session VII, Part II, 1235, 1326, 1821, VII, Part III, 2704 f, 3558 f, VII, Part IV, 3889 f; 45th Congress, 3rd Session VIII, 1082 ff, 1221, 1237, 1413; *Court of Claims Reports* (Washington, D.C., 1874) IX, 346-356; "Enter Portia," *Public Ledger* [Philadelphia] (February 12, 1879) p. 2; *The Evening Star* [Washington, D.C.] (February 8, 1879) p. 1; Lydia Hoyt Farmer, ed., *The National Exposition Souvenir What America Owes to Women* (Buffalo, Chicago & New York 1893) pp. 395 f; Information from Mr. John T. Fey, Clerk, Supreme Court of the United States; Frederick H. Gillett, *George Frisbie Hoar* (Boston & New York 1934) p. 87; Information from Mr. Willard L. Hart, Clerk, United States Court of Claims; Hays, *op. cit.*, pp. 120 f; *History of Woman Suffrage, op. cit.*, III, 64 f, 106 ff, 110, 138 ff, 141, IV, 33; Inez Haynes Irwin, *Angels and Amazons* (Garden City, N.Y., 1933) pp. 178 f; Kerr, *op. cit.*, *passim*; King, *op cit.*, p. 423; Belva A. Lockwood, "My Efforts to Become A Lawyer," *op. cit.*, pp. 225-229; Belva Lockwood, "Mrs. Lockwood, and the Late Associate Justice Knott [sic] of the Court of Claims now retired" (MS, Swarthmore College Peace Collection); Belva Lockwood, Brief, Sustaining Petition of Belva A. Lockwood, Asking That Congress May Pass A Declaratory Act Or Joint Resolution . . . "That no woman otherwise qualified shall be debarred from practice before any United States Court on account of sex or coverture" (National Archives); Belva Lockwood, Petition . . . that no woman otherwise qualified shall be debarred from practice before any United States Court on account of sex or coverture (National Archives); Martin, *op. cit.*, p. 80; Meyer, *op. cit.*, pp. 224 f; Gustavus Myers, *History of the Supreme Court of the United States* (Chicago 1912) p. 528; *The Nation* XXVIII:711 (February 13, 1879) p. 110 & XXVIII:719 (April 10, 1879) p. 247; *National Equal Rights* III:11 (November 1884) p. 4 & I:5 (March 1885) p. 7; *The New York Herald* (February 9, 1879) p. 6; [Charles C. Nott], *The New Woman and the Late President of Williams* [Washington, D.C., 1895] pp. 2 f; "Charles Cooper Nott," *DAB*; Stanton J. Peelle, "History and Jurisdiction of the United States Court of Claims," *Records of The Columbia Historical Society* (Washington, D.C., 1916) Vol. 19, p. 18; Proctor, "Belva Ann Lockwood," *op. cit.*, pp. 197 f; Proctor, ed., *Washington Past and Present, op. cit.*, I, 267; *Progress A Mirror for Men and Women* I:15 (February 22, 1879) pp. 282 f; Mrs. M.L. Rayne, *What Can A Woman Do* (Petersburgh, N.Y., n.d.) pp. 54 f; Reed, *op. cit.*, p. 67; William A. Richardson, *History, Jurisdiction, and Practice of the Court of Claims (United States.)* (Washington, D.C., 1885) p. 18; "Aaron Augustus Sargent," *DAB*; *The Sunday Star* [Washington, D.C.]

(July 7, 1940) p. C-4; Information from Mrs. Dorothy Thomas, New York City; Charles Warren, *The Supreme Court in United States History* (Boston 1922) III, 272 f; *The Washington Post* (February 8, 1879) p. 2; Willard and Livermore, *op. cit.,* p. 469; *Woman's Herald of Industry* III:10 (October 1884); *The Woman's Journal* X:10 (March 8, 1879) p. 77.

Belva's House on F Street

Proctor, "Belva Ann Lockwood," *op. cit.,* p. 203; Reed, *op. cit.;* Information from Mr. Peter S. Ridley, Deputy Recorder of Deeds, D.C.; *Woman's Herald of Industry* III:10 (October 1884).

Belva's Cases, Legal Acumen, & Characteristics

Buffalo Express (October 21, 22, 1881) p. 4; Frank G. Carpenter, *Carp's Washington* (New York, Toronto & London [1960]) pp. 33, 229 f; Clark, "Belva Ann Lockwood," *op. cit.,* pp. 215 f; Clark, "More About The Fourth Ward," *op. cit.,* p. 73; *History of Woman Suffrage, op. cit.,* III, 106, IV, 571; Belva A. Lockwood, "How I Ran for the Presidency," *National Magazine* XVII:6 (March 1903) pp. 729 f; *National Equal Rights* III:11 (November 1884) p. 4, III:12 (December 1884) pp. 2, 4, I:5 (March 1885) p. 7, I:6 (April 1885) p. 7; *The Peacemaker* XXXI:10 (October 1912) p. 211; Peelle, *op. cit., passim;* Richardson, *op. cit., passim;* Marilla M. Ricker, *I Don't Know Do You?* (East Aurora, N.Y., 1916) p. 57; Lelia J. Robinson, "Women Lawyers in the United States," *The Green Bag* II:1 (January 1890) p. 27; Willard and Livermore, *op. cit.,* p. 469; *Woman's Herald of Industry* II:[1] (January 1883).

According to [Rollin H. Kirk], *Many Secrets Revealed; or Ten Years Behind the Scenes In Washington City. By A Washington Journalist* (Washington, D.C., 1885) p. 38, Southern war claimants should send a copy of schedules of losses "to some lawyer of National reputation at Washington —such as Belva A. Lockwood, who is on friendly terms with all political parties, and who is esteemed throughout the Nation for her sterling integrity and fine abilities." In the same work there is an advertisement of "Belva A. Lockwood, Attorney and Solicitor" who makes "Southern War Claims A Specialty."

According to *The Woman's Journal* XII:51 (December 17, 1881) p. 405, Mrs. Belva A. Lockwood presented the "first instance of a woman lawyer appearing before a court in Massachusetts" in her scheduled appearance in the United States Circuit Court of Massachusetts, December 27, 1881, to argue a cause in equity.

Belva's Campaigns for the Presidency

Although Victoria Woodhull was nominated in 1872 for the Presidency, her party disintegrated before the election. Thus Belva Lockwood becomes the first woman formally to run for the office.

Roger Butterfield, *The American Past* (New York [1947]) p. 217; *The Evening Star* [Washington, D.C.] (September 4, 1884) p. 1 & (May 16, 1888) p. 4; Kerr, *op. cit., passim; Frank Leslie's Illustrated Newspaper*

LIX:1513 (September 20, 1884) pp. 72, 74, LIX:1519 (November 1, 1884) pp. 169, 171; Belva A. Lockwood, "How I Ran for the Presidency," *op. cit., passim*; Belva A. Lockwood, Letter of Acceptance, September 3, 1884 (Copy, Courtesy Mrs. Arthur C. Holden); Belva A. Lockwood, "Women In Politics," *The American Journal of Politics* (April 1893) II, 387; "Belva A. Lockwood," *Case and Comment, op. cit.,* p. 253; Miller, "She Chose to Run," *op. cit.; National Equal Rights* III:11—III:12 (November 1884—December 1884), I:4—I:6 (February 1885—April 1885) *passim; The New Northwest* (November 6, 1884) p. 4 (Courtesy Mr. Henry J. Dubester, Chief, General Reference & Bibliography Division, Library of Congress); *New-York Daily Tribune* (September 5, 1884) p. 2, (September 29, 1884) p. 1, (October 20, 1884) p. 1, (November 4, 1884) p. 1, (May 17, 1888) p. 6; *The New York Herald* (September 4, 1884) p. 3, (September 5, 1884) p. 6, (May 16, 1888) p. 4, (July 26, 1888) p. 3, (August 6, 1888) p. 3; Mignon Rittenhouse, *The Amazing Nellie Bly* (New York 1956) pp. 138 ff; Mrs. J.W. Stow, *Probate Confiscation, and the Unjust Laws which Govern Women* (San Francisco [1876]) pp. 1 f, 245; *The Sunday Star* [Washington, D.C.] (July 7, 1940) p. C-4; *Syracuse Herald-Journal* (January 18, 1957); *Today's Health* (December 1957) (Courtesy Mrs. Arthur C. Holden); *The Washington Post* (July 6, 1952) p. 8 S; Willard and Livermore, *op. cit.,* p. 469; *Woman's Herald of Industry* I:1—III:10 (September 1881—October 1884) *passim* [Mrs. Lockwood's letter on "Women Rulers" as well as her letter accepting the nomination appear in the October 1884 issue]; *The World* (May 19, 1888) p. 1.

Broken down, the vote read: New York 1336, Illinois 1008, California 734, New Hampshire 379, Michigan 374, Maryland 318.

According to *The Women Lawyers' Journal* VII:4 (January 1918) pp. 27 f (Courtesy Mrs. Dorothy Thomas, New York City) the nomination was originally meant as a kind of joke, but when she was informed of that fact, Belva, undaunted, continued to lecture for $100 a night under the auspices of the Slayton Lyceum.

Belva Lockwood's Public Activities: Suffrage & Peace
    Alumni Record . . . of Syracuse University, op. cit., p. 220; Olympia Brown, *Acquaintances, Old and New, Among Reformers* (N.p. 1911) p. 89; *Bulletin de Ier Congrès Universel de la Paix Paris 1889* (Berne 1901) *passim; Bulletin Officiel du IVme Congrès Universel de la Paix . . . à Berne . . . du 22 au 27 août 1892* (Berne 1892) *passim; Bulletin Officiel du VIme Congrès* (Antwerp 1895), *. . . du VIIe Congrès* (Berne 1896), *. . . du IXe Congrès* (Berne 1901), *. . . du XVme Congrès* (Berne 1906) *passim*; Clark, "Belva Ann Lockwood," *op. cit.,* p. 218; Mrs. J.C. Croly, *The History of the Woman's Club Movement in America* (New York [1898]) p. 349; *Declaration of Rights of the Women of the United States by the National Woman Suffrage Association* [Philadelphia 1876] unpaged; *IIme Congrès International D'Assistance et IIme Congrès International de la Protection de L'Enfance Genève, 14-19 Septembre 1896. Procès-Verbaux et Résolutions* (Geneva 1897) *passim; Equal Franchise Bulletin* I:4 (August

1, 1912) *passim*; *History of Woman Suffrage, op. cit.*, IV, 343, 569, VI, 700; *Der Internationale Kongress für Frauenwerke und Frauenbestrebungen in Berlin 19. bis 26. September 1896* (Berlin 1897) *passim*; *Joan of Arc Magazine* I:2/3 (April/May 1910) p. 77; Kerr, *op. cit., passim*; Belva Lockwood to Prof. Frank Gardner, October 30, 1911 (Swarthmore College Peace Collection); Belva Lockwood to Lella, May 2, August 11, November 10, November 18, December 1, 1912, January 12, April 30, May 13, 1913 (Swarthmore College Peace Collection); Belva Lockwood, "How I Helped to settle the Shirt Waist Strike in Philadelphia," (MS, Swarthmore College Peace Collection); Belva A. Lockwood, *Arbitration and the Treaties* (N.p. n.d.) *passim*; Belva A. Lockwood, *The Central American Peace Congress* ([Washington, D.C.?] 1908) *passim*; Belva A. Lockwood, *A Complete List of all The Treaties Entered into by the United States* (Washington, D.C., 1893) *passim*; Belva A. Lockwood, *Congrès Internationale De La Paix, Novembre, 1891. Le Creation D'un Bureau Internationale De La Paix* [Washington, D.C., 1891] *passim*; Belva A. Lockwood, *Peace and the Outlook* (Washington, D.C., 1899) *passim*; "Belva A. Lockwood," *The Suffragist* V:70 (May 26, 1917) p. 5; Logan, *op. cit.*, p. 397; Sidney Morse, *The Siege of University City* (University City & St. Louis 1912) pp. 772 & *passim*; *New-York Daily Tribune* (January 2, 1899) p. 5; *Official Report of the Fifth Universal Peace Congress held at Chicago, . . . August 14 to 20, 1893* (Boston [1893]) *passim*; *Official Report of the Thirteenth Universal Peace Congress . . . at Boston, . . . October . . . 1904* (Boston 1904) *passim*; *The Peacemaker* VIII:7—VIII:10 (January 1890—April 1890), XI:1—XVIII:12 (July 1891—June 1900), XX:3—XXVI:12 (March 1901 —December 1907), XXVII:4—XXX:6-7 (April 1908—June-July 1911), XXXI:1—XXXII (January-February 1912—Midsummer 1913) *passim*; *Proceedings of the Tenth Universal Peace Congress, . . . Glasgow, . . . September 1901* (London & Berne 1902) *passim*; *Proceedings of the Universal Peace Congress, . . . London, From 14th to 19th July, 1890* (London n.d.) *passim*; *Troisieme Congrès International de la Paix Rome Novembre 1891* (Rome 1892) *passim*; *Who's Who in America 1916-1917* IX, 1501; Willard and Livermore, *op. cit.*, pp. 469 f; *Woman's National Liberal Union. Report of the Convention for Organization* (Syracuse 1890) p. 79; *The Woman's Tribune* VII:17 (April 26, 1890) p. 136.

The Cherokee Case; Mrs. Lockwood's Later Legal Activities

The Cherokee case dragged on and was still before the Court of Claims at the 1909-1910 Term (See *Court of Claims Reports* XLV, 104-108, 137). The insanity case to which Mrs. Lockwood refers in her letter to Lella, April 7, 1912 (Swarthmore College Peace Collection) was that of Mary E. Gage (Mental Health No. 4542). However, the Clerk's Office of the United States District Court for the District of Columbia "fails to find" that she appeared as attorney of record in the case. Mrs. Lockwood mentions the Myra Gaines case in a letter to *The Peacemaker* [XIII:3 & 4 (September & October 1894)]: "I will . . . sail home . . . arriving in New York in time to be at the trial of the Gaines Will case." According to *Who's Who in America 1916-1917* IX, 1501, she was one of the attorneys in the probate of the Gaines will. Her part in the case was, however, doubtless a minor one.

For details, see Clark, "Belva Ann Lockwood," *op. cit.,* pp. 215 f; *Court of Claims Reports* (Washington, D.C., 1905) XL, 252-365; *History of Woman Suffrage, op. cit.,* IV, 571; Kerr, *op. cit., passim*; List of Documents Filed by Mrs. Belva Lockwood and Found Among the Records in United States Court of Claims Cases 23212 and 23214 (Courtesy Miss Bess Glenn, National Archives); Belva Lockwood to Sisters of the Equity Club, April 30, 1887 (Equity Club letters in Dillon Collection, Radcliffe College, Courtesy Mrs. Dorothy Thomas, New York City); Belva Lockwood to Prof. Frank Gardner, October 23, 1911 (Swarthmore College Peace Collection); Belva Lockwood to Lella, March 27, April 7, May 2, December 30, 1912 (Swarthmore College Peace Collection); Belva Lockwood, "For Biography" (MS, Swarthmore College Peace Collection); Belva Lockwood, "Mrs. Lockwood, and the Late Associate Justice Knott [sic] of the Court of Claims now retired," and "The Eastern Cherokee Case" (MSS, Swarthmore College Peace Collection); "Belva A. Lockwood," *Case and Comment* XXIV:3 (August 1917) p. 253; *New-York Daily Tribune* (March 28, 1893) p. 4, (April 27, 1895) p. 3, (May 4, 1895) p. 6; *The New-York Times* (June 16, 1894) p. 1, (October 2, 1894) p. 4, (May 20, 1917) p. 23; *The Peacemaker* XI:10 (April 1893) p. 186, XIII:3 & 4 (September & October 1894) p. 44, XVIII:9 (March 1900) pp. 175 f, XXV:11 (November 1906) p. 253, XXVI:8 (August 1907) p. 183, XXVIII:7 (July 1909) p. 164, XXIX:4 (April 1910) pp. 77 f; Peelle, *op. cit.,* p. 10; Reed, *op. cit., passim*; Richardson, *op. cit.,* pp. 26 f; *United States Reports* (New York 1906) Vol. 202, pp. 101-132; *Washington Directories* 1887—1895 (Courtesy Mrs. Margaret Billings, Columbia Historical Society); *Who's Who in America 1916-1917* IX, 1501; *Woman's National Liberal Union. Report of the Convention for Organization* (Syracuse 1890) p. 78; *The Woman's Tribune* VII:17 (April 26, 1890) p. 136, XXII:9 (May 13, 1905) p. 33.

Belva's Honors, Financial Troubles, Death
Information from Madeline L. Brown, Medical Records Department, The George Washington University Hospital; Clark, "Belva Ann Lockwood," *op. cit.,* pp. 217 ff, 220; *The Evening Star* [Washington, D.C.] (May 19, 1917) Part I, p. 7, (May 21, 1917) p. 2, (May 22, 1917) p. 2, (May 23, 1917) p. 3; Kerr, *op. cit., passim*; Belva Lockwood to Lella, May 2, November 4, November 18, 1912, January 5, April 30, 1913 (Swarthmore College Peace Collection); Belva A. Lockwood, "The Present Phase of the Woman Question," *The Cosmopolitan* V:6 (October 1888) p. 469; Belva Lockwood, Certificate of Death (Vital Statistics Section, District of Columbia Department of Public Health); "Belva A. Lockwood," *The Suffragist* V:70 (May 26, 1917) p. 5; "Belva Lockwood," *The Woman Citizen* N.S. I:1 (June 2, 1917) p. 6; "Belva Lockwood In Dire Need," *The Woman's Journal* XLV:14 (April 4, 1914) p. 111; Information from Edwin A. Mooers, Washington College of Law, American University);

The New York Times (May 20, 1917) p. 23; *The Peacemaker* XXVIII:7 (July 1909) p. 164; Information from Mrs. Evelyn Perry, Office of the Registrar, Syracuse University; "The Pioneer Suffragist," *The Literary Digest* LIV:24 (June 16, 1917) p. 1890; Proctor, "Belva Ann Lockwood," *op. cit.*, pp. 203 f; *Public Ledger* [Philadelphia] (May 21, 1917) p. 10; Reed, *op. cit.*, *passim*; Information from Peter S. Ridley, Deputy Recorder of Deeds, D.C.; *The Sunday Star* [Washington, D.C.] (May 20, 1917) p. 8; Information from Dorothy Thomas; *The Women Lawyers' Journal* IV:5 (February 1915) p. 37 (Courtesy Mrs. Dorothy Thomas, New York City).

The portrait of Belva Lockwood by Nellie Mathes Horne now hangs in the Rotunda of the Natural History Building in Washington (Information from Thomas M. Beggs, National Collection of Fine Arts, Smithsonian Institution).

The letter in which Belva Lockwood summed up her accomplishments was written to Jas. A. Cruikshank, November 21, 1897. The original is owned by Mrs. Arthur C. Holden of New York City and is quoted with her permission.

CHAPTER 10

REBECCA W. LUKENS

Change of Name of Brandywine Iron Works
"A Century And A Quarter In Iron And Steel," *The Iron Age* 136:1 (July 4, 1935) p. 44; Gilbert Cope & Henry Graham Ashmead, eds., *Historic Homes and Institutions . . . of Chester and Delaware Counties, Pennsylvania* (New York & Chicago 1904) I, 142; J. Smith Futhey & Gilbert Cope, *History of Chester County, Pennsylvania* (Philadelphia 1881) p. 349; Stewart Huston, "The Iron Industry of Chester County," In J. Bennett Nolan, ed., *Southeastern Pennsylvania* (Philadelphia & New York [1943]) I, 279 [Hereinafter Huston in Nolan]; Lukens Steel Company, [*Handbook*] (Coatesville, Pa., [1924]) p. 8; "One Hundred and Thirty Years of Iron and Steel Making," *The Iron Trade Review* XLVI:26 (June 30, 1910) p. 1266; Information from Dr. John B. Riggs, Eleutherian Mills Historical Library; James M. Swank, *History of The Manufacture of Iron in All Ages* (Philadelphia 1892) p. 195.

Early Life, Background & Characteristics of Rebecca Pennock Lukens
The writer is especially indebted to Mr. Stewart Huston of Lukens Steel Company for information regarding this and all phases of Rebecca Lukens' life and career. For further details, see *The Biographical Cyclopaedia of American Women* (New York 1924) I, 12-15; Rebecca Lukens, Unpublished Autobiography (Courtesy Mr. Stewart Huston) *passim*; "Rebecca Webb Pennock Lukens," *DAB*; George Valentine Massey II, *The Pennocks of Primitive Hall* (West Chester, Pa., 1951) p. 95; Clara Huston Miller, *Reminiscences*. For Private Circulation only (Courtesy Mr. Stewart Huston)

passim; Toni Taylor, "Rebecca Lukens, Iron Master," *Steelways* [I]:12 (September 1947) *passim* [This article was reprinted in the *Bulletin* of the Commonwealth of Pennsylvania Department of Internal Affairs XVI:5 (April 1948) pp. 3-7]; Robert W. Wolcott, *A Woman in Steel—Rebecca Lukens (1794-1854)* ([New York] 1940) *passim* [Newcomen Address] (Courtesy Mrs. Arthur Holden).

For the legend of the "Brandywine," see Elizabeth Montgomery, *Reminiscences of Wilmington* (Philadelphia 1851) p. 8.

Federal Slitting Mill & Brandywine Works under Isaac Pennock

The Biographical Cyclopaedia of American Women, op. cit., I, 12; "Centennial of the Lukens Iron & Steel Company's Plant," *The Iron Age* 85:26 (June 30, 1910) p. 1562; "A Century And a Quarter In Iron And Steel," *op. cit.,* pp. 37-43; Cope & Ashmead, *op. cit.,* I, 142 f; Futhey & Cope, *op. cit.,* p. 349; Huston in Nolan I, 275 ff; Ruth Lawrence, ed., *Colonial Families of America* (New York n.d.) V, 333, 335 f; Lukens, Autobiography, *op. cit.;* Lukens Steel Company, [*Handbook*], *op. cit.,* pp. 7, 9; Lukens Steel Company, *Steel Plates And Their Fabrication* (Coatesville, Pa., [1947]) p. 5; Miller, *op. cit.,* p. 44; "One Hundred and Thirty Years of Iron and Steel Making," *op. cit.,* pp. 1263 f, 1267; "The Story of Lukens is the Story of Steel," *The Iron Age* 136:1 (July 4, 1935) p. 99; Swank, *op. cit.,* p. 195; Taylor, *op. cit.,* p. 6; Wolcott, *op. cit.,* pp. 12 ff.

Rebecca's Formal Education

The school, described but not identified by Rebecca Lukens in her unpublished Autobiography, has been identified by the writer as the Hilles Boarding School for Young Ladies in Wilmington, for details of which, see *Friends in Wilmington 1738-1938* (N.p. [1938]) p. 52; Samuel E. Hilles, *Memorials of the Hilles Family* (Cincinnati 1928) pp. 12 ff; Information from Mrs. W. Francis Lindell, Librarian, Historical Society of Delaware; Montgomery, *Reminiscences, op. cit.,* p. 269; Lyman P. Powell, *The History of Education in Delaware* (Washington, D.C., 1893) p. 49; J. Thomas Scharf, *History of Delaware 1609-1888* (Philadelphia 1888) II, 687 f.

Courtship of Dr. Charles Lukens; Married Life

Isabella P. Huston, *Autumn Leaves* (Philadelphia 1873) pp. 25, 87 f, 92 (Courtesy Mr. Stewart Huston); Lukens, Autobiography; Miller, *op. cit.,* pp. 31, 42; Wolcott, *op. cit.,* p. 11.

Charles Lukens' Activities in Iron Industry; The Codorus; Lukens' Death

The Biographical Cyclopaedia of American Women, op. cit., I, 12; Alexander Crosby Brown, "The Sheet Iron Steamboat Codorus," *The American Neptune* X:3 (July 1950) *passim*; "Centennial of the Lukens Iron & Steel Company's Plant," *The Iron Age, op. cit.,* p. 1562; "A Century And A Quarter In Iron And Steel," *The Iron Age, op. cit.,* pp. 38 f, 43 f; Cope & Ashmead, *op. cit.,* I, 142 f; Chauncey M. Depew, ed., *1795-1895 One*

Hundred Years of American Commerce (New York 1895) I, 323 f; John Elgar to Dr. Charles Lukens, York, Pa., March 31, 1825 (Courtesy Mr. Stewart Huston); Futhey & Cope, *op. cit.*, p. 349; Isabella P. Huston, *op. cit.*, p. 24; Huston in Nolan I, 278; Information from Mr. Stewart Huston; Lawrence, *op. cit.*, V, 333 ff, 336; Rebecca Lukens, Autobiography; Rebecca Lukens, Unpublished Statement . . . In connection with adjustment of her interest in her Father's estate, and a History of her Labors in conducting her business affairs, Brandywine, September 10, 1850 (Courtesy Mr. Stewart Huston); Lukens Steel Company, [*Handbook*], *op. cit.*, p. 7; Lukens Steel Company, *Steel Plates And Their Fabrication, op. cit.*, p. 5; Miller, *op. cit.*, pp. 31 ff; Miscellaneous Docket 17 p. 129 (Orphans Court, Chester County Court House); "The Story of Lukens is the Story of Steel," *The Iron Age, op. cit.*, pp. 99 f; Taylor, *op. cit.*, p. 7; Wolcott, *op. cit.*, pp. 14, 17 f.

Rebecca Lukens in the Iron Industry: Her Control of Brandywine, Her Problems & Achievements; Her Death & Growth of the Plant

Of particular importance is the splendid collection of Lukens MS material at Eleutherian Mills Historical Library. This consists of ledgers, daybooks, cash books, correspondence, shipments, letter books and accounts. The material was made available to the writer through the courtesy of Dr. Charles David and Dr. J.B. Riggs.

In addition, see Accounts of Rebecca W. Lukens Administratrix of Charles Lukens (No. 7700, Chester County Court House) & A Supplement to the Account of Rebecca W. Lukens Administratrix (Chester County Court House); Articles of Copartnership . . . between Abraham Gibbons Jr and Rebecca W. Lukens (October 1, 1847) (Courtesy Mr. Stewart Huston); Robert M. Barr, *Pennsylvania State Reports* II, 129-138; Gertrude Bosler Biddle & Sarah Dickinson Lowrie, eds., *Notable Women of Pennsylvania* (Philadelphia 1942) p. 123; *The Biographical Cyclopaedia of American Women, op. cit.*, I, 15; Brandywine House, Account Book (Chester County Historical Society); "Centennial of the Lukens Iron & Steel Co.," *The Iron Trade Review* XLVII:1 (July 7, 1910) pp. 13 f; "Centennial of the Lukens Iron & Steel Company's Plant," *The Iron Age, op. cit.*, pp. 1563 f, 1566; "A Century And A Quarter In Iron And Steel," *The Iron Age, op. cit.*, pp. 40, 44, 48, 50; Cope & Ashmead, *op. cit.*, I, 142 ff; *Documents relating to the Manufacture of Iron in Pennsylvania* (Philadelphia 1850) pp. 19, 23, & folding table at end; *The Friend* XXVIII:33 (April 28, 1855) p. 264 (Courtesy Mrs. Betty Liveright, Friends Historical Library of Swarthmore College); John Fritz, "Early Days in the Rolling Mills," *The Iron Trade Review* XLVII:2 (July 14, 1910) pp. 89, 92; George W. Harris, *Pennsylvania State Reports* XIII, 253-260, XX, 268-280; Charles Lukens Huston, "Rebecca Webb Lukens," MS (Courtesy Mr. Stewart Huston); I.P. Huston, *op. cit.*, pp. 24 f, 88 ff, 91; Huston in Nolan I, 278 ff, 281 ff; Information from Mr. Stewart Huston; Lawrence, *op. cit.*, V, 322, 336 f; Letters of Administration in estate of Dr. Charles Lukens (Chester County Court House); R.W. Lukens to her daughter, Martha, Northumberland, August, n.y. (Chester County Historical Society);

Rebecca Lukens to Mrs. Hannah Pennock Steel, Brandywine, May 22, 1837 (Courtesy Mr. Stewart Huston); Rebecca Lukens, [Diary] begun August 14, 1849 (Chester County Historical Society); Rebecca Lukens, Receipt Book (Chester County Historical Society); Rebecca Lukens, Unpublished Statement, *op. cit.* [This, with the materials at Eleutherian Mills Historical Library, is the most important single source for Rebecca Lukens' business career]; Rebecca W. Lukens, Will in Will Book U, Vol. 20, p. 351 (Chester County Court House); "Rebecca Webb Pennock Lukens," *DAB*; Lukens Steel Company, [*Handbook*], *op. cit.*, pp. 7 ff, 10; Lukens Steel Company, *Steel Plates And Their Fabrication, op. cit.*, pp. 5 f; "Lukens Steel Co. 'Then And Now,'" *Lukens Plate* I:13 & 14 (November 23, & December 21, 1934) pp. 1-2, p. 3 (Courtesy Mr. Stewart Huston); Miller, *op. cit.*, pp. 32 f, 43 ff, 46 ff, 53 f, 69, 71 ff, 106 ff, 141; "One Hundred and Thirty Years of Iron and Steel Making," *The Iron Trade Review, op. cit.*, pp. 1264 ff, 1267 f; *Paper Book. In the Matter of Isaac Pennock's Estate, passim* (Courtesy Mr. Stewart Huston); John B. Pearse, *A Concise History of the Iron Manufacture of the American Colonies . . . and of Pennsylvania* (Philadelphia 1876) pp. 180 f; Isaac Pennock, Will of April 5, 1824 & Codicil (Book P, Vol. 15, p. 60, No. 7484, Chester County Court House); Records of Administration Accounts & Auditors' Reports, Account Docket 3 p. 129 (Chester County Court House); Taylor, *op. cit., passim*; *Village Record* (August 10, 1825) (Clipping, Chester County Historical Society); Wolcott, *op. cit., passim*; "Woman Managed Lukens In 1825," *Lukens Plate* II:7 (July 2, 1935) p. 4 (Courtesy Mr. Stewart Huston).

The family litigation in connection with the estate of Isaac Pennock arose from the ambiguity in the latter's Will and Codicil. He had bequeathed to his wife "the use, benefit, and profits of all my real estate during her natural life, and also all my personal estate . . . . absolutely, having full confidence that she will leave the surplus to be divided, at her decease, justly, amongst my children." The case was carried from the Orphans Court of Chester County to the Supreme Court of Pennsylvania to determine whether Isaac Pennock's Will had bestowed a gift upon his wife or created a trust in favor of his children. The decree was rendered on January 27, 1853, that absolute ownership of Isaac Pennock's personal property had been given to his widow.

CHAPTER 11

VICTORIA C. WOODHULL

Opening of Woodhull, Claflin & Company
"The Bewitching Brokers," *The New York Herald* (February 9, 1870) p. 9; Henry Clews, *Fifty Years In Wall Street* (New York [1908]) p. 442; *The New York Herald* (January 20, 1870) p. 9; Matthew Hale Smith, *Bulls and Bears of New York* (Hartford & Chicago 1874) pp. 272-276; "Sunbeams," *The Sun* (April 11, 1870) p. 2; Theodore Tilton, *Victoria C.*

Woodhull. A Biographical Sketch. The Golden Age Tracts. No. 3 (New York 1871) p. 27; "Woman On 'Change," *The World* (February 8, 1870) p. 5; *The Woman's Journal* I:7 (February 19, 1870) p. 50; "Women in Wall Street," *The New York Herald* (January 22, 1870) p. 6; "Women in Wall Street," *The World* (February 8, 1870) p. 4; Victoria Claflin Woodhull & Tennessee C. Claflin, *The Human Body The Temple Of God* (London 1890) pp. 275, 286-293, 299; "Woodhull, Claflin & Co.," *The Sun* (February 7, 1870) p. 1.

Early Life of Victoria Woodhull
Beril Becker, *Whirlwind in Petticoats* (Garden City, N.Y., 1947) *passim* [fictionalized account]; *Brief Sketches of The Life of Victoria Woodhull (Mrs. John Biddulph Martin)* (N.p., n.d.) pp. 11-15, 27 f; Tennie C. Claflin, *The Ethics of Sexual Equality* (New York 1873) p. 11; G.S. Darewin, *Synopsis of the Lives of Victoria C. Woodhull, . . . and Tennessee Claflin* (London n.d.) pp. 10, 33 f; [M.F. Darwin], *One Moral Standard For All* (N.p., n.d.) pp. 2-8; Stewart H. Holbrook, *Dreamers of The American Dream* (New York 1957) p. 197; Gerald W. Johnson, *The Lunatic Fringe* (Philadelphia & New York [1957]) pp. 83-91; "A Lamp Without Oil," *The New-York Times* (February 22, 1872) p. 4; *Leaflet of the Manor House Club, Norton Park, near Tewkesbury. No. III* (N.p., n.d.) *passim*; *Men And Women of The Time. . . . Thirteenth Edition Revised . . . by G. Washington Moon* (London 1891) pp. 610 f; Emanie Sachs, *"The Terrible Siren"* (New York 1928) *passim* [the most substantial attempt to document Victoria Woodhull's career]; Tilton, *op. cit., passim*; Irving Wallace, *The Square Pegs* (New York 1957) pp. 101, 107-111; Charles Henry Wight, *Genealogy of the Claflin Family* (New York [1903]) p. 257; Mary Gould Woodhull & Francis Bowes Stevens, *Woodhull Genealogy* (Philadelphia 1904) p. 211; "Victoria Claflin Woodhull," *DAB.*

Although Victoria declared that she married Blood in Dayton, Ohio, in 1866 [See Woodhull & Claflin, *The Human Body The Temple Of God, op. cit.,* p. 602] their marriage record of July 14, 1866 (Probate Court, Montgomery County, Ohio, Record G p. 518) does not actually show a return for marriage, but rather an intention for marriage.

Brokerage & Banking Business of Woodhull, Claflin & Company: Vanderbilt Connection, Firm Projects, Accounts, Activities & Wall Street Background
Wayne Andrews, *The Vanderbilt Legend* (New York [1941]) pp. 147 ff; "The Bewitching Brokers," *The New York Herald* (February 9, 1870) p. 9, (February 10, 1870) p. 9 & (February 13, 1870) p. 7; *Brief Sketches, op. cit.,* p. 15; Emily Edson Briggs, *The Olivia Letters* (New York & Washington 1906) p. 238; Junius Henri Browne, *The Great Metropolis* (Hartford 1869) pp. 41-48, 337 f; Thomas Byrnes, *Professional Criminals of America* (New York [1886]) p. 313; "The Check Frauds," *The World* (March 20, 1870) p. 8; Claflin, *The Ethics of Sexual Equality, op. cit.,* pp. 21 ff; Clews, *op. cit.,* pp. 437-445; "The Coming Woman," *The World*

(January 28, 1869) p. 7; Kinahan Cornwallis, *The Gold Room And the New York Stock Exchange and Clearing House* (New York [1879]) pp. 31, 35; Darewin, *op. cit.*, pp. 10-13; [Darwin], *op. cit.*, pp. 11-15; *The Evening Telegram* [New York] (February 18, 1870) p. 1; "Finance And Trade," *The Evening Post* (February 5, 1870) p. 3; William Worthington Fowler, *Twenty Years of Inside Life in Wall Street* (New York 1880) p. 456; Robert H. Fuller, *Jubilee Jim* (New York 1928) p. 151; John Hickling & Co., *Men and Idioms of Wall Street* (New York 1875) *passim*; Holbrook, *op. cit.*, p. 197; Johnson, *op. cit.*, p. 94; Wheaton J. Lane, *Commodore Vanderbilt* (New York 1942) pp. 310 ff; Lloyd Morris, *Incredible New York* (New York [1951]) pp. 129 f; *New York City Business Directories* 1870-1876; *New-York [Daily] Tribune* (March 2, 1878) p. 3, (October 16, 1878) p. 4; Leon Oliver, *The Great Sensation* (Chicago 1873) pp. 37, 58; "The Queens of Finance," *The New York Herald* (January 22, 1870) p. 10 & (February 5, 1870) p. 8; *The Revolution* V:8 (February 24, 1870) pp. 123 f, V:10 (March 10, 1870) pp. 154 f & V:12 (March 24, 1870) p. 188, VI:2 (July 14, 1870) p. 31; Sachs, *op. cit.*, pp. 49-54 & *passim*; *Scrapbooks of Clippings Relating to the Beecher-Tilton Trial* (New York Public Library); Robert Shaplen, *Free Love and Heavenly Sinners* (New York [1954]) pp. 124 f, 138; Arthur D. Howden Smith, *Commodore Vanderbilt* (New York 1927) pp. 293, 295 f, 299 f; Smith, *Bulls and Bears, op. cit.*, pp. 272-276; Tilton, *op. cit.*, p. 27; *Theodore Tilton against Henry Ward Beecher. Verbatim Report of the Trial* (New York n.d.) III, 392; [Joseph Treat], *Beecher, Tilton, Woodhull, The Creation of Society* (New York 1874) pp. 4, 10 f; Wallace, *op. cit.*, pp. 104 ff; "Woman On 'Change," *The World* (February 8, 1870) p. 5; Woodhull & Claflin, *The Human Body, op. cit.*, pp. 272-310, 458; "Woodhull, Claflin & Co.," *The Sun* (February 7, 1870) p. 1; *Woodhull & Claflin's Weekly* I:19 (September 17, 1870) p. 11, I:24 (October 29, 1870) p. 9, VI:3 (June 21, 1873) p. 9, VI:20 (October 18, 1873) p. 12.

Woodhull Bid for Presidency
  The New York Herald (April 2, 1870) p. 8.

Woodhull & Claflin's Weekly
  Woodhull & Claflin's Weekly I:1 (May 14, 1870)—XI:20 (April 15, 1876) *passim* [Many of these issues were examined through the courtesy of Mrs. Arthur C. Holden, whose library provided numerous sources for this chapter]. The exposure of swindles began with the issue of I:18 (September 10, 1870) from which (p. 8) the quotation regarding that exposure is taken.
  See also Clews, *op. cit.*, pp. 442 f; [Darwin], *op. cit.*, p. 15; Holbrook, *op. cit.*, p. 198; Frederic Hudson, *Journalism in the United States, from 1690 to 1872* (New York 1873) p. 499; *Leaflet of the Manor House Club, Bredons Norton, near Tewkesbury. No. II* (N.p., n.d.) p. 2; Frank Luther Mott, *A History of American Magazines* (Cambridge 1938) III, 95, 443-452; *The New York Herald* (May 15, 1870) p. 6; Oliver, *op. cit.*, p. 40;

Sachs, *op. cit., passim*; Tilton, *op. cit.*, p. 27; *Troy Daily Whig* (September 15, 1871) p. [2]; Wallace, *op. cit.*, pp. 113 f; Woodhull & Claflin, *The Human Body, op. cit.*, pp. 310, 482 f.

Victoria & The IWA

John R. Commons, *History of Labour in The United States* (New York 1918) II, 210 f, 213; [Darwin], *op. cit.*, p. 24; Philip S. Foner, *History Of The Labor Movement In The United States* (New York [1947]) pp. 415 f; William Z. Foster, *History of the Three Internationals* (New York [1955]) pp. 121 f; Samuel Gompers, *Seventy Years of Life And Labor* (New York [1925]) I, 55, 57 f; Morris Hillquit, *History of Socialism in the United States* (New York & London 1906) pp. 197 f; *Frank Leslie's Illustrated Newspaper* XXXIII:849 (January 6, 1872) pp. 263 ff; Charles A. Madison, *Critics & Crusaders* (New York [1947]) p. 449; Mott, *op. cit.*, III, 302 n. 141; Maximilien Rubel, *Bibliographie des Oeuvres de Karl Marx* (Paris 1956) p. 63 #70; Shaplen, *op. cit.*, p. 139; Wallace, *op. cit.*, p. 115; *Woodhull & Claflin's Weekly* III:15 (August 26, 1871) p. 7, IV:7 (December 30, 1871) p. 3 [issue containing "Communist Manifesto," courtesy Mrs. Arthur C. Holden].

According to Frederick B. Adams, Jr., *Radical Literature in America* (Stamford, Conn., 1939) p. 49, Victoria Woodhull's *A New Constitution for the United States of the World* (New York 1872) was "an early step in the direction of a League of Nations."

Victoria Woodhull's Writings & Speeches

Goethe's Elective Affinities: with an introduction by Victoria C. Woodhull (Boston 1872) pp. iii-vii; "A Lamp Without Oil," *The New-York Times* (February 22, 1872) p. 4; Morris, *op. cit.*, pp. 131 f; *New-York Commercial Advertiser* (August 4, 1871) p. 2; *The New York Herald* (April 16, 1870) p. 5, (April 25, 1870) p. 5, (May 2, 1870) p. 8, (May 9, 1870) p. 8, (May 16, 1870) p. 8, (May 27, 1870) p. 4, (June 4, 1870) p. 5, (June 19, 1870) p. 8, (July 4, 1870) p. 12, (July 11, 1870) p. 11; *The New-York Times* (August 4, 1871) p. 8; Shaplen, *op. cit.*, p. 129; Victoria C. Woodhull to Charles Haseltine, New York, October 17, 1873 (Special Collections, Columbia University); Victoria C. Woodhull, *The Origin, Tendencies And Principles of Government* (New York 1871) *passim*; Victoria C. Woodhull, *A Speech on the Impending Revolution* (New York 1872) *passim*; Victoria C. Woodhull, *A Speech on The Principles Of Finance* (New York 1871 & London 1894) *passim*; Victoria C. Woodhull, *A Speech on The Principles of Social Freedom* (New York 1871) *passim*; Woodhull & Claflin, *The Human Body, op. cit., passim*; *Woodhull & Claflin's Weekly* IV:11 (January 27, 1872) p. 3, IV:18 (March 16, 1872) pp. 9 f, V:6 (June 22, 1872) p. 4, VI:11 (August 16, 1873) p. 7, VI:15 (September 13, 1873) pp. 2-7, 9, 14, VI:17 (September 27, 1873) pp. 3, 6, VI:22 (November 1, 1873) pp. 2, 4-7, 9 f, VI:26 (November 29, 1873) p. 9.

The Woodhull Memorial, Attempt to Vote, & Candidacy for Presidency
   Brief Sketches, op. cit., pp. 16 f; Briggs, *op. cit.,* pp. 229 ff, 232, 237;
Olympia Brown, *Acquaintances, Old and New, Among Reformers* (N.p.
1911) pp. 90 f; *The Congressional Globe* (Washington 1871) pp. 838, 888;
Ibid, Third Session Forty-First Congress. Part I, 218, 272; *The Correspond-
ence between The Victoria League and Victoria C. Woodhull* (printed
brochure, courtesy Mrs. Arthur C. Holden); [Darwin], *op. cit.,* pp. 15 ff,
18 f, 21, 28 ff; Paulina W. Davis, *A History of the National Woman's
Rights Movement, for Twenty Years* (New York 1871) *passim;* Rheta
Childe Dorr, *Susan B. Anthony* (New York 1928) pp. 233 ff; *The Golden
Age Tracts No. 2* (New York 1871) p. 8; Ida Husted Harper, *The Life
And Work of Susan B. Anthony* (Indianapolis 1898—1908) I, 375 ff; Hol-
brook, *op. cit.,* p. 205; *House of Representatives. 41st Congress, 3d Session.
Report No. 22 & Report No. 22, Part 2, passim; The Humanitarian* IX:1
(July 1896) pp. 1-8; *Frank Leslie's Illustrated Newspaper* XXXI:801 (Feb-
ruary 24, 1871) pp. 347, 349; Alma Lutz, *Created Equal A Biography of
Elizabeth Cady Stanton* (New York [1940]) pp. 209, 220; Alma Lutz,
Susan B. Anthony (Boston [1959]) pp. 180-186, 191-195; Morris, *op. cit.,*
pp. 130, 133, 136; *New-York Daily Tribune* (January 16, 1871) p. 8;
The New York Herald (January 12, 1871) p. 3, (November 8, 1871) p. 4
& (January 12, 1872) p. 10; *The New-York Times* (November 8, 1871)
p. 2; Sachs, *op. cit., passim;* Elizabeth Cady Stanton, Susan B. Anthony,
and Matilda Joslyn Gage, eds., *History of Woman Suffrage* (Rochester,
N.Y., 1887) II, 443-446, 448, 461, 464, 482; Wallace, *op. cit.,* pp. 106,
116 ff, 130-134, 139; Victoria C. Woodhull, *The Argument for Woman's
Electoral Rights* (London 1887) *passim* (Courtesy Mrs. Arthur C. Holden);
Victoria C. Woodhull, *Carpenter and Cartter Reviewed* (New York 1872)
passim; Victoria C. Woodhull, *A Lecture on Constitutional Equality* (New
York 1871) *passim;* Woodhull, *The Origin, Tendencies And Principles of
Government, op. cit., passim;* Woodhull & Claflin, *The Human Body, op.
cit., passim; Woodhull & Claflin's Weekly* II:1 (November 19, 1870) p. 8,
IV:11 (January 27, 1872) p. 5, IV:27 (May 18, 1872) p. 13, IV:28 (May
25, 1872) *passim,* [IV]:29 (June 1, 1872) *passim,* [IV]:30 (June 8, 1872)
p. 8, V:5 [sic] (June 15, 1872) pp. 8 f, V:6 (June 22, 1872) pp. 9, 12,
V:7 (November 2, 1872) p. 15, V:25 (May 24, 1873) p. 16.

Claflin Scandal; Beecher-Tilton Scandal; Victoria's Lectures
   The literature is voluminous. For the most pertinent material, see Katha-
rine Anthony, *Susan B. Anthony* (Garden City, N.Y., 1954) p. 314; "The
Arrest of Woodhull & Claflin," *The Sun* (February 3, 1873) p. 3; *The
Beecher-Tilton War* (N.p., n.d.) *passim;* William C. Beecher & Rev. Samuel
Scoville, *A Biography of Rev. Henry Ward Beecher* (New York 1888) *pas-
sim;* "Blood, Woodhull, Claflin. The Great Scandal at Essex Market," *The
New York Herald* (May 16, 1871) p. 3; Heywood Broun & Margaret Leech,
Anthony Comstock (New York 1927) *passim;* "A Card From Mrs. Wood-
hull," *The World* (May 22, 1871) p. 3; *Court of Appeals. Theodore Tilton,
Respondent. v. Henry Ward Beecher, Appellant* (N.p., n.d.) *passim;* Dare-

win, *op. cit.*, pp. 24 f; [Darwin], *op. cit.*, pp. 38 ff, 43 ff, 46; Walter Davenport & James C. Derieux, *Ladies, Gentlemen and Editors* (Garden City, N.Y., 1960) pp. 117-122; *The Day's Doings* X:235 (November 30, 1872) p. 3; J.E.P. Doyle, *Plymouth Church And Its Pastor* (Hartford 1874) p. 13; *The Great Brooklyn Romance* (New York 1874) *passim* [Here it is suggested that Tilton published his biography of Mrs. Woodhull to disarm her and prevent her from revealing his family secret]; *Harper's Weekly* XVI:790 (February 17, 1872) p. 140; Paxton Hibben, *Henry Ward Beecher* (New York [1927]) pp. 283 ff, 293, 310 f; Holbrook, *op. cit.*, pp. 203 f; *The Independent* XXIII:1172 (May 18, 1871) p. 4; Inez Haynes Irwin, *Angels and Amazons* (Garden City, N.Y., 1933) pp. 252-257; Johnson, *op. cit.*, pp. 100 ff, 103; S.M. Landis, *The Prohibited Lecture! on Woodhull and Beecher, analyzing Free-Love* (Philadelphia [1873]) *passim*; "A Legend Of Good Women," *The Golden Age* I:18 (July 1, 1871) p. 6; *Frank Leslie's Illustrated Newspaper* XXXV:897 (December 7, 1872) p. 198; Lutz, *Created Equal*, *op. cit.*, p. 213; Charles A. Madison, "Benjamin R. Tucker: Individualist and Anarchist," *The New England Quarterly* XVI:3 (September 1943) *passim*; Charles F. Marshall, *The True History of the Brooklyn Scandal* (Philadelphia, Chicago & St. Louis [1874]) *passim*; *The Memphis Sunday Appeal* (November 17, 1872) p. 1; Morris, *op. cit.*, pp. 136 f; James M. Nelson, "America's Victoria," *Bulletin of the Historical and Philosophical Society of Ohio* XVI:4 (October 1958) pp. 324-339; *New-York Daily Tribune* (March 28, 1873) p. 2; *Official Report of The Trial of Henry Ward Beecher* (New York 1875) *passim*; Oliver, *op. cit.*, *passim*; Richard H. Rovere, *Howe & Hummel* (New York 1947) pp. 131 ff; Sachs, *op. cit.*, *passim*; *Scrapbooks of Clippings Relating to the Beecher-Tilton Trial* (New York Public Library); Shaplen, *op. cit.*, *passim*; Harriet Beecher Stowe, *My Wife and I* (Boston [1871]) *passim*; Lyman Beecher Stowe, *Saints Sinners and Beechers* (Indianapolis [1934]) pp. 309, 316; *The Sun* (June 30, 1873) p. 2; "Tennie And Vic," *New York Dispatch* (November 3, 1872) p. 1; *The Thunderbolt* (New York, Albany & Troy, May 1873) No. 1, *passim* (In *Scrapbooks of Clippings Relating to the Beecher-Tilton Trial* Vol. II); Tilton, *Victoria C. Woodhull*, *op. cit.*, *passim*; *Theodore Tilton against Henry Ward Beecher. Verbatim Report of the Trial* (New York n.d.) *passim*; George Francis Train, *My Life in Many States and in Foreign Lands* (New York 1902) pp. 323 ff, 328, 331; [Treat], *op. cit.*, *passim*; Earle F. Walbridge, *Literary Characters Drawn from Life Supplement* [Separate from the *Papers of the Bibliographical Society of America* 47:2 (1953)] p. 24; Wallace, *op. cit.*, pp. 120 ff, 123, 129 f, 134 ff, 137 ff, 139 ff; Francis P. Williamson, *Beecher and His Accusers* (Philadelphia [1874]) p. 105; Forrest Wilson, *Crusader in Crinoline* (Philadelphia, London & New York [1947]) pp. 568 f, 581, 587 f; Victoria C. Woodhull, *The Elixir of Life* (New York 1873) *passim*; Victoria C. Woodhull, *A Speech on The Garden of Eden* (New York 1876) *passim*; Victoria C. Woodhull, *Tried As By Fire; . . . An Oration* (New York 1874) *passim*; Woodhull & Claflin, *The Human Body*, *op. cit.*, pp. 359 f, 363 f, 369-374, 379, 382, 393, 591 ff & *passim*; *Woodhull & Claflin's Weekly* V:7 (November 2, 1872)— V:[10] (February 8, 1873) *passim*, V:18 (April 5, 1873) pp. 3 f, V:19 (April 12, 1873) p. 7, V:24 (May 17, 1873) *passim*, V:27 (June 7, 1873) p. 2, VI:2 (June 14, 1873) *passim*, VI:5 (July 5, 1873) *passim*, VII:16 (March 21, 1874) p. 8, VIII:18 (October 3, 1874) p. 4; "Victoria Claflin Woodhull," *DAB*; "Mrs. Woodhull and Her Critics," *The New-York Times* (May 22, 1871) p. 5; "The Woodhull War," *The New York Herald* (May 17, 1871) p. 10; "Woodhull," *The Memphis Sunday Appeal* (November 17, 1872) p. 2.

Vanderbilt Will Case
Brief Sketches, op. cit., p. 26; Holbrook, op. cit., p. 204; Johnson, op. cit., pp. 103 f; The Last Will and Testament of Cornelius Vanderbilt (N.p., n.d.) passim; Sachs, op. cit., pp. 287 f; Vanderbilt Will. Scrapbook of Newspaper Clippings 1877-78 (New York Public Library) passim; Wallace, op. cit., pp. 141 f; Woodhull & Claflin, The Human Body, op. cit., pp. 568 ff, 579; "Victoria C. Woodhull," DAB.

Victoria's Life in England; J.B. Martin; Victoria's Death
Brief Sketches, op. cit., pp. 21 ff, 27; "Tennie Claflin Married," The World (October 25, 1885) p. 3; Clews, op. cit., p. 444; Clipping & Broadsheets 1889 in Miscellaneous Papers, New York Public Library, Manuscript Division; Herbert Cook, ed., A Catalogue of the Paintings at Doughty House (London 1913-1915) passim; "Lady Cook Dies In London At 77," The New York Times (January 20, 1923) p. 13; Darewin, op. cit., pp. 30, 35; [Darwin], op. cit., pp. 8, 47; The Humanitarian I:1 (July 1892)—III:4 (October 1893), VIII:1 (January 1896)—XI:5 (November 1897) passim [many issues courtesy Mrs. Arthur C. Holden]; Henry James, "The Siege of London," The Great Short Novels (New York [1944]) p. 236 & passim [The novel first appeared in Cornhill Magazine January-February 1883]; Leaflet of the Manor House Club. No. III, op. cit., p. 39; Madeleine Legge, "Two Noble Women, Nobly Planned" (N.p. [1893]) passim; John Biddulph Martin, The Future of the United States (London 1884) passim; John Biddulph Martin, "The Grasshopper" in Lombard Street (London 1892) passim; Victoria Woodhull (Mrs. John Biddulph Martin), Humanitarian Money (London 1892) passim; Victoria C. Woodhull Martin, The Rapid Multiplication of The Unfit (London & New York 1891) passim; Victoria Claflin Woodhull Martin, Stirpiculture; or, The Scientific Propagation Of The Human Race (London 1888) passim; "Victoria Martin, Suffragist, Dies," The New York Times (June 11, 1927) p. 19; Men And Women of The Time, op. cit., p. 611; Mott, op. cit., III, 452 n. 19; T.H. Packer, Round Bredon Hill (Cheltenham 1903) p. 25; Sachs, op. cit., passim; The Times [London] (February 24, 1894) p. 11, (March 5, 1894) p. 3, (April 20, 1894) p. 13; Wallace, op. cit., pp. 142 ff, 145 ff; Who's Who In America (1926-1927) XIV, 1275; Woman's Who's Who of America 1914-1915 p. 545; The Women's International Agricultural Club, The Manor House, Bredon's Norton (N.p., n.d.) pp. 1 f; Woodhull & Claflin,

The Human Body, op. cit., pp. 568 f, 571 ff, 580 ff, 596 f; "Victoria C. Woodhull," *DAB.*

CHAPTER 12

CANDACE WHEELER

Influence of the Centennial Exposition of 1876
  Catalogue of Louis Prang's Collection of Oil and Water-Color Paintings (Boston 1899) p. 4; *Catalogue of the Pedestal Fund Art Loan Exhibition, at the National Academy of Design, ... December, 1883* preliminary page; Maud Howe Elliott, ed., *Art And Handicraft in the Woman's Building of the World's Columbian Exposition Chicago, 1893* (Paris & New York 1893) p. 62; Mrs. Burton Harrison, *Recollections Grave And Gay* (New York 1912) p. 308; Information from Prof. Robert Koch, Southern Connecticut State College, New Haven, to whom the author is deeply indebted for his help in the preparation of this chapter; James D. McCabe, *The Illustrated History of the Centennial Exhibition* (Cincinnati, Philadelphia, Chicago, etc., [1876]) pp. 144, 368; Candace Wheeler, *The Development of Embroidery in America* (New York & London 1921) p. 109; Candace Wheeler, ed., *Household Art* (New York 1893) p. 122; Candace Wheeler, *Yesterdays In a Busy Life* (New York & London [1918]) pp. 210 f.

Candace Wheeler's Early Life (1827-1877); Her Marriage & Travels
  Gertrude A. Barber, *Marriages Taken from the [Delaware] Gazette From Nov. 1819 to August 28, 1844. Delhi, Delaware County, New York* (Typescript, New York Public Library) p. 91; *The Biographical Cyclopaedia of American Women* (New York 1925) II, 186 ff; Sarah K. Bolton, *Successful Women* (Boston [1888]) pp. 182 ff, 185 f, 194; Information from Mr. John H. Brinckerhoff, Prospect Cemetery Association, Jamaica, N.Y.; "Home of Stimson's Grandparents," *Long Island Forum* XIX:5 (May 1956) p. 92; Information from Marjorie H. Leek, Librarian, Long Island Collection, The Queens Borough Public Library; Marriage Certificate of Thomas M. Wheeler & Candace Thurber, June 28, 1844 (Courtesy Mr. Richard Simpson, Anaheim, California); *New York City Directories* 1860-1876; Theodore Sizer, ed., *The Recollections of John Ferguson Weir* (New York & New Haven 1957) pp. 49 f; Candace Wheeler, *Content In A Garden* (Boston & New York 1902) pp. 100, 105; Wheeler, *The Development of Embroidery, op. cit.,* pp. 43, 48 f; Wheeler, *Yesterdays, op. cit., passim;* "Mrs. Candace T. Wheeler Dies at 96," *The New York Times* (August 6, 1923) p. 11; *Who Was Who In America I 1897-1942* (Chicago 1942) p. 1327; *Woman's Who's Who of America 1914-1915* p. 871.

Society of Decorative Art
  The Art Interchange I:1 (September 18, 1878) p. 4, III:3 (August 6,

1879) p. 24; Bolton, *op. cit.,* pp. 189 f; *Catalogue of the Loan Exhibition in aid of the Society of Decorative Art, . . . at the National Academy of Design* [1877] *passim*; *Catalogue of the Loan Exhibition, 1878 in aid of the Society of Decorative Art* (New York 1878) *passim*; *First Annual Report of the Society of Decorative Art of the City of New York. Organized March 1877. . . . Presented January 1st, 1878 passim*; *Second Annual Report, . . . Presented January 1st, 1879 passim*; *Third Annual Report* [1880] *passim*; Mrs. Burton Harrison, *Recollections, op. cit.,* p. 308; Constance Cary Harrison, *Woman's Handiwork in Modern Homes* ([New York] 1881) p. 4; Dora Wheeler Keith, "The American Tapestry as Invented by Candace Wheeler," *Wellesley College Bulletin The Art Museum* II:1 (January 1936) Supplementary p. 9 b (Courtesy Alice C. Moore, Secretary, Department of Art, Wellesley College); "The Loan Exhibition," *New-York* [*Daily*] *Tribune* (October 16, 1878) p. 3; "The Society of Decorative Art," *Scribner's Monthly* XXII:5 (September 1881) pp. 699, 706; Candace Wheeler, "Art Education for Women," *The Outlook* LV:1 (January 2, 1897) pp. 85 f; Wheeler, *The Development of Embroidery, op. cit.,* pp. 102, 106, 109 f, 112-118, 121; Candace Wheeler, *How to Make Rugs* (New York 1902) p. 5; Wheeler, *Yesterdays, op. cit.,* pp. 212-224, 226; *The Woman's Book* (New York 1894) II, 217.

The Ladies' Art Association of New York had earlier made the "first effort to engraft decorative needlework upon any existing growth in this country." [See Mrs. Candace Wheeler, "Embroidery In America," clipping, courtesy Mr. H. Keith Simpson, Santa Barbara, California].

Woman's Exchange

The Art Interchange I:3 (October 16, 1878) p. 20, I:7 (December 11, 1878) p. iii; *The Biographical Cyclopaedia of American Women, op. cit.,* II, 187 f; Bolton, *op. cit.,* p. 190; Wheeler, *Yesterdays, op. cit.,* pp. 147, 224, 226 ff, 230.

Candace Wheeler & Tiffany's Associated Artists; Work Done

The Art Amateur XII:5 (April 1885) advertisement on verso of back cover; *The Art Work of Louis C. Tiffany* (Garden City, N.Y., 1914) *passim*; *Artistic Houses* (New York 1883-1884) Vols. I & II, *passim*; "The Associated Artists," *The Art Amateur* XII:2 (January 1885) p. 38; "The Associated Artists' Needlework," *The Art Amateur* VI:1 (December 1881) p. 13; *The Biographical Cyclopaedia of American Women, op. cit.,* II, 189; Bolton, *op. cit.,* pp. 191 ff; William C. Brownell, "Decoration in the Seventh Regiment Armory," *Scribner's Monthly* XXII:3 (July 1881) pp. 370 f, 375, 379 f; *Bulletin of The Metropolitan Museum of Art* XXIII:5 (May 1928) pp. 137 f; Oliver B. Bunce, *My House: An Ideal* (New York 1884) p. 69; Col. Emmons Clark, *History of the Seventh Regiment of New York* (New York 1890) II, 284 f, 295 f; "Samuel Colman," *DAB*; Clarence Cook, *"What Shall We Do With Our Walls?"* (New York 1881) p. 31; "Draperies of the Union League Club," *The Art Amateur* V:1 (June 1881) p. 17; Bess Furman, *White House Profile* (Indianapolis & New York [1951])

p. 232; Georgiana Brown Harbeson, *American Needlework* (New York 1938) p. 161; Mrs. Burton Harrison, "Some Work of the 'Associated Artists,'" *Harper's New Monthly Magazine* LXIX:411 (August 1884) pp. 343, 350; Harrison, *Woman's Handiwork in Modern Homes, op. cit.,* pp. 4 ff & *passim*; Charles Hurd, *The White House* (New York & London [1940]) p. 196; "Interior Paradises," *Appletons' Journal* N.S. VIII:46 (April 1880) p. 377; A.E. Ives, "A Talk About Wall-Paper," *The Art Amateur* XXVII:6 (November 1892) p. 160; Edgar Kaufmann, Jr., "At home with Louis C. Tiffany," *Interiors* CXVII:5 (December 1957) pp. 120, 122 ff, 125; Keith, *op. cit.,* p. 9 b; Robert Koch, *The Stained Glass Decades A Study of Louis Comfort Tiffany (1848-1933) and the Art Nouveau in America* (Doctoral Dissertation, Yale University, 1957) *passim*; Ethel Lewis, *The White House* (New York 1937) pp. 210 f; Mrs. John A. Logan, *The Part Taken By Women In American History* (Wilmington, Del., 1912) p. 753; "Movable Theater Stages," *Scientific American* L:14 (April 5, 1884) p. 208; "The New Decorations At The White House," *Harper's Weekly* XXVII:1359 (January 6, 1883) p. 11; "Notes on Decoration," *The Art Amateur* XII:3 (February 1885) p. 72; George C.D. Odell, *Annals of the New York Stage* (New York 1939) XI, 20; Information from Mary L. Peck & Mrs. Charles B. Salsbury, Mark Twain Library and Memorial Commission; "Recent Church Decoration," *The Art Amateur* V:6 (November 1881) p. 126; Information from Mrs. George Riggs, Port Washington, N.Y.; Aline B. Saarinen, *The Proud Possessors* (New York [1958]) pp. 153 f; Esther Singleton, *The Story of the White House* (New York 1907) II, 174; Gertrude Speenburgh, *The Arts of the Tiffanys* (Chicago 1956) *passim*; *The Spirit of the Times* XCVIII:26 (January 31, 1880) p. 638; Information from Mrs. Thomas K. Stevenson, New York City; "A Suggestive Exhibition of Designs," *The Art Amateur* V:6 (November 1881) p. 112; Information from Mrs. Herbert A. Taylor, Princeton, N.J.; *Third Annual Report of the Society of Decorative Art* [1880], *op. cit.,* p. 5; *Louis Comfort Tiffany 1848-1933. Museum of Contemporary Crafts of the American Craftsmen's Council, New York* [New York 1958] *passim*; "Louis Comfort Tiffany," *DAB*; "The Union League Club House," *Harper's Weekly* XXV:1260 (February 19, 1881) pp. 118 f; *The Union League Club of New York. Annual Reports, . . . March 1, 1882* (New York 1882) pp. 7, 73 f; "The Veterans' Room," *Harper's Weekly* XXV:1278 (June 25, 1881) pp. 413 f; *The Veteran's Room Seventh Regiment N.G.S.N.Y. Armory* ([New York] 1881) *passim*; Wheeler, "Art Education for Women," *op. cit.,* p. 86; Wheeler, *The Development of Embroidery, op. cit.,* pp. 121-126; Wheeler, ed., *Household Art, op. cit.,* pp. 57 ff, 71 f; Wheeler, *Yesterdays, op. cit.,* pp. 145, 147, 231-256; *The Woman's Book, op. cit.,* p. 218; "Work of the Associated Artists," *The Art Amateur* VII:1 (June 1882) p. 20.

The author examined the Veterans' Room of the Seventh Regiment Armory through the courtesy of Mr. William Hein & Col. G.F. Johnston.

The records of the Office of Public Buildings and Public Parks of the National Capital, now in the National Archives, include some correspondence between that office and Louis Tiffany (information from Jane F. Smith, Archivist in Charge, Interior Branch).

The Wheeler Tapestry; Pedestal Fund Art Loan Exhibition; Mrs. Wheeler's Development & General Credo on Decoration; Break with Tiffany

"The Associated Artists," *The Art Amateur* (January 1885) *op. cit.,* p. 38; Bolton, *op. cit.,* pp. 179 ff; *Catalogue of the Pedestal Fund Art Loan Exhibition, op. cit., passim*; Harbeson, *op. cit.,* p. 161; Harrison, "Some Work of the 'Associated Artists,'" *op. cit.,* pp. 343, 346 f; Rossiter Johnson, ed., *A History of the World's Columbian Exposition* (New York 1898) IV, 338-342; Keith, *op. cit., passim*; Koch, *op. cit.,* pp. 106 f; *Needle Woven Tapestry. Letters Patent to Alfred Julius Boult, ... A communication from abroad by Candace T. Wheeler. March 14, 1882. No. 1233, passim*; "The Pedestal Fund Art Loan Exhibition," *The Art Amateur* X:2 (January 1884) p. 46; *Specifications and Drawings of Patents issued from the United States Patent Office for November, 1882* (Washington, D.C., 1882) p. 1705 . . . . *January 23-30, 1883,* p. 1665; Speenburgh, *op. cit.,* p. 84; United States Patent Office. Candace Wheeler, Of Jamaica, New York. Art Of Embroidering And Embroidery. Specification forming part of Letters Patent No. 268,332, dated November 28, 1882. Application filed July 20, 1881, *passim*; United States Patent Office. Candace T. Wheeler, Of New York, N.Y. Fabric For Needle-Woven Tapestries. Specification forming part of Letters Patent No. 271,174, dated January 23, 1883. Application filed March 27, 1882, *passim*; *Wellesley College Bulletin The Art Museum* I:4 (June 1934) p. 9 (Courtesy Alice C. Moore, Secretary, Department of Art, Wellesley College); Candace Wheeler, "Country House Interiors," *The Christian Union* XLV:18 (April 30, 1892) pp. 840 f; Candace Wheeler, "Decoration of Walls," *The Outlook* LII:18 (November 2, 1895) pp. 705 f; Candace Wheeler, "Decorative Art," *The Architectural Record* IV:4 (April-June 1895) pp. 409-413; Wheeler, *The Development of Embroidery, op. cit.,* pp. 67 f, 108, 126, 137 f; Candace Wheeler, "Furnishing of Country Homes," *The Christian Union* XLV:17 (April 23, 1892) pp. 792 f; Wheeler, ed., *Household Art, op. cit., passim*; Candace Wheeler, "Interior Decoration," MS & Typescript (Courtesy Mr. Richard Simpson, Anaheim, California); Candace Wheeler, "Interior Decoration As a Profession for Women," *The Outlook* LI:14 & 16 (April 6 & 20, 1895) pp. 559 f & 649; Candace Wheeler, "Interiors of Summer Cottages," *The Christian Union* XLV:16 (April 16, 1892) pp. 741 f; Candace Wheeler, *Principles of Home Decoration With Practical Examples* (New York 1903) *passim.*

Candace Wheeler's Associated Artists: Textiles, Tapestries, Interior Decoration

The Art Amateur XVIII:1—6 (December 1887—May 1888) pp. 19 f, 46, 71, 99, 123, 147, XIX:1—2, 6 (June—July, November 1888) pp. 21, 46, 141, XX:3 (February 1889) p. 73; *The Art Digest* XV:8 (January 15, 1941) p. 30; "The Associated Artists," *The Art Amateur* (January 1885), *op. cit.,* pp. 38 ff; Clara Barrus, ed., *The Heart of Burroughs's Journals* (Boston & New York 1928) p. 141; *The Biographical Cyclopaedia of Amer-*

ican Women, op. cit., II, 187; Bolton, *op. cit.,* pp. 175-182, 192 ff, 195; Mary D. Brine, *My Boy And I* (N.p. 1881) [Illustrated for Tiffany's Associated Artists by Dora Wheeler]; *Bulletin of The Metropolitan Museum of Art* (May 1928), *op. cit.,* pp. 137 f; *Catalogue of Louis Prang's Collection of . . . Paintings, op. cit.,* pp. 4 f, 83, 92; Clippings & Typescript (Courtesy Mr. H. Keith Simpson, Santa Barbara, California); Collection of portières & textiles by Candace Wheeler & Associated Artists in Textile Study Room, Metropolitan Museum of Art (Courtesy Miss Edith Standen, Curator); *The Eighteenth* [through] *Fifty-Second Annual Report of the Trustees of the Cooper Union* (New York 1877—1911) *passim;* Elliott, ed., *op. cit.,* pp. 35, 59-67; Lydia Hoyt Farmer, ed., *The National Exposition Souvenir What America Owes To Women* (Buffalo, Chicago & New York 1893) p. 457; Harbeson, *op. cit.,* pp. 161 f; Harrison, "Some Work of the 'Associated Artists,' " *op. cit.,* pp. 343-351; Johnson, ed., *op. cit.,* IV, 338-342; Moses King, *King's Handbook of New York City* (Boston 1893) pp. 310 f; Koch, *op. cit.,* pp. 106 ff, 109 f; *The Literary News* X:1-4, 6, 8-10 (January— April, June, August—October 1889) frontispieces; H. H. Manchester, *The Story of Silk & Cheney Silks* (N.p. [1916]) *passim;* Anne Shannon Monroe, "Years and the Woman," *Good Housekeeping* LXIX:3 (September 1919) pp. 41 & 187-193; *New York City Directories* 1883-1907; *N.Y. Institute for Artist-Artisans. . . . 1st Annual Report,* 1888-9 pp. 14, 19, 27; C.F. Ober & C.M. Westover, *Manhattan Historic And Artistic* (New York [1892]) pp. 80 f; Information from Mrs. George Riggs, Port Washington, N.Y.; Katharine Metcalf Roof, *The Life And Art of William Merritt Chase* (New York 1917) p. 85; Information from Mrs. Thomas K. Stevenson, New York City; Ulrich Thieme & Felix Becker, *Allgemeines Lexikon der Bildenden Künstler* (Leipzig 1927) XX, 83; *Louis Comfort Tiffany 1848-1933. Museum of Contemporary Crafts, op. cit.,* p. 9; Candace Wheeler, "Art Education for Women," *op. cit.,* pp. 84, 86; Candace Wheeler, "The Art of Embroidery," *Home Needlework Magazine* I:2 (April 1899) pp. 99-102; Wheeler, "Decoration of Walls," *op. cit.,* pp. 705 f; Wheeler, "Decorative Art," *op. cit.,* pp. 409, 412; Wheeler, *The Development of Embroidery, op. cit.,* pp. 126, 132-135, 137 f, 141 f; Candace Wheeler, "Home Industries and Domestic Manufactures," *The Outlook* LXIII:7 (October 14, 1899) pp. 402-406; Candace Wheeler, *Home Industries and . . . Domestic Weavings* (New York: Associated Artists, n.d.) advertisement at end (Courtesy Mr. Richard B. Simpson, Anaheim, California); Wheeler, ed., *Household Art, op. cit.,* pp. 57, 59-73, 162 ff, 165; Mrs. Candace Wheeler, "How I Devised an Attractive Kitchen," *The Ladies' Home Journal* XX:8 (July 1903) p. 20; Wheeler, *How to Make Rugs, op. cit., passim;* Wheeler, "Interior Decoration As a Profession for Women," *op. cit.,* pp. 559 & 649; Candace Wheeler, "The New Woman and Her Home Needs," *The Christian Union* XLIII:26 (June 25, 1891) p. 845; Candace Wheeler, "Practical Use of Art Education," *The Christian Union* XLIV:13 (September 26, 1891) pp. 582 f; Candace Wheeler, "The Principles of Decoration," *The Outlook* LIII:7 (February 15, 1896) pp. 284 f; Wheeler, *Principles of Home Decoration, op. cit., passim;* Mrs. T.M.

Wheeler, "The Study of Design," *The Art Amateur* XXVI:1 (December 1891) p. 18; Candace Wheeler, Two Embroidered panels at The Cleveland Museum of Art; Wheeler, *Yesterdays, op. cit.,* pp. 107, 147, 237 ff, 246 f, 256-265, 406, 414 ff, 417 ff, 420 f; *Who's Who in America (1914-1915)* VIII, 1290; *The Woman's Book,* op. cit., p. 218.

Mrs. Wheeler's Work for the Columbian Exposition
    Addresses and Reports of Mrs. Potter Palmer (Chicago 1894) pp. 129, 145; *The Art Amateur* XXVIII:4 (March 1893) p. 117, XXIX:6 (November 1893) p. 154; Hubert Howe Bancroft, *The Book of The Fair* (Chicago & San Francisco 1893) pp. 261 f, 289; *The Biographical Cyclopaedia of American Women, op. cit.,* II, 189; *Condensed Catalogue of Interesting Exhibits . . . in the World's Columbian Exposition* (Chicago 1893) p. 149; Mary Kavanaugh Oldham Eagle, ed., *The Congress of Women* (Chicago & Philadelphia 1894) pp. 818 f; Elliott, ed., *op. cit., passim*; Moses P. Handy, ed., *The Official Directory of the World's Columbian Exposition* (Chicago 1893) p. 25; Johnson, ed., *op. cit.,* I, 245, 248 ff, IV, 338-342; *List Of Books Sent . . . to the Library of the Woman's Building, World's Columbian Exposition, Chicago, 1893* (N.p. n.d.) pp. 44 f; Logan, *op. cit.,* p. 753; *Report of the Board of General Managers of the Exhibit of the State of New York at the World's Columbian Exposition* (Albany 1894) pp. 156-218; *Report of the Board of Women Managers for the Exhibit of the State of New York at the World's Columbian Exposition, 1893* (New York n.d.) *passim*; Major Ben C. Truman, *History of The World's Fair* (Philadelphia & Chicago [1893]) p. 175; Candace Wheeler, "A Century of Progress. . . . What the Century Has Done for the Household," *The Outlook* LVII:4 (September 25, 1897) p. 229; [Candace Wheeler, ed.], *Columbia's Emblem Indian Corn* (Boston & New York 1893) *passim*; Wheeler, "Decorative Art," *op. cit.,* p. 411; Wheeler, *The Development of Embroidery, op. cit.,* p. 109; Candace Wheeler, "A Dream City," *Harper's New Monthly Magazine* LXXXVI:516 (May 1893) pp. 830-846; Candace Wheeler, "Embroideries . . . Shown At The World's Fair," *The Art Amateur* XXVIII:6 (May 1893) p. 167; Wheeler, ed., *Household Art, op. cit., passim*; Wheeler, *Yesterdays, op. cit.,* pp. 146 f, 340-356, 364; "Women's Work In The Applied Arts. New York State Preliminary Exhibition," *The Art Amateur* XXVIII:5 (April 1893) pp. 146 f.

Candace Wheeler's Writings; Later Activities & Life; Her Death
    Many of Mrs. Wheeler's voluminous writings have already been cited among the sources for this chapter and will not be listed here. Among those not previously cited are "The Decorative Use of Wild Flowers," *The Atlantic Monthly* LXXXXV:5 (May 1905) pp. 630-634; *Doubledarling and the Dream Spinner* (New York 1905); "The Fine Arts Group Exhibitions," *The Critic* XXVI (N.S.XXIII):675 (January 26, 1895) p. 70; "Weaving Rugs from Rags," *The Ladies' Home Journal* XXII:12 (November 1905) p. 56.

For further details, see *American Art Annual* (Washington, D.C., 1923) XX, 266; Clara Barrus, *The Life And Letters Of John Burroughs* (Boston & New York 1925) I, 316, II, 275, 393; *The Biographical Cyclopaedia of American Women, op. cit.,* II, 189 f; Bolton, *op. cit.,* pp. 195 ff; Information from Mrs. Mary G. Bryan, Department of Archives & History, Atlanta, Georgia; Information from Mr. James B. Burch, Thomasville, Georgia; Clippings (Courtesy Mr. H. Keith Simpson); *Corticelli Home Needlework* [*Home Needlework Magazine*] I:1-3 (January, April, July 1899) *passim; Corticelli Home Needlework. 1899 A Manual of Art Needlework, Embroidery and Crochet* (Florence, Mass., 1899) *passim;* Elliott, ed., *op. cit.,* p. 40; Robert Underwood Johnson, *Remembered Yesterdays* (Boston 1923) p. 324; Keith, *op. cit.,* p. 9 b; Information from Marjorie H. Leek, Librarian, Long Island Collection, The Queens Borough Public Library; Logan, *op. cit.,* p. 753; Russell Lynes, *The Tastemakers* [New York 1954] pp. 181 f; Monroe, *op. cit.,* pp. 41, 187-193; *New York City Directories* 1895-1907 (Courtesy Dr. James J. Heslin, New-York Historical Society); *The New York Times* (April 27, 1895) p. 5, (August 6, 1923) p. 11, (August 8, 1923) p. 15, (October 25, 1925) p. 30; Information from Mrs. George Riggs; Information from Mrs. Thomas K. Stevenson; *The Trow Copartnership and Corporation Directory of the . . . City of New York* 1898 & 1899; Mrs. Candace Wheeler to Henry L. Stimson, Collection of Letters, 1898-1921 (Henry L. Stimson Collection, Yale University Library [Quoted letters are those of January 10, 1909, May 9, 1918, May 22, 1918, July 27, 1919, March 31, 1920, October 5, 1920, November 7, 1920, August 1, 1921, August 17, 1921]; Candace Wheeler, *Annals of Onteora 1887-1914* (New York n.d.) *passim* (Courtesy Mr. John Cook Wyllie, Alderman Library, University of Virginia); Candace Wheeler, "Art Education for Women," *op. cit.,* p. 84; Candace Wheeler, *Content In A Garden, op. cit., passim;* Wheeler, *Yesterdays, op. cit., passim;* "Mrs. Candace T. Wheeler," *The Art News* XXI:39 (August 11, 1923) p. 6; Dora Wheeler, "The Vacation Home on the Mountain," *The Christian Union. Supplement* XLI:22 (May 29, 1890) pp. 785 f.

INDEX